The World of Music

Seventh Connect Edition

The World of Music

Seventh Connect Edition

David Willoughby

Elizabethtown, Pennsylvania
Professor Emeritus, Eastern New Mexico University

The McGraw·Hill Companies

Connect
Learn
Succeed™

Published by McGraw-Hill, an imprint of The McGraw-Hill Companies, Inc., 1221 Avenue of the Americas, New York, NY 10020. Copyright © 2012, 2010, 2007, 2003, 1999. All rights reserved. No part of this publication may be reproduced or distributed in any form or by any means, or stored in a database or retrieval system, without the prior written consent of The McGraw-Hill Companies, Inc., including, but not limited to, in any network or other electronic storage or transmission, or broadcast for distance learning.

This book is printed on acid-free paper.

2 3 4 5 6 7 8 9 0 RJE/RJE 10 9 8 7 6 5 4 3 2

ISBN: 978-0-07-802516-7
MHID: 0-07-802516-8

Developmental Editor: *Sarah E. Remington*
Marketing Manager: *Tara Culliney*
Production Editor: *Holly Irish*
Design Manager: *Allister Fein*
Cover Designer: *Cassandra Chu*
Photo Research: *Brian J. Pecko*
Buyer: *Louis Swaim*
Media Project Manager: *Katie Klochan*
Digital Product Manager: *Jay Gubernick*
Composition: 10/12 Gill Sans *by Macmillan Publishing Solutions*
Printing: *45# New Era Matte Plus, RRD, Jefferson City*

Editor in Chief: *Michael Ryan*
Editorial Director: *William R. Glass*
Publisher and Sponsoring Editor: *Christopher Freitag*
Director of Development: *Rhona Robbin*

Cover: *Jazz Band by Coco Masuda.* © *Images.com/Corbis.*

Credits: The credits appear on page 329 of the book and are considered an extension of the copyright page.

Library of Congress Cataloging-in-Publication Data

Willoughby, David.
  The world of music/David Willoughby.—7th [updated] ed.
      p. cm.
  Includes bibliographical references and index.
  ISBN-13: 978-0-07-802516-7 (alk. paper)
  ISBN-10: 0-07-802516-8 (alk. paper)
  1. Music appreciation. I. Title.

  MT6.W533W7 2014
  781.1'7—dc23
                            2011037362

The Internet addresses listed in the text were accurate at the time of publication. The inclusion of a Web site does not indicate an endorsement by the authors or McGraw-Hill, and McGraw-Hill does not guarantee the accuracy of the information presented at these sites.

www.mhhe.com

BRIEF CONTENTS

CONTENTS

PREFACE

The World of Music is designed for teachers who want to focus on listening to music as it exists in the real world of their students. My book goes beyond the traditional repertoire used for music study; it captures students' interest immediately, by beginning with music they know. I start with American folk, religious, jazz, popular and ethnic music, then introduce some world music, and conclude with a thorough overview of Western classical music. My intention is to capture and convey the essence of each repertoire—whether popular, traditional, or classical music—in order to enhance students' musical understanding. Students who read this text will be able to recognize different styles and appreciate their different functions, and they will acquire a solid foundation for continued learning in areas of personal interest. These three statements summarize the philosophy on which *The World of Music* is based:

- It is critical for students to develop solid listening skills, including the ability to describe and comment on the music they hear.
- Listening skills can be taught through music from any period or place.
- No repertoire is too small to be studied, and all repertoires are important, differing only in style and function.

My text introduces students to the many styles of music currently enjoyed by people in the United States, and it will help them to appreciate the roots of these various styles. The text encourages readers to reach out to cultures around the world to learn about—and perhaps enjoy—music with which they may not now be familiar.

The World of Music presumes no prior musical training on the part of the student. Its broad scope and introductory nature make it ideal for any first course in music listening/appreciation.

Repertoire

The repertoire offered in *The World of Music* is comprehensive and is presented, as much as possible, without bias. The choices reflect my belief in the musical and educational validity of including in the college curriculum music other than western

European classical music. This expanded repertoire also indicates some other important beliefs:

- The United States includes people from many cultures, and curricula should reflect this diversity; thus, a strong emphasis on American ethnic music and on music as it exists in our own nation is appropriate.
- In our increasingly globalized society, we need to acknowledge the importance and the study of world music.

To support the notion that American music is in fact world music, I include a variety of repertoires within American music that have non-Western roots or influences: the music of Native Americans, music valued by various American ethnic and immigrant groups, and music from Latin America and the Caribbean. This broad coverage affirms my belief that all repertoires make important contributions to the study of music.

When discussing a specific repertoire, I focus on both its historical and its cultural aspects. I note the significant influences and contributions of the repertoire's creators and performers to a particular society and to that society's musical development. This background, in some cases, is balanced with coverage of a culture's contemporary musical elements. Thus, this new edition of *The World of Music* is both historical and contemporary—a valuable musical resource for today's students.

Listening Emphasis

The sequential development of substantive listening and descriptive skills is my central goal. Starting with simple music and progressing to more complex pieces, students learn the vocabulary with which they can talk about a style and describe their reactions to it. What ties the chapters together more than the study of specific repertoires, though, is the study—through listening—of musical concepts common to nearly all repertoires. Chapter 2 provides an introduction to the elements of music. Listening goals, musical concepts, and terminology are introduced throughout the book.

Listening Guides

In chapters 2–13, Listening Guides allow students to examine in detail a recorded musical example from the CD set available with the textbook. I carefully selected the musical examples to reinforce the concepts discussed in the text, and in each Listening Guide I provide strategies to help students listen to and understand each piece. For every recorded example on the CD set, there is a Listening Guide in the textbook that presents:

- Background information on the composer or piece.
- Goals for developing listening and descriptive skills.
- An outline of and commentary on the music and its structure and style.
- Reflections on the listening experiences that can spark discussion in and out of class.

I developed the goals for each listening experience sequentially so that as students progress, their listening and descriptive skills and use of vocabulary improve gradually but steadily. The guides direct this listening experience. But because listening is to some extent subjective, individual listeners may hear the music in different ways, and these multiple perceptions may be entirely valid. The reflective comments and questions in each Listening Guide are intended to serve only as possibilities and as models. Teachers can modify them and ask students to create their own reflective statements or questions for discussion.

Organization

Chapters, sections, and Listening Guides can be omitted or given emphasis different from mine to suit individual instructors' interests and needs. Teachers who tailor the text to fit a course may want to consider modifying the goals and descriptions in the Listening Guides in order to retain the sequential development of listening skills.

New to the Connect Edition

Connect Music is the most successful digital platform in music: a truly integrated teaching and learning program that has been tailored to *The World of Music*. *Connect Music* provides students with new ways to read the text, listen to the music, and demonstrate their understanding.

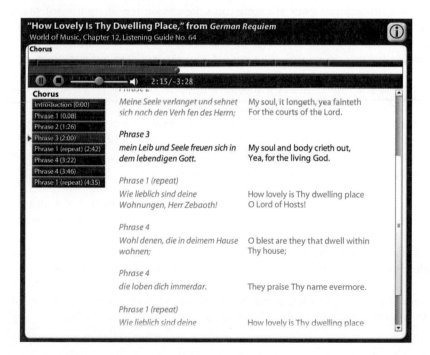

Connect Music for *The World of Music* offers:

- A web-based assignment and assessment platform.
- Interactive Listening Guides with streaming audio for all musical selections.
- Listening identification quizzes for all selections.
- Critical listening and comparison activities help students improve their active listening skills.

Additional Resources

Blackboard and McGraw-Hill Higher Education have teamed up! Now, all McGraw-Hill content (text, tools, and home-work) can be accessed directly from within your Blackboard course—all with a single sign-on. McGraw-Hill's content is seamlessly woven within your Blackboard course. Connect assignments within Blackboard automatically (and instantly) feed grades directly to your Blackboard grade center. No more keeping track of two grade books! Even if your institution is not currently using Blackboard, McGraw-Hill has a solution for you. Ask your sales representative for details.

Tegrity Campus is a service that makes class time avail-able all the time by capturing audio and computer screen shots from your lectures in a searchable format for stu-dents to review when they study and complete assignments. With classroom re-sources available all the time, students can study more efficiently and learn more successfully.

CourseSmart, the largest provider of eTextbooks, offers students the option of receiving *Experience Music* as an eBook. At CourseSmart your students can take advantage of significant savings off the cost of a print textbook, reduce their impact on the environment, and gain access to powerful web tools for learning. CourseSmart eTextbooks can be viewed online or downloaded to a computer. Visit www.CourseSmart.com to learn more.

McGraw-Hill Create allows you to create a customized print book or eBook tailored to your course and syllabus. You can search through thousands of McGraw-Hill texts, rearrange chapters, combine mate-rial from other content sources, and include your own content or teaching notes. Create even allows you to personalize your book's appearance by selecting the cover and adding your name, school, and course information.

The complete content of *The World of Music* is available to instructors and students in traditional print format as well as online with integrated and time-saving tools.

A set of 3 audio CDs (ISBN 0077493168) is available for purchase. It contains all of the selections discussed in the Listening Guides in *The World of Music*.

The Online Learning Center, which includes the instructor manual, test bank, and lecture PowerPoints, can be found at www.mhhe.com/willoughby7e.

ACKNOWLEDGMENTS

I would like to thank the reviewers who read and commented on previous editions. I incorporated many of their suggestions for improvement. I am grateful to

Felix Cox,
East Carolina University

Lon Denhart,
University of Central Oklahoma

Constance Edwards,
Fairmont State University

Billie Gateley,
Jackson State Community College

George Halsell,
College of Southern Idaho

Ronald Horner,
Frostburg State University

Vicki Pierce Stroeher,
Marshall University

Todd Queen,
Colorado State University

Brenda Romero,
University of Colorado, Boulder

I especially want to thank my wife, Barbara English Maris, whose professional background in music and writing enabled her to offer numerous helpful suggestions, of which I continue to be most appreciative.

Finally, I am deeply appreciative of my McGraw-Hill book team for their competence, support, and help in moving this project to its completion: Chris Freitag (Publisher), Rhona Robbin (Director of Development), Sarah Remington (Development Editor), Tara Culliney (Marketing Manager), Holly Irish (Production Editor), Allister Fein (Design Manager), Cassandra Chu (Cover Designer), Brian J. Pecko (Manager, Photo Research), and Louis Swaim (Buyer II).

David Willoughby
Elizabethtown, Pennsylvania

ABOUT THE AUTHOR

David Willoughby is a graduate of Lebanon Valley College (Pennsylvania), Miami University (Ohio), and the Eastman School of Music of the University of Rochester (New York). He is Professor Emeritus of Music at Eastern New Mexico University (ENMU), where he taught for 20 years while serving as dean of the School of Music and then the College of Fine Arts. Following his retirement in 1993, he moved to Pennsylvania and became head of the Music Department at Susquehanna University (Selinsgrove).

Willoughby has long been active in the College Music Society (CMS), a national organization of music teachers in higher education. His leadership roles with CMS have included board member for Music in General Studies (MGS; 1980–1985), director of several MGS conferences and teacher institutes (1980–1985), president (1987 and 1988), and editor of the CMS Newsletter (1997–2006).

Throughout his musical career, Willoughby has played bass in symphony orchestras in Pennsylvania and New Mexico, as well as jazz bass with a wide variety of groups.

During his years at ENMU, he hosted a weekly music and talk program that explored music and musicians from diverse periods, styles, and cultures. Those one-hour programs, presented on public radio, created a foundation that expanded Willoughby's world of music and established the philosophy for *The World of Music,* first published in 1990.

David Willoughby and his wife, Barbara English Maris, live in Elizabethtown, Pennsylvania, with Taffy, their very special maltese/poodle.

The
World of Music

PART one

Preparation for Listening

This is a book about music as it exists in the United States—our world of music. It encourages the study of music from a global perspective. This perspective can help us develop a greater respect for the music of other cultures and for any of our own cultural or ethnic groups. A global approach can also deepen our understanding of the predominant or mainstream musical styles of the United States, especially jazz, classical music, and popular music.

The primary purpose of *The World of Music* is to help you become a more perceptive listener by giving you more knowledge about music in general. In order to enhance your experience of listening to music, the text seeks to

- Help you improve your ability to listen to music intelligently. Listening is the core of the book and also the link that ties the chapters together.

- Cultivate an awareness and knowledge of musical traditions from around the world.

- Deepen your understanding of musical context—that is, the historical, social, political, and economic contexts within which music is created and used.

Although many people have become sophisticated in their use of music by learning to play instruments and perhaps even read music notation, significant musical experiences can happen with or without formal training. Not everyone creates or performs music, but we all listen to it.

Music is a part of our experience from birth to death. We experience it through games at recess, rituals in our places of worship, and curricula in our schools, as well as singing in the shower with no one listening. Our musical experiences may involve a stereo system and DVD player in our home entertainment center, a multidisc CD player at home or in the car, downloads to a computer, MP3 player, iPod, or some new, technologically advanced piece of equipment that we can't even imagine now.

Part One of this text, "Preparation for Listening," consists of two chapters:

- Chapter 1 draws attention to the enormous variety of music that we discover when we examine music from a global perspective. This chapter also discusses the various ramifications of the music business and the ways in which music functions in our communities.

- Chapter 2 explores the musical vocabulary used by English-speaking westerners and how we use this vocabulary to describe ways that sounds become music, how music is both an art and a science, and how it is sometimes lofty—perhaps challenging—yet other times part of our daily experiences. You will discuss ways we all use music as listeners, sometimes performers, and even creators of music. Chapter 2 also presents a beginning vocabulary based on the elements of music. It stresses how creators of music organize these elements to create a style, and it is intended to assist you in describing and understanding the structure and style of music—that is, what it is that makes something a piece of music. Additional vocabulary is presented in later parts of the book.

The goals of this book are to help you

- Develop listening skills by using basic musical concepts and applying them to any music you hear.

- Gain an understanding of the structure of music by examining various ways in which music is organized.

- Learn how musicians at any level manipulate sounds in a personal way to create a style.

- Recognize stylistic differences—the characteristics that distinguish one piece from another.

To reach these goals, you will need to understand certain musical concepts and learn the relevant vocabulary. All **boldfaced** terms are defined in the glossary. The glossary can help you understand new concepts, so consult it often.

1 Introducing the World of Music

Chapter Outline

In This Chapter

How is music a global phenomenon?

How is ethnic diversity important in our culture?

What are some cultural characteristics of the United States?

How helpful is the use of labels in music?

What does it mean, in music, to be an "artist"?

How is music both a business and an art?

How can we participate in the arts in our communities?

Throughout *The World of Music,* we discuss the roots and development of the musical styles that have had the greatest impact on American society. The music that we discuss comes from the American cultural mainstream (the historically predominant culture), as well as from the diverse subcultures within the United States. The roots of many of these diverse musics lie in the musics of other cultures—notably those of Europe, sub-Saharan Africa, and Asia—which were brought to the United States by immigrants from those regions.

In this text, we acknowledge and respect the similarities and differences among these various musical styles and traditions that make up the composite we call "American" music. Thus, a key goal of this chapter—and this book—is to convey the diversity of the world's music, particularly the music important to large or small groups of people in American society.

The course begins by encouraging the development of listening skills through a sampling of the seemingly endless styles of music from around the globe. One goal is to acquire a sense of what exists beyond our own experience.

The sitar, a plucked stringed instrument from northern India, is a widely accepted instrument in India's classical music tradition. Pictured is Ravi Shankar, India's foremost sitar player, who is known internationally. Here he is shown performing in Athens, Greece.

The koto, a plucked string instrument (13 strings), is part of Japan's classical music tradition. Accomplished koto players, in addition to plucking, use slides, scrapes, and striking to produce ornaments and other effects typical of traditional Japanese music.

The Infinite Variety of Music: A Global Perspective

We live in a world that seems to grow smaller and smaller thanks to tremendous advances in communication and transportation technologies and to the resultant increase in social mobility. So it seems not merely appropriate but necessary to approach music from a **global perspective.** This worldwide point of view requires awareness of and respect for the lifestyles, traditions, values—and music—of different nations and cultures. Such an approach also acknowledges the great diversity of musical traditions within our nation—a diversity that has contributed significantly to the richness of our national culture.

The musical traditions in the United States include western European classical music, folk music, and popular music, much of which is based on European traditions. Other styles, however, including jazz, blues, and various ethnic musics, have evolved from a blending of cultures and traditions. All these styles constitute an important part of music in American society.

The American Mainstream and Ethnic Diversity

The primary factor in the development of America's cultural mainstream was the predominance of English-speaking settlers in North America in the seventeenth and

The guitarrón (left) and vihuela (right) are plucked stringed instruments. These folk instruments, primarily from Mexico, are used in mariachi bands worldwide.

eighteenth centuries. When our society and our government were taking shape, English culture defined America's politics, religion, and language. All succeeding immigrant groups had to choose **assimilation** with the English-speaking mainstream or isolation from it.

Groups that retained a substantial part of the language, customs, or social views of their original cultures became what we call **ethnic** minorities. Part of the cultural richness of our nation is derived from its ethnic diversity and the large number of ethnic groups living here. Some immigrant groups have partially assimilated into mainstream American society while retaining the songs, dances, instruments, languages (or at least accents and inflections), fashions, cuisines, and lifestyles of their traditional cultures.

In many cases, new styles and modes of behavior have been formed by the merging of cultural traditions. For example, jazz developed in the early twentieth century, in part from a merging of songs and dances of Anglo-Americans with songs and dances of Creoles (people of mixed French or Spanish and perhaps African heritage who were born in the West Indies and the southern United States), and in part from a further merging of this Anglo-American and Creole music with the songs and dances of African Americans (many the descendants of black slaves).

European influences in early American music were dominant in part because (1) most early religious, folk, and popular songs were derived from traditions and styles from the British Isles and mainland Europe; (2) Americans, particularly throughout the nineteenth century, were exposed to European classical music by traveling to Europe or listening to music performed by visiting or immigrant European

Israeli-Arab rappers are shown recording a song in one of their homes in Akko, a town in northern Israel. Rap, born of inner-city poverty and the struggles of black Americans, has been adopted by youths around the world.

musicians; and (3) European Americans rejected the music of Native Americans as primitive and unworthy. Thus, most of America's popular and classical music is based on the melodic, harmonic, rhythmic, and performance practices of western Europe. The instruments we Americans have used are, for the most part, the same as or derived from those used in mainland Europe and the British Isles. At the beginning of the twenty-first century, however, the American mainstream is becoming less European and more global.

Music in Culture

Music is part of a culture. We learn much about a culture or a subculture from its arts: its songs, dances, and other forms of expression that depict or suggest feelings, attitudes, and important events.

The study of the music of other cultures, as well as our own, means describing music in musical terms. The problem with this approach is that the language we use to talk about music is not universal. It is based on western European musical concepts and often cannot describe other music equally well. Furthermore, studying the music of a culture implies much more than simply describing music. It also involves considering the **context** of music in a society, music as it relates to human behavior, and the general attitude of a people toward their music.

Scholars of music in cultures—or "world music"—are known as **ethnomusicologists.** They do the research on the music of a culture, write about it, and teach others about it. They may live for a time in the country or region where that music is produced. They record the music, talk to the people who make the music, and find out why and how it is created, performed, and heard. In other words, they try to understand the music the way members of the culture understand it. And this is true not only when they study the music of faraway places but also when they study the music within their own national boundaries.

Ethnomusicologists, through their research, seek to learn about the *social aspects* of music in a culture, asking such questions as "Who creates?" "Who performs?" and "Who listens?" These scholars try to determine what the life of a musician is like and what this person's status is—that is, whether a musician is highly respected or more like a servant, is professional or amateur, is formally schooled or unschooled, and so on. They also discover how the musician acquires and develops skills.

This research produces information about a culture's ideas about music, how music ties into a belief system, and whether music is intended for immediate use or preserved in some way for future generations. Ethnomusicologists explore how a group perceives music in relation to nature and to society. They observe a culture's musical preferences. Do the people consider music beautiful, or is beauty no concern at all? What sounds do people consider to be pleasing and satisfying? Is there "good" and "bad" music? Does the culture have popular music and classical music?

In addition, ethnomusicologists ask where music is performed, how musicians dress when they perform, and on what occasions music is performed—for rituals, entertainment, concerts, ceremonies, sports, dance, drama, or religion. They examine the relationship between performer and audience: what the audience does during a presentation and whether the spectators are active or inactive, quiet or noisy, attentive or inattentive.

In addition to examining the social aspects of music in a culture, ethnomusicologists study the music itself, to determine musical styles, genres, forms, and the history and theory of a culture's music. They also try to discover what can be learned about the culture from the texts of its songs, what the music sounds like, and what linguistic problems arise in describing the music. They find ways to describe the creative process, the use of melody, the rhythmic organization, the choice of instruments, and the preferred qualities of vocal and instrumental sounds. These scholars determine how music is taught, learned, and passed on from one generation to the next, and whether it is notated or transmitted mainly by oral tradition (that is, by example, imitation, or memory).

Ethnomusicologists discover what tangible things a community uses to produce music: instruments, equipment, printed music, or recordings. They also study the extent to which technological and urban—perhaps Western—influences are evident: mass media, sound reinforcement, concert and touring performances, professional musicians, and the music industry.

Ethnomusicologists examine the extent of **acculturation**—the process by which a culture assimilates, blends with, or adapts to the characteristics and practices of other cultures. They study the extent to which people accept or accommodate outside influences, making such influences a part of their culture—and to what extent people reject outside influences to preserve the purity of their culture.

Cultures change—sometimes rapidly, sometimes imperceptibly. In this modern technological age, few cultures are unaffected by outside influences. Most have accepted some of these influences and changed their behaviors and practices as a result. Ethnomusicologists have taught us much about the music of non-Western cultures, subcultures of American society, and Western-influenced cultures in other parts of the world. They have taught us to take a global rather than an ethnocentric perspective—that is, they have taught us to be interested in more than our own culture and our own music.

Acoustic guitars, such as the one pictured, are used primarily for playing folk and classical music.

Music Labels: Help or Hindrance?

When we develop a global perspective and examine diverse musical styles, the problem of labels arises. How do we identify different types of music? Categories or labels are sometimes useful for organizing knowledge, and this book does use them for that purpose. But ambiguity and overlap frequently occur, and stylistic distinctions are often blurred. Consider, among many influences, the current popularity of crossover and fusion styles, overlapping and frequently changing sales charts, classical composers who incorporate jazz or ethnic music, and jazz musicians who incorporate classical or religious music. Here are a few examples of the ambiguity of labels:

- George Gershwin was a composer of classical music and popular music—in the same pieces! *Rhapsody in Blue* (symphonic music) and *Porgy and Bess* (an opera) contain elements of both classical and popular styles. Gershwin also wrote songs for Broadway that were later arranged for string quartet. Are those songs then a part of the classical music repertoire?
- A folk song typically grows out of a cultural group, and usually its composer or creator is unknown. Yet the writers or composers of many well-known contemporary folk songs are known. Woody Guthrie, Pete Seeger, and Bob Dylan wrote songs that seemed very personal, were learned by memory, and became commercially successful. These composed songs started out as popular music, then became part of the folk music tradition.
- A popular song falls into the category of commercial music—that is, music intended to become commercially successful, even a hit. But if such a song doesn't become popular, it still remains in the category of popular music.
- Classical music is not popular or commercial music, yet contemporary composers want their music to sell and be performed. And even very old classical pieces remain popular—for example, Handel's *Messiah,* Beethoven's Fifth Symphony, and Tchaikovsky's *The Nutcracker.*

- Music composed for symphony orchestra, such as a Beethoven symphony, falls in the genre of classical music. But, for example, music for the *Star Wars* movies was composed by John Williams and scored for large orchestra, and it has been performed by countless symphony orchestras and bands, including the Boston Pops Orchestra, which Williams conducted for a time. Thus, is it classical music? Or is film music a distinct musical genre?
- Operas, operettas, and musicals are usually thought of as separate genres, but considerable overlap exists. The following musical and stage productions use sets, costumes, orchestras, solo and ensemble singing, and dramatic action, yet they represent different genres: Puccini's *Tosca* and Bizet's *Carmen* are operas; Victor Herbert's *Naughty Marietta* and Sigmund Romberg's *The Student Prince* are operettas; and Rodgers and Hammerstein's *Sound of Music* and Andrew Lloyd Webber's *Phantom of the Opera* are Broadway musicals.

What is the difference between a popular song and a pop song? Between pop music and soul or rock? Between blues, rhythm and blues, and soul? Does soul include blues or rap? What is the difference between rap and hip-hop? Which became popular first? What are the differences between hip-hop and contemporary R&B? What is the currently popular label (or labels)? What artists today best represent rap/hip-hop and contemporary R&B? What labels will we use five years from now?

How do we classify New Age music? Is it jazz, classical, or pop? Is it all or neither? What is alternative music? Is it a separate and distinct category? What is it an alternative to? As alternative artists or albums become more popular and move into the mainstream, does their music continue to be alternative music?

When is a popular song traditional and when is it contemporary? When is it pop and when is it rock? When is a song gospel and when is it Christian? When is it soul and when is it rhythm and blues (R&B)? Afropop and worldbeat are different from Anglo-American folk music, yet there can be similarities.

When stylistic differences are obvious, the choice of a label is clear. But frequently, labeling is not so easy. Within the category of popular music, but also between classical and popular or jazz styles, there is considerable overlap, given today's propensity for crossover and fusion. Many artists reflect characteristics of more than one style from album to album, from song to song, and even within a song. Some music defies any label.

What matters and what doesn't? Labels can be helpful for organizing information and classifying music. Use labels and benefit from them, but do not adhere to them rigidly. Do not spend much time and energy defending one label or another. Do not assume that another person—particularly your instructor—is wrong about a label!

Artists and Artistry

When we think of an "artist," we often picture someone who paints or sculpts, but this person is simply a visual artist. More broadly, an artist is someone who performs in any medium with creativity and sensitivity and with the ability to communicate with an audience. A person plays music artistically when it is played in a manner that is expressive, consistent in style, and based on musical, cultural, and historical knowledge. Often we associate musical artistry only with the creation and performance of Western art music—that is, classical music. But musical artistry is found in all styles and traditions of music. We should not think of it only in association with Western art music.

This piano quartet, a western chamber music ensemble, takes on an international character, judging, if for no other reason, by their names: (left to right) Japanese violinist Eiji Arai; South Korean pianist Chung Myung-whun; Japanese violist Crown Prince Naruhito; and Latvian cellist Mischa Maisky.

In the context of the popular music industry, anyone who performs music, regardless of style, is usually said to be an artist. How many times have you heard a singer with some successful CDs referred to as a "talented artist"?

Many of the artists included in this book are well known; others are little known or unknown. Many of those who are well known have gained national and international reputations from sales of recordings, tours, prestigious performances, rave reviews, and awards and honors. Yet many outstanding artists live in your community and region, perhaps never attempting national or international careers. They play at street festivals and county fairs and in churches, symphony orchestra halls, and nightclubs. Active local artists often have excellent CDs to sell. Read the performing arts calendars in your local or regional newspapers. Get to know and support your local artists.

The Business of Music

Understanding the basics of a complex industry—the music business—provides a context for understanding how Americans support music's creators, performers, and listeners. To a large extent, the musical life of communities—amateur or professional—could not exist without the vast number of people who participate in this support. The roles that people play in support of musicians and the musical life of their communities, regions, or nation may be categorized as follows:

- *Manufacturing and merchandising*—making and selling music and merchandise for profit.
- *Performance of music*—producing and selling live or recorded music for profit or as a service; this involves recording technicians, agents, managers, and copyright attorneys, among others.
- *Music publishing*—for performance and instruction of music and the administration of copyright laws, where applicable.
- *Advertising*—includes radio, television, the Internet, and print media.

An electric guitar, amplified electronically, is used primarily for playing pop, rock, blues, rap/hip-hop, and other forms of vernacular music worldwide. Pictured is Eric Clapton, noted British pop/rock guitarist.

- *Music in local communities*—encompasses professional, semiprofessional, and amateur musical organizations and activities, and the promotion and development of music and the other arts.

Manufacturing and Merchandising

Manufacturing and merchandising is the actual making of goods and includes research, design, and development; promotion, sales, and distribution; and customer service. The variety of manufactured goods essential to the music industry provides a good illustration of its scope, diversity, and impact on our lives. These goods include the following:

- Band and orchestra instruments and the repair people who keep those instruments functioning.
- Electronic instruments, some with links to computers, that serve the vast professional, semiprofessional, and amateur entertainment industry.
- Pianos and pipe or electronic organs that serve homes, schools, churches, and concert halls.

Performance of Music

Music performance permeates every aspect of the music industry and, indeed, of society itself. Music is performed live on street corners and in concert halls, gymnasiums, parks, fairgrounds, hotel lounges, nightclubs, and churches, temples, and synagogues. It is performed, recorded, distributed, and sold to consumers; broadcast over radio and television; used on the soundtracks of films and commercials; and played in elevators, offices, and department stores.

Among the biggest patrons of those musicians who tour are colleges and universities. Most institutions of higher education offer an "artist series." Communities also sponsor artist series featuring touring performers. Symphony orchestras typically

This early version of electric multiple-keyboards was used primarily in popular music and rock groups. Today, electronic keyboards take up less space and are more versatile in creating combinations of musical sounds.

offer a series of concerts. Any concert series is usually sold as a package—a subscription series or season tickets—always with considerable savings over the cost of individual concerts.

Most communities offer their own local music performances in many different styles and traditions, depending on the size and population mix of the area. Cities with ethnically diverse populations usually offer live musical performances of such great diversity that they appeal to almost every taste. Many communities sponsor festive occasions such as folk festivals, bluegrass concerts, or fiddle contests. Larger cities often maintain symphony orchestras, community bands, and even opera companies, some of them fully professional and some strictly volunteer.

Most community orchestras hire musicians who play for pay, but at a level that requires them to earn most of their income elsewhere, often from teaching. Other performers choose careers outside of music and play for their own enrichment, enjoyment, and perhaps supplemental income. Many semiprofessional or amateur musicians are primarily public school or college music teachers. Symphony musicians frequently supplement their income by playing jazz, rock, or country music in local nightclubs, lounges, and private social clubs and for school or community dances—or they may be hired or volunteer to perform church music regularly or on special occasions.

Music Publishing and Copyright Laws

Some publishers specialize in printed music for churches, schools, and colleges—that is, the Christian, educational, and concert music markets. Another market for printed music is the large group of amateur music makers who purchase pianos, organs, electronic keyboards, and guitars for home use and who need to buy sheet music, collections, and instructional how-to books.

One area of music publishing that is quite large but typically not considered part of the music industry is the music book industry, including textbooks and magazines about music. These materials usually are published by houses that specialize in writing, producing, and distributing books or other materials on a variety of subjects.

With the establishment of the copyright law in 1909, composers, lyricists, and publishers became the copyright owners of popular songs and were able to make a profit from the royalties earned when these songs were performed live and in recordings. Copyright holders were granted exclusive rights to authorize the use of their music for a limited time and to collect fees for such use. Today, anyone performing copyrighted material for profit has to obtain *performance rights* by paying for a license or by paying a royalty. Anyone recording copyrighted material for profit has to obtain *mechanical rights* and pay the established fees. Anyone using copyrighted music in a film for profit has to obtain *synchronization rights* and pay the appropriate fees.

Downloading copyrighted music, whether recorded or on film, presents unique problems. One involves the violation of copyright law, and another the enforcement of that law. It is clear, today, that downloading copyrighted music or movies (*intellectual property*)—without paying—is no less a crime than stealing *physical property*. People who create artistic works that contribute to their livelihood, whether on land or in cyberspace, are entitled to fair compensation. To copy copyrighted property without permission or without paying a legal fee is **piracy** and is illegal.

Music in Advertising

Nearly all commercials on radio and television use music to help sell a product or service. This music has to be created and performed, providing jobs for jingle writers (composers) and performers, as well as for everyone associated with its production. Given the prominence today, however, of electronically produced sound, especially **MIDI** (Musical Instrument Digital Interface) technology, many commercials use only one performer. The same person who composes the music also creates and records the sounds.

Both anecdotal evidence and documented scientific research suggest that music powerfully affects the conscious and subconscious emotions of listeners. Music in advertising can be in the foreground, might accompany dancing, or may serve as background for spoken material. It can create an image or a mood, establish an association, and enhance the positive or minimize the negative attributes of a product or service. It can attract attention, create unity, and provide a style that is memorable. It can be catchy, simple, and repetitive, and it can serve as a catalyst for an entire ad campaign. Music for an ad may be derived from a popular song or converted into a popular song. Either way, the intent of those who reuse the music is to capitalize on the exposure and popularity of the original.

Examine the qualities of familiar commercials or almost any current ones on radio or television. What are their attractive qualities? What makes them potentially effective? How do you respond to them?

Music in the Community

Both music making and music listening are favorite pastimes for large numbers of Americans. Much of this musical involvement takes place outside of the formal music education programs in schools and colleges. It occurs in the community in locations such as streets, malls, playgrounds, civic auditoriums, community music schools, senior citizen centers, churches, prisons, and mental health clinics, and at home with family and friends.

The extent and nature of the musical activities taking place in communities reflect the vast amount of amateur music making in our society. These examples also suggest that Americans value and enjoy a wide range of musical styles, from children's songs to chamber music, from square dance music to ballet, from mariachi to blues. Also, when we consider the extent to which Americans attend live concerts, buy CDs and DVDs, and listen to the radio and to music downloaded to their MP3 players or iPods, we see that both listening to music and making music are valued activities in our society.

In the entertainment industry, people who hold jobs as agents, managers, bookers, and promoters fulfill nonmusical functions in order to make the industry work. Similarly, in both small and large communities, many paid professionals and many more unpaid volunteers—from box office personnel and ushers to publicists and lawyers—fulfill nonmusical functions in support of the community's artistic life. In many communities, arts programs are supported through grants from federal, state, and local agencies and the resources of local industry.

Local community support from the private sector comes from the volunteer work of boards of directors of professional arts organizations, committees of chambers of commerce and local government, local arts councils, and volunteer support groups (such as Friends of Music, the Symphony Auxiliary, and the Opera Guild).

Large and active volunteer organizations also cause a ripple effect in increased contributions and larger and perhaps better-informed audiences at live concerts. Arts organizations would not exist without the dedication and hard work of community volunteers.

Typically, business and industry support arts programs in the communities in which they operate as a means of providing their employees with a better place to live. Such support acknowledges and communicates to others that the arts are important in the workplace and contribute to an improved quality of life in local communities.

For many communities, the maintenance of a vital and active musical life is a source of civic pride; a symbol of a progressive attitude that stresses human, cultural, and artistic values; and a strategy for economic development, including the promotion of tourism and the recruitment of new business and industry.

Summary

Music serves different purposes: to entertain, to uplift, to stimulate feelings and responses, and to enhance certain rituals—from music at a football game to music for a High Mass. Music that is unfamiliar to some can be profoundly important to others.

Music exists throughout the world. It is part of all cultures, and we can learn about other cultures from their music. Ethnomusicologists help us learn about musical acculturation and assimilation. They also help us realize that many cultures, traditions, and ethnic groups produce an infinite variety of music, of which any one person can come to know only a small part.

People make judgments about music and develop their own attitudes, tastes, and preferences. Most of us have a relatively narrow range, preferring styles we know well, perhaps grew up with, and feel comfortable with.

This book will help you build and expand on what you already know, so that you can gain an understanding of what is less familiar and can discover relationships, similarities, and differences among a variety of musical styles. In addition, *The World of Music* may stimulate you to find new music that you like and value, and it may help you acquire a sense of what exists beyond the limits of your own experience.

When we recognize the diversity of music and acquire a global perspective, categorizing music, defining terms, organizing musical styles and genres, and giving them labels can be useful. But labels can be problematic when applied too rigidly. Musical styles frequently overlap, and lines of distinction frequently are ambiguous.

An example of fuzziness in the use of terms is *artist* and *artistry*. A visual artist paints and sculpts. In classical music, a concert pianist may be a great artist and play artistically. But in the vernacular—in jazz and popular music—anyone who performs is said to be an artist. Some performers are well known; others are not. Some outstanding artists are well known in a local community or region, without aspiring to achieve national or international fame.

Music is a business, and we should be aware of the people who support the *artists:* the agents, manufacturers, and retailers of music-related goods and services, publishers, recording technicians, and community volunteers.

2

The Nature of Music: Vocabulary for Listening and Understanding

Chapter Outline

In This Chapter

When do sounds become music?

In what ways is music both an art and a science?

What are expressive qualities in music?

What factors create the various tone qualities we hear in music?

How is music organized horizontally and vertically?

What are the elements of a musical style?

As you explore the world of music, your sense of what music is and what music means to you will become clearer and more inclusive. We begin this exploration by considering three possible definitions of music. We then look at the physical, or acoustical, characteristics of music and at its aesthetic, expressive, and functional qualities.

Definitions of Music

What is music? All music includes the elements of sound and time, but the nature of music involves much more. Consider the following three ways we can think about the nature of music.

"Music is sound that is pleasing to the ear." Most of us respond well to sounds that we like. But if *pleasing* means only "pretty or beautiful," then this definition excludes a great deal of music. Music can be noisy, loud, raucous—anything but pleasing (unless your concept of what is beautiful or pleasing is very broad!). And what about music that may sound pleasing to you, but not to others? Or what about music that may have a larger purpose than to sound pleasing? Defining music solely on the basis of how pleasing it seems to us may exclude much western European art music composed in the past hundred years, as well as much music from non-Western cultures—music that may not be intended to be pleasing to Western ears.

"Music is sound and silence organized in time." This definition is relatively objective, because it includes all music from any place at any time, but it avoids the subjective. A person listening to music that may seem noisy, weird, displeasing, and ugly may think, "To my ear, this isn't music!" We cannot really define music without subjective factors—taste, judgment, and personal reactions—as exemplified in the common expression "I don't know anything about music, but I know what I like."

"Music is sound that you want to hear as music." Sound that is not organized in some fashion typically cannot be called music. Yet the roar of a waterfall, the sound of rain falling on a tent, or the chirping of birds can be "music to my ears." Though not music in the objective sense, these sounds are pleasing and thus, perhaps, musical sounds. In fact, the sounds of birds, water, and whales have been taped and used in "organized" music. Conversely, all sorts of drums, cymbals, and gongs; harsh, dissonant harmonies; and abstract, totally unsingable melodies have been organized into music. However, are such creations really music? As at least one student has asked, "What would prompt a person to write something like that?" Still, sounds that some listeners might perceive as noise can be incorporated into music if the composer or performer wants them to be. If you do not like a certain style of music, you can still respect it, value the creative process that produced it, and learn from it. Perhaps you will create your own definition of music.

Music as a Science

The physical characteristics of music involve principles of acoustics, physics, mathematics, and engineering. **Acoustics** is the science of sound and the physical basis of music. People who are aware of the scientific aspects of music include those interested in the specifications (specs) of stereo components, sound reinforcement at recording studios and concerts, the creation and performance of electronic or computer music, and the acoustical design of rooms and concert halls. Acoustical principles are applied to the construction of musical instruments, audio equipment, auditoriums, recording studios, homes, and offices and to medical technology through sonar (sound-related) diagnostics and treatment.

Audio enthusiasts refer to principles of acoustics when they use such terms as *frequency range, echo, graphic equalizers,* and *signal-to-noise ratios.* For example, the quality of audio speakers is measured in part by their frequency response as specified by the range of frequencies they can produce. To reproduce music, an audio enthusiast will want a speaker system with the widest frequency response.

Acoustical engineers design recording studios and auditoriums according to certain principles, such as resonance and reverberation (echo). Saying that a room has good acoustics means that the degree of resonance and reverberation is suited to the room's purposes. A facility constructed of porous material will absorb sound waves, creating "dead" acoustics. A facility constructed of hard, dense material will bounce the sound waves around the room, resulting in "live," or highly resonant, acoustics. Computer technology has taken most of the guesswork out of sound design and the acoustical treatment of auditoriums, concert halls, sanctuaries, and similar facilities.

Expressive and Functional Qualities of Music

Music is a science, but it is also an art possessing the power to elicit feelings and images to which individuals respond in a variety of ways. Through music, performers and creators are able to communicate a wide range of feeling, whether in simple children's songs or in highly structured art music. And much music is functional, serving nonmusical purposes—ceremonial, therapeutic, or religious.

Music Is Sound and Silence

Music is an aural phenomenon; we listen and respond to it as sound. Yet silence—from short rests to long, dramatic pauses—is also very much a part of music. Many composers and performers recognize that, rather than being merely a rest from sound, silence is an important compositional technique with its own aesthetic and dramatic effects.

Music Moves through Time

Music, like motion pictures, moves from one moment to the next. To appreciate music (or movies), it is important to remember what happened before and to anticipate what is about to happen. By contrast, arts such as photography, painting, and pottery are static: What the viewer sees at one moment will still be there the next.

Much music moves forward with energy and momentum, in a predictable progression, to a clear conclusion such as the end of a phrase (phrases in prose and poetry function in much the same way). Other music may move through time with less noticeable forward energy; such music may seem static, suspended in time, and lacking a clear phrase structure.

Music Is an Art

Music exists on a continuum ranging from folk music (music for the masses) to classical music (music for the connoisseur). Much music has attributes of both extremes. Classical music is "art music." In the western European concert tradition, symphonies and string quartets, operas and oratorios, and music for bands and choruses are considered to be classical music. Other cultures, too, may have their own classical music.

The best music of any tradition, regardless of its style, lasts. It may have universal appeal. It may be remembered through decades and generations. Some forms, such as notated concert music, may be remembered even longer. The best notated concert music is substantial enough to challenge listeners and performers.

A great piece of music encourages repeated listening, performance, and study. We can explore the best music again and again without tiring of it, yet still discover subtleties of expression and depths of meaning. The characteristics of art music can also be found in some vernacular music, especially jazz.

The creation of great music that will last for generations is very important in Western civilization. Worldwide, the more common attitude is to create something for immediate use, not for preservation. In either case, music from every culture, like all the arts, is a reflection of the society in which it was created.

Music Is Universal

Music exists in all cultures and among all people, and it has existed as far back in time as we know. Musical languages, styles, and functions, however, differ considerably. People in different cultures value music for different reasons. For example, music varies from culture to culture because social groups or societies develop their own tastes and their own ideas about what sounds beautiful. Each culture has developed its own musical traditions and reasons for using music in its communities, whether for purposes of religion, recreation, or entertainment. Cultures use different instruments and have different ways of creating music; thus, they develop stylistic differences. They also have different attitudes about performance practices and about the relationship between listeners and performers.

Still, all cultures have music because of its power to stimulate emotional responses and to convey powerful feelings, moods, images, and associations. Music also provides a means of communication for people who share a common identity and have common values and aspirations.

Music Is a Means of Expression

Music is an expressive language by which people can communicate feelings and images and generate **aesthetic** responses that may transcend cultural boundaries or be unique to a specific culture. Music can communicate such feelings as joy, sorrow, pain, love, merriment, and spiritual exaltation. It also can stimulate physical reactions such as foot tapping, weeping, or shouting and physiological reactions such as goose bumps.

Music can be romantic and sentimental; it can be simple and beautiful; and it can bring to mind special memories and pleasant associations. Yet it can also evoke unpleasant associations and be harsh and complex—even noisy—reflecting certain aspects of our modern technological society.

Music Can Be Functional

Music serves many functions in human societies. It is a part of ceremony and ritual and something to march and dance to. It affects our moods by its capacity to entertain, enrich, or relax us. It can help people escape momentarily from the real world.

Music therapists use music to alter people's feelings and attitudes. They use music therapeutically to help people who are physically or mentally challenged. Many colleges and universities offer degrees in music therapy. Graduates of such programs work in mental health clinics and hospitals, public schools, and private practice. Among other purposes, music therapists use music to help people of all ages improve their self-esteem, find joy in self-expression, achieve success through music, and learn better ways of interacting socially.

Some music is intended to improve our feelings when we are alone—such as when we are riding in an elevator or are put on hold during a telephone call. This

These street musicians, a "rockabilly" group, are seen making music on a street corner in Moscow.

background or *elevator* music is not to be listened to attentively and with discrimination. Although it serves a purpose in our society, such music promotes passive listening or nonlistening.

Music Is a Changing Art

Music changes as a society changes and because people's needs and tastes change. Music evolves because of new or refined instruments and other sources of sound and new ways of creating music, even new musical languages. Music also changes because of artists' innate need to grow, to advance in knowledge and understanding, and to stretch their performance skills. The rate and extent of change have differed throughout history and among various cultures and subcultures.

The Creative, Performing, and Listening Experiences

People of all ages experience music as creators, performers, and listeners. Without these three overlapping groups, music would not exist.

When music is notated, a **score** (a printed version of a piece of music) contains the composer's symbols, which performers can transform into musical sounds. **Notation** in music is the use of written or printed symbols to represent musical sounds. The notated tradition provides for the preservation and dissemination of music by means of handwritten or printed music. The performer reads and interprets the creator's symbols, transforming them into music that has the power to communicate feelings and images and to generate in listeners a variety of responses. In contrast, music that is **improvised** is simultaneously created, performed, and listened to by the performer.

For public performers, an important motivating force is the listeners. Professional performers rely on a paying audience, but all performers—amateurs as well as professionals—value interaction with an audience: a full house of enthusiastic,

These pre-kindergarten children are making music in their classroom. They are playing a "xylophone" and other percussion instruments.

supportive listeners. For most performers, the audience is likely to be a small group of friends or family or perhaps only the performer him- or herself. As one dedicated performer observed, "I would still perform music for myself even if no one else listened."

The creative process may be simple or sophisticated; it may result in a lullaby or a grand opera. We may recognize a composer's name, or the composer may be completely unknown (anonymous)—like the composers of much folk music. In either case, the creative process is fundamentally the same. The composer chooses elements of sound and organizes them to achieve a desired result: the creator's own piece of music. Keep in mind, however, that although music is created by individuals, these individuals are part of a culture and share with their intended audience a particular view. Thus, a creator usually chooses elements and organizes them in ways that are culture-specific.

The process of creating music may be spontaneous or painstakingly deliberate. The music may or may not be notated. The process may be loosely controlled, allowing the performer considerable freedom to make creative choices, such as in jazz improvisation. Or the process may be tightly controlled, with detailed notation and meticulous instructions that the performer is expected to follow, such as in much orchestra and band music.

The performance process is interpretive. Its goal is adherence, as closely as possible, to the intentions of the creator. Within certain styles, however, the performer may deliberately deviate from the creative work. Performing thus has its own creative element, whether spontaneous or planned.

Performers sometimes interpret a piece of music on the basis of deliberate choices, but at other times, they follow their musical instincts. Any pop or jazz singer will

Professional musicians represent another way of making music. Pictured is the Lincoln Center Jazz Orchestra.

sometimes perform a notated melody by adding personal interpretations within stylistic limitations. For example, singers may interpret romantic ballads and upbeat tunes in a different manner. A performer's interpretation brings life to a composer's symbolism (notation) and increases the communicative power of the music.

In a band, chorus, or orchestra, the conductor is the primary interpreter. Members of the ensemble must, to some degree, relinquish their own, perhaps different, interpretations and submit to the authority of the conductor.

The listening process can be passive, such as when we hear background or "homework" music, or active, such as when we go to a concert or listen attentively to a favorite CD. Active listening requires commitment, energy, and a desire to become personally and intensely involved. Although passive listening is valued by many people, active listening is the most important part of developing an appreciation for any type of music.

Participating in Active Listening

Many people participate in music as performers and creators, but everyone participates as a listener.

Begin now to develop **perceptive listening** skills as you listen to music anywhere, anytime. Be an active listener. Concentrate when listening, and make a commitment to hear all that there is to hear in the music. Listen attentively in an attempt to understand the musical processes and structure that give the music its characteristic qualities. Develop curiosity and a desire to know why the music came to be, what its purpose is, how it serves the people who listen to or otherwise use it, and what you need to know to understand it better. Think about what you are hearing, and use words to describe what you hear. Write about your reactions to the music that you listen to in this course, and describe how any of the pieces are similar to or different from music that you already knew and enjoyed.

As performers, most people sing the popular tunes of the day. Many sing in school and church choirs, others play in high school bands and orchestras, and a few even organize small groups of people to play jazz, rock, or country music. Sometimes people play well enough to perform in public for pay. Sometimes performing is very private, intended only for the performers themselves. Only a relatively small percentage of people learn to read music notation.

As creators, people of any age may make up tunes for their own private enjoyment. A few may have learned to create while performing—that is, to improvise—or they may have learned enough about a system of notating music and about various instruments and voices to compose a written piece of music that someone else can read and perform.

Recorded musical examples are available on the three CDs that accompany this book, and for each example, a Listening Guide in the text presents information to help you listen actively. Collectively, the musical selections provide an overview of the vastness, richness, and diversity of music.

Musical skills are not necessary to understand that music exists throughout the world and has existed for many centuries, that people make music a part of their lives for many different reasons, and that the world's musical styles are as varied as the world's people.

The Elements of Music

As you familiarize yourself with the music presented in this text and listen to music outside of class, you may find that your awareness of, and your ability to describe, what is happening in the music gradually increases. In general, listeners are seldom aware of the intricacies and subtleties of composition techniques; these factors, however, determine how effectively a piece of music communicates.

All sounds have **pitch, duration, loudness,** and **tone quality.** Combining these elements can result in the musical characteristics of melody, harmony, and rhythm. To create music, one organizes melody, harmony, and rhythm and adds varying

Pictured is wave form generated by an oscilloscope. This instrument is used in acoustics, which is the science of sound—the physical basis of all music. In this wave form, the horizontal line by itself is silence; the peaks and troughs represent sound, which may be music. One can visualize sound by watching an oscilloscope.

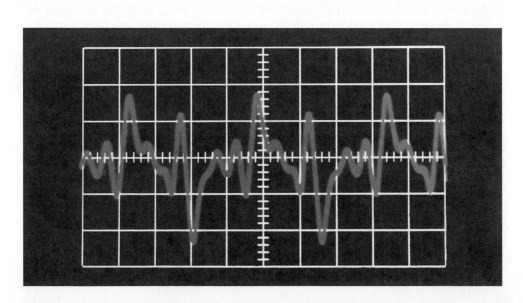

degrees of loudness and tone qualities. Music then can be characterized by its **texture** and **form.**

When people perceive a single tone, we call it a pitch. Most melodies are made up of individually recognizable pitches. However, music includes sounds that are less precise. We cannot hum the pitch of a triangle, a cymbal, or a bass drum, but we can perceive these sounds according to their **register** (an area of the sound spectrum—high, middle, or low). Although we identify the frequency of the vibrations as fast or slow, we identify both pitches and pitch areas (registers) as high or low: the faster the frequency, the higher the pitch; the slower the frequency, the lower the pitch. The entire **range** of frequencies sounding at once is called **white sound** or **white noise.** Examples of sounds very similar to white noise are static on a radio and the roar of a waterfall. The absence of frequencies is, of course, *silence.* Silence and even noise are sometimes used in musical compositions.

We can also relate pitches visually in a variety of ways, although some of these ways may seem contradictory, for they differ according to the construction of the instruments producing the pitches. On the piano keyboard, for example, low pitches are to the left, and higher pitches to the right. On any member of the violin family, you move down on the fingerboard to go higher in pitch and move up to go lower; the high strings are thinner, and the low strings thicker. Small drums produce higher-frequency **clusters;** bigger drums produce lower-frequency clusters. Likewise, small, thin instruments are higher in pitch range, and big and wide instruments lower. A piccolo is higher in pitch than a flute, a clarinet higher than a bass clarinet, and a trumpet higher than a tuba.

Melody

Because music moves through time, all music has sounds that occur *horizontally*—that is, as a sequence of pitches occurring one after the other. Making the pitches differing lengths of time (varying durations) can produce a melody.

We often think of melody as a tune, something easily recognized and remembered. It can be described according to the smoothness and wideness of its range. A melody may be smooth (moving mostly stepwise), have a flat **contour** or melodic shape, and sound "tuneful" or singable, especially if the range of the melody does not span so many tones that it extends beyond the normal singing range. However, a melody also may have many large skips and a range spanning more tones than are comfortable for one voice. Such a melody is described as having a *jagged* contour—that is, many wide intervals that typically can be sung only by highly trained singers. Much of our traditional folk and pop music features smooth, tuneful melodies.

Melodies for instruments may be patterned after vocal lines, but they need not be limited by the range of the normal singing voice. Thus, they often have wider ranges, wider skips, and greater complexity.

In most familiar Western music, the notes chosen by the creator of the music are derived from certain **scales,** which are systems of organizing pitches. Scales often give cohesion and form to a piece of music. They also establish the concept of **tonality**—the "home tone" or tonal center of a key (for example, the key of C or the key of F). This system of scales or keys produces the musical sounds with which we are most familiar.

The tones commonly chosen for a piece of music are derived from a specific scale. The pitches and rhythms are usually arranged to convey a musical thought—a **theme**—that has musical meaning and causes the listener to respond.

Harmony

When music is organized *vertically* and then performed, pitches are heard simultaneously. Most music incorporates simultaneous sounds, but some does not. The system of using chords in western European art music and in most of America's folk and popular music is known as harmony. Much music that we know is based on rather simple harmonies and chord progressions (movements from one chord to the next).

In harmonic music, we usually hear two simultaneous sounds as an interval and three or more simultaneous sounds as a **chord.** Chords may sound simple or complex, familiar or unfamiliar, repetitive or changing. They may or may not change frequently. To many people, certain chords and chord progressions sound very familiar because they are used widely in nearly all styles of American folk and popular music. A 12-bar blues progression is one example.

Rhythm

Music moves through time. It continues from one moment to the next. We see a painting all at once, but we cannot hear a piece of music all at once. As we listen to music, we remember what went before and anticipate what is to come. Musicians can visualize a short piece of music in its totality in printed form, as in sheet music. But **notation** is not music; it is only symbols. The symbols do not become music until a performer transforms them into sound.

Music can be perceived in various levels of duration: the length of an entire piece of music, a section of a piece, a phrase or musical thought, and each individual tone. A piece of music may last one minute or several hours. A sound event, such as a single tone, a melodic fragment, or a phrase, can be short or long. An eight-bar phrase typically but not always lasts longer than a four-bar phrase. Duration depends on the rate of speed—the **tempo**—so a slow four-bar phrase could last longer than a fast eight-bar phrase.

The variety of changes in the duration of pitches creates rhythm. Rhythm can be regular or irregular, simple or complex, floating or driving. However, rhythmic activity is not merely a mechanical arrangement of pitches and note values. Combinations or patterns of durations can generate a rhythmic feel, an energy, or a vitality that contributes to one of the most powerful aesthetic forces in the arts: the rhythmic impulse. Music having a strong rhythmic impulse stimulates us to tap our feet, dance, or march.

The tempo may be described as fast, slow, speeding up, or slowing down. Most of the music we listen to has a **pulse** or a steady beat—the "heartbeat" of a large portion of traditional Western music. Many listeners respond with greater enthusiasm to the strong beat of a piece of music than to its melody or harmony.

The pulse of music is usually organized into groups of two or three beats, creating **meter.** By stressing (accenting) every other beat, we get a two-beat or **duple meter** (STRONG, weak; STRONG, weak). By grouping the beats into patterns of three, we get **triple meter** (STRONG, weak, weak; STRONG, weak, weak). The "strong" beat may be depicted by a boldfaced number. Thus, duple meter is **1** 2/**1** 2/**1** 2, or **1** 2 3 4/**1** 2 3 4 (four beats are a multiple of two; thus, a grouping of four beats is duple meter, although quadruple meter would also be correct). Triple meter is **1** 2 3/**1** 2 3.

Nonmetric music has no pulse, a weak pulse, or an irregular pulse. **Mixed meter** has a clear pulse, but the strong beats occur in different patterns. One example of mixed meter is STRONG, weak; STRONG, weak, weak; STRONG, weak, or **1** 2/**1** 2 3/**1** 2. These shifts of accents may occur irregularly, or they may create regular patterns of shifting accents, as in this sequence (">" above a number represents an accented tone):

```
>     >    >       >    >    >       >    >    >
1  2  1  2  1  2  3/1  2  1  2  1  2  3/1  2  1  2  1  2  3
```

Placing accents on weak beats or on weak parts of beats produces **syncopation**— for example, weak, STRONG, weak, weak; weak, STRONG, weak, weak; or **1** 2 3 4/**1** **2** 3 4. Here syncopation takes place on the second beat of each group (bar or measure in notated music). In a four-beat measure, beats 2 and 4 are considered weak. The following is another example:

```
>        >         >      >        >          >
1  +  2  +  3  +  4  +  /1  +  2  +  3  +  4  +
```

In this example, syncopation occurs only on the second half of the second beat and on the first half of the fourth beat of each bar.

As previously indicated, each group constitutes a measure or bar. In much music, a group of measures can constitute a phrase—a longer unit of duration. Common groupings include an 8-bar phrase, a 12-bar blues tune, and a 32-bar chorus. Bars are perceived as part of our awareness of strong beats; the number of **downbeats** (the first beat of each bar) equals the number of bars in a phrase. In 12-bar blues, for example, we can typically count 12 downbeats to each 12-bar phrase.

Loudness

The loudness or softness of music—sometimes referred to as **dynamics**—varies with the intensity or energy expended in producing the sound. The greater the intensity, the louder the sound; less intensity generates a softer sound. In audio technology, volume controls can be used to adjust loudness.

An **accent** is achieved by increasing the intensity (increased stress or emphasis) on a single note or chord. You might think that if more musicians were performing, loudness would increase, but this is not necessarily so. For example, it is quite possible for a group of 20 musicians to perform as softly as a group of 4.

Tone Quality

All sound-producing devices possess their own distinctive tone qualities, or **timbres** (pronounced TAM-burs). A flute sounds different from a clarinet; a man usually sounds different from a woman; a guitar sounds different from a banjo; and a snare drum sounds different from a bongo. Learn to recognize the sounds of various instruments and voices, because they are relatively consistent in tone quality. The reason for this consistency lies in the acoustical construction of the devices, whether natural (the human voice) or manufactured (musical instruments).

In Western classical music, instruments are generally classified according to the way their tones are produced—that is, according to their characteristic timbre. There are brass instruments, string instruments (usually thought of as the violin family), woodwinds, and percussion. These classifications are useful when we are referring to band and orchestra instruments, but they may not be sufficient when we are describing the large number of instruments used in many other cultures.

Interaction of the Elements

The elements of music (pitch, duration, loudness, and timbre) always work together in a piece of music. As you listen to music, practice recognizing the following aspects of musical organization, and use your growing musical vocabulary to describe what you hear:

- Highs and lows of pitches and how they change and are combined (melody and harmony).
- Relative durations of pitches and how they are organized (rhythm and meter).
- Dynamic levels in relation to the relative loudness of the music and how they change.
- Tone qualities of different sources of sounds (voices or instruments).
- Pulse, measures (bars), meter (duple, triple), and phrases.
- Tempo (rate of speed).

To Create a Style: Musical Concepts

Let us now consider how creators of music organize sounds to develop a piece and create a style that communicates their intentions to, and evokes a particular response from, the listener. The purpose is to increase our understanding of how the creative process works in music and how composers or creators organize sound into music.

If music had no variety, would it be intolerable? If music did not have unifying characteristics, would it ramble? Western music incorporates some aspects of **variety** (departure) and **unity** (return). A *departure* is a musical idea (theme) that is different from what has already been presented; this is a point of **contrast**. A *return* is either an exact or a modified **repetition** of the original theme. It can be rhythmic, melodic, harmonic, or any combination of the three. Sometimes a melodic or rhythmic pattern is repeated, or a melody is based on a constantly repeated pattern. Repetition of musical patterns gives unity and cohesion to a piece of music and provides familiarity, which helps listeners feel comfortable.

Much music around the world and in American culture creates in us a sense of forward motion, of being drawn from one point to the next, from the beginning of a phrase to the end, and from one tone or chord to another. This **forward energy** can be derived from **tension** followed by a release of tension; it arises from an unstable feeling that drives the music forward to points of relative stability, such as at the end of a phrase. If a composer chooses to avoid forward energy, the music may be described as static, floating, or lacking a tendency to move forward.

Forward energy in traditional Western music is often generated by melodies and harmonic progressions. The musical tension that drives the forward energy is created by an increase in harmonic or rhythmic complexity, an increase in the dynamic level (loudness), a rise in the pitch of the melody, a change of key or tonal center, or an increase in the thickness or density of sound. Musical tension typically needs **resolution** (release of tension) to make the listener relate comfortably to the music. Just as continuous variety would seem uncomfortable, so would continuous tension. A release of tension is accomplished by a return from complex to simple, from high to low, from loud to soft, or from less comfortable to more comfortable sounds.

One kind of tension is **dissonance.** Dissonance, like other forms of tension, traditionally requires resolution: a release, or a move, from the unstable dissonance or tension to a more stable or consonant sound. **Consonance** is caused by intervals or chords that create repose, resolution, and comfort rather than tension. Often, tension and dissonance, in particular, are stronger in the middle of phrases, and repose or the release of tension occurs at the end of phrases.

Instability is a desired attribute in music because it contributes to tension, dissonance, and other characteristics that provide variety and interest. Instability is generated by departures—that is, elements of musical contrast that set up returns to passages that have **stability,** that are more familiar, comfortable, and satisfying. A **modulation,** or change of key, can create a feeling of instability that is satisfied when the music returns to the original key.

Texture

In Western music, **texture** is sometimes described as *thick* and *full,* such as when many lines of music are heard simultaneously, and sometimes as *thin* and *transparent,* such as when only a few lines of music are sounding together. Music played by a large ensemble such as a symphony orchestra certainly can provide a full texture, but it also can include passages of thin texture (only a few lines sounding at one time). Likewise, in piano music, six or eight tones sounding simultaneously have a thicker, more complex texture than just two or three tones sounding at a time.

Texture also relates to the various ways musical lines are combined, some of which are listed here:

- A single-line melody without harmonic accompaniment or other melodic lines: a chant, a lullaby, or an unaccompanied song.
- Melody with accompaniment: most familiar hymns, art songs, and popular songs.
- One melody combined with the same melody in two or more parts; each line has equal emphasis but starts at different times, such as a two- or three-part round.

Genres and Forms

A **genre** is a type or category of music, such as a symphony, hymn, song, march, or opera. **Form** is the shape or structure of a piece. For example, some forms of organization are described as a b a or a a b a. The "a" represents the main theme or its repetition; the "b" represents a theme that contrasts with the main theme. A "c" would indicate a second contrasting theme. Patterns of departures and returns—contrasts and repetitions—are important in establishing the form of a piece of music.

Forms can be perceived at various levels, from the form of a complete four-movement symphony to that of a familiar hymn or a popular song. Small forms can be perceived within large forms. For example, we can describe the structure of the first section of the first movement of a symphony and the overall scheme of the symphony's various movements. The 32-bar **song form** (a a b a) is found in nearly all styles derived from western European musical traditions: art songs, religious music, folk songs, and both old and current jazz and popular tunes.

In many American popular songs and religious music, a **verse-chorus** or verse-refrain form can easily be found. Typically, the text varies in each repetition of the verse (a musical narrative), but the text of the chorus or refrain is repeated with each return. In popular music, the chorus or refrain usually is more tuneful and memorable than the verse.

Twelve-bar blues is a form derived from a style of American folk song called the **blues,** but it is now used in almost every style of jazz and popular music. Typically, the 12 bars are divided into three 4-bar segments using a specific set of chord progressions.

Nearly all musical genres and forms change and evolve. They reflect existing practices and serve as flexible models for the work of future creators of music.

Melodic Growth and Character

We conclude our development of a working vocabulary for listening by looking again at the components and characteristics of melody. Melody is the part of music that most listeners can understand, remember, and "tune in to." However, much rock emphasizes a strong beat over melody or harmony, and much twentieth-century classical music de-emphasized melody in preference to rhythm and timbre (creative uses of existing and new instruments).

In most music of Western culture, the melody does not exist in isolation from other musical factors, such as harmony, timbre, and texture. If you heard only the melody of a piece of music without the support of these other musical elements, you would find it a very different piece of music and probably not nearly as satisfying. Again, all these elements interact and work together to make a piece of music cohesive, satisfying, and memorable.

Typically, a melody is made up of phrases—complete or relatively complete musical thoughts (themes). Phrases end when the music comes to points of repose: points of release of tension, of forward energy, or of harmonic, melodic, and rhythmic rest. These points are called **cadences.** Some cadences, sometimes called *open cadences,* give a feeling of temporarily stopping, but with an awareness that musical movement will continue. Others, sometimes called *closed cadences,* convey a strong feeling of finality, such as at the end of a piece of music.

A melody or phrase often begins with a **motive,** the smallest group of notes having an identifiable character, from three or four notes to one or two bars. A motive may be the basis of the music that is to follow. A motive is not necessarily melodic; it may be harmonic or rhythmic. Most likely, it incorporates a combination of musical elements.

Music evolves; it develops and grows. A motive often is the basis for this development and growth. It is usually repeated—perhaps exactly but more often in a modified version. Generally, contrast occurs when a new motive is introduced and the character of the music changes.

Goals for Listening

The Listening Guides in this chapter will help you throughout this book, because the skills that you need become increasingly sophisticated (see Preface, page ix). You should begin to develop an awareness of the following musical elements, all present in the most common music in American society:

- *Basic characteristics of melody:* Describe melody—its character and range.
- *Basic elements of rhythm:* Identify pulse, tempo, downbeats (bars), and meter.
- *Basic elements of harmony:* Begin to recognize chord changes and concepts of chord progressions.

- *Degrees of loudness:* Describe varying levels of loudness.
- *Qualities of tone production:* Describe differences in vocal and instrumental qualities and begin to identify specific instruments.
- *Basic elements of musical structure and style:* Become aware of the interaction of these musical elements by recognizing simple phrase patterns, contrast and repetition, and clearly perceivable forms, such as a a b a, verse-chorus, and the 12-bar blues.

The following is a suggested procedure for listening to the musical examples, here and in subsequent chapters: (1) Read about the piece at the beginning of each Listening Guide. (2) Read the "Goals" section and listen to the music, trying to absorb the goals without referring to the "Guide" section that follows. (3) Read the "Reflections" section and listen again, this time following the "Guide" while thinking about the goals and reflections. You will find repeated listening particularly useful for less familiar or for especially complex musical examples.

As the course progresses, become aware of certain musical concepts, and determine whether they exist in the music. Doing this will help you develop the listening skills you will need to use later Listening Guides effectively.

Listening Guide   No. 1

"Sylvie"

CD1, Track 1, 2:02

Composer: Huddie Ledbetter ("Leadbelly").

Performer: Sweet Honey in the Rock.

Genre: Folk music (see chapter 3).

Context: Leadbelly created many of his songs while in prison. His themes dealt with the plight of poor farmworkers and black immigrants in large cities. Sweet Honey in the Rock is an a cappella ensemble of African American women whose roots are in the gospel music of the black church—with a sprinkling of folk, jazz, blues, and pop. The group was founded in 1973 by Bernice Johnson Reagon, then a curator at the Smithsonian Institution in Washington, D.C. Reagon retired from Sweet Honey in 2004.

Goals

Recognize and identify pulse, downbeats, and rate of speed.

Recognize and describe any prominent changes in the music.

Identify phrases and any patterns of repetition or contrast.

Describe the melody (smoothness, range), harmony (simple or complex, repetitive or changing), and rhythm (regular or irregular; two-, three-, or four-beat).

–Continued

Listening Guide –Continued   No. 1

Guide

The pulse can be counted in a slow two, although you could perceive it in a moderately fast four. Each phrase is four bars (divided 2 + 2) and corresponds to two lines of poetry.

Chorus

Bring me little water, Sylvie;
Bring me little water now.
Bring me little water, Sylvie
Every little once in a while.

Verse 1

Don't you see me comin';
Don't you see me now?
Don't you see me comin'
Every little once in a while.

Chorus

Verse 2

Bring it in a bucket, Sylvie;
Bring it in a bucket now.
Bring it in a bucket, Sylvie
Every little once in a while.

Sweet Honey in the Rock performing.

Listening Guide –Continued   No. 1

Chorus

Verse 3 (solo)   *See me come a 'runnin';*
                 See me comin' now.
                 See me come a 'runnin' in
                 Every little once in a while.

Verse 4 (solo)   *Sylvie come a 'runnin';*
                 Sylvie comin' now.
                 Sylvie come a 'runnin'
                 Every little once in a while.

Chorus

Reflections

The words and music for each chorus are the same.

Each fourth line of poetry ("Every little once in a while"), whether part of a verse or chorus, has the same music.

How is the music of verses 3 and 4 different from that of the other verses?

The end of the first musical phrase of each verse (end of second line of text) gives the expectation of continuing. The end of the second phrase of each verse (end of fourth line of text) conveys a strong sense of finality.

Notice how the pulse is steady and falls into regular patterns of strong and weak beats (duple meter; strong-weak, strong-weak). In this song, is a two-beat pulse preferable to a four-beat pulse? Why or why not?

Describe your response to this music. What moods do the singers create?

Listening Guide   No. 2

"Body and Soul"
CD1, Track 2, 1:22

Performers: Benny Goodman, clarinet; Teddy Wilson, piano; Gene Krupa, drums. Recorded in 1935 in New York City.
Genre: Jazz from the swing era (see chapter 5).

Goals

Describe the contrasting sections, and identify the phrase patterns (structure).
Recognize the sound of a clarinet.
Be aware of the timekeeping role of the drums.

–Continued

Listening Guide –Continued   No. 2

Benny Goodman playing the clarinet.

Guide

Count in four at a moderate tempo. This example consists of four 8-bar phrases. It is in a a b a form. Listen to what the pianist is doing while the clarinetist is playing the lead.

a   Clarinet lead: a jazz interpretation of a standard tune

a   Clarinet lead repeated

b   Piano lead: contrasting phrase (the **bridge**); jazz improvisation

a   Clarinet lead repeated

Reflections

With Benny Goodman's clarinet lead in the first phrase, the melody is always recognizable, although Goodman embellishes it with slides, **pitch bending,** and added tones.

Notice how Goodman's tones fluctuate up and down in pitch. He is using **vibrato,** an oscillating ("wobbling") variation of pitch that enhances a tone, providing richness and warmth particularly to sustained pitches or to a slow, lyrical melody. Also, rather than placing tones precisely on each beat, Goodman often plays "around the beat," providing a mild syncopation.

When Teddy Wilson takes the lead on the piano in the "b" section, the melody is not recognizable. His piano style is more elaborate and complex than Goodman's interpretation, contributing to the contrasting character of this phrase.

Notice Krupa's machinelike timekeeping on the drums.

Listening Guide   No. 3

String Quartet, op. 33, no. 2 ("The Joke") (II. Scherzo) (excerpt)
CD1, Track 3, 1:15

Composer: Franz Joseph Haydn (1791).
Performer: Tátrai Quartet.
Genre: Classical chamber music (see chapter 11).

Listening Guide –Continued   No. 3

Background: The number of this quartet, op. 33, no. 2, indicates that the quartet is the second composition of a group of Haydn's works cataloged by his publisher as opus 33. "The Joke" is a nickname for this piece. It was given the nickname because Haydn supposedly put some extensive pauses (rests or silences) near the end of the quartet in order to catch people off guard who may have been talking while the music was being played. This excerpt is from the second of four movements of the quartet: Scherzo—a fast, dancelike style.

Goals

Recognize beginnings and ends of phrases and points of rest (cadences) where forward energy subsides and the phrases end.

Distinguish between melodic line and supportive accompaniment.

Recognize melodic contour (melodic shape).

Notice the sounds of bowed stringed instruments (the violin family).

Guide

The music is in triple meter; its stately mood can be counted in a moderately fast three,

1 2 3/ **1** 2 3

or in a slow one,

1 - -/ **1** - -

In either case, the phrases begin ahead of the downbeat (with a pickup). The following numbers coincide with each downbeat; thus, they will guide you in counting the bars. As you listen, count the numbers, making sure they match the music's strong beats.

0:00	First phrase	a		1--2--3--4--5--6--7--8--9--10
0:11	First phrase repeated	a		1--2--3--4--5--6--7--8--9--10
0:22	Contrasting phrase (notice descending pattern)	b		1--2--3--4--5--6--7--8--9--10
0:35	Transition			1--2--3--4
0:38	First phrase repeated	a		1--2--3--4--5--6--7--8--9--10
0:49	Contrasting phrase repeated (notice descending pattern)	b		1--2--3--4--5--6--7--8--9--10
1:00	Transition			1--2--3--4
1:05	First phrase repeated	a		1--2--3--4--5--6--7--8--9--10

–Continued

Listening Guide –Continued   No. 3

Reflections

A four-bar passage after each contrasting phrase serves as a transition to the first phrase. These transitions do not constitute self-contained musical thoughts; thus, they are not usually considered phrases.

Be aware of the complete musical thoughts (phrases). They are separated at points where musical energy comes to a rest (cadences). Identify when the music returns to tonic.

Listen for changes in thought (a different melody, a different instrument playing the melody, or anything that seems to contrast with whatever preceded it). Remember the original melody, and listen for when it changes and when it returns to its original character.

Is the melody singable?

Listening Guide   No. 4

"Nkende yamuyayu" ("The Waist of the Wild Cat")
CD1, Track 4, 1:08

Performer: Plays on a four-holed, V-notched flute made of bamboo.
Genre: Traditional African music from Uganda (see chapter 8).

Goals

Identify the metric characteristics. Is this musical example metric or nonmetric?

Describe the melodic characteristics and the relative importance of melody and harmony in this example.

Guide

0:00	The music starts with solo flute playing the opening melodic idea; the drum enters when the opening fragment is repeated
0:07	A second, higher motive is played and is extended in various forms; a singer chants a background line throughout this section
0:27	The first motive returns with the singer joining the flute melody in unison; handclapping soon begins
0:35	The second motive enters and continues with many modifications and, again, with the singer chanting in the background; ends with a "tag"

Reflections

Notice how the phrases are modified.

Describe how the piece is built on one short melodic idea, which is the basis for the two motives. Compare the motives.

Listen for the quiet singing and clapping in the background. Does this contribute to or detract from the music? Explain.

Summary

Music eludes a clear definition. It is both a science and an art. It has physical (acoustical) properties, and it has artistic and expressive attributes. It has the power to communicate and to elicit emotional responses. It exists for many different reasons, and we use it for many different purposes. We need to be aware of the various ways we participate in music and how music functions in our daily lives.

This chapter sets the stage for developing listening skills that will allow you to reach a higher level of musical perception. It presents the beginnings of a musical vocabulary for listening: words that describe musical concepts—the elusive, subjective characteristics that happen in music to make it communicate and to make listeners respond. Most important, this chapter provides a vocabulary that will allow you to begin describing any music that you listen to.

Consider what music is, how it is put together, what makes some music different from other music, and what is basic in music and common to all musical styles. One of the most significant points made in this chapter is that the basic elements of music—pitch, duration, loudness, and tone quality—interact to create structure, form, and style.

PART two

Listening to American Music: Folk, Religious, Jazz, and Pop

Most music is created in a language that the majority of listeners understands and enjoys. This music, in the language of the people of a nation, region, or cultural group, is known as **vernacular** music, as opposed to classical music or art music. It is created and performed by and for the common people of a group—the general community. In Chapters 3–6, we explore American vernacular music, with a focus on the following:

- Influences on and styles of folk music.

- Protestant religious songs and hymns.

- The historical and stylistic development of jazz.

- Various styles of popular music.

Our national culture includes differing regional, ethnic, and religious cultures, among others. Music important to a particular group, typically, is modest, unpretentious, immediately gratifying, and enjoyed and valued by the majority of people within the group.

The United States is a nation of immigrants; thus, American folk music has roots in many traditions. In addition to having British roots, American folk music includes, for example, the music of Native Americans, Jews, Cajuns, and African, Mexican, Irish, Italian, and Polish Americans. The vernacular music of these groups generally includes their dance music, religious music, and commercial (popular) music.

It is common for some people within a cultural group to have musical preferences that differ from others. People in rural areas may have preferences different from people living in metropolitan areas. People in the Southwest may enjoy different styles from those living in New England or on the West Coast. Older people usually prefer different music from younger people. And many Americans from ethnic subcultures have tastes in music based on their ethnic heritage.

Many cultures also have their own classical or art music. Classical music is not vernacular music. In our society, classical music, such as the music of Bach, Beethoven, and Brahms, is in a language and context that many Americans do not include in their daily experiences. Many people do not understand this more formal music, do not frequently listen to it, and do not feel comfortable in the settings in which it is usually heard, such as concert halls and opera houses (chapters 9–13 are intended to improve your understanding and perhaps appreciation of Western classical music).

Chapter 3 presents a variety of American folk music, including traditional and urban blues songs. The music of Cajuns, Native Americans, and immigrants from Mexico, the Caribbean, and Central and South America is discussed briefly in chapter 7.

Chapter 4 discusses American religious music, including early hymns, black and white gospel and revival music, and contemporary "praise and worship" music.

In chapter 5, we present an overview of American jazz as a vernacular music having at times characteristics of sophisticated art music.

Chapter 6 discusses the many aspects of American popular music: its roots, styles, influential artists, and roles in our society. This chapter emphasizes the roots of Tin Pan Alley, Nashville, Motown, rockabilly, and the "British Invasion" (the Beatles). It concludes with a summary of several styles of popular music flourishing in the early years of the twenty-first century.

3 *Folk Music Traditions*

Chapter Outline

In This Chapter

What are the various ways this music was preserved?

What music was notated? What music was not?

What are the contributions of immigrant music to our culture?

Folk music is, for many Americans, close to the heart and to everyday life, and it has influenced much of the music around us today. It is a living, ever-changing music. Authentic folk music, or traditional music, is understood by participants within a cultural group: singers, players, dancers, and listeners. The music reflects the spirit and personality of the people who produce, use, and value it. Folk music grows out of the lives of the people and conveys in song their joys and sorrows, their relationships and romances, and the events and circumstances that are important to them.

In American society, the predominant folk music originally was the songs of Anglo-Americans—white New Englanders whose roots were in Britain. Later, it included the songs of African Americans—black people in the rural South whose roots were in Africa. As British immigrants moved southward, their sounds mingled with those of freed black slaves and their descendants who were moving north; the songs of one cultural group influenced those of another. From these cross-cultural influences, new musical styles and practices developed, combining traits of northern and southern and black and white cultures. This interweaving of British and African styles and influences is perhaps the single most important factor in the development of American traditional music.

Goals for Listening

The "Goals for Listening" section near the beginning of this and the following chapters is intended to help you increase your awareness of and your ability to describe the recorded music presented in the Listening Guides. As you proceed through the Listening Guides in this chapter, focus on the following individual and interactive musical elements:

- *Basic characteristics of melody.* Describe melodic character: How simple and how singable is the melody? Begin to recognize musical lines other than melody.
- *Basic elements of rhythm.* Identify characteristics of tempo, downbeats, measures (bars), and meter. Describe rhythmic impulse—the character of the rhythm (a driving beat, a fluid rhythm, or a weak or uneven pulse).
- *Basic elements of harmony and tonality.* Become more skillful at recognizing the sounds of different chords, chord changes, the sounds of chord progressions, and modulation (when the tonality changes). Recognize the sounds of the three primary chords—the I, IV, and V chords. Their names signify their relationship to one another: The tonic chord (I) is a chord of rest, and the dominant (V) and the subdominant (IV) are chords of movement.
- *Degrees of loudness.* Describe varying levels of loudness. Notice changes within a piece of music.
- *Qualities of tone production.* Increase your skill at describing differences in vocal and instrumental qualities and at identifying instruments.
- *Basic elements of musical structure.* Recognize and describe the interaction of these musical elements through phrase patterns, contrast and repetition, tension and release of tension, and clearly perceivable forms (verse-refrain, a a b a, and 12-bar blues). Recognize and identify deviations from standard characteristics of these forms. Identify strophic form.

The Roots of Traditional Folk Music

America's folk music traditions helped shape its culture from the time of the earliest European settlers in the early 1600s. All this music is part of America's "roots music"—music at the core of America's collective culture, derived from and related directly to the everyday lives of its people.

African American folk music is rooted largely in the musical expressions of slaves and their descendants in the Deep South, whereas Anglo-American folk music grew out of the folk culture of the northeastern United States combined with British-influenced hymns and songs. But America's roots music also includes folk music associated with various American subcultures, such as Appalachian and Ozark mountain music, Native American music, Irish dance music, Tex-Mex (*tejano*) dance music, Cajun and zydeco music, and Jewish klezmer music. American ethnic (immigrant) music is discussed in detail in chapter 7. And although space precludes covering all these cultural traditions, we could consider the indigenous music of Alaska and Hawaii and the increasing importance of the music of the Asian and Arab immigrant communities.

Traditional folk music is considered informal, aesthetically and musically unsophisticated, and usually simple. Typically, it is preserved and transmitted by learning songs from memory, rather than from notated, printed music. Thus, we can think of folk music as a body of music consisting of traditional songs and dances derived from an **oral tradition.** Folk songs are preserved by oral tradition within communities and cultural groups, but music scholars—usually folklorists—have collected, classified, and transcribed them into notation, and published traditional folk songs, thus preserving them in print.

Most folk music is not created by professional composers and lyricists. The creators are often unknown because their names are lost in the process of oral transmission. It is true, however, that some commercial popular songs and other simple songs may appeal to a traditional folksinger, and a composed song may enter the oral tradition as a result of this memory process. People of all ages, and particularly children, routinely learn songs from memory rather than from notation: pop songs from radio and television, songs from well-known musicals, and camp songs.

Traditional songs, learned by hearing and memorizing, typically go through many changes as they are sung father to son, uncle to nephew, grandmother to granddaughter, neighbor to neighbor, musician to musician, and community to community, for generations and sometimes centuries. Songs may change because singers want to improve them, add their own personal interpretation, or adapt them to suit the taste of a community. A song may also change because of inaccurate memorization or misunderstood words and meanings, or simply forgetting—in which case a singer may create new lines on the spot.

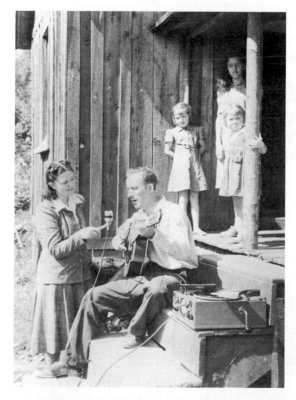

This field recording took place in North Carolina in 1941. To preserve traditional folk music, without songbooks or recordings, folk song collectors took their portable recording equipment and recorded songs where the people were—in their homes or community gathering places.

Roger D. Abrahams and George Foss in their book *Anglo-American Folksong Style* (1968) illustrate the concept of how texts change. They list multiple versions of a single line: "Save rosemary and thyme":

Rosemary in time.
Every rose grows merry in time.
Rose de Marion Time.
Rozz marrow and time.
May every rose bloom merry in time.
Let every rose grow merry and fine.
Every leaf grows many a time.
Sing Ivy leaf, Sweet William and thyme.
Every rose grows bonny in time.
Every globe grows merry in time.
Green grows the merry antine.
Whilst every grove rings with a merry antine.
So sav'ry was said, come marry in time.

It is probable that successive singers misheard the words they were memorizing or did not know the herbs—rosemary and thyme—the words referred to.

Change is an accepted—and valued—part of an oral tradition. Changes may weaken a song, but more often they give it new life or make it more meaningful to a community. Songs that are not accepted by a community are soon forgotten or changed. As songs are passed from community to community over time, those that do survive may be changed to such an extent that they bear little resemblance to the original version. In fact, the original version may no longer be known.

One of the most prominent folklorists was the nineteenth-century collector Francis James Child, who published 305 traditional English and Scottish ballads that are now known as the "Child ballads." One Child ballad is "Barbry Allen." As many as 243 variants of "Barbry Allen" have been identified. Such variation is an outgrowth of an oral, rather than a notated, tradition.

Types of Folk Music

The broad spectrum of American traditional folk music includes a wide variety of songs and dances. Spirituals and the blues, derived from African American traditions, are discussed in a later section of this chapter.

Narrative Ballads (Story Songs)   Narrative songs came from New England, having originally been brought to America in the seventeenth, eighteenth, and nineteenth centuries by immigrants from the British Isles, particularly Scotland and Ireland. A ballad singer is a storyteller. The music often is strophic (see Listening Guide 5 in this chapter).

Lyric Songs   Lyric songs are not narrative. Many were derived from British folk music in New England. They include love songs, ceremonial songs, folk hymns, songs about farming and rural life, songs about industrialization, and songs about freedom. Lyric songs convey emotions and moods in a more private context than a ballad. Action and drama are minimal, the subject matter is wide ranging, and musical forms and poetic structures are diverse.

Listening Guide No. 5

"Barbry Allen"
CD1, Track 5, 1:12

Performer: Jean Ritchie (1922–), vocal and dulcimer. One of the best-known traditional singers in America, Ritchie is from a family of prominent folksingers in Kentucky. This unaccompanied rendition represents a typical southern white singing style from the Kentucky mountains.
Genre: Narrative ballad (story song).
Background: "Barbry Allen" is perhaps the best-known, most durable, and most widely sung narrative ballad in English. It is derived from English, Scottish, and American traditions and may be one of the longest-lived songs learned through oral tradition. Originally, this was a Scottish song; it can be traced to 1666.

Goals

Recognize **strophic** form. (Each stanza is set to the same music regardless of the meaning and mood of the text.)
Recognize a fluid and flexible rhythm.
Describe the singing style.

Guide

Each verse begins on the third beat of the bar (with a "pickup"). Considerable rhythmic flexibility is evident.
The tempo is moderately slow.
There are two phrases to each verse. Three of 12 verses are included.

Reflections

Is a strong metric feeling important?
Discuss how this tune is different from music that is more familiar to you.

Work Songs   Both black and white Americans have work songs. These include sea chanties, railroad songs, and lumbermen's songs. Such songs offered rhythm, pace, and a spirit that helped make long hours of hard work—and even oppression—bearable. Work songs often used a call-and-response pattern and were sung to a beat compatible with that of the oar, a sledgehammer, or an ax.

Children's Songs   Children's songs, such as lullabies, camp songs, and game songs, are usually short, simple, and functional. They are extremely varied in type and style; all are easily remembered.

Protest Songs   Protest songs that encouraged social and political change emerged in the mid-nineteenth century. For example, in the late 1800s, the Hutchinsons, a prominent musical family, expressed their commitment to social reform through their music and gave concerts in settings that ranged from labor halls to the White House. In developing this repertoire, the Hutchinsons helped establish a new genre of American music: the protest song. This tradition in American folk and popular music reached its peak during the 1960s with the protest songs of Woody Guthrie, the Almanac Singers, Pete Seeger, Bob Dylan, and Joan Baez (see pages 52–53). More recent popular artists have also created songs to describe, reflect on, and perhaps advocate the improvement of social conditions. Such artists include Bruce Springsteen (the working class), Willie Nelson (farmers), Elton John and many other artists (AIDS), and many rap performers (urban conditions). Contemporary performers often participate in benefits for their favorite causes, using their music to mobilize support and help raise funds.

Rally Songs   Rally songs have been used to promote union organization, political candidates, and patriotism. Protest songs have promoted causes (prohibition, civil rights) and condemned wars (the Mexican-American War, the Vietnam War). A rally or protest song may be composed, or someone may write new words to a well-known folk or popular song, in effect creating a new folk song.

Dance Music   Dancing has been an important part of the lives of Americans of almost all backgrounds; thus, instrumental dance music is a vital part of traditional folk music. The fiddle has been the primary instrument in nearly all European American folk dance traditions, and fiddle tunes were a common genre of folk dance music. These tunes were arranged for various instrumental groups—notably, the string band, which in the nineteenth century featured fiddle and banjo. Today, they are performed by many bluegrass bands (see chapter 6). The guitar became a part of this music only in the twentieth century. Listening Guide 6 provides an example of a popular fiddle tune.

The fact that composed folk songs are also discussed briefly in chapter 6 as a form of popular music reflects the ambiguity of music composed in folk style. A composed folk song may have been published in printed form, recorded, and sold commercially, and then learned from memory. Thus, at times, the line between a folk and a popular song is not very clear. Examples of familiar, composed folk songs include Woody Guthrie's "So Long, It's Been Good to Know You" and "This Land Is Your Land"; Bob Dylan's "Blowin' in the Wind"; and Pete Seeger's "Where Have All the Flowers Gone?"

The Blues

Western European notation cannot adequately reproduce the slides, **tone bending** (slight lowering of the pitch and then a return to the original pitch), and other fluctuations in pitch and rhythm that were and are an integral part of the performance style

Listening Guide   No. 6

"Soldier's Joy"
CD1, Track 6, 1:42

Performer: Gid Tanner and His Skillet Lickers, a rural string band from northern Georgia (two fiddles, banjo, guitar, and vocal). Recorded in 1929.
Genre: Folk dance tune for fiddle.

Listening Guide –Continued   No. 6

Context: The fiddle has been the primary melody instrument in almost all instrumental folk dance traditions, and fiddle tunes were a common genre of folk dance music. These tunes were arranged for various instrumental groups—notably, the string band, which in the nineteenth century featured fiddle and banjo. Today, they are performed by many bluegrass bands (see chapter 6). The guitar became popular only in the twentieth century.

Goals

Describe the melodic style.

Focus on the bass line to help recognize chord changes.

Identify phrase patterns.

Guide

0:00	Intro	One guitar chord and commentary designed to get the listener into a mood for dancing—followed by Instrumental Instrumental Chorus
0:13	aa	Descending motive at the beginning 1 2 3 4 5 6 7 8
		I – – V I IV V I
0:29	b b	Ascending motive at the beginning I IV I V I IV V I
0:44		Instrumental phrases repeated from above (a, a).
		c a b b Phrase c is vocal.
		a I – – V I IV V I
		b I IV I V I IV V I
		c I – – V I – I V I
1:15		c a a b Phrase c is vocal.
		Instrumental phrases repeated from above (a, a).
		(Excerpt fades to 1:42.)

Reflections

Can "Soldier's Joy" be perceived as duple meter with four beats to the bar instead of two?

What are the advantages and disadvantages of the many repeated patterns and phrases?

Each phrase begins and ends on the tonic chord (I), with midpoints (fourth bar) ending on the dominant (V); listen for these sounds. Which are the chords of movement? Which are the chords of rest?

Describe the style of the fiddle tune and the fiddle playing.

of black folk singing and that more accurately reflect the black experience that inspired this music. Rather than adhering to strict notation, black singers would adjust the pitch up or down slightly to interpret or emphasize the "feel" of the music.

The blues is a style of music that has exerted considerable influence on jazz, rhythm and blues, soul, rock, and other, more recent forms of American popular music. Some performers specialize in "singing the blues." This is a very powerful means of musical communication; the feelings evoked by the music and the text may be mournful or melancholy. The original intent was to lift the spirits of people who were "feeling blue." It is significant that the blues is discussed or at least referred to in four chapters of this book, suggesting the importance of its role in American folk, jazz, popular, and classical music.

Blues evolved into specific forms: the three-line poetic stanza form of poetry and the 12-bar blues form of music. These are common structures, but each has many variations. The first line of poetry is usually repeated and followed by a contrasting third line (a a b form). The poetry most frequently expresses a sense of mistreatment or injustice—the misery of an oppressed people or of someone who has lost or been abandoned by a lover or a loved one. Consider these lines:

I got a brownskin woman, she's all right with me.
I got a brownskin woman, she's all right with me.
Got the finest woman that a man most ever seen.

Lord, I can't stay here, and my lover gone.
Lord, I can't stay here, and my lover gone.
Sometimes I wonder, my brownskin she won't come home.

The music reflects the poetic structure, with four bars of music to each of the three lines of poetry, adding up to the common 12-bar blues. Over time, this 12-bar musical structure has evolved into the following:

- A regular pattern of chords—a relatively consistent chord progression.
- A blues scale created by alterations to certain pitches, known as "blue notes."
- A blues feeling that performers enhance by bending tones or sliding into or out of pitches to enhance their moaning, mournful "bluesy" quality.

A gifted blues singer uses all these patterns and alterations to create the feel of the blues, as we'll see in Listening Guides 7 and 8.

The 12-bar blues form is found in all styles of jazz and in much popular music, including rock. It forms the basis of **boogie woogie** (see chapter 5) and much popular music of the mid-twentieth century, such as urban blues, popular forms of early rock and roll (see chapter 6), and **zydeco** (the music of French-speaking African Americans from southwestern Louisiana; see chapter 7).

Folk Music: An Expanded View

Only a thin line separates some genres of American popular music from their roots in folk music. For example, there is a close relationship between the traditional folk music of the southern Appalachians and hillbilly music, between string band music and early bluegrass, and between camp-meeting and revival songs and southern gospel music. Thus, to some extent, the roots of certain contemporary genres of American popular music—especially country, blues, and gospel—lie in America's southern folk music.

Listening Guide

No. 7

"Bourgeois Blues"
CD1, Track 7, 1:41

Words and music: Huddie Ledbetter.
Performer: Huddie Ledbetter ("Leadbelly"), vocal and guitar.
Genre: Traditional blues.
Background: Huddie Ledbetter (1885–1949) was born in Louisiana and became a world-renowned singer and songwriter. His songs reflect his African American culture in the first half of the twentieth century. "Bourgeois Blues" is a song about black immigrants to large cities, in this case, Washington, D.C. Other well-known songs by Leadbelly include "Grey Goose," "Good Night Irene," and "Sylvie" (see Listening Guide 1, page 33).

Huddie Ledbetter ("Leadbelly"), American folk-blues songwriter and performer.

Goals

Describe the vocal and instrumental style, the form, and the blues chord progressions.

Guide

Duple meter in four. Strong rhythmic impulse. One guitar chorus followed by three vocal choruses. The chord progression for each chorus is the standard 12-bar blues (approximately).

One guitar chorus followed by three vocal choruses: I – – I – – I – – I – –
IV – – IV – – I – – I – – V – – V – – I – – I – –.

Spoken intro followed by four vocal choruses.

Bars:	1	2	3	4	5	6	7	8	9	10	11	12
	I	–	–	–	IV	–	I	–	V	–	I	–

Reflections

Describe the vocal quality and style.
Notice Leadbelly's rhythmic and harmonic flexibility.

A significant factor in this broadening of the sources of folk music was and continues to be the thousands of concerts and festivals of folk, blues, bluegrass, and jazz that take place each year. Many of them are huge commercial enterprises. Among the best known are the Newport Folk Festival, the Newport Jazz Festival, the New Orleans Jazz and Heritage Festival, the San Francisco Blues Festival, and the Smithsonian Folk Arts Festival.

The Urban Folk Revival

A *revival* is a resurgence or a return to popularity of an existing style. Examples of music traditions that have enjoyed recent revivals are ragtime (see chapter 5), klezmer (see chapter 8), Native American songs and dances (through powwows that are popular tourist attractions; see chapter 7), and folk music in the United States and elsewhere. A revival usually involves the interest and participation of performers outside the tradition that originally produced the genre. The revival discussed here is the urban folk revival of the 1960s.

This revival, according to some scholars, began in 1958 with the recording of a version of an old folk ballad, "Tom Dooley," by an aspiring pop group called the Kingston Trio. In that year, this song soared to number 5 on the charts in the United Kingdom and number 1 in the United States. In the music industry, that kind of success generates interest by other artists and other record companies. By the early 1960s, recordings of folk songs and, more commonly, songs composed in the manner of folk songs, had become an extremely important part of the music industry and of popular culture. Many of these songs were versions of traditional folk songs and ballads; others served as rally and protest songs; still others were contemporary ballads and more lyrical, folklike pop songs. Most were recorded with minimal instrumentation; often the singers were accompanied by a guitar. Typical settings were hootenannies (gatherings at which folksingers entertained and audience members frequently joined in), coffeehouses, small clubs in Greenwich Village (New York City), and eventually similar places in other urban areas. Newsletters, magazines, books, and radio shows were devoted to this new folk music. It was the typical popular music environment of the early 1960s—urban folk music, until Bob Dylan added the electric guitar in 1965, puzzling the purist devotees of folk music and stimulating a new genre: folk rock. Among the best known urban folksingers of the 1960s, in addition to Dylan, were Arlo Guthrie; Joan Baez; Peter, Paul, and Mary; and Simon and Garfunkel.

Bob Dylan is a legendary folk singer and songwriter. His first period was as a traditional folk singer of protest songs (early 1960s); this music featured his guitar and harmonica playing. In 1965, he added electric guitar, which led to a new style known as folk rock. He then pursued a style much like country rock with a twinge of hillbilly. Throughout his career, he has written his own music and lyrics.

B. B. King—urban blues singer and guitarist—is the king of the blues.

Traditional folk music is often created anonymously, learned through the process of oral tradition, and performed by amateurs in nonprofessional settings. But the music of the 1960s was none of these, especially after electric instruments were added. Was it, then, not folk music, or had the definition of folk music changed?

Urban Blues

In the early twentieth century, country blues singers, particularly from the Mississippi Delta, moved to northern cities. Classic blues singers, notably Ma Rainey and Bessie Smith, performed with jazz and blues bands and paved the way for later jazz-blues singers such as Billie Holiday, Ella Fitzgerald, and Sarah Vaughan.

In the 1940s and 1950s, blues singers added electric guitar, a rhythm section, and sometimes horns; their new style came to be known as *urban blues,* one of several categories of blues. Urban blues had moved beyond traditional folk blues. The songs were now composed, recorded, and sold, though they were not produced and distributed by mainstream record labels until the second half of the twentieth century.

In 1949, *Billboard* magazine gave this genre the name **rhythm and blues,** or **R&B.** It has become a recognized and important genre of American popular music and of the music industry. The king of R&B (urban blues) was B. B. King. However, today, R&B is the preferred label for a wide spectrum of African American pop, notably R&B/hip-hop (the *Billboard* category), rather than only blues-based music (see "Early African American Influences" in chapter 6).

Other prominent blues artists include Muddy Waters, T-Bone Walker, Lightn'n Hopkins, and Howlin' Wolf. Several early rock artists based much of their repertoire on the blues, including the Rolling Stones, Jimi Hendrix, and Cream (with Eric Clapton). Contemporary rock-oriented blues musicians include Etta James, Robert Cray, John Hammond Jr., and Eric Clapton. Blues bands are currently popular; they are heard regularly at blues festivals and at clubs and community events in almost any city.

Listening Guide   No. 8

"(I'm Your) Hoochie Coochie Man"
CD1, Track 08, 3:55

Composer: Willie Dixon

Performers: Muddy Waters, lead vocals and guitar; Willie Dixon, bass; Little Walter, harmonica; Otis Spann, piano; Jimmy Rogers, guitar; Fred Below, drums. Recorded at Chess Records in Chicago (1954).

Genre: Urban blues from Chicago

Background: "(I'm Your) Hoochie Coochie Man" is a blues standard written by Willie Dixon. Dixon, who gave up boxing for a career in music, was a Chicago blues composer, producer, and performer who had a huge influence on rock and blues musicians of the 1960s. Working at Chess Records, Dixon wrote songs for Muddy Waters, Chuck Berry, Howlin' Wolf, Bo Diddley, and others. Muddy Waters, known as the "Godfather of the Blues," first performed this song in 1954. A major hit upon its release, it reached #8 on *Billboard* magazine's Black Singles chart.

Goals

Recognize the blues scale, tone bending, and distinctive rhythm of the blues style. Recognize the "stop time" in the verses.

Recognize the blues progression that underpins the verses, choruses, and instrumental rides. All blues progressions follow this basic chord pattern, in which each Roman numeral represents one measure of 4/4 time: I-I-I-I-IV-IV-I-I-V-IV-I-I. The most common length is the 12-bar format, but 8- and 10-bar groupings are common variations. Even within these variations, the basic pattern remains consistent. In this blues, notice the differing lengths of the blues progressions in the verses and choruses compared with the instrumental ride.

Guide

Eight repetitions of the blues progression in slow 4/4 time. Introduction and verses are in "stop-time." **Stop-time** was originally a jazz technique in which the rhythm section stops playing for one or more beats each measure while a soloist continues to play.

Intro	2-bar (pick up and one full bar) in "stop-time"	
First chorus	8-bar blues	*The gypsy woman told my momma, before I was born* *You got a boy-child's comin', gonna be a son-of-a-gun* *He gonna make pretty womens, jump and shout* *The world will only know, a-what it's all about*
Chorus	8-bar blues	*Y'know I'm here* *Everybody knows I'm here* *And I'm the hoochie coochie man* *Everybody knows I'm here*
Second Verse	8-bar blues	*I got a black cat bone, I got a mojo too* *I got John the Conqueror, I'm gonna mess with you*

Listening Guide –Continued   No. 8

		I'm gonna make you girls, lead me by the hand
		Then the world will know, the hoochie coochie man
Chorus	8-bar blues	*Y'know I'm here*
		Everybody knows I'm here
		And I'm the hoochie coochie man
		Everybody knows I'm here
Instrumental	12-bar blues progression repeats twice	
Third Verse	8-bar blues	*On the seventh hour, of the seventh day,*
		on the seventh month, the seventh doctor said:
		"He's born for good luck, and I know you see;
		Got seven hundred dollars, and don't you mess with me
Chorus	8-bar blues	*Y'know I'm here*
		Everybody knows I'm here
		Well you know, I'm the hoochie coochie man
		The whole round world know we here

Reflections

How similar is Chicago blues to early rock and roll? How is it different?

Compare this performance with the Leadbelly (Listening Guide 7), Little Richard (Listening Guide 25), and Clifton Chenier (Listening Guide 32); which selection most closely resembles the Chicago blues?

Why do you think the blues progression is shortened in the verses of this song?

Do you think the change from the 8-bar progression in the verses and choruses to the 12-bar progression in the instrumental section enhances or detracts from the blues style?

Summary

American folk music derives from common musical practices of millions of Americans from the beginning of our nation to the present. Some practices have changed little over the past hundred years. Others have adapted to recent changes in taste and style and to advances in audio technology, electronic music, and media.

The study of folk music provides two important benefits: (1) insight into America's musical history through a recognition of the styles that continue to be important to many Americans and (2) an understanding of how music evolves and what influences generate change. In addition, the relatively simple form of much folk music provides a way to study musical characteristics and techniques that will contribute to your development of listening skills as you prepare for more complicated music in later chapters.

American folk music is rooted in the traditions and styles of the British and Europeans and influenced by African cultures. The story of America's folk music was in its development and evolution as it moved from the northeastern cities to the rural South and West and merged with music of other cultures, particularly African-based music.

4 *Religious Music Traditions*

Chapter Outline

In This Chapter

What do the terms psalter, shape-note system, *and* lining out *mean?*

What do the terms hymnody, psalm-singing, revival music, black gospel, *and* praise music *mean?*

The religious traditions of our nation, as with our folk traditions, helped shape American culture from the time of the earliest European settlers in the early 1600s. Much of the traditional religious music—its hymns and songs—is part of America's "roots music." It is music at the core of America's culture, derived from and related directly to the everyday lives of its people.

Goals for Listening

As noted in chapter 3, the goal throughout the text is to focus on individual and interactive musical elements such as basic characteristics of melody, rhythm, tonality, and harmony; degrees of loudness; qualities of tone production; and basic elements of musical structure.

The Roots of American Protestant Music

American Protestant religious music grew out of America's rural and small-town folk cultures, from both white and black populations. This religious music is emphasized in this book, not because music from other traditions did not exist or was not important, but because these various styles of Protestant music were prominent and had a deep impact on American culture. Music from two other religious traditions is discussed elsewhere in the book: (1) the liturgical music of the Roman Catholic Church in chapter 9 (page 187), discussed as part of western European classical music, and (2) the religious music of the Jewish people in chapter 8 (page 174), considered as part of world music.

Psalm Singing and Psalters

When the English Pilgrims and Puritans first settled in Massachusetts in the early 1600s, they brought with them the practice of **psalm singing.** Both groups had fled religious persecution and wanted to establish colonies where they could worship in freedom. The religious practices of these early immigrants included the unaccompanied singing of metered and rhymed versions of the Psalms.

Two divergent styles of psalm singing emerged during this nation's first hundred years: (1) a European, formal musical style, found among the more urban and musically literate populace, and (2) a folklike style, found among the less musically educated people, who typically lived in rural and small-town environments. The formal style required learning hymns from notated music; the singers had to be able to read music. The folk style required learning songs by memory (the oral tradition).

Both the Puritans and the Pilgrims used English **psalters**—hymnbooks containing the psalms to be sung during worship, sometimes with notated melodies. The Pilgrims used Henry Ainsworth's psalter, *The Book of Psalmes: Englished both in Prose and Metre,* published in 1612. This book included 39 melodies, one of which was "Old Hundredth," commonly known today as the "Doxology." The first American psalter, the *Bay Psalm Book,* was published in 1640 in Cambridge, Massachusetts. Printed on a press brought from England, it was the first book of any kind published in British North America. It included no musical notation. The first edition with notation appeared in 1698.

Psalm singing had a profound effect on the development of American religious music. It was preferred by the early settlers over the liturgical music of the Roman Catholic Church and over the hymns of the Lutheran Church, because these English immigrants were averse to state religion and ecclesiastical power.

Lining Out, Singing Schools, and the Shape-Note System

Psalm singing began with notated music, but the oral tradition eventually became prevalent. The music in the psalters did not benefit people who could not read music;

and there were many such people, particularly in rural areas. Like most musical practices derived from oral tradition, consistency and accuracy were not ensured, nor necessarily desired. Local variants developed; fragments of one tune would find their way into others; thus, the number of totally different tunes in common use diminished.

To sing the hymns, many rural congregations practiced **lining out,** a technique that involved their own memory and the leadership of someone with a powerful voice. The leader would sing one line at a time, and the congregation would sing it back. A form of call and response, lining out was not a new idea; it had begun in England and Scotland. In fact, it is still a common practice today in some rural regions of the southeastern United States.

People changed the melodies according to their own musical taste and ability. Without strong direction, singers tended to sing in their own way, at tempos that accommodated the slowest singers. By the early eighteenth century, however, many of the college-educated ministers were expressing dissatisfaction with the state of psalm singing in New England. Essays were written and sermons preached decrying this folk style and the practice of lining out. Many people felt that the "proper" tradition of psalm singing had been lost. The critics urged a return to singing from musical notation.

Around 1720, a few New England ministers decided to do something to improve this "deplorable" state of psalm singing. They began to establish **singing schools** to encourage people to sing together "decently" and with "some semblance of art." The leader was usually an itinerant "singing master." The participants, many of them teenagers and young adults, would come together for an evening or, in some cases, for two or three days to learn to read music and to sing hymn tunes. The young people also came to the singing schools to make friends and to have a good time.

In eighteenth-century New England, the church served not only as a place for worship but also as a town meeting place and a center of community life, both sacred and secular. The need for improved singing grew from the church, but the nondenominational singing schools—like the churches—also met the social needs of the community. Since psalm singing took place not just in the church but throughout the community, some psalm or hymn tunes and secular folk tunes became closely related and even interchangeable.

Church music was meant for the performer, rather than the listener. The idea was to participate in singing, not to be sung to. How the music sounded to a nonparticipant was of little importance. What was important was the experience of singing, which allowed the congregation to be active participants in worship.

The Easy Instructor, published in Philadelphia in 1801, introduced a **shape-note system,** whereby each pitch of a hymn tune was notated on a staff. Each note had a note head and a stem, and each note head had a distinctive shape that represented a specific pitch, as can be seen in the illustration on page 60. These books were used in the singing schools that were organized throughout the South, and so the shape-note system spread.

The singing school was the main vehicle for disseminating shape-note music. Many of the hymns sung today, at least in some Protestant churches, such as "Nearer, My God to Thee" and "Rock of Ages," were by urban composers and later became part of the shape-note repertoire. Singing schools and efforts to teach people to read music created a demand not only for hymnbooks but also for new texts and harmonized tunes. The musical benefits of the singing school movement included

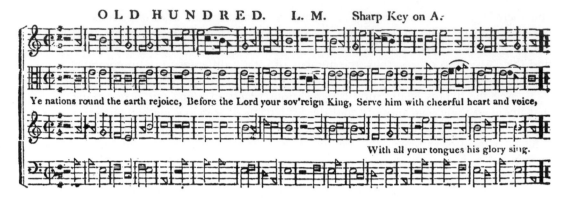

This shape-note hymn, known to many people as the "Doxology," was included in the oldest known shape-note hymn book, *The Easy Instructor* (1801). The shape-note system helped singers learn to read music.

Source: White Spirituals in the Southern Uplands, by George Jackson Pullen.

raising the general level of music literacy, creating new hymns, and encouraging local composers.

These new collections included three- and four-part hymn settings of melodies that resembled the ballads, songs, and fiddle tunes of the southern oral tradition. The composers were presumably arrangers of **indigenous** folk melodies. In effect, they captured in notation hundreds of these traditional melodies, arranged them as "folk hymns," and published them in shape-note hymnbooks. The best-known of these hymnbooks were *The Southern Harmony* (1835) and *The Sacred Harp* (1844). Both collections were used widely in singing schools, by church congregations, at social meetings, and at conventions. Conventions and all-day "sings" were organized around these hymnbooks. Organizers included the United Sacred Harp Musical Association, the Chattahoochee Musical Convention, and the Southern Musical Convention.

Listening Guide   No. 9

"Sherburne"

CD1, Track 9, 1:44

Composer: Daniel Read.

Performer: A weekend meeting of the Alabama Sacred Harp Convention, in a country church in northern Alabama. Recorded in 1959.

Genre: Folk hymn, fuging tune.

Listening Guide –Continued   No. 9

"Sherburne," a fuging tune, was included in *The Sacred Harp*, a hymn book first published in 1844.

Context: "Sherburne" is from the early New England period. It was first included in *The Sacred Harp,* a collection of four-part settings of folk hymns first published in 1844. It is a shape-note hymn that reveals a singing style that was common in singing schools, Sacred Harp Conventions, worship services, and other gatherings throughout the nineteenth century.

Goals

Recognize and describe the texture and form of each hymn.
Describe the meter and rhythm of each hymn.

Guide

This hymn can be felt in a two-beat meter at a moderate tempo. The first time through, the participants utilize the **"fasola"** style of reading the shaped notes (a method to help singers learn new hymns). After singing the syllables, they use the hymn text. The phrase structure is the same with the hymn text as with the fasola. Refer to the accompanying notation.

The first phrase is in a chordal or hymnlike style. In the remaining phrases, you hear the same melody sung independently (the fuging tune—sung like a round)

–Continued

Listening Guide –Continued   No. 9

except at the cadences of the third and fifth phrases. Both times, the first two beats of the first phrase are not in strict time. The singers start on the downbeat but hold it slightly before feeling the second beat.

1–2–3–4–5–	While Shepherds watched their flocks . . .
1–2–3–4–5–6–7–8–	The Angel of the Lord . . .
1–3–4–5–6–7–	The Angel of the Lord . . .
1–2–3–4–5–6–7–8–	The Angel of the Lord . . .
1–2–3–4–5–6–7–	The Angel of the Lord . . .

Reflections

The singers make no attempt to "pretty up" their voices; they sing at full volume at a quick tempo. One hears no embellishments or ornamentations.

The rhythm is steady and straightforward.

Notice the four-part vertical structures (harmony) common in hymn singing and also how, in the second phrase of each verse, the treatment of both harmony and rhythm changes.

At first, all the vocal parts (soprano, alto, tenor, and bass voices) move rhythmically at the same time. At the sixth bar, the music shifts texture. Each voice then moves separately, one in imitation of the other; thus, each vocal line has the melody.

Melodic fragments are passed around from voice to voice.

Traditional Black Gospel Music

In the mid-twentieth century, *gospel music* referred to a style of music that emerged from black worshipers and the way they worshiped—their manner of religious musical expression. As noted before, this style became a vital part of music in black churches and also in popular culture. Its roots lie in black spirituals, camp-meeting hymns and songs, adaptations of revival hymns, the lively services of black churches, and the intense, songlike sermons of black preachers—all combined with cultural and performance qualities growing out of the slave culture and the black experience.

The infusion of blues and jazz into the religious musical expression of African Americans in the early twentieth century created modern, black gospel music. It became a style that comfortably merged sacred and secular influences. This music combines passionate religious feelings with dramatic stage presentation. The more popular black gospel music grew out of the Church of God in Christ and similar churches. These churches functioned as folk theaters, community centers, and houses of worship.

Black gospel is emotional, vocal, physical, theatrical, and musically skillful, and it arouses an enthusiastic physical and emotional response in the audience.

Thomas A. Dorsey (1899–1993), a former blues singer, became known as the "father of black gospel music," largely because of his success as a promoter, teacher, choir director, and organizer.

Mahalia Jackson (1911–1972), perhaps the foremost black gospel singer of all time, toured with Thomas A. Dorsey for five years, then pursued a career that gave her worldwide recognition.

The sound of black gospel has been a dominant vocal influence in the rhythmic and theatrical aspects of much contemporary popular music, particularly soul and rhythm and blues (R&B). The appeal of black gospel transcends sectarian boundaries. The music has syncopation and rhythmic vitality. Singers decorate, embellish, and vary the music in all sorts of ways; they frequently use a wide vocal range and perform intricate melodic and rhythmic patterns with remarkable dexterity. Hard-driving energy is typical. The style frequently features interplay between a leader and respondents, who may be the choir, the congregation, or both.

The father of *modern* black gospel music was Thomas A. Dorsey (1899–1993), a former blues singer (he sang under the name of Georgia Tom) who became a successful promoter, composer, publisher, teacher, choir director, and organizer. Black

Listening Guide   No. 10

Tramaine Hawkins, a gospel singer and recording artist for more than 25 years, sings one of the all-time great spiritual songs, "Amazing Grace."

"Amazing Grace"
CD1, Track 10, 3:35

Words: John Newton (1725–1807), a slave trader from England who was converted to Christianity and became a preacher.

Performer: Tramaine Hawkins, with orchestra, keyboards, bass, and drums. Recorded in Hollywood with the L.A. Love Crusade Choir in 1993.

Genre: An American folk melody in a contemporary black gospel setting.

Goals

Recognize and describe melodic embellishments: **rubato** (flexible rhythm), **melisma** (several notes, perhaps many, to one word or one syllable of a word), **vibrato** (a stylistic vocal technique featuring an up-and-down variation—a gentle wobbling—of the pitch).

Recognize and follow the verses of the hymn.

Describe the setting of the song.

Guide

All verses have two phrases. Verses 1–3 of the hymn text follow.

Listening Guide –Continued   No. 10

Verse 1   0:00   **A cappella;** slow tempo; highly embellished; extended when the orchestra enters on final cadence

Amazing grace! How sweet the sound,
That saved a wretch like me!
I once was lost, but now am found,
Was blind, but now I see.

Verse 2   1:28   Similar in style to verse 1, but with the orchestra playing an underlying, unchanging texture; chord changes begin near the end of the first phrase

'Twas grace that taught my heart to fear,
And grace my fear(s) relieved.
How precious did that grace appear
The hour I first believed!

Verse 3   2:39   In a new key; stronger rhythmic impulse; modulates to another new key

Through many dangers, toils, and snares,
I have already come.
'Tis grace has brought me safe thus far,
And grace will lead me home.

Reflections

What is the musical interest in this example? What is the cultural interest?
Does Hawkins capture the spirit of this song?
Describe the nature and extent of the melodic embellishment.
Is this church music? Concert music? Gospel music? Other?

gospel music influenced the development of jazz, soul, and rhythm and blues, and became known worldwide, mostly because of the efforts of Dorsey and the popularity of gospel singers like Mahalia Jackson and Aretha Franklin.

The Edwin Hawkins Singers helped create the sound of contemporary gospel music. Their recording of "Oh Happy Day" (1967) became the first big crossover hit (gospel-pop); yet, not surprisingly, it sounds very traditional today. Aretha Franklin, Sam Cooke, and Little Richard were also among the artists who moved successfully from gospel to popular music. In recent years, many singers who remained in black gospel have incorporated elements of popular styles in their music. Black gospel remains in the church but also has made its mark in the world.

White Gospel Music: Revival and Evangelical Hymns

Gospel music originally referred to hymns and songs with texts related to the first four books of the New Testament—Matthew, Mark, Luke, and John—rather than to the Psalms. The term came to describe an extensive body of evangelical hymns and songs used at revival services, at religious camp meetings, in Sunday schools, and in churches. This music became prevalent during the early nineteenth century, when itinerant preachers and evangelists stimulated a remarkable revival of religion. Present-day southern gospel music grew out of this tradition.

This revival spread quickly throughout the South as preachers traveled and conducted mass meetings to spread the Gospel and win converts to Christianity. These public religious rallies or revival services were often held nightly for one or two weeks. The preachers understood very well the role of congregational singing and special music in stimulating the emotions of a crowd.

The gospel music sung at revivals and camp meetings in the early nineteenth century was to a large extent derived from the oral folk tradition. Religious poetry was adapted to familiar songs. Gospel music originally appealed to both white and black Americans; however, by the second half of the nineteenth century, distinct styles began to emerge, though mostly in performance practices rather than in the hymns themselves. That is, the hymns were frequently the same, but the style of singing them came to differ, as can be seen in the various hymn and song collections used in revivals.

The revival or camp-meeting hymn, created out of the oral tradition, remained popular in the rural churches and in the Pentecostal or Holiness denominations and sects. The gospel or church hymns, composed by writers and musicians, became important in urban churches, which wanted music that was more "classical" and more European—with four-part harmony that combined psalm tunes and the music of classical composers with more traditional folk hymns.

The interest in gospel hymns resulted in a tremendous number of compositions and published collections; many hymns sung in American churches today came from these collections. Thomas Hastings composed 600 hymn texts, more than 1000 hymn tunes, and 50 collections. William Bradbury published more than 50 collections, one of which sold over 250,000 copies. Lowell Mason composed, adapted, and arranged hymns and published more than 20 collections; his *Carmina Sacra* alone sold half a million copies in 1844. According to Mason himself, a professor at the Boston Academy of Music, this collection comprised the "most popular Psalm and hymn tunes in general use, together with a great variety of new tunes, chants, sentences, motets, and anthems, principally by distinguished European composers: the whole constituting one of the most complete collections of music for choirs, congregations, singing schools and societies."

Toward the end of the nineteenth century, revivals shifted from rural to urban settings. Great buildings called *tabernacles* were built to house the revival meetings. Preachers, to an even greater extent than before, became religious salesmen, sometimes establishing complex organizations. Realizing the importance of music at these revivals, they became associated with song leaders who conducted congregational hymn singing and sang solos.

One of the first influential pairings was evangelist Dwight Moody and his song leader, Ira Sankey. Sankey made the gospel hymn a popular song. Many hymns were in verse-refrain form—simple, repetitive, emotional, and memorable. At the turn of the century, evangelist Billy Sunday recognized the value of his song leader, Homer Rodeheaver, who helped make his revivals entertaining and popular. In the mid-twentieth century, Billy Graham—with his featured soloist, George Beverly Shea, and his musical director, Cliff Barrows—held revivals worldwide. Shea became a successful recording artist in his own right. Graham's crusades were urban and international and made extensive use of the media, particularly radio and television.

Listening Guide No. 11

"I'm Headed for the Promised Land"
CD1, Track 11, 1:13

Performer: The Chuck Wagon Gang, a vocal quartet with guitar. Recorded in 1956.
Genre: Southern gospel.

Goals

Describe the overall style: melody, harmony, rhythm, tone quality, form, and text.
Describe the vocal quality.
Describe the style of guitar accompaniment.

Guide

Duple meter in four at a moderate tempo; strict, regular rhythm; men's and women's voices with guitar accompaniment; two verses, each with two equal phrases; very repetitive; little melodic, harmonic, or rhythmic embellishment. The opening guitar arpeggio is a tonic chord; an arpeggio is a chord with each note sounding separately.

Intro	A short, tonic guitar chord (arpeggio); free rhythm
Verse 1	Quartet: 8-bar phrase, open cadence (four 2-bar segments) 8-bar phrase, closed cadence (four 2-bar segments)
Verse 2	Vocal solo with quartet: same structure as above and for the following verses
Verse 3	Quartet
Verse 4	Vocal solo with quartet

Reflections

Discuss the repetitiveness. Does it add to or detract from your appreciation of this song?
Compare the style of this performance with that of black gospel and other styles.

Popular Contemporary Styles

A modern counterpart of the music of the revival movement, particularly southern gospel, is the music that is an integral part of the programs (services) of TV "televangelists." The purposes of television revival meetings and "old-time religion" are the same: to win souls to Christianity and to use music to help make that happen. The music is familiar in style to large numbers of people: simple, catchy, repetitive, and easy to sing. In recent decades, this music has influenced and been influenced by new styles of commercial popular music: contemporary Christian music, or CCM.

The contemporary manifestation of white gospel music (southern gospel) can be found in the early-twentieth-century gospel quartets and family groups, many centered in Tennessee, and many who later crossed over into more commercial country, such as Elvis Presley, Johnny Cash, the Statler Brothers, Ricky Skaggs, the Gaither Vocal Band, and the Oak Ridge Boys.

Music that incorporates elements from pop, rock, and rhythm and blues (R&B) styles is increasingly becoming a part of the contemporary church. Popular styles, with electric guitars, electric bass, and drum sets (live or on tape), have become standard fare in many churches that seek new audiences (parishioners).

Gospel music today seems to have transcended, to some degree, the stylistic distinctions between white gospel and black gospel. Black, white, and mixed groups are creating music in styles with which they feel comfortable—styles that they believe will appeal to the widest audience, regardless of categories and labels. Much of this music consciously incorporates elements of pop and rock and even rap/hip-hop; as a result, the only difference between a contemporary white or black gospel song and a pop or rock song may be in the lyrics—one being sacred, the other secular. It has become acceptable (and perhaps commercially practical) to use popular culture to proclaim the Christian message.

Listening Guide   No. 12

"Lord of the Dance" (excerpt)
CD1, Track 12, 3:15

Performer: Steven Curtis Chapman, from the album *Signs of Life* (1996).
Genre: Contemporary Christian.
Background: Steven Curtis Chapman is one of the most successful singer-songwriters in contemporary Christian music, beginning with his first album, *First Hand*, in 1987. Among his many honors, the Gospel Music Association has awarded him 45 Dove Awards from 1989 through 2002, including multiple awards for Artist of the Year, Songwriter of the Year, Male Vocalist of the Year, and various albums of the year. He also won four Grammy awards during the 1990s, including two for Best Pop-Contemporary Gospel albums.

Listening Guide –Continued No. 12

Contemporary
Christian singer Steven
Curtis Chapman.

Goals

Identify the instruments.

Describe characteristics of the choruses and of the verses.

Describe Chapman's vocal quality.

Guide

0:00 Intro—instrumental

0:30 Chorus (**vamp**—a short, repetitive pattern connecting one section with another)

0:40 Verse 1

1:03 Chorus (vamp)

1:14 Verse 2

1:37 Chorus (vamp)

1:59 Chorus extended

2:07 Verse 3

2:30 Chorus

2:52 Chorus extended

3:02 Fade

–Continued

Listening Guide –Continued   No. 12

Reflections

Consider the music in relation to the words—for example, the chorus of verse 3:

> *I am the heart, He is the heartbeat*
> *I am the eyes, He is the sight*
> *And I see clearly, I am just a body*
> *He is the life*
>
> *I move my feet, I go through the motions*
> *But He gives purpose to chance*
> *I am the dancer*
> *He is the Lord of the dance*

Does this song reflect pop, contemporary Christian, gospel, or something else? What aspects of this music can be considered sacred? What aspects would be considered secular?

Christian music is promoted largely through Christian bookstores and Christian programs on radio and television, including Christian cable networks and radio stations. The more popular Christian and gospel recordings are evident in any major full-service record store. The Gospel Music Association (GMA), through its annual Dove Awards, continues to influence the style of contemporary Christian/gospel music—having moved from its southern gospel roots to sophisticated, lush, sometimes symphonic arrangements of newly composed songs in a pop style. As our culture has become more inclusive, as styles have merged, and as existing labels have become less useful, GMA has included and honored increasingly more gospel artists from the African American community.

Summary

American religious music, like its folk music, is based on common musical practices of millions of Americans throughout our nation's history. Some practices have been slow to change; others have adapted to recent shifts in taste and style and to advances in audio technology, electronic music, and media.

The study of America's religious music, as with its folk music, provides insight into American history and to musical styles that continue to be an important part of the lives of many Americans. Additionally, the relatively simple forms of much religious music provide a way to study musical characteristics and techniques that can contribute to your development of listening skills as you prepare for more complicated music in later chapters.

Like other aspects of American culture, American religious music is rooted in the traditions and styles of the British and Europeans and was later influenced by African cultures. The story of America's religious music is in its development and evolution as it moved from the northeastern cities to the rural South and West and merged, particularly, with African-based spirituals and gospel music.

White and black gospel music since the 1990s has, for the most part, become less differentiated. Black artists have, in increasingly larger numbers, been winners at the annual Gospel Music Association's Dove Awards. It is becoming more common to simply refer to pop-oriented, commercial, religious music—whether by black or by white artists—as "gospel" or "Christian."

5 *Jazz Styles*

Although jazz is a relatively recent, twentieth-century American phenomenon, jazz artists and styles are recognized worldwide. Jazz includes widely divergent styles ranging from entertainment music to art music. It is ever changing and defies simple definition.

Jazz began in the early part of the twentieth century in the bars and nightclubs of poor urban neighborhoods, particularly in New Orleans. These bars and clubs were the places where musicians who aspired to a career playing jazz were able to find employment. The jazz they played emerged from a combining of the songs, dances, and musical instincts and preferences of people of African and European (particularly French and Spanish) heritage.

Jazz has come a long way over the past hundred years. Today it is international in scope—performed and listened to nearly everywhere—and it has a strong following, especially in continental Europe, Scandinavia, Japan, Africa, South America, and Canada. It is heard not only in bars and nightclubs but also in the finest hotels, on college campuses, in concert halls, and even in churches. Jazz has become an accepted part of the music curriculum in schools and colleges. Courses are devoted to the study of jazz, and music students in many schools can pursue degrees in jazz. Students can play in jazz ensembles for academic credit in American colleges and universities, and most high schools have stage bands. The International Association of Jazz Educators was organized to further the study and performance of jazz in our educational system.

Many women, such as Mary Lou Williams, Shirley Horn, Hazel Scott, Marian McPartland, Toshiko Akiyoshi, and Diana Krall have achieved distinction as jazz musicians, not to mention the large number of distinguished women jazz singers, such as Billie Holiday, Ella Fitzgerald, and Sarah Vaughan. In addition, many women have been influential as composers or arrangers, as leaders of jazz groups, or as writers and teachers.

Goals for Listening

The primary purpose of this chapter is to develop your ability to recognize and describe these elements of the jazz style:

- Musical concepts: syncopation, improvisation, swing rhythm, and characteristic formal structures, such as the 32-bar chorus (four 8-bar phrases with bridge—a a b a), 12-bar blues, riffs, and ostinato (repeated) patterns.
- Common jazz instruments, common ensembles (big band, combo), characteristic tone qualities (vibrato, use of mutes), and unique performance practices, such as comping, scat singing, and walking bass.
- Sounds of individual instruments and instrumental combinations (sections).

In addition, continue developing the ability to recognize and describe these basic melodic, harmonic, and rhythmic characteristics:

- Repetitive and characteristic patterns, motives, and themes; phrases, phrase groupings (question-answer phrase patterns), and cadences (open and closed endings).

Billie Holiday was one of the most respected and revered jazz/blues/big band singers of the 1930s.

Ella Fitzgerald sings in an NBC television studio in Manhattan in 1959. Fitzgerald considered herself as "one of the band." She would "take choruses," improvising (scat singing) like an instrumentalist. But she could also sing a tender ballad with great sensitivity. Her long career extended from the late 1930s through the 1980s. She is considered by many to be the greatest jazz singer of all time.

- Musical lines other than melody (drum patterns, bass lines, comping).
- Personal interpretation and melodic embellishment.
- Rhythmic impulse: the character of the rhythm (a driving beat, a fluid rhythm, a weak or uneven pulse).
- Chord changes and chord progressions. Become more skillful in recognizing the sounds of the three primary chords (I, IV, and V).

The Listening Guides in this chapter feature various styles of jazz: traditional (through the 1920s), big band (1930s and 1940s), bebop (late 1940s and through the 1950s), cool (primarily 1950s) and modern jazz, fusion (jazz rock), and smooth jazz.

What Is Jazz?

Jazz began in the early days of radio and recordings, and these media brought it to the attention of the public. Recordings, especially, brought the music of jazz musicians to other jazz musicians and to the public—a valuable way to share, learn, grow, and influence other musicians and, indeed, the future course of jazz.

Today, jazz is part of a large and complex entertainment industry. Jazz musicians make recordings to sell—to become popular—but not at the expense of the integrity of their art. Elements of jazz have become evident in many styles of popular music.

Jazz aspires to do more than entertain, and the great jazz musicians strive for better ways of expression, sometimes in very sophisticated forms and styles. Perhaps for these reasons, jazz has never achieved mass popularity except during the swing era. Most jazz today is not considered pop music, commercial music, or music created for the sole purpose of entertaining; rather, for many musicians, jazz is a genuine form of art music. The great jazz artists have a high level of musicianship, a sense of what jazz is, an appreciation of its power to communicate feelings, and a desire to share their art with others.

The Jazz Style

Jazz includes many styles and techniques. This list describes the common characteristics of jazz:

- The music **swings;** this is the feel of jazz—the jazz rhythm.
- Musicians improvise, for **improvisation** is at the heart of jazz.
- The rhythm includes much **syncopation**—off-beat rhythms.
- The music is played on certain instruments, such as the saxophone, trumpet, trombone, drums, bass, and piano. These are jazz instruments only when they are played in a jazz style in a jazz context. Sometimes jazz is played on instruments that are not commonly used in jazz performance, such as the flute, tuba, organ, and harp.

Listen to popular songs, hymns, folk songs, marches, or any pieces that do not fall into the category of jazz. Do they swing? Are they syncopated? What instruments are used? Identify the factors that distinguish any of these pieces from jazz.

The Feel of Swing

Swing is a manner of performance—perhaps more a feel than a precise, describable, easily analyzed technique. At the risk of being too simplistic, we might say that swing is the product of some combination of the following:

- *Swing rhythm.* Jazz is played rhythmically in a way that creates heightened energy and vitality. Repeated, evenly spaced rhythms are unusual, and syncopation is common.
- *A unique combination of timekeeping and syncopation.* The drummer may keep time with the bass drum and a cymbal while emphasizing off-beat accents with the snare drum or another cymbal. When accompanying a soloist, the bass player often keeps time by playing a note on each beat (known as **walking bass**) while the pianist plays syncopated chords at irregular time intervals, providing rhythmic energy and vitality (known as **comping**). In big band jazz, this rhythmic energy is also generated by **riffs.** These are short, syncopated patterns usually written for specific groups of instruments. They provide punctuated background material while another section or a soloist is playing the melody or improvising. Occasionally, an entire chorus is made up of riffs without a recognizable melody.

- *Melodies that are not played as written.* A jazz musician always interprets a melody to make it swing. The musician may vary the rhythm, slide into or out of pitches, shift accents, bend pitches, add notes, and do whatever else feels right to give a tune the feel of jazz—to make it swing.
- *Vibrato.* A shaking or wobbling of tones—particularly of sustained tones in a melody—is essential to the jazz style. This is frequently a slow, wide vibrato, sometimes a combination of a straight tone followed by vibrato. Compare the clarinet vibrato of Benny Goodman (in Listening Guide 2, page 35) with that of any classical clarinet soloist. Compare the vibrato of Miles Davis's trumpet playing (in Listening Guide 18 in this chapter) with that of trumpet players in bands, orchestras, or brass quintets.
- *Instruments played in ways unique, or nearly unique, to jazz.* For example, in jazz, the drummer plays a drum set that has a variety of percussion instruments—snare drum, tom-toms, several different cymbals, and bass drum—whereas in a band or orchestra, these instruments, if used, are likely to be played by different musicians. In jazz, the bass player usually plucks the strings rather than using a bow as bassists most commonly do in an orchestra. In jazz, the trumpet or trombone player frequently uses a mute to alter the quality of the sound; mutes are less common in bands and orchestras.

Instruments

The development of jazz has resulted in some standard jazz instruments and instrumentation, but there are many exceptions. Here we consider **combo jazz**, which involves between 2 and 9 players (usually 3–5), and **big band jazz**, which involves 10 or more players (usually 15–18).

Groups of instruments in big band jazz are known as **sections**: the rhythm section (piano, bass, and drums), the brass section (three or four trumpets and three or four trombones), and the sax section (traditionally, two altos, two tenors, and one baritone). On occasion, a big band includes French horns or a tuba, a guitar, and sometimes a featured singer. The most basic instrumental group is the rhythm section: piano, bass, and drums. The rhythm section is basic to both combo and big band jazz and frequently functions as a self-contained jazz combo. When it does, the piano is the primary lead or solo instrument, with occasional solos from the bass or drums. Particularly in modern jazz, the conventional, acoustic piano is often replaced by the electric piano, synthesizer keyboards, or a combination of electric and acoustic keyboard instruments. The guitar is sometimes included in the rhythm section, although it frequently functions as a lead or solo instrument. The rhythm section, incidentally, is also common in most forms of popular music.

A common jazz combo adds one or more lead instruments to the rhythm section: trumpet and tenor or alto sax are most common. Sometimes we find trombone, clarinet, vibraphone (vibes), flute, soprano sax, or baritone sax. In Latin jazz and some forms of modern jazz, groups often add a percussionist to play instruments such as bongos, claves, and castanets to add color and vitality to the rhythm.

Improvisation

To improvise music is to make it up as you go along. Improvisation is a fundamental characteristic of jazz and is important in every jazz style. This concept does not imply total freedom; to improvise is not simply to play whatever you feel like playing. In all jazz styles, there is structure on which creative improvisation is based. In some styles, the structure is clear and controlling. In others, the control or guideline is minimal. A structure might be an 8-bar phrase of a 32-bar chorus; it might be a specific chord progression that underlies a popular tune or a 12-bar blues tune; or it might be a meter that the improviser adheres to (listen to Listening Guide 2, page 35, and to Listening Guide 16 in this chapter).

The ability to swing and the ability to improvise often set the jazz musician apart from other musicians. Many of the best classically trained musicians, for example, do not have these skills. A musician who is not skilled in jazz will play without a sense of "swing," and the jazz "feel" will be absent. Many musicians, however, are able to excel at playing both Western classical and jazz styles.

The Roots of Jazz

Jazz—like American society—is the product of many cultures and influences. In some ways, it represents a merging of cultures and musical styles; in other ways, it retains distinct ethnic characteristics. In the late nineteenth and early twentieth centuries, Americans—both black and white, from both North and South—sang and danced to "jazzy" music—the syncopated popular music of the time. That music included several song types:

- *Popular songs.* These are the syncopated melodies and rhythms of minstrel songs, cakewalks, vaudeville songs and dances, and the dance music of New York City and other emerging centers of popular music. For the most part, these notated songs had considerable rhythmic vitality. They typically had a syncopated melody and a strongly pulsating accompaniment (see Listening Guide 21, page 109).
- *Blues songs. Blues* is not synonymous with *jazz.* Originally, it was part of the African American oral tradition (see chapter 5). After the blues culture shifted from rural communities to cities in the early decades of the twentieth century, blues songs came to be performed by women accompanied by a New Orleans–style jazz combo. The music and spirit of the blues were compatible with the emerging jazz style. By the 1920s, blues and jazz had become inseparable, always influencing each other. One of the greatest blues singers of that time was Bessie Smith.
- *Rags.* **Ragtime** became a notated form of popular music, originally for solo piano. It developed in and around St. Louis, and its most popular creator and performer was Scott Joplin (1868–1917). Through performances by various traveling musicians and the sale of popular pieces, ragtime arrived in New Orleans and other southern cities. It was then arranged for instruments used in the popular black brass bands.
- *Brass band marches and dances.* Brass bands of New Orleans and other southern cities were associated with private black lodges, social clubs, and fraternal organizations that employed black musicians to play at dances, parties, parades, and especially funerals. A typical instrumentation included clarinets, trombones, cornets (similar to a trumpet), banjos, bass horns (tubas), and drums.
- *Gospel songs.* Early **gospel music,** particularly that of rural and nonliterate blacks, combined the shouts and moans of the blues with exciting rhythms, high energy, religious fervor, theatrical presentations, and religious texts. This style developed through the nineteenth century and still exists today. It has become popular among both blacks and whites.

Bessie Smith was a jazz and blues singer in vaudeville
shows in the 1920s and the big bands of the early 1930s.

Jazz Styles

The history of modern jazz style begins with New Orleans jazz. Musicians increasingly
found that the music they wanted to play and the public wanted to hear had jazzy
characteristics. Jazz music became established in New Orleans when artists devoted
to jazz began to emerge, particularly in the second decade of the twentieth century.

New Orleans and Chicago Jazz

New Orleans jazz, or traditional jazz, was performed mostly in the area of New
Orleans known as Storyville, which contained bars, nightclubs, and brothels that
hired jazz musicians to provide entertainment and dance music. In 1917, Storyville
was closed down as part of "urban reform." With that closing, opportunities for
aspiring jazz musicians were lost, so they left New Orleans. Some traveled on boats
up the Mississippi River. Many went to Chicago. Others settled as far afield as New
York and Los Angeles. By 1920, so many of the most accomplished musicians of
New Orleans had moved elsewhere that no recordings of New Orleans jazz were ever
made in New Orleans.

The most notable recording artists to come out of New Orleans were Jelly Roll
Morton, piano; Kid Ory, trombone; King Oliver, cornet; Louis Armstrong, cornet;
Sidney Bechet, clarinet; and Nick LaRocca, clarinet. LaRocca headed a jazz group

Pictured is the George Williams Brass Band from New Orleans. The instrumentation of the New Orleans brass bands helped shape the instrumentation of the early jazz bands, particularly those that became identified with New Orleans jazz.

from New Orleans that later became known as the Original Dixieland Jazz Band. While in New York City in 1917, this group made the very first jazz recording.

New Orleans jazz reemerged in Chicago in the 1920s, largely through the music of transplanted New Orleans musicians. In its new location, it was called Chicago or Dixieland jazz, and it remains popular to this day (see Listening Guide 13 in this chapter).

New Orleans and Chicago jazz are actually quite similar:

- Both styles have high energy and rhythmic vitality.
- Both styles have clarinet, trumpet or cornet, and trombone as solo instruments; there are not many exceptions. Both styles have a rhythm section of piano, bass—either string bass or tuba—and drums. Sometimes there is no bass; sometimes there are no drums; sometimes there is no piano. If there is no piano, there will be a banjo or a guitar.
- Both styles use **"head" arrangements**—arrangements that are worked out in rehearsal and then performed from memory according to traditional jazz style (they are not notated).

- Both styles use group improvisation among the solo instruments. This improvisation follows rather strict conventions: (1) Musicians create melodic lines that fall within the chords dictated by the melody. (2) The trumpet plays the **lead** (the main melodic or solo part), the clarinet an obbligato (a higher, decorative part), and the trombone a lower melodic line derived from the main chord tones. (3) All parts move in independent lines but follow the same progression and interact with each other.
- The role of the rhythm section is timekeeping. Sometimes the performers put equal emphasis on each beat. Other times they may stress the first and third beats or the second and fourth beats. The piano (or banjo or guitar) plays chords in the same manner; none of them plays lead.
- The music has occasional **breaks** (stop time). All musicians stop except for a soloist who improvises for two bars. This usually happens at the end of a phrase.
- Musicians sometimes use **fills** to provide movement while the rhythm of a pattern or phrase stops. Fills provide **embellishment** between phrases.

The most successful and most famous of the New Orleans musicians unquestionably was Louis Armstrong (listen to Listening Guide No. 13). He had an illustrious career as a trumpet player, singer, and entertainer well into the 1960s. His primary influence was on jazz musicians through the recordings he made in Chicago in the 1920s with his combos the Hot Five and the Hot Seven. They not only educated the public about New Orleans jazz but established a model for Armstrong's greatest contributions to the development of jazz: (1) the possibility of innovative jazz improvisations extended for more than a two-bar break, and (2) the possibility of solo, improvised jazz singing, a style known as **scat singing** (vocal improvising similar to instrumental improvising).

Listening Guide No. 13

"Hotter Than That"
CD1, Track 13, 3:00

Composer: Lil Hardin Armstrong.
Performer: Louis Armstrong and His Hot Five: Louis Armstrong, cornet and vocal; Kid Ory, trombone; Johnny Dodds, clarinet; Lil Hardin Armstrong, piano; Johnny St. Cyr, banjo; and Lonnie Johnson, guitar. Recorded in Chicago in 1927.
Genre: Chicago jazz.

Goals

Recognize syncopation, breaks, and scat singing.
Identify the style of traditional jazz (Chicago jazz).

—Continued

Listening Guide –Continued   No. 13

Louis "Satchmo" Armstrong, one of the most influential, durable, and well-liked musicians in jazz history—from traditional New Orleans jazz, to Chicago jazz, to appearances in nearly 20 movies, to becoming a major touring and television star.

Identify instruments from their sounds.

Describe group improvisation.

Describe the relationship between improvisation and structure.

Guide

Count in a fast four or a moderately slow two.

0:00	Intro	8 bars	Full ensemble; group improvisation
0:09	First chorus	32 bars	Solo improvisation, cornet
			First break, cornet
			Second break, clarinet
0:45	Second chorus	32 bars	Solo improvisation, clarinet
			First break, clarinet
			Second break, vocal
1:21	Third chorus	32 bars	Solo improvisation, vocal (scat singing)
			First break, vocal
			Second break extended; vocal and guitar dialogue
2:14	Vamp	4 bars	Piano
2:18	Fourth chorus	16 bars	Solo improvisation, muted trombone; cornet break
		20 bars	Group improvisation, cornet lead, includes stopped time patterns; guitar break; brief cornet and guitar dialogue, the guitar having the "last word" with the final, unresolved chord

Reflections

Be aware of the group improvisation among the cornet, clarinet, and trombone in the introduction and the final chorus.

Recognize the two-bar breaks and the improvised dialogues between the voice and guitar and between the voice and trumpet.

Describe the vocal improvisation known as scat singing.

Stride and Boogie Woogie

During the 1930s, the economic difficulties of the Depression meant that many clubs could no longer hire jazz groups, so peoples' craving for jazz was in large measure satisfied by the solo pianists that were hired instead. Ragtime, a notated popular music (see p. 78), evolved into the improvised, more energetic **stride** piano style. This style, like ragtime, featured a strongly rhythmic, walking or striding left hand and a syncopated right-hand melody, but it was typically improvised and more upbeat than ragtime. The stride style—the first pure jazz form to feature solo pianists—inspired the artistry of a series of great pianists: Fats Waller, Earl "Fatha" Hines, Art Tatum, Erroll Garner, and Oscar Peterson.

Boogie woogie was the 12-bar blues form combined with a unique style of piano playing. It featured a constantly repeated left-hand **ostinato** pattern moving through the blues chord progression along with energetic, syncopated right-hand patterns that varied with each 12-bar repetition.

Swing and Big Band Jazz

The 1930s featured a big band form of jazz: swing, the only style of jazz to become popular with the masses. Thus, this period is commonly known as the "swing era." Swing was the popular music of the day, and many of these jazz tunes were on the Hit Parade (the equivalent of the top-40 **charts** or current *Billboard* charts). As Americans rebounded from the Great Depression, they wanted to be entertained and to dance, and they were willing to pay for both. It was a great time for popular music, jazz, jazz musicians, radio, and the recording industry.

The swing era also emerged from jazz artists' need to explore, innovate, and apply a higher standard of musicianship and jazz sense than was available to them through the relatively confining style of traditional jazz. In the late 1920s, a number of musicians became interested in creating jazz arrangements for big bands. To perform these arrangements successfully, musicians had to read music, play precisely with others, and improvise in the context of notated music. The most important arrangers of early big band jazz pieces were Fletcher Henderson in New York; Don Redman, who played with Henderson's group and later became an influential jazz musician in Kansas City; and Duke Ellington, who became one of the most durable and successful of all jazz composers, arrangers, and big band leaders.

In the swing era, jazz took three different forms:

- *Sweet swing.* Sweet swing groups had existed since the early decades of the twentieth century; in the swing era, they took the form of dance bands, society bands, or syncopated dance orchestras. Sweet swing was, and is, intended for entertainment, dancing, and easy listening. Some people do not consider this music jazz, because improvisation and the feel of jazz swing are minimal. Among the most prominent leaders of sweet swing dance bands were James Reese Europe in the late 1910s, Paul Whiteman in the 1920s, Guy Lombardo from the 1940s through the 1970s, and Lawrence Welk as recently as the 1980s. Their bands, particularly Paul Whiteman's, frequently employed some of the best jazz musicians available.
- *The jazz of Benny Goodman, the "King of Swing."* Probably the best known of all jazz musicians, Benny Goodman (1909–1986) formed big bands and combos that played hot jazz and gentle swing. He received the highest honors from his peers and from governments. Books and articles have been written

about Goodman, and a Hollywood movie about his life had wide exposure. He did more than any other jazz performer to make jazz respectable, and he did much to racially integrate jazz groups and jazz audiences. He also performed as a clarinet soloist with major symphony orchestras.

- *Hot swing or big band jazz.* This jazz served the more serious jazz composer, arranger, and performer. It included more musically sophisticated charts, featured more extended improvised solos, and was more demanding musically than sweet swing. During the 1930s, the recording industry was flourishing, but long-play recordings (LPs) had not yet come into existence. Most compositions and arrangements were limited to three minutes, the duration of one side of a 78-rpm record. This greatly restricted the possibility of extended improvisations by the leading jazz artists, except in live performance.

The most sophisticated big band charts were aimed at listeners rather than dancers. Among the best and most durable of the big bands were those of Duke Ellington and Count Basie. Other prominent bands included those of Glenn Miller, Woody Herman, and Tommy Dorsey. The next generation of big band leaders included Stan Kenton and Maynard Ferguson.

The recordings of some big bands, notably Glenn Miller, Duke Ellington, and Count Basie, are reissued on CDs. These bands also continue to perform in concerts, though under new leadership. Their compositions and arrangements are the same as or similar to the originals.

Duke Ellington was one of the most influential big band leaders in jazz history, in large measure because of the high skill of the musicians and arrangers he hired.

Benny Goodman was an outstanding jazz and classical clarinetist and big band leader. He deservedly was known as the "King of Swing."

Listening Guide   No. 14

"Mood Indigo"
CD1, Track 14, 3:04

Performer: Duke Ellington and His Orchestra, featuring Shorty Baker, trumpet. From the album *Indigos* (1989), recorded in New York in 1957.
Genre: Big band jazz.

Goals

Recognize the style of big band jazz.

Describe the style of the first and second choruses, with walking bass and muted trumpet.

Describe the style of the third chorus.

Recognize the form of the third chorus: four 4-bar phrases (a a b a). Identify the bridge.

—Continued

Listening Guide –Continued   No. 14

Guide

Count in a moderately slow four. All phrases are four bars.

0:00	Intro	Four bars; strong to gentle mood
0:11	First chorus	Muted trumpet and walking bass
1:01	Second chorus	Muted trumpet and walking bass
1:54	Third chorus	Full ensemble; last phrase slower and extended to a slow, quiet ending

Reflections

What was your response to "Mood Indigo," with its quiet, mellow mood and gentle beat?

How popular is big band jazz today?

Listening Guide   No. 15

"'Round Midnight"

CD1, Track 15, 2:15

Performer: Carmen McRae, jazz singer, from *Carmen Sings Monk* (1988)—a recording of tunes written by Thelonious Monk (see Listening Guide 17). The pianist is Clifford Jordon, although bass and drums are added in the second chorus (not included).

Genre: Bebop.

Background: Carmen McRae is a highly respected jazz vocalist. Significantly, she is highly respected as an artist by other jazz musicians and by jazz critics. Born in Harlem, she emerged first as a songwriter, then as a singer in the 1940s. Her most productive years were from the 1950s through the 1980s. Her influences were primarily Billie Holiday and the later bebop style.

Goals

Recognize her flexible pulse, known in this style as "behind the beat" phrasing.

Describe phrasing in the context of McRae's interpretation of this song.

Describe how her vibrato contributes to this jazz style.

Listening Guide –Continued   No. 15

Guide

Slow; free rhythm and flexible interpretation.

0:00	Intro		8 bars
	First chorus		32 bars—each phrase is eight bars
0:09		a	
0:41		a	
1:11		b (bridge)	
1:38		a	

It begins to tell at midnight, 'round midnight.
I do pretty well, till after sundown,
Suppertime I'm feelin' sad;
But it really gets bad, 'round midnight.

Memories always start 'round midnight,
Haven't got the heart to stand those memories,
When my heart is still with you,
And ol' midnight knows it, too.

When some quarrel we had needs mending,
Does that mean that our love is ending.
Darlin' I need you, lately, I find
You're out of my heart,
And I'm out of my mind.

Let our love take wings 'round midnight,
Let the angels sing of your returning.
Let our love be safe and sound.
When old midnight comes around.

Words (excerpt) by Thelonious Monk, Bernie Hanighen, and C. Wilson

Reflections

How does McRae's interpretation enhance the text?

Can music without a steady beat really be jazz?

What is meant by McRae's "behind the beat" phrasing?

How do you respond to this music emotionally? Physically?

Is the purpose of this music for dancing, listening, or something else? Explain your answer.

Is this art music? Why or why not?

Bebop

Three major economic and musical factors created **bebop** (listen to Listening Guide 16 in this chapter):

- Many jazz musicians wanted to find new ways of playing the same chords, improvising imaginative and unexpected chords, and creating new interpretations of melodies. However, notated swing arrangements, restricted by the three minutes available on 78-rpm records, offered little opportunity for serious jazz musicians to engage in creative exploration. Combo jazz, common to bebop, allowed greater opportunities for more substantial and extended jazz improvisation.
- Late-night jam sessions provided a venue for experimentation and creative exploration. People partied and danced at night; thus, jazz musicians worked at night. Too often, however, the style of jazz preferred by their paying audience—and thus required by their employer—did not allow room for creativity. So creative exploration took place in after-hours **jam sessions** frequently lasting all night. Bebop was born at these sessions.
- During World War II, people had less time and money for dancing and entertainment. Gasoline was rationed, restricting travel, and many men had gone to war, making it more difficult for bandleaders to find the needed musicians. Consequently, in the 1940s, big band music declined in popularity. One response to these circumstances was a return to combo jazz and the creation of the bebop style.

The roots of bebop date to the 1930s, but it was not until the early 1940s in New York City that Dizzy Gillespie, Thelonious Monk, Kenny Clark, and others gathered to explore new musical possibilities and to satisfy their own unfulfilled musical

This photo of jazz being performed in a nightclub shows a typical venue for jazz and a typical jazz combo: piano, bass and drums.

desires. Gillespie played the trumpet, Monk the piano, and Clark the drums. Their search for a new style, however, did not solidify until a saxophonist named Charlie Parker arrived in New York from Kansas City. Parker's skillful improvisation and musical instincts led to a clarification and synthesis of the bebop style.

Bebop is usually combo jazz. The standard instrumentation consists of one or two solo lead instruments and a rhythm section of piano, bass, and drums. The most common leads are tenor or alto sax, trumpet, and piano; but the lead can also be a trombone, vibraphone (vibes), flute, or guitar, or any other melodic instrument.

Bebop is often complex, intense, and very fast. The emphasis is on unusual harmonic, melodic, and rhythmic treatments of a song and on the performer's virtuosity. The song itself is often a popular song of the day or a **standard;** but usually, all that remains of this song are its title and its underlying chords. The melody of the song is likely to be obscure or not present at all, and improvisations are based mostly on harmonic progressions rather than on melodic patterns.

The 32-bar, a a b a song form is common. Here is a model of what a bebop piece might be like:

- First chorus:
  a The first eight-bar phrase may begin with the full ensemble, the lead instruments in a unique duet, often in unison.
  a Second phrase repeats.
  b Third phrase (the bridge) provides contrast, usually with an improvised solo.
  a Fourth phrase returns to the original theme.
- Subsequent choruses: After the first chorus, the sax may play a full chorus or more. The trumpet player takes one or more choruses, and the pianist does likewise. The bass and drummer may share a chorus. The end of the piece is similar to the beginning, with a return to the ensemble chorus.

Listening Guide   No. 16

"Ko-Ko"
CD 1, Track 16, 2:56

Composer: Charlie Parker

Performers: Charlie Parker and His Re-Boppers: Charlie Parker, alto saxophone; Dizzy Gillespie, trumpet; Curly Russell, bass; Max Roach, drums. Recorded in New York City on November 26, 1945.

Genre: Bebop (combo jazz).

Background: This is one of the earliest Bebop recordings. It was Parker's first recording session as a leader, and this piece features one of his most famous solos. The session got off to a rocky start. The trumpet player for the session was Miles Davis, then just 19 years old. The tempo of this piece is 300 beats per minute, and Davis could not play fast enough to suit Parker. Instead, veteran musician Dizzy Gillespie, who was at the session as an observer, played on "Ko-Ko." Gillespie also ended up comping on the piano during Parker's solo because Parker could not find his preferred pianist.

–Continued

Listening Guide –Continued   No. 16

Charlie Parker in a 1954 photo. His alto sax playing and his musical instincts contributed significantly to the development of the bebop style.

"Ko-Ko" is extremely complex, and can more easily be understood when thought of as a broad ABA form. Most jazz players think of combo tunes in three broad sections: the "head" (the melody of the piece), the solo section (improvisation), and the "head out" (the restatement of the original melody). Compare this to the sonata form in chapter 11, which similarly consists of an exposition (statement), development (improvisation), and recapitulation (restatement).

In "Ko-Ko," solos are improvised over the chord progression of the tune "Cherokee," which is in the AABA form but which contains 64 bars per chorus; this might explain why the solo sections are 64 bars in length. The head, which normally is based on pre-composed melody, is replaced by an elaborate improvisation. In combo jazz, the drummer usually has the option of soloing over the form or soloing openly. In this case, Roach solos openly over approximately 29 bars, which are not a part of the AABA form.

Goals

Listen to the virtuosity of these legends of jazz; their ability to "get around" on their instruments and to move with considerable complexity through basic harmonies. Do not try to recognize familiar chord progressions as these are more elaborate, especially the harmonic foundation of the bridge (B).

Recognize the styles, roles, and functions of the various musicians: lead, timekeeping, harmonic foundation, comping, and so on.

Recognize the extremely fast tempo, continuous stream of notes, and technical virtuosity which is a hallmark of the bebop style.

Guide

			Head (statement of melody)
0:00	A	8 bars	Alto saxophone and trumpet play melody in unison octaves, accompanied by drums
0:07	B	8 bars	Improvised solo trumpet break
0:12	B	8 bars	Improvised solo saxophone break
0:19	A	4 bars	Alto saxophone and trumpet in thirds
		4 bars	Alto saxophone and trumpet in octave unison
			Solo section (first solo chorus)
0:25	A	16 bars	Improvised saxophone solo starts, and walking bass and piano enter
0:38	A	16 bars	

Listening Guide –Continued   No. 16

0:51	B	16 bars	Saxophone repeats melodic sequence
1:04	A	16 bars	

Solo section (second solo chorus)

1:16	A	16 bars	Saxophone solo continues and builds energy
1:29	A	16 bars	
1:42	B	16 bars	Saxophone plays sequence of descending arpeggios
1:55	A	16 bars	
2:08		29 bars	Extended open drum solo (not over form)
			Drums cue saxophone and trumpet back into the head. The drums are tuned higher than normal to give the drum solo a sharper, brighter sound.

Head out (ending melodic statement)

2:31	A	8 bars	Alto saxophone and trumpet restate beginning melody, accompanied by drums
2:37	B	8 bars	Improvised solo trumpet break
2:43	B	8 bars	Improvised solo saxophone break
2:50	A	4 bars	Trumpet and alto saxophone restate melody in last unison passage; bass and drums play a "hit" to end the piece.

Reflections

Which elements of the music seem prominent in this style?

Describe the musical interaction of the musicians.

Compare the trumpet sound (cup mute) of Gillespie's playing on this tune to the trumpet sound of Davis' (Harmon mute) on "Summertime" (Listening Guide 18). How do the mutes change the color of the trumpet?

In what ways is this entertainment music? In what ways is it art music?

Are Charlie Parker and Dizzy Gillespie as important to American music as say, Willie Nelson, Ray Charles or Bruce Springsteen? Why or why not?

Listening Guide   No. 17

" 'Round Midnight"

CD1, Track 17, 1:45

Composer: Thelonious Monk, in the early 1950s.
Performer: Thelonious Monk, bop pianist, composer, and innovator. Recorded in 1968.
Genre: Bebop.

–Continued

Listening Guide –Continued   No. 17

Thelonious Monk in a 1950 photo. Monk was a jazz bebop pianist and composer.

Goals

Describe tempo, mood, instrumentation, and improvisational style.

Recognize sounds of the various instruments.

Recognize places where soloists adhere to or depart from the main melody, and describe ways they depart.

Guide

All phrases are eight bars, counting four beats to the bar at a moderately slow tempo.

0:00	Intro		(eight bars)—highly syncopated; obscure pulses in bars 1 and 5, but constant beat
	Chorus 1		
0:24	Phrase 1	a	Main theme presented with considerable embellishment
0:48	Phrase 2	a	More improvisatory than the first phrase and played in a higher range; ends on tonic with an ascending flourish
1:13	Phrase 3	b	Contrasting phrase (the bridge); a steady "boom-chick" (or stride) bass line
1:37	Phrase 4	a	The main melody repeated but modified; tune obscure in the first four bars; phrase ends on tonic—fades

Reflections

Distinguish between the interpretation of a melodic line and improvisation.

Be familiar with the use of the term *chorus* in jazz and popular music (a cohesive group of phrases, a stanza), often four 8-bar phrases in a a b a form: a 32-bar chorus.

Notice ways in which Monk improvises by adding notes to the main melody; filling in spaces, such as the ends of phrases; using a wide range of the keyboard; and creating complex and imaginative harmonies and textures.

Consider the skills needed not only to create a lasting piece of music but to do so while performing in such an elaborate and effective manner.

Cool Jazz, Hard Bop, Soul Jazz, and Free Jazz

Because the bop of the 1940s and 1950s was complex and sophisticated, it never achieved widespread popularity with the public or even among jazz musicians. Immediately, musicians began to explore alternatives. Many styles and influential artists emerged in the 1950s and 1960s, a period of diversity in the history of jazz. Four important styles from these years are cool jazz, hard bop, soul jazz—sometimes called funky jazz—and free jazz. Again, keep in mind that very few artists adhere to only one style.

Cool jazz began with Lester Young in the late 1930s and was given impetus by Miles Davis, a bebop trumpet player, in an album called *The Birth of the Cool* (1949). It was an attempt to apply musically sophisticated ideas in a softer, more relaxed, more accessible manner than bebop. Cool jazz is typified by the early music of Miles Davis and by the music of the Modern Jazz Quartet, Dave Brubeck, Gerry Mulligan, Stan Getz, and Chet Baker.

Listening Guide   No. 18

"Summertime," from *Porgy and Bess*
CD1, Track 18, 1:29

Composer: George Gershwin.

Lyricist: Ira Gershwin.

Performer: Miles Davis, trumpet. Recorded in New York City in 1958.

Genre: Cool jazz.

Background: The music, arranged and conducted by Gil Evans, was written for 19 pieces, a large and unusual instrumentation: 4 trumpets, 4 trombones, 3 French horns, 1 tuba, 1 alto sax, 2 flutes, 1 bass clarinet, 1 string bass, drums, and soloist Miles Davis on trumpet and flugelhorn.

Goals

Recognize characteristics of cool jazz.

Distinguish between interpreting a melody in a jazz style and jazz improvisation.

Identify muted trumpet and other instruments.

Notice the ostinato pattern in the background. It is a series of block chords played mostly by woodwinds, sometimes with flutes predominating. Observe the subtle variations to the usually ascending line.

Miles Davis, a jazz innovator, perhaps best known for his influencing the development of cool jazz (1950s and 1960s). This 1989 photo reveals an aspect of his later career in which he contributed to modern jazz, electronic jazz, and fusion—and perhaps to jazz fashion.

—Continued

Listening Guide –Continued   No. 18

Guide

Count in a moderate four; no introduction. It starts with a pickup.

0:00	a	8 bars	Ostinato in background; open cadence
0:20	a	8 bars	Repeat of first phrase but ends with closed cadence
0:37	b	8 bars	Contrasting phrase ends with open cadence on bar 7
0:55	a	16 bars	Solo improvisation; open cadence on bar 15—fade

Reflections

Describe Davis's inventive interpretation on muted trumpet.

To what extent and in how many ways does Davis deviate from the established melody?

Be aware of his use of vibrato, the role of the drums and cymbals, and the bass line.

What aspects of this music belong to Gershwin the composer, to Evans the arranger, or to Davis the interpreter?

Describe the energy and the mood of this piece.

Describe your reactions.

Hard bop is a catchall name for the music of the next generation of bop musicians, who attempted to maintain the principles of bop in a way that would not alienate the listening public. Three of the most popular hard bop jazz musicians of this period were Bill Evans (piano), Clifford Brown (trumpet), and Sonny Rollins (tenor sax). Other jazz musicians continued to experiment with new styles and techniques. One of the most outstanding was John Coltrane (tenor and soprano sax), whose tone quality and approach to improvisation have influenced countless other jazz musicians.

Funky jazz or *soul jazz* are the names sometimes used to describe the music of jazz performers who created a style that returned to the roots of jazz. These musicians explored a new style of jazz that capitalized on harmonic and rhythmic simplicity, a strong beat, and influences from gospel music, R&B, and, later, soul. Influential artists who represented funky jazz are Horace Silver, Art Blakey, Jimmy Smith, and Ramsey Lewis.

Listening Guide   No. 19

"The Preacher"

CD 1, Track 19, 4:21

Composer: Horace Silver

Performers: Horace Silver and the Jazz Messengers: Horace Silver, piano; Kenny Dorham, trumpet; Hank Mobley, tenor sax; Doug Watkins, bass; Art Blakey, drums. Recorded in New York City in 1955.

Listening Guide –Continued   No. 19

Genre: Hard bop.

Background: This recording session was the first to feature Horace Silver as a combo leader. The musicians who played this laid permanent claim to the title "The Jazz Messengers," a name Blakey had used previously for his 17-piece band. The tune is based on a traditional 16-bar format and features a swinging melody that is reminiscent of the American folk tune "I've Been Working on the Railroad." Each player takes a turn "preaching" his solo. Some of the piano harmonies sound like gospel, but the overall sound is bluesy, drawing upon old time barroom blues with a bit of a backbeat. "The Preacher" became one of the biggest hits in this particular style, which eventually came to be known as "funk" or "soul."

Goals

Recognize the sound of hard bop, which combines elements of rhythm and blues and gospel into the existing jazz sound.

Describe the mood of this jazz.

Recognize the style of playing "hard on the beat."

Describe the role of each musician. For example, who leads, who comps, and who keeps time?

Recognize the 16-bar format.

Guide

0:00	Head: trumpet solo
0:23	Repeat of the head: trumpet solo
0:45	Trumpet solo; gospel-sounding harmonies in the piano
1:06	Second trumpet solo in the upper register
1:27	Saxophone solo with comping in the piano
1:38	Increased complexity in the repeated saxophone solo
2:04	Repeated notes are syncopated over rising harmonies
2:09	Piano solo
2:31	Continued piano solo, descending melodic motive
2:43	Piano features cross accents between the two hands
2:50	Saxophone and trumpet in a unison melodic figure with piano solo riffs
3:11	Repeat of the same style as above
3:31	The original duet of the opening returns
3:51	Final chorus is a repeat of the duet
4:13	Final chord

Reflections

Compare this selection to the bebop of Charlie Parker (Listening Guide 16). Do you think this sound is more accessible to a broader audience? Why or why not?

Does this sound more like gospel or more like jazz? Why?

Three modern jazz/
fusion artists—British
bassist Dave Holland,
Miles Davis, trumpet,
and Chick Corea,
keyboards—perform at
a jazz festival in Dallas,
Texas, in 1969. Hear
Corea and Holland in
Listening Guide 20,
page 98.

The jazz styles of George Benson, guitarist and singer, and Grover Washington, Jr., saxophonist, span bebop, modern jazz, funk
(or soul jazz), rhythm and blues, and smooth jazz. Benson's career has spanned 50 years; Grover Washington's lasted about
25 years; he died in 1999.

Free jazz was pioneered in the 1950s and 1960s by Ornette Coleman (alto sax and violin). He created a style that is almost pure improvisation, with no adherence to predetermined chord structures, meter, or melodic motives. The idea was for the musicians to interact musically with each other, building on what others in the group were doing, but also being free to create according to their musical instincts. Like bebop, free jazz was not one of the more popular forms of jazz with the public or among many jazz musicians. Some people were averse to it because it lacked the structures on which jazz improvisation was traditionally based. It did, however, attract avid supporters who respected its level of creativity and its new sounds.

Modern Jazz, Fusion, and Smooth Jazz

Modern jazz began in the mid-1960s, with Miles Davis, again, as the driving force. It was not just Davis's music that was important but the people he hired as **sidemen.** Many have since become the biggest names in modern jazz.

A popular form of modern jazz is **fusion.** Fusion artists merge the jazz style with pop, classical, or rock styles to create *fusion jazz.* The most dramatic change involves instruments and techniques borrowed from rock: electronic keyboards, electric bass, and rock drumming. Synthesizers, computers, **MIDI** (Musical Instrument Digital Interface), and other technological advancements have become widely used in contemporary ("modern") jazz. Some writers have argued that fusion has been the most popular form of jazz since the swing era. Perhaps the most successful fusion artists are Herbie Hancock (keyboards), Chick Corea (keyboards), and Pat Metheny (guitar) (see Listening Guide 20 in this chapter).

Fusion, however, was a term more widely used in the 1970s and 1980s than in recent years. The styles of jazz today are extremely varied, ranging from the easy-listening jazz of many contemporary musicians to the extremely complex postbop jazz of many others. Again, diversity is a major characteristic of this music. Without question, the impact of rock and electronic instruments is significant. But the term *fusion* may also signal a synthesis of jazz with other styles and traditions: jazz and classical music (third stream—Gunther Schuller, John Lewis), Caribbean and South American music (salsa and Latin jazz—Tito Puente and Stan Getz), country (bluegrass and jazz—David Grisman), and the blues (some B. B. King and some Van Morrison).

Among the artists who, in the early years, moved easily between traditional jazz, pop, and—in some cases—blues styles were singers such as Billie Holiday, Ella Fitzgerald, Tony Bennett, Frank Sinatra, and Mel Tormé. In recent years, Diana Krall (vocal and piano), Norah Jones (vocal and piano), and Cassandra Wilson (vocal) have also made this move.

Smooth jazz is the newest genre under the label "modern jazz," having emerged in the 1990s. Some call this genre "new adult contemporary"; some don't call it jazz! Many well-known fusion and traditional jazz artists have adopted this less intense and more easy-listening style. The popularity of smooth jazz has increased as more and more radio stations have adopted a "smooth jazz" format. Tours and festivals have attracted huge followings, and hundreds of recordings of smooth jazz artists are readily available in stores and online. Many smooth jazz artists today were once considered performers of fusion or mainstream jazz. Among the currently popular artists are Boney James, David Sanborn, George Benson, Grover Washington Jr., Kirk Whalum, and Fourplay—a group that has included jazz greats Bob James, Lee Ritenour, and Larry Carlton.

In some styles of modern jazz, it is sometimes difficult to identify jazz in the traditional sense. The style of jazz—indeed, the definition of jazz—is changing. But traditional jazz is not a thing of the past. Many great modern jazz artists value the instruments, rhythms, harmonic changes, and forms of traditional jazz; some call it "straight-ahead jazz." The most prominent current jazz musician who builds directly on the past is the gifted trumpeter Wynton Marsalis. Marsalis, who is also an accomplished classical musician, received two Grammy awards in 1983, one for jazz and one for his recording of classical trumpet concertos. In 1997, he was awarded the Pulitzer Prize in music for *Blood on the Fields,* a three-hour work about slavery for solo singers and jazz band.

As in any art, some musicians are motivated artistically, others commercially. Some look backward and value history and traditions. Others look forward, valuing experimentation and new forms of expression. Future styles of jazz will almost certainly blend all these influences, for most artists respond to the challenges from various sources of inspiration and creativity.

Listening Guide   No. 20

"Futures"
CD1, Track 20, 2:30

Composer: Chick Corea.
Performers: Gary Burton, vibraphone (vibes); Chick Corea, piano; Pat Metheny, guitar; Dave Holland, bass; and Roy Haynes, drums—from the album *Like Minds* (1998).
Genre: Modern jazz.
Context: "Futures" and the other pieces in this CD were performed by five of the greatest artists in modern jazz. All of them have been active since the 1970s and have moved through a succession of jazz styles. "Futures" is musically sophisticated yet has an elegance and a simplicity that borders on smooth jazz.

Goals

Assign a label to this music: Experimental? Easy listening? Cool? Bebop? Something else?

Compare what each of the instrumentalists does in this piece with the traditional roles for their instruments—for example, melodic, harmonic, or rhythmic roles; dance music; timekeeping; walking bass; and comping, lead or supportive.

Is the pulse typically strong, varied in strength, weak, or nonexistent?

Guide

0:00	Vibraphone (vibes) lead with piano support
0:22	Bass added—equal in emphasis to the vibes; drums very light
1:11	Guitar lead
1:46	Ascending pattern in full ensemble—a transition to the next chorus
2:04	Chorus fades

Listening Guide –*Continued* No. 20

Reflections

Discuss your reaction to this music (more than "I like it" or "I don't like it"). Give reasons for your reactions.

Is this jazz? How does it fit or not fit traditional definitions of jazz?

Compare this piece with others you have enjoyed (or not enjoyed) throughout this course or with other jazz you may have listened to or perhaps performed.

Summary

This chapter on jazz is designed to help you know, appreciate, and respect the literature, heritage, people, and sounds of jazz.

Jazz is complex and always changing. The best jazz artists are driven to reach for new possibilities, to experiment, to resist permanent labels. For example, Miles Davis was at first a bebop musician, then an influential cool jazz artist, and later a leader in fusion and electronic jazz. Max Roach, one of the best bop drummers, has also performed on many cool jazz recordings. You can find cool jazz, bebop, and other styles all in the same piece. The big band jazz of Stan Kenton, for example, frequently has elements of bebop, cool jazz, and swing in one arrangement. Many of the great artists defy classification because they continue to grow and change.

6 *Popular Music*

Chapter Outline

In This Chapter

What characterized minstrel shows and vaudeville?

What were the influences of Tin Pan Alley?

How important were musicals on stage and in film?

How did radio contribute to the development of popular music?

What was the significance of Nashville to the music industry?

What is the significance of Motown to popular music?

What is the relationship between rap/hip-hop and popular music?

This chapter presents the major genres of American popular music, their historical backgrounds, the trends and influences that helped shape them, and representative artists that made them an important part of American popular culture. After discussing the nature of popular music and its history before the twentieth century, we introduce the popular music of the twentieth century and beyond in four broad categories:

1. The music of Tin Pan Alley: the beginning of modern American popular music and the music industry.
2. Country music: its shift from a regional folk music to a major part of the music industry.
3. Music having African American influences: blues, gospel, Motown, and rap/hip-hop.
4. Pop and rock: from rockabilly and the "British Invasion" to a wide array of contemporary sounds and styles.

These discussions will help you learn more about musical styles with which you already may be familiar, increase your awareness and understanding of less familiar styles, and, again, use relatively simple music to sharpen your listening skills, musical vocabulary, and awareness of the elements of music.

Goals for Listening

In this chapter, listening skills are based on skills that you developed in previous chapters, especially chapter 3. Thus, rather than responding to new musical concepts, you will further develop those listening skills to which you already have been introduced.

The purpose of the Listening Guides is to reveal a breadth of styles (though not a complete overview) and provide listening experiences in popular music styles with which you may not be familiar.

The Listening Guides provide a small sampling of the many styles of American popular music, including examples from an early Broadway musical, traditional bluegrass and contemporary country, rock and roll of the 1950s, and a variety of current popular musical styles.

The Definition and Scope of Popular Music

Popular music is music known by the majority of interested people at any given time, yet many listeners focus on and appreciate a limited number of styles. For example, you may know the sound and style of Keith Urban or Carrie Underwood, but know little if anything about Usher or Alicia Keys. To know a name is important, but to recognize and know a person's musical style requires a higher level of experience and understanding.

One goal of this chapter is to help you learn the common characteristics that cause a piece to be classified "popular music," as opposed to jazz, classical, or folk music—any of which may be popular, but among smaller groups or specialized audiences.

A second goal is to perceive and articulate the factors that distinguish one popular style from another. What makes a country tune different from a Tin Pan Alley tune? What makes rock music different from R&B, or R&B different from blues, or contemporary rock different from classic rock? What makes 1970s R&B different from R&B today?

Music that is popular has the widest appeal and is purchased and enjoyed by the largest number of people. It is cross-cultural and transcends regional, ethnic, economic, political, and educational boundaries. It speaks directly to the people in ways to which they can respond, both musically and emotionally.

Traditional pop songs and romantic ballads typically are easy to listen to. The dominant attributes are the melody and the **lyrics.** The sound and the style are easily recognizable. These songs are simple and tuneful, easily singable, repetitive, and based on the familiar tonic, dominant, and subdominant (or sometimes fewer) chords. The music usually has a strong beat, regular meter, repetitive rhythmic patterns, and clear phrases.

In rap and rock, however, it is the beat—the rhythmic vitality—that is dominant. In live concerts, the artist's persona is influenced by clothing styles and often highly energetic stage movement and stylistic behavior. Use of state-of-the-art sound and lighting technology and equipment is typical.

Popular music is music that is or has been well known and easily recognizable—if not a specific piece, then at least its style. If it is not well known now, it may have been at an earlier time. Today, for a song to become well known, successful marketing, advertising, distribution, and sales strategies are critical. These strategies influence tastes in popular music, maintain continued interest in the music, and create and promote hits and star performers. The public tends to be swayed by musical fads, rapidly changing tastes, and manipulation by advertising media and the music industry. As a result, songs typically do not remain popular for a long time; they come and go, frequently in a matter of months. Only a few songs remain popular for decades or generations. Songs that do remain popular for a long period of time are sometimes called **standards**. Examples are presented in these Listening Guides: 2 ("Body and Soul," page 35), 14 ("Mood Indigo," page 85), 18 ("Summertime," page 93), and 21 ("I Get a Kick Out of You," page 109).

The popularity of songs is measurable and has been regularly measured for decades: by the number of times a song was played on a jukebox or on the radio (**airplay**) and by the sales figures of LPs, then cassettes, then CDs, and now downloads. Before recordings, popularity was measured by the sales of sheet music. During the early radio era, popularity was reported to the public by means of *The Hit Parade,* a long-running radio show of the 1930s and 1940s, and *Billboard* magazine, which still provides weekly charts of sales in a wide variety of categories, including Christian and Gospel, Country, Adult Contemporary, Blues, Latin, New Age, Rock, World Music, R&B, and Rap/Hip-Hop. Nearly every country or region of the world has its own charts, easily accessed via the Internet.

The shift from printed music to recordings had a profound impact on American musical culture. Since sheet music is a printed song arranged usually for voice and piano accompaniment, a person wanting to learn a song from sheet music had to perform it, either by singing or by accompanying the singer. Thus, the consumer was an active participant.

With recordings and radio, even television, we need only listen to know and appreciate a popular song. Thus, instead of making music (performing), the listener is a nonperforming participant. Consumers may listen intently to a song, memorize the lyrics, and learn to sing the song from listening to it. Without this active participation, however, listening is too often passive.

Pre-Twentieth Century

Because popular music is ever changing, it will be helpful to consider the roots of American popular music: the events, artists, and styles that created it. What are the influences that shaped today's popular music?

Popular music did not flourish in colonial times, particularly in the Northeast. Although religious music and concert art music were acceptable, moral and religious scruples—some codified into law—prohibited "entertainment" music, particularly music for the stage. After the Revolutionary War, however, many of these strictures were relaxed, and entertainment music became commonplace.

Songs that colonial Americans enjoyed were mostly imported from Europe and the British Isles and included melodies from European operas fitted with English texts, settings of traditional Scottish and Irish airs, hymns and religious songs, German art songs, and simplified arrangements of vocal solos originally composed for professional singers. By the early part of the nineteenth century, Americans were learning to read music and play the piano. The earliest popular songs were composed for amateurs to sing and enjoy in their homes with small groups of family and friends. Here are some examples of early American popular songs:

"The Blue Bells of Scotland"—traditional Scottish air.

"Auld Lang Syne" and "Coming through the Rye"—traditional Scottish airs with texts by Robert Burns.

"Ave Maria" and "Serenade"—from music by Franz Schubert, an Austrian composer of classical music.

"Home Sweet Home"—text by Sir Henry Bishop (sold 100,000 copies in 1832, its first year, and several million by the end of the nineteenth century).

"The Last Rose of Summer" and "Believe Me If All Those Endearing Young Charms"—traditional Irish tunes with texts by Thomas Moore.

By the middle of the nineteenth century, American popular music had begun to take on a more diverse character. Songs influenced by British music and European opera were still popular, but others assumed a more distinctively American character.

Henry Russell, an influential American songwriter, was born in England but came to America to enhance his performing and composing career. During his career, he concertized widely. His songs and performances were intended to appeal to many different types of people. Russell had a good sense of what type of song would be popular for the time. Although his songs were influenced by European opera, he was able to infuse them with an American spirit that helped shape the course of popular songwriting. He influenced others, most notably the greatest of all nineteenth-century composers of American songs, Stephen Foster.

Like Russell, Stephen Foster was trained and knowledgeable in the art music of the day. Both composers wanted to "speak to the American people in song."

This sheet music cover of Stephen Foster's first edition of "Jeanie with the Light Brown Hair" (1854) represents one of many of Foster's songs that became so widely known that they now are a part of the American folk song tradition.

However, no composer provided more songs known by Americans of this era than did Stephen Foster. His songs included minstrel songs, plantation songs, and sentimental and dramatic songs. In his later minstrel songs, Foster began offering an image of blacks as human beings who experience pain, sorrow, and love. Many of his songs have become identified with American culture to such an extent that they now are a part of the American folk song tradition.

His best-known songs are these:

"Old Folks at Home" (also known as "Swanee River")

"Oh! Susanna"

"My Old Kentucky Home"

"Old Black Joe"

"Jeanie with the Light Brown Hair"

"Come Where My Love Lies Dreaming"

"Beautiful Dreamer"

The mainstay of the **minstrel show** was the minstrel song. A product of rural American folk traditions and emerging urban composed music, it may be considered the first distinctively American music genre. Typically, it was lively, syncopated, and humorous. Minstrel songs originally were written by and for white Americans and were sung by white Americans in blackface (white faces painted black). The songs were a caricature of the "Negro" way of life, often portraying black Americans as comical and illiterate. This portrayal had little or nothing to do with the realities of black culture, but the songs became an important part of American popular music. An early composer of minstrel songs was Dan Emmett, who wrote "Dixie" and "Old Dan Tucker."

By the mid-nineteenth century, minstrel songs had become popular in both America and Europe. This popularity resulted from the success of traveling minstrel troupes such as the Virginia Minstrels, with Dan Emmett, formed in New York in 1843; and the Christy Minstrels, also formed in New York in the 1840s. Their success paved the way for hundreds of successors and imitators. It was a logical step to take the popular minstrel songs and dances performed by troupes and individual entertainers and put them in a sequence of acts on stage; thus, the minstrel show was created. Hundreds of such shows were produced in America and Europe in the late 1800s.

The music for a minstrel show was drawn from traditional folk material, popular songs of the day, songs from Italian opera, and songs newly composed for the show. These shows also included comic dialogue, dances, acrobatics, black-face songs, and instrumental pieces. Since the plot was minimal, the music was incidental to, and did not necessarily enhance, any dramatic action.

Ironically, white performers' blackface minstrel shows were so popular that blacks themselves began writing and performing in such shows. Black minstrel shows began in 1865 in Georgia with the Georgia Minstrels. The style and content were essentially the same as white minstrel shows. The first black songwriter of note was James Bland, who wrote "In the Evening by the Moonlight," "Carry Me Back to Old Virginny," and "Oh, Dem Golden Slippers."

Twentieth Century and Beyond

Twentieth-century American popular music included many genres and styles derived from a merging of European and African musical traditions. It was influenced by a dramatic expansion of the music industry and the advent of recordings, radio, and television. In this section, we consider the extent to which certain artists were innovative, influenced other artists, and helped shape the future of popular music, although this is difficult to judge after only a short time has elapsed. Sometimes it takes decades to gain sufficient perspective to assess the significance of a particular artist.

Tin Pan Alley

The 1890s through the 1950s saw the greatest period of songwriting in the history of American popular music. These were the years of the **Tin Pan Alley** tradition. The most productive years were the 1920s and the 1930s. From Tin Pan Alley came America's pop tunes and standards, including our most beloved songs: songs for amusement, entertainment, and escape. They included sentimental love songs, syncopated songs and dance tunes, Latin American music, nonsense songs, and show tunes.

The origin of the name "Tin Pan Alley" is unclear, but some say it refers to the stretch of Twenty-eighth Street in New York City where major music publishers and sheet music retailers were located. Each firm promoted this music by having either staff or customers play it on the piano; thus, potential customers could hear the music before they purchased it. "Tin Pan" presumably came from the sound created by the multitude of pianos in the neighborhood sounding at once.

Eventually, the term *Tin Pan Alley* came to represent important aspects of popular music of that era, particularly the part of the music industry devoted to the production, promotion, and sale of popular songs. Tin Pan Alley publishers assessed the public's taste and proceeded to write and publish more of the songs the public liked. They retained their own composers (sometimes called "hacks"), who ground out the songs daily. Most of these songs were forgotten shortly after they were published.

Tin Pan Alley also refers to the type of song written during these decades. Typically, it was a song in verse-chorus form with the chorus usually consisting of 32 bars with four equal phrases. The chorus had the more memorable lyrics and melody. The lyrics of a Tin Pan Alley song ranged from those having no "message" to those that expressed strong feelings about contemporary social conditions (see Listening Guide 21, page 109).

Tin Pan Alley songs were performed in vaudeville, the Ziegfeld Follies, and other revues; in Broadway musicals, Hollywood films, and nightclubs; on radio and recordings; and by featured singers in big band jazz and swing bands. The most durable and popular of American songs are the Tin Pan Alley standards, sometimes called *classics*.

Despite the widespread use of hacks, Tin Pan Alley had a way of encouraging genius among America's popular composers, lyricists, and performers. Among the best composers who flourished within the Tin Pan Alley tradition were Jerome Kern, Cole Porter, George Gershwin, Irving Berlin, and Richard Rodgers. Among its outstanding performers were Al Jolson, Eddie Cantor, Rudy Vallee, Kate Smith, Paul Whiteman, and Bing Crosby.

Vaudeville   The entertainment form that eventually replaced the minstrel show in popularity was a type of variety show known as **vaudeville**. Vaudeville shows included a sequence of unrelated acts: singers (usually not in blackface), dancers, comedians, jugglers, child performers, trained animals, and dramatic sketches. Its more sophisticated counterpart on Broadway was the **revue**. These variety shows

The sheet music cover of Irving Berlin's "Mandy" depicts one of the musical numbers included in the 1919 Ziegfeld Follies. Many of the follies, revues, musicals, and vaudeville productions featured songs written by Tin Pan Alley composers who became legends in American popular music, such as Jerome Kern, George Gershwin, Irving Berlin, and Cole Porter. Hear Ethel Merman sing a song by Cole Porter in Listening Guide 21, page 109.

were known at different times as *follies, scandals,* or *vanities*. The most famous of them was the Ziegfeld Follies, produced from 1907 through 1932.

Tin Pan Alley songs were the essential musical element of vaudeville and included sentimental popular songs, the occasional blackface minstrel song, and racial or ethnic dialect songs. Vaudeville songs represented a new direction in American popular music; they dealt with contemporary city life in what was still a predominantly rural, agrarian society.

Musicals The Broadway musical was a theatrical work that included songs, dances, staging, and drama. In contrast to minstrel and vaudeville shows, it was a unified work with dramatic flow—a musical play. Musicals were created by songwriters of genius such as Jerome Kern, George Gershwin, Cole Porter, and Irving Berlin. Though centered in New York, the American musical reached the entire country. The Broadway musical tradition continues to this day.

The best Tin Pan Alley composers wrote Broadway musicals. George Gershwin wrote *Girl Crazy, Strike Up the Band, Lady Be Good* (including the songs "Fascinating

Composer Irving Berlin rehearses with Ethel Merman.

Rhythm" and "The Man I Love"), and *Porgy and Bess* ("Summertime"; see Listening Guide 18, page 93). Other notable composers and their works were Cole Porter with *Anything Goes* ("I Get a Kick Out of You"; see Listening Guide 21 in this chapter); Jerome Kern with *Roberta* and *Showboat* ("Ol' Man River"); Irving Berlin with *Annie Get Your Gun* ("There's No Business like Show Business"); and Richard Rodgers with *Oklahoma* and *Carousel* ("If I Loved You").

The tradition of the Broadway musical continues to the present in the music or lyrics of, among many others, Stephen Sondheim (*West Side Story, Gypsy, A Funny Thing Happened on the Way to the Forum, Company, A Little Night Music,* and *Sweeney Todd*) and Andrew Lloyd Webber (*Jesus Christ Superstar, Evita, Cats,* and *Phantom of the Opera*).

Film   Film music was born in 1927 with *The Jazz Singer,* the first commercial movie with a synchronized sound track. In the decade that followed, composers, arrangers, singers, dancers, and producers headed for Hollywood. The early movie musicals featured large orchestras, lavish sets and costumes, large casts, and expensive stars. They provided marvelous opportunities for talented artists.

These movies were entertaining spectacles. They presented an unreal world of glittering sophistication, the carefree world of show people, the exciting world of exotic travel, and the make-believe world of childhood. They brought escape from the hardships of the Great Depression and projected a lifestyle that was not available to most Americans. Ironically, people who were deprived of any luxury wanted to be entertained by seeing excesses of it.

Many songs from these movies were very popular. Tin Pan Alley composers became important creators of film music, and many of their most successful songs came from films. Also, many successful popular singers had successful careers in film, including Al Jolson, Bing Crosby, Doris Day, Frank Sinatra, and Barbra Streisand.

Radio and Recordings   Music for radio and recordings began in the 1920s. Network radio, along with the national marketing, advertising, and sales of recordings, changed the face of the music industry. It created the "hit" song, determined what songs produced profits for the creators and producers, and developed a way to report the hits: first the *Lucky Strike Hit Parade* and later the charts of *Billboard* magazine and other polls of the industry. To a large extent, the media determined who would be the "stars" of popular music, what songs Americans would listen to, and, in effect, what their tastes in popular music would be. Tin Pan Alley stars such as Rudy Vallee, Bing Crosby, and Kate Smith achieved great success as radio artists.

In the 1920s, commercial record companies recognized the financial benefit of doing field recordings of the folk songs of various immigrant groups, the blues of black singers, and white rural folk songs, ballads, and dances. These companies, while realizing commercial gain by selling the recordings back to these specialized audiences, also preserved a diverse folk repertoire, created an invaluable musical resource of American culture, and transformed many traditional folksingers into professional recording artists.

The most popular jazz bands or swing bands achieved national exposure from touring and, particularly, from network radio broadcasts. This made them prime targets for Tin Pan Alley song pluggers. Publishers marketed (plugged) their songs through the big swing bands, particularly those featuring vocalists such as Ella Fitzgerald, Frank Sinatra, Peggy Lee, and the Andrews Sisters, whose recording of a song would practically guarantee its commercial success.

Listening Guide   No. 21

"I Get a Kick Out of You," from *Anything Goes*
CD1, Track 21, 1:17

Composer: Cole Porter (1891–1964).
Performer: Sung by Ethel Merman in 1934.
Genre: Tin Pan Alley song from a Broadway musical.

Goals

Recognize the style of a Tin Pan Alley song.
Identify patterns of contrast and repetition in the standard Tin Pan Alley verse-chorus song form.

–Continued

Listening Guide –Continued   No. 21

Recognize open and closed cadences.

Recognize motives, *a tempo* (a return to the original tempo), extension, and tag.

Guide (music ends near the second phrase of the Chorus)

Count in a slow two.

0:00	Intro	2 bars	Instrumental
0:36	Verse	20 bars (8 + 12)	Vocal; ritard in bar 10 of the second phrase, then returns to the original tempo in bar 11 (*a tempo*); leads into the chorus

My story is much too sad to be told,
But practically everything leaves me totally cold.
The only exception I know is the case
When I'm out on a quiet spree
Fighting vainly the old ennui
And I suddenly turn and see
Your fabulous face.

Chorus	a	16 bars	Based on an ascending stepwise motive; title phrase "I Get a Kick Out of You" repeated in the last four bars of each "a" phrase; closed cadence
	a	16 bars	Closed cadence
	b	16 bars (8 + 8)	Contrasting section (bridge); based on another ascending stepwise motive at another pitch level; open cadence
	a	18 bars	Phrase extended by two bars after closed cadence
	b	16 bars (8 + 8)	Bridge, piano lead; open cadence
	a	20 bars	Ritard in bars 13 and 14, resolves to tonic in bar 15, then continues *a tempo* for the final six bars

I get no kick from champagne.
Mere alcohol doesn't thrill me at all,
So tell me why should it be true
That I get a kick out of you?

Some get a kick from cocaine.
I'm sure that if I took even one sniff
That would bore me terrifically too . . .

Listening Guide –Continued No. 21

Reflections

In the verse, do the phrases repeat or contrast? In the chorus, identify the form.
Listen for repetition within each phrase.
How important is syncopation in this example?

Two important factors contributed to the decline of the Tin Pan Alley song: (1) the beginnings of rock and roll and (2) the shift to Nashville as the center of songwriting, publishing, and the subsequent popularization of country music.

Country Music

Chapter 3 presented the "roots music" of the rural South. In this chapter, the phrase *country music* refers to songwriting, recording, and the creation of "stars" in a popular style that is closely related to this southern folk music. It is a regional music made national. This music includes hillbilly, bluegrass, and the Nashville sound, and it represents the beginning of modern, commercial country music.

Hillbilly Originally, the label **hillbilly** was used in a deprecating way to describe the "culturally and musically inferior" songs of poor, white, rural, uneducated southerners. This music was a product of the rural South; it was a regional music for a regional audience.

The 1920s saw a tremendous national effort by commercial record companies to record music by hillbilly performers, in addition to that of blues, jazz, gospel, folk, Tin Pan Alley, and vaudeville artists. Radio created additional demand for performers. Among the first hillbilly recording artists were Uncle Dave Macon, the Carter Family, and Jimmie Rodgers.

In the second quarter of the twentieth century, hillbilly records were sold widely, and hillbilly music was broadcast from Atlanta, Chicago, Nashville, and many other cities. Its widespread popularity as measured by record sales may have resulted from several factors: (1) Hillbilly music represented an image of an older and simpler America; (2) it provided an alternative to jazz and the popular dance music of the

1920s; and (3) it reflected a yearning for the "good old songs" of the nineteenth century. Hillbilly music was often projected as wholesome, down-to-earth, family-style entertainment.

Cowboy Songs and Western Swing   As singers from the South headed west in search of greater opportunity, taking with them their religion and their songs, the gulf widened between hillbilly and its folk roots. Western hillbilly dealt with loneliness and infidelity rather than religion, sentiment, and nostalgia. Some western music was performed on the piano in small-town saloons and was called **honky-tonk.**

By the 1930s, the movie industry was making westerns with music and singing cowboys that romanticized the "wild west" and caused the production of a vast quantity of cowboy songs. Gene Autry, Tex Ritter, and Roy Rogers were the most famous of the singing cowboys. Their most famous songs, such as "Tumbling Tumbleweed," "Back in the Saddle Again," "The Yellow Rose of Texas," "Deep in the Heart of Texas," "Don't Fence Me In," and "I'm an Old Cowhand," were newly composed, many by Tin Pan Alley composers.

A brand of western music that used a larger instrumental ensemble including saxes, brass, and a standard jazz rhythm section of piano, bass, and drums is **western swing.** The most influential exponent of western swing was Bob Wills, who, with His Texas Playboys, flourished in Tulsa from 1934 to 1942. He popularized his music through radio broadcasts, recordings, dances, and personal appearances throughout the Southwest.

Listening Guide   No. 22

"New San Antonio Rose"
CD1, Track 22, 2:32

Performer: Bob Wills and His Texas Playboys (1940).
Genre: Western swing.
Background: Adapted from the fiddle tune "Spanish Two Step." The word *new* in the song title differentiates the vocal from Wills's earlier instrumental version.

Goals

Identify solo instruments and sections of instruments.

Recognize motives as a means of identifying phrase structure and form. Identify the phrase structure.

Recognize open and closed cadences, question-answer phrases, and modulation.

Recognize the sounds of western swing.

Listen for repetitive patterns of harmonic change—for example, I – IV – V – I.

Listening Guide –Continued No. 22

Guide

Count in a moderately fast two.

0:00	Intro		Four bars, instrumental
0:04	First chorus		Instrumental, with muted trumpets prominent
		a 8 bars	Ascending-descending motive at the beginning
		a 8 bars	First theme repeated
		b 8 bars	Second theme with a descending-ascending motive at the beginning
		b 10 bars	Modulation in last two bars providing transition to the vocal chorus
0:43	Second chorus		Vocal; four phrases, each 8 + 8, paired in question-answer relationships (open-closed cadence patterns)
		a 16 bars	First question-answer phrase group; new key
		b 16 bars	Second motive
		c 16 bars	Second new theme suddenly in a second new key; modulates in last bar
		a 16 bars	Return to the original motive in the tonic key of this chorus
1:55	Third chorus		Instrumental
		c 16 bars	The second new key; trumpets in parallel motion giving a hint of a mariachi sound (see chapter 7); modulates in last bar
		a 18 bars	Sax section prominent (8 + 10); in tonic
		a	key of second chorus; concludes with two-bar tag

Reflections

Does this music sound like hillbilly? Jazz? Pop music? Cowboy music?
Folk music? Mariachi?

Does western swing have contemporary counterparts?

Does music that incorporates elements of several different styles add to or detract from the listening experience?

What effect do the several modulations have?

What do the little shouts ("a-ha") contribute to the music?

Henry Tanner, an African American painter, created one of
his most famous paintings, "The Banjo Lesson," in 1893. The
banjo has become a popular musical instrument in modern
country music, especially bluegrass.

Bluegrass   The word *bluegrass* refers to mountain music that originally was the
music of Appalachian ethnic groups and is now an internationally popular style
of country music. **Bluegrass** includes story songs, part singing, fiddle tunes, and
religious music. The typical instrumentation of a bluegrass group includes the
acoustic guitar, fiddle, mandolin, bass fiddle, and five-string banjo—no electric
guitars, drums, or keyboards. Indeed, whereas hillbilly music became commercialized with Hawaiian steel guitars and electronic instruments, bluegrass continued
in the style of the old-time songs and dances. The goal was not to produce regional
and culturally isolated music, but to have bluegrass expand from a rural folk music
to a part of the national popular culture. Eventually bluegrass was performed in
urban settings, such as parks, and nightclubs, on college campuses, and at bluegrass festivals.

     The pioneer of the style that came to be known as bluegrass was Bill Monroe,
who in 1945 headed a group called the Bluegrass Boys, thus creating the name of
the style. Lester Flatt and Earl Scruggs split away from Monroe in 1948 and formed
a bluegrass group called the Foggy Mountain Boys. Many other groups followed as

Bill Monroe on the right, with his group the Bluegrass Boys, is credited with defining modern bluegrass, an extension of hillbilly. Then, bluegrass was a regional, rural folk music. Today, it is a genre listened to in rural areas and in cities, at festivals, and in large performance halls.

the popularity of bluegrass spread. Current bluegrass artists include Alison Krauss and Union Station, Ricky Skaggs, and the Nashville Bluegrass Band.

Successful artists develop and maintain loyal audiences for their live concerts and, more important, their recordings. For example, an artist like Alison Krauss must balance her loyalty to the bluegrass audience with her desire to develop a wider audience for herself and for bluegrass. How does she do this without alienating the bluegrass traditionalists? How does she manage to stay in touch with bluegrass traditions while at the same time infusing her music with nontraditional elements? The line between tradition and innovation is not always clear.

The Nashville Sound In 1925, radio station WSM in Nashville started a hillbilly program that, in time, was to become the Grand Ole Opry. In 1938, Roy Acuff was engaged as a regular performer, achieving national success. His celebrity was responsible, in part, for the Opry's new prominence—one attracting national interest. All the great country artists appeared on the Grand Ole Opry—a tradition that survives today.

The New York record companies were aware of the emerging nationalization of country music. Many opened studios in Nashville to be close to the stars of country music. They began producing records and attracting songwriters. Chet Atkins, a talented and successful guitarist, singer, and songwriter, was employed as RCA's recording director in Nashville. He was a prime force in the innovations that took place in the music industry in response to the popularity of rock and roll in the 1950s. These innovations, collectively, became known as the **Nashville sound.** Its period of greatest popularity and influence spanned the years 1957–1971.

Listening Guide   No. 23

Ricky Skaggs and the Kentucky Thunder.

"Uncle Pen"
CD1, Track 23, 2:23

Performer: Ricky Skaggs, country singer, guitarist, mandolinist, violinist, and producer. From the album *Country Gentleman: The Best of Ricky Skaggs* (1998), a collection of his greatest hits originally recorded for the Sugarhill label, 1981–1992.

Genre: Bluegrass.

Background: Ricky Skaggs' career spans the 1980s to today. At the time many country artists were crossing over into pop styles, Skaggs kept his country roots. His 10 Grammy awards from 1983 through 2004, including two Best Bluegrass Album awards (1999 and 2004), attest to his popularity and commercial success. This song, "Uncle Pen," was written by Bill Monroe, who was considered the Father of Bluegrass (see page 114). The name of this genre was taken from the name of Monroe's group, the Bluegrass Boys. Today Skaggs heads a group known as Kentucky Thunder.

Goals

Describe the distinctive sounds and style of bluegrass.
Recognize the "a a b a" form in both the vocal and instrumental verses.
How does the "b" pattern differ from the "a"?

Guide (each number represents one 2-beat bar)

0:00	Intro	Two beats
	Instrumental	1 – 2 – 3 – 4 – 5 – 6 – 7 – 8 –
	(a a b a)	1 – 2 – 3 – 4 – 5 – 6 – 7 – 8 – plus three beats
0:17	Vocal	1 – 2 – 3 – 4 – 5 – 6 – 7 – 8 – plus three beats
	(a a b a)	1 – 2 – 3 – 4 – 5 – 6 – 7 – 8 – plus two beats
0:34	Instrumental	1 – 2 – 3 – 4 – 5 – 6 – 7 – 8 –
	(a a b a)	1 – 2 – 3 – 4 – 5 – 6 – 7 – 8 – plus three beats
0:51	Vocal	1 – 2 – 3 – 4 – 5 – 6 – 7 – 8 – plus three beats
	(a a b a)	1 – 2 – 3 – 4 – 5 – 6 – 7 – 8 – plus two beats
1:08	Instrumental	1 – 2 – 3 – 4 – 5 – 6 – 7 – 8 –
1:15	Guitar solo	1 – 2 – 3 – 4 – 5 – 6 – 7 – 8 – plus three beats

Listening Guide –Continued   No. 23

1:24	Vocal	1 – 2 – 3 – 4 – 5 – 6 – 7 – 8 – plus three beats
	(a a b a)	1 – 2 – 3 – 4 – 5 – 6 – 7 – 8 – plus two beats
1:41	Instrumental	1 – 2 – 3 – 4 – 5 – 6 – 7 – 8 –
	(a a b a)	1 – 2 – 3 – 4 – 5 – 6 – 7 – 8 – plus one beat
1:56	Vocal	1 – 2 – 3 – 4 – 5 – 6 – 7 – 8 – plus two beats
2:05	Instrumental	1 – 2 – 3 – 4 – 5 – 6 – 7 – 8 –
	(a a a a)	1 – 2 – 3 – 4 – 5 – 6 – 7 – 8 – plus tag

Reflections

Compare this style with those developed by other country artists, such as Bob Wills and the Texas Playboys (Listening Guide 22).
In what ways is this music contemporary country? In what ways is it pop?

The longtime director of the Country Music Foundation, William Ivey, offers these insights on the nature and influences of the Nashville sound:

- It was an era in which the Nashville music industry responded to the pressures and demands of the marketplace; it would create a product that would have the widest possible appeal, become a part of the larger popular music spectrum, yet preserve as much as possible the traditional attributes of country music.
- It was an era in which the music changed, partly because of commercial forces at work, but also because of the interests, talents, and instincts of the record producers. They were more inclined toward popular music than toward the "primitive ruralisms" of hillbilly music, the style that is now called "hard country."
- The instrumentation became standard, including as many as six guitars of different types—including the Hawaiian steel guitar and electronic instruments—backup singers, small or even large string sections (violins and cellos), and horn sections. Sometimes the background music was laid down on separate tracks after the main core of musicians was finished.

With the Nashville sound, the roots of country music (as found in the folk tradition) were becoming increasingly obscure. It was hillbilly made popular by adding pop sophistication to country performance style. Nashville now symbolized the full-scale commercialization of country music. To this day, it reigns as the recording capital of the industry.

Hank Williams, a country music legend, became a "star" in a way and at a level that helped define what that meant for future country artists. He influenced countless country singers and songwriters. All this took place within a career in the limelight that lasted approximately five years: from 1949, with his debut with the Grand Ole Opry and his first No. 1 hit, to January 1, 1953, when he died on his way to perform a concert.

Willie Nelson, born in 1933, was a Texan who tried to make it big in Texas. That effort did not suit Willie; his ambition caused him to head for Nashville, where he became financially successful as a songwriter. But he liked to perform, and perform he did and is still doing so today.

Contemporary Country   Country music in the United States has produced many great entertainers, whether their specialty was honky-tonk (Hank Williams and Patsy Cline), bluegrass (Bill Monroe and Alison Krauss), cowboy music (Roy Rogers and Gene Autry), mainstream or traditional country (Johnny Cash, Emmylou Harris, and Chet Atkins), or young country (Vince Gill, Garth Brooks, Tim McGraw, and Faith Hill). Relatively new (twenty-first century) artists include Kenny Chesney, Keith Urban, Carrie Underwood, and Miranda Lambert.

The most successful country artists today—like pop and rock artists—measure their success largely by tours and individuals concerts, which in turn promote their sale of CDs and DVDs—and frequently nonmusical paraphenalia. All successful artists have developed effective fan bases through attractive and sophisticated means of communication, such as e-mail networks and websites. Music business, as discussed in the beginning of this book, continues to be an integral part of the entertainment industry, particularly for those seeking national and international exposure.

Listening Guide

"Don't Forget to Remember Me"
CD1, Track 24, 4:00

Performer: Carrie Underwood, from *Some Hearts* (2005).
Genre: Contemporary country.
Context: At the time of this writing, Carrie Underwood is one of the biggest stars in country music. She is an *American Idol* winner (2005), a multiplatinum recording artist, and a multiple Grammy Award winner. *Some Hearts* (2005) was one of the fastest-selling debut albums in recording history. This album produced four number-1 country hits, including "Don't Forget to Remember Me." It was the best-selling solo female debut album in country music history. Her most recent album is *Carnival Ride* (2007). Underwood was inducted as a member of the Grand Ole Opry in 2008.

Goals

Describe the vocal style. What makes it effective? Not so effective?

How is this style different from bluegrass singing or contemporary pop music?

Guide

0:00	Intro—Instrumental
0:24	Verse 1
1:00	Chorus
1:42	Verse 2
2:18	Chorus
2:48	Instrumental interlude
2:58	Verse 3
3:38	Coda

Carrie Underwood performing.

Reflections

Compare this song and the singing style with the previous two songs (Bob Wills' western swing (page 112) and Ricky Skaggs' bluegrass (page 116).

Compare this musical style with an earlier style exemplified by Ethel Merman's Tin Pan Alley song (page 109) and with any other currently popular singing style.

Early African American Influences

African American music has traditionally included gospel, R&B, and soul. Each of these styles, and the artists that created them, has made a profound contribution to the development of American popular music.

Seldom, however, does music fit neatly into categories and definitions. Any music conceived to "rise on the charts" has to have a wide enough appeal to sell a sufficient number of records to be declared a hit—a status intensely desired by professional performers and producers of popular music. Thus, some music is intentionally "watered down" (commercialized) so that listeners unfamiliar with the style will be more likely to appreciate the music. This is particularly true of some gospel music, and it is definitely true of a style of black music produced in Detroit in the 1960s—the **Motown sound.**

Motown   Berry Gordy was a songwriter from Detroit who, in the early 1960s, founded his own record production company, Motown Records. At first, he drew talent exclusively from the black population of Detroit. He had an instinct for making black music widely popular among both black and white populations. He stressed arrangements in a style derived more from the black gospel than from blues or jazz traditions. He exerted firm control over the recordings and produced a stylistic consistency.

Motown recordings with their studio-produced sounds climbed to the top of both the R&B charts and the white pop charts. The most common recording artists were singing groups with featured soloists: Gladys Knight and the Pips, Diana Ross and the Supremes, Smokey Robinson and the Miracles, and Martha and the Vandellas. The Motown superstar was Stevie Wonder.

Gospel   Modern black gospel music represents the urbanization of the spirituals and hymns sung in rural churches and at camp meetings. This style of music is covered in more detail in chapter 4.

The Temptations, a group of five male singers, began in the Motown tradition of the 1960s and have been performing ever since. One person from the original five-man group, Otis Williams, continues today. They take pride in having been able to stay with the original Temptations style.

Rhythm and Blues   As noted in the blues discussion in chapter 3, there are many different ways of singing the blues. Country blues is a genre of American folk music. Urban or classic blues of the 1920s and 1930s was often sung by women, such as Ma Rainey and Bessie Smith, with accompaniment by an instrumental jazz ensemble. Traditional rhythm and blues (R&B) was blues singing with a boogie-woogie style of piano and electric guitar accompaniment. This style resulted from the migration of blacks from the rural South to the cities, primarily to Memphis and Chicago. R&B, which flourished during the 1940s and early 1950s, was black music intended for black audiences. Record companies produced blues music for black Americans on what were then called *race records*. *Billboard* published R&B charts from 1949 through 1969. Today, R&B is a different style of music from this early R&B.

Country blues singers who could adapt to the city music and the electrified sound became part of this early R&B tradition. The most notable of these were Lightn'n

James Brown, the "Godfather of Soul," is shown performing in 2005 in Indonesia, where he joined a star-studded lineup of jazz greats. He had been singing—and dancing—since the 1950s. Brown began dancing on street corners for tips; the more elaborate his dance steps, the greater the tips. He then started singing in groups in Augusta, Georgia, and found that he wanted to be "out front." So began his style that involved a wild stage act: dramatic and energetic vocal embellishments and high-energy "dancing," likely influenced by the success of his childhood street-corner dancing. He died on Christmas day, 2006.

(a) Tina Turner is shown performing in 2000 in Zurich, Switzerland. Tina's career began in 1956 when she joined Ike Turner's Kings of Rhythm. Tina, who later married Ike, contributed much to the success of Ike's band with her high energy and dazzling presentation, and the band later became the Ike and Tina Turner Review. The abusive marriage ended, Tina turned to a solo career and achieved international success.

(b) Ray Charles is seen singing in Pasadena for a National Easter Seals fundraising event—a 20-hour telethon. A singer and pianist, he is one of the few soul singers who never performed gospel music in churches. However, he regularly incorporated elements of the gospel style in his R&B performances.

(c) Little Richard is seen performing during a Rock and Roll Hall of Fame show. His performances are marked by fast tempos and high energy. Throughout his career, he incorporated both rock and religion. His style featured rock and roll tunes supported by a boogie-woogie beat, a style that became known as rockabilly.

Hopkins, John Lee Hooker, Howlin' Wolf, T-Bone Walker, and Muddy Waters. These were older blues men, some of whom came from the Mississippi Delta, who didn't find fame until they moved to Memphis or Chicago. The most famous traditional R&B artist is B. B. King (see Listening Guide 8, page 54), also a bluesman from the Mississippi Delta who moved to Memphis. Part of his phenomenal success originally was due to his popularity among the British rock musicians of the 1960s.

Soul   Soul was an extension of R&B and, in fact, was popularized by previous R&B singers. In 1969, *Billboard* magazine changed the name of its R&B chart to Soul, its new name for black popular music. This sound was intended only for black audiences, with singing styles derived from blues and jazz as well as black gospel.

Soul became the black music for black audiences that Motown no longer served. The music was identifiable with and a product of the black experience in the United States.

It represented a communication and sharing of strong emotions and of a wide spectrum of life experiences among blacks. It was the music of northern-born former Motown blacks and of southern-born former Memphis blacks—the music of Ray Charles, Otis Redding, Aretha Franklin, Ike and Tina Turner, Sam Cooke, and James Brown.

Contemporary Styles

Rock   **Rock,** or rock and roll, began in the mid-1950s. It was essentially an underground, antiestablishment, protest music. The older generation (the "establishment" of the 1950s) believed that this music was a fad and would contribute nothing substantial to America's musical culture. They were wrong. Rock not only survived but became a commercial product that soon became a powerhouse of the recording industry.

Rock was an amalgamation of several styles and influences, especially R&B and country and western—one essentially black, the other white. From its beginning, rock performers and their audiences were interracial and international. Rock was an umbrella for young people that provided common symbols, language, and dress codes for white and black people alike. Rock appealed to urban and rural people; to wealthy, middle-class, and poor people; and especially to rebellious young people.

Before rock, most radio stations, catering to white audiences, did not play songs performed or written by blacks. Concerts typically were segregated. However, this was the period in which the U.S. Supreme Court handed down its landmark decision desegregating education in *Brown v. Board of Education* (1954), and it was a time of intense national awareness of racial issues, particularly relating to segregation and integration.

White Americans discovered that they enjoyed listening and dancing to R&B music. White artists began recording R&B songs previously recorded by blacks. Their recordings sold considerably better than the originals, but much of the earthy quality of the originals was lost. These versions were refined, "watered down," and more acceptable to white consumers than the original R&B arrangements.

Since many of the R&B artists were from the South, and a number of country artists had rubbed elbows with southern blacks, it was no surprise that country performers were attracted to rock and roll music. The resulting form often has been called **rockabilly.**

Listening Guide   No. 25

"Good Golly, Miss Molly"
CD1, Track 25, 1:37

Performer: Little Richard. Recorded in 1958.
Genre: Rock and roll.

Goals

Recognize the 12-bar blues form.
Recognize breaks, riffs, and boogie-woogie patterns.

–Continued

Listening Guide –Continued   No. 25

Guide

The blues chord progression of each phrase of this 12-bar blues is the same:
I – – – IV – I – V IV I –.

Chorus

0:00	1	Piano: boogie-woogie pattern
0:22	2	Vocal chorus
0:39	3	Vocal chorus
0:57	4	First four bars: "break" or "stop time" (rhythmic activity in accompaniment stops—a common jazz technique; notice the extra two beats)
		Last eight bars: the second and third lines of the text
1:15	5	Chorus with big band jazz accompaniment and riffs; 11 bars plus brief extension (tag) in free rhythm

Reflections

What is the main function of the piano part in this piece?

Notice, as in previous pieces, the frequent repetition of phrases that give the piece conciseness, cohesion, and identity.

Describe any relationship of this music to jazz and to bluegrass. What musical characteristics make this music different?

How is this music different from current popular music? How have tastes changed since the late 1950s?

The success of rock and roll cannot be traced to a single song or a single artist. Significant contributions were made by Bill Haley and the Comets, Chuck Berry, Little Richard, and Elvis Presley through their popular hits of the 1950s. "Rock around the Clock" was the first rock and roll song to climb to the top of the pop charts, symbolizing the power and popularity of early rock and roll. Through television, recordings, and personal appearances, Elvis Presley became a superstar of popular music to an unprecedented degree, eliciting frenzied responses from his audiences. He then retreated into more conventional, conservative styles that appealed to a wider market.

Mainstream white popular music (the conservative, Tin Pan Alley–type music) was controlled by several major recording companies. These major labels were considered the music establishment. All the early rock and roll hits were produced by much smaller, independent labels. However, the popularity of their songs made the established record companies sit up and take notice.

At first, this new teenage music was discredited by the major labels. When this tactic did not succeed in redirecting aesthetic tastes, the major labels countered with *covers* (new recordings of the same material) sung by their own white artists, such as Pat Boone and the old crooners: Bing Crosby, Frank Sinatra, and Perry Como. They then "manufactured" teenage idols: Fabian, Frankie Avalon, Ricky Nelson, Bobby Vinton, Bobby Rydell, and others. Their music was white, urban, and only remotely related to R&B. It dealt almost solely with teenage romance. The music of these teen idols was given considerable exposure on *The Ed Sullivan Show* and, most important, on Dick Clark's *American Bandstand,* a show that unquestionably was a powerful force in "taming" the controversial rock and roll and making it acceptable to the establishment.

The establishment won out for a time. Rock and roll diminished in popularity by the early 1960s—until February 8, 1964, when the Beatles appeared on *The Ed Sullivan Show.* The "British Invasion" had begun.

The birthplace of the "British Invasion" was Liverpool, England—a seaport city with a large working-class population that supported hundreds of local musical groups. British sailors who had been to America brought back to Liverpool rhythm and blues and rock and roll records. This music influenced the local musicians so profoundly that its popularity was sustained in England even after it had waned in the States. Local favorites were the Everly Brothers, Buddy Holly, Chuck Berry, and Little Richard.

The most durable and influential groups that came from England were the Beatles, the Rolling Stones, the Who, and Pink Floyd. In 1967, the Beatles' *Sgt.*

The Beatles' performing in 1964 on *The Ed Sullivan Show.* This historic performance contributed significantly to "Beatlemania" in the United States and internationally. From the left: Paul McCartney, George Harrison, and John Lennon, with Ringo Starr at the drums.

Pepper's Lonely Hearts Club Band was the first album with music clearly and completely in the new rock style to climb to the top of the pop charts. It became known to almost everyone interested in popular music. This album was many people's first exposure to the style of popular music now simply called *rock*. It became more than dance music. It was music for listening and was respected as "legitimate music" by many educated musicians. This album signaled a new age in American popular music.

The music of the Beatles and other British groups served mostly urban white people. It did not achieve popularity among the black and country and western audiences. Thus, in bringing new life to popular music, it did not recapture the cross-cultural feature of early rock and roll.

Styles of rock music result from advanced electronic technology, including sound amplification, studio manipulation of sound, synthesizers, MIDI applications, sampling, studio mixing, a wide range of instruments, and flexible and varied forms. Performances stress both audio and visual impacts. Performers stress unique if not bizarre dress and onstage behavior. Outlandish presentations were particularly popular in the 1980s among artists such as Mötley Crüe, Kiss, Alice Cooper, and other heavy metal bands.

The rise of rock inspired the study of popular culture by music scholars, sociologists, journalists. and writers of theses and dissertations. It also gave birth to a diversity of subgenres that included acid rock, art rock, blues rock, folk rock, gospel rock, industrial rock, jazz rock, metal, heavy metal, alternative heavy metal, new wave, pop rock, punk rock, southern rock, and others that came and went in the continuously evolving world of American popular music.

Many artists change styles from album to album or within an album. Others may create blended styles, such as jazz and rock or gypsy music and punk or blues. Artists who regularly perform in more than one style, especially blended styles, are known as **"crossover"** artists. Crossover artists can have hits on more than one chart; they include those performers whose multifaceted talents and interests defy classification.

Rap/Hip-Hop   The roots of rap date to the 1970s in the streets of New York City. Rap is one part of the "hip-hop" culture, which originally included inner-city manifestations of four distinct arts: street poetry, rap music, graffiti, and break dancing. Rap was a black, male-dominated genre, but before long Latinos came to enjoy its beat and empathize with its poetry. They developed rap groups, as did women and white performers. The first successful female rap group was Salt-n-Pepa. Other early groups (1980s) included Run-D.M.C and the Beastie Boys.

Now, like all previous forms of black popular music—the blues, R&B, gospel, and soul—rap has moved into the mainstream of American popular music. The music today is known more as hip-hop, with the chanting or recitation of poetry sometimes called "rapping."

As rap evolved, the "singer" recited socially aware street poetry that ranged from light, entertaining lyrics intended to increase public awareness of social concerns to those that promoted sexism, bigotry, black supremacy, and violence. Typically, the poetry described the harsh realities of American street life for urban blacks: drugs, poverty, racial injustice, gang violence, AIDS, battered women, and child abuse.

A unique "instrument," typical of some rap groups, is the turntable; the performer "plays" the turntable by generating very tiny moves of the tone-arm needle across the vinyl (33⅓ LP records), producing highly rhythmic scratching sounds. This has sometimes been called "turntabalism."

Listening Guide

No. 26

"Un-break My Heart"
CD1, Track 26, 4:30

Performer: Toni Braxton, from *Ultimate* (2003), a collection of greatest hits.

Music and lyrics: Diane Warren.

Genre: R&B.

Context: Toni Braxton had huge hits and won Grammy awards throughout the 1990s. This song first appeared on *Secret* (1996). A few phrases from "Un-break My Heart" are sufficient to reveal the sadness and the longing in this song:

Don't leave me in all this pain.
Don't leave me out in the rain.
Undo this hurt you caused. Un-cry these tears
I cried so many nights. Un-break my heart.

Goals

Describe the vocal quality—and range—in relation to the mood of the song.
Describe the relationship of music and words.
Recognize the form.

Guide

0:00	Intro—wordless singing
0:21	Verse 1
0:55	Chorus
1:30	Verse 2
2:02	Chorus
2:35	Interlude—guitar solo then vocal
3:10	Chorus
3:56	Extension—fade

Toni Braxton performing. Braxton was one of the most popular and commercially successful female R&B singers of the 1990s, thanks to her ability to straddle seemingly opposite worlds. Braxton was soulful enough for R&B audiences, smooth enough for adult contemporary listeners, sophisticated enough for adults, and sultry enough for younger listeners. Braxton had two albums that sold over 8 million copies each; her song "Un-break My Heart" ranks among the top pop hits of the rock era.

Reflections

Describe the vocal style and how it is or is not appropriate to the mood of the lyrics.
Discuss any musical elements that are or are not rooted in the R&B tradition.

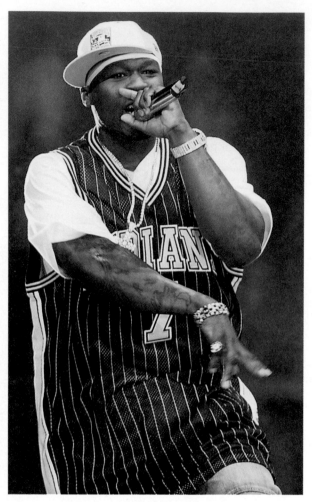

Eminem is seen performing in 2004 at the MTV-Europe Awards show in Rome. Eminem is able to present dazzling lyrics, violent and vulgar, yet memorable. He released his debut album, *Infinite*, in 1996 and made his major radio debut on the world-famous "Wake Up Show with Sway and Tech." Realizing that this was the opportunity of a lifetime, Eminem delivered a furious medley of lyrics that wowed his hosts and radio audience alike.

50 Cent is seen performing in Moline, Illinois, in 2003. Born Curtis Jackson, 50 Cent is a man of the streets, intimately familiar with its codes and its violence. Born into a notorious Queens drug dynasty during the late 1970s, he lost those closest to him at an early age. 50 Cent was signed to Columbia Records in 1999. Among his best-selling albums so far are *Massacre* (2005) and *Get Rich or Die Trying* (2003).

Today, rap/hip-hop is very big business. *Billboard* now includes two related categories: Rap and R&B/Hip-Hop. The Grammy category is still Rap.

Other Genres

A genre of popular music that has become increasingly successful since it emerged in the 1970s is New Age music (not to be confused with New Age religion). It combines elements of jazz, classical, popular, or rock styles to create a mellow, soothing, "back-to-nature" mood, although in recent years it has become much more diverse. Much of New Age music is processed sound (electronically produced) and occasionally is combined with acoustic instruments such as piano, guitar, or harp.

International and ethnic styles have become important in American popular culture. This music includes Irish or Celtic songs, long-lasting reggae and salsa styles of the Caribbean, Afropop, and other "worldbeat" styles from southern Africa (see Listening Guide 38, page 168), and Celtic music from the British Isles (see Listening Guides 42 and 43 on pages 179 and 180).

Global genres and styles are discussed further in chapters 7 and 8 as part of world and ethnic musics. Nearly every country and region have their own forms of popular music.

Summary

This chapter focuses on the musical development, social implications, and economic impact of American popular music. We are all affected in one way or another by our relationship to popular music.

Popular music has developed in clear stages, and this growth has been recorded in the literature of music. For these reasons, we can approach the study of vernacular music (music other than art music) from a scholarly perspective. Many universities offer programs and degrees in the study of popular music or popular culture.

In this chapter, we examine the roots and trends that have contributed to the development of popular music as it exists today. We explore styles, influences, and artists that represent the beginning and other important stages of various popular styles in music, from minstrel song to Tin Pan Alley, country and western, several manifestations of black popular music, rock, and other contemporary styles.

The tastes of the masses often change rapidly, causing styles of popular music also to change. In order to study popular music, it is necessary to understand something of the impact of mass media and advertising on popular taste and something about the music industry and how it functions.

PART three

Listening to World Music

Chapters 7 and 8 present a sampling of music from both Western and non-Western cultures. Non-Western musical sounds and structures may be quite different from the more familiar ones found in western European and American music.

In Chapter 7, we look at music from the Western Hemisphere, including music of Native Americans and music from Mexico, South America, and the Caribbean. In addition to brief discussions of folk and classical music from these nations and regions, the chapter also includes music and information on a variety of world musical styles popular in the United States, including reggae (Jamaica), salsa (Cuba and Puerto Rico), bossa nova (Brazil), mariachi (Mexico), Tex-Mex and *tejano* (border music of Mexico and south Texas), and Cajun and zydeco (southwestern Louisiana).

In Chapter 8, we discuss some musical styles found in other parts of the world, beyond the Americas. We introduce the traditional and contemporary styles of India, Japan, and sub-Saharan Africa, and we discuss briefly Bulgarian choral music, Jewish music including klezmer, gamelan music from Indonesia, and both Celtic and traditional Irish music.

Attempting to understand the music of various cultures may help you understand music from your own culture. Reaching out to new and therefore unfamiliar music may broaden your own musical tastes and listening choices. These chapters provide opportunities for sampling a variety of musics. The purpose is not to prompt you to change your musical tastes and listening habits; however, on occasion, one experience may lead to another.

In providing musical examples from a few of the world's cultures, we acknowledge the following:

• Music plays an important role in both developed and developing societies throughout the world.

• Just like music in our own culture, music in other cultures has a tradition, a history, and a profound value within its society. Like Western art music, with which we may be more familiar, music of other cultures may also be involved, disciplined, and intellectually well founded.

• Any culture or nation has subcultures and regional differences, and its music is likely to reflect those variations.

• People in different parts of the world like and dislike different elements of musical style and performance practices. Differences are evident in style of dress, performance sites, and audience behavior.

Our musical tastes are shaped from birth by our environment. No matter what region of the world we live in, we tend to prefer the music that our culture produces. This natural bias in favor of what is familiar may make it difficult for us to respond favorably to unfamiliar music. Music that is based on different musical systems or performed in contexts that seem strange to us can be perceived as "all sounding the same" or simply "weird." Try to listen to the music of another culture on its own terms, not in the context of our Western biases. Remember that the sounds and performance contexts of Western music that are familiar to us may "all sound the same" or seem "weird" to listeners from other cultures.

Most westerners are culturally conditioned to listen to the melody or to a distinctive rhythm. In contrast, other cultures may create music with no perceivable melody or no distinctive beat, or they may value instrumental or vocal tone qualities that sound quite different, even uncomfortable, to our ears. On the other hand, the popular music of various nations and cultures worldwide may not sound that unfamiliar, for such music is frequently a fusion of native traditional music and contemporary Western styles. Popular artists everywhere are mobile, recording their music in major metropolitan cities such as Paris, London, or New York, and also touring and otherwise marketing their music internationally. That's why world music and its various subgenres (Afropop, Celtic, world fusion, reggae, and dozens more) are known internationally. Styles of international popular music have generated new audiences, instruments, and performance **venues.**

7 *Music of the Americas*

In This Chapter

What is the role of music in the Native American cultures?

What was the impact of immigrants on American music and culture?

How would you describe the vernacular music of South America, Mexico, and the Caribbean?

What is an indigenous folk culture? What is mestizo culture?

How would you describe the folk culture and the popular culture of the nations and regions of the Americas?

This brief discussion is intended to give impressions of and insights into "American" music outside our own culture and experience.

Bridges to other cultures do not necessarily span great distances; world music exists within the boundaries of the United States. We can study the music of Native Americans, including those from Alaska and Hawaii, and we can listen to the songs and dances that immigrant groups brought to the United States and retained as ethnic repertoires.

When we speak of "American" music, we tend to think of music from the continental United States, rather than music from elsewhere in the Western Hemisphere—Canada, Mexico, Central and South America, and the Caribbean. Geographically, however, these are all part of the "Americas."

From this chapter, you will gain a sense of some of the musical traditions and influences found within the Americas. We focus first on the music of the original Americans (the American Indians). Then we explore ethnic music in the United States and the traditions and characteristics of the music of South America, Mexico, and the Caribbean.

Goals for Listening

Most of the musical concepts and vocabulary presented thus far apply to the music presented in chapters 7 and 8. However, world music also reveals some interesting differences:

- Pitch patterns, particularly pentatonic and other gapped scales, which form the basis of melodies that may sound different from Western melodies.
- Styles in which harmony is not valued.
- Rhythms that may be quite complex and not based on the Western sense of meter.
- Musical instruments and different ways of singing that provide a vast array of new sounds.
- Ensembles uncommon in Western culture.
- Functional and ceremonial music whose purposes are neither entertainment nor art.
- Music that combines the sounds of American popular music with the traditional sounds of a culture or region.

Among the new musical material to be recognized are phrase groupings other than a a b a and 12-bar blues, chants, **vocables, glissandos,** minor **modes,** pentatonic scales, **fermatas,** and other terms and symbols related to musical expression. We also give attention to relationships between music and text.

The Listening Guides for this chapter offer Native American music, indigenous Peruvian music, Latino music (a Mexican *ranchera,* Tex-Mex conjunto, and maria-chi), zydeco, and reggae.

Native American Music

The indigenous music of North America is the music of Native Americans in the United States, Canada, and Mexico. It is ironic that *Native* American music is often treated more as world music than as a type of American music. This may be so for several reasons:

- Native American cultures are essentially different from any European-based cultures.
- The traditions, functions, and styles of Native American music are substantially different from those of any other American music.
- Native American music is essentially different from any European-based music, both vocally and instrumentally and also in its functions and aesthetic qualities.
- Native American music is ignored by most Europeans and Americans.
- Native American music has been of little consequence in the development of music in American society, particularly when compared with the influence of European music or music from Africa.

Many Native American cultures were nonliterate and thus had no recorded history. Knowledge of their music has come from anthropology and archaeology, from stories told by the "old people," and from the findings of scholars who began studying Indian cultures in the mid-nineteenth century. Through the annihilation and acculturation of the native peoples, however, most of the old songs have been lost.

In the United States, each native people had its own culture, language, and music. Even among peoples living in close proximity, there was only minimal cultural

Native American elders from the Santa Clara Pueblo in New Mexico are seen drumming during a Corn Dance ceremony.

interaction and exchange. The long-term result was cultural isolation and very little **acculturation.** Thus, although some broad shared characteristics and recurring patterns can be found in the music of Native American peoples, on close scrutiny, we become aware of tremendous diversity.

The native cultures of Mexico and South America came under the influence of Europeans, particularly the Spanish, much earlier than did their northern counterparts. These groups adopted the cultural behaviors, traditions, and language of Europeans more thoroughly than did those in North America. Consequently, the native cultures of Mexico and South America were more assimilated, and less is known of their original music than of the music of the more segregated indigenous cultures of the United States and Canada.

Style and Context

In contrast to European cultures, the native cultures of North America considered music an essential part of daily life. Music was mainly functional, consisting primarily of songs and dances intended to achieve some purpose, such as good health, a successful hunt, victory in war, rain, or contact with the spirit world. Therefore, music was usually associated with rituals, although some songs and dances were performed purely for entertainment. Music was transmitted by oral tradition rather than notation.

Music was sometimes composed deliberately for recreation rather than for religious purposes or rituals. Such songs were frequently borrowed from other native peoples or even from Christians. Other songs were said to be received in dreams or visions, as if they came directly from the spirits.

Unlike a modern concert or a recording, Native American music was not intended to be listened to alone or apart from its function. We might even say that this music should not exist out of its original context. Many songs were valued for their power and were "owned" by individuals, who would protect that power by performing these songs only under special, often ceremonial, circumstances.

The words to a song may have told a story, expressed a prayer or a wish, or described an emotion. Sometimes the words carried no meaning but were intended only as vocal sounds known as **vocables.** In some songs, these vocables, through the total experience of the ritual or dance, conveyed a meaning or a mood. Vocables sometimes appeared in recognizable, perhaps quite intricate patterns that native listeners identified with particular songs or kinds of songs. Some songs combined meaningful words with vocables, but some vocables may never have had any meaning, or their meanings may be obscure or long forgotten.

Instrumental music was seldom performed by itself, and melody instruments were rare. The most common instruments were drums of all shapes and sizes, rattles, and tambourines or bells and other percussion instruments. Drums were made of clay, iron, wood, or aluminum with heads of buckskin, chamois, or rubber. A drum was typically played with a single drumstick. One drum that was unique in its construction was the water drum, prevalent throughout the Americas. Drum rhythms were usually very simple—a steady four-beat pattern. The drums typically accompanied singers or dancers. The most common wind instruments were the vertical flute, whistle, and, in some cultures, **panpipes.** The flute was seldom used in religious ceremonies; it was more often used to accompany love songs.

Most songs had a small range, seldom more than an **octave,** and often encompassed only a few tones. Many songs were based on scales that approximated the European major scale; the most common scale, however, was the **pentatonic** (five tones). Songs were made up of short phrases with considerable repetition or sometimes subtle variation. The singing was intense, earthy, and harsh; was sometimes performed in a high-pitched voice; and included **ornamentation,** slides, shouts, and animal calls. There was no **harmony,** only a single-line **melody** with percussion accompaniment. Melodies were often quite rhythmic and were supported by the timekeeping of the drums. Nearly all traditional songs accompanied dancing. In ceremonies, musicians and dancers were usually dressed in elaborate costumes with feathers, wore makeup, and held sticks or other objects.

Assimilation and Preservation

The pressures and the attractions of the "white man's" world have led some Native Americans to reject their own culture and enter the **mainstream** of American life. In recent decades, however, there seems to be increased awareness among Native Americans of the importance of their culture and the necessity of preserving it.

Although many ceremonies and rituals remain private within the Native American community, public events such as intertribal ceremonies and powwows contribute to preserving the Indian culture today. These ceremonies take place on reservations and in cities with large Native American populations; they typically include songs and dances, colorful costumes, and concessions selling native food and gifts. The performers include professional musicians making the powwow circuit. Such events help to preserve the culture as a whole, rather than the characteristics and behaviors of specific peoples.

Despite the extent to which Native Americans have been assimilated into American society, their music has not significantly merged with or influenced European-based music, probably because of its radically different style and functions. However, although their own music remains separate, Native Americans have accepted the popular music of America. They listen to rock and country music. They have formed their own performing groups and have made recordings in both rock and country styles. A few radio stations in the Southwest regularly program for the Native American population, playing tribal music, Western popular music, and religious music.

Indigenous American music still exists, although most of the old songs and dances and the old traditions have long since died. Native Americans seem to be truly multicultural, keeping some of their own ways and adopting other ways from Europeans and Americans.

Listening Guides Nos. 27 and 28

Native American Songs and Dances
CD1, Tracks 27 and 28, 4:06 (3:16 and 1:40)
A. "Rabbit Dance"

Source: Music of the Northern Plains Indians. Recorded in 1975.
Context: This type of dance is one of the few in which men and women are allowed to dance together. It is a social dance and a time for merriment.

B. "Butterfly Dance" (excerpt)

Source: Music from the San Juan Pueblo, New Mexico. Recorded in 1975.
Context: "Butterfly Dance" is associated with warfare, for the butterfly (considered a symbol of elusiveness, of always getting away, of escaping just in the nick of time) has qualities desired in a warrior.

Goals

Recognize textures, vocal qualities, timbres, and other characteristics of Native American music.
Describe the musical relationship of the singing and instrumental accompaniment.
Describe vocal and instrumental qualities. Compare them with other familiar styles.
Describe length of phrases, pitch registers, formal elements, and rhythmic organization.
Recognize melodic sequence.

Guide for "Rabbit Dance"

This dance is in three easily distinguishable parts (Indian words, then English, then Indian). The melody is similar in each part. Listen carefully to the second part. The words are in English:

Hey, sweetheart, I always think of you,
I wonder if you are alone tonight,
I wonder if you are thinking of me.

–Continued

Listening Guides —Continued Nos. 27 and 28

Guide for "Butterfly Dance"

This musical example, the opening of a set of nine songs performed for "Butterfly Dance," calls the participants to get into position. The instruments are a double-headed cylindrical rawhide drum played by the lead singer and a set of bells worn behind the knees of the male dancer. In many places throughout the song, the pulse and the length of phrase are irregular. Count according to the drumbeats, and follow the phrases and patterns.

0:00	Instruments introducing the song
0:03	Low register, then a slightly higher register
0:11	Descending patterns (melodic sequence); first two patterns, seven beats each; third pattern extended with several pauses
0:30	Low register; short patterns—all similar
0:51	Middle register; short pattern
0:56	High register; more melodic than previous patterns; descends in pitch; speed of pulse shifts
1:24	Pitch changes only with slight embellishments; tempo slows; big pause at the end
1:30	Very slow ending; low register

Reflections

Notice the earthy intensity with which these Native Americans sing and the pulsating effect they achieve with their voices. Notice also that the singing and instrumental accompaniment are not always exactly synchronized.

In example A, the English words in the second section match the sounds of the Indian words; the rhythms, pitches, and tonal qualities are very similar. You may hear the English words merely as a continuation of the Indian words.

Discuss the vocal quality and compare it with other familiar singing styles.

Discuss the functions of Native American music.

Ethnic Music in the United States

During the nineteenth and early twentieth centuries, more than 35 million Europeans immigrated to the United States. At first they came from England; then from Ireland, Germany, and the Scandinavian countries; and then from Italy, Poland, and other eastern European countries. Today, such a journey may take less than a day, but in earlier times, it could take as much as three months and entail considerable hardship.

Immigrants often left their families and friends behind, never to return. Their departure—a family decision—was decisive and permanent. There was no organized exodus, no grand plan. Although some immigrants may have been seeking adventure, others were desperate peasants, craftsmen, and artisans who had lost their jobs in societies that were being transformed from an agrarian to an industrialized economy. Others were fleeing political or religious oppression or persecution. All were seeking a better life in a land of opportunity.

Although many immigrants may have hoped to reach the wide open spaces of the United States, most of them could not afford to go farther than the cities where they landed. Thus, rural Europeans became urban Americans. Typically, they became isolated in a society of strangers, so they cherished the coherent and stable traditional cultures of their homeland. Often, they retained their native languages, foods, and customs and expressed their nostalgia through folktales, songs, and dances.

By the late nineteenth century, executives of the developing American recording industry became aware that it could be profitable to make recordings in foreign languages for these immigrants. By the 1890s, recordings of folk music were available in Yiddish, Polish, Czech, Spanish, and many other languages. These recordings brought back memories of the immigrants' homeland and reinforced the worth of retaining old languages and customs in the new land.

At first, the performers on these recordings were trained artists, and the music was recorded in Europe using sophisticated arrangements; however, this approach robbed the peasant and village music of its original flavor and did not fill the need for "real" folk music. Peasants had brought with them a taste for rougher music—the kind sung in the fields and mountains of their homelands—that did not find acceptance in the more sophisticated cities of America.

As these immigrants became acculturated in their new communities, they came to enjoy new singers and instrumental groups. At the same time, the record companies found a way to provide music that was more pleasing for them, namely the music of the people from the Deep South who migrated north: the blues and jazz of African Americans and the hillbilly music of rural white people. This was music with guitarists and fiddlers, rough-voiced singers, village orchestras, and other representations of authentic folk styles. Suddenly, the importation of urbanized folk music from eastern Europe and elsewhere became less accepted as the immigrants developed new tastes, new loyalties, and new traditions.

Today, the diverse culture of the United States provides an abundance of musical styles from various immigrant and minority groups, homogeneous communities, and other identifiable groups—immigrant Polish, Italian, Ukrainian, German, Irish, Jewish, and Asian groups, among many others. All these groups hold on to valued parts of their original culture, such as certain songs and dances—sometimes in their original forms but more often in modified forms reflecting various degrees of assimilation into the host culture. This is American ethnic music. Some of it is marketed beyond the homogeneous immigrant communities, even becoming nationally popular genres.

Music of Native Americans may be considered an ethnic repertoire, as may Appalachian folk music (see chapter 3), country blues (chapter 3), and hillbilly (chapter 6). African-based popular music, such as early R&B, jazz, gospel, blues, and soul, is now considered mainstream rather than ethnic.

Examples of ethnic music important to many people in the United States include the following:

- Reggae music, a Jamaican style derived from African nationalism, Jamaican rhythms, and American R&B (see chapter 7).
- Latino music, including salsa, a popular Afro-Cuban dance style related to Latin jazz; bossa nova, a popular music style originating in Brazil; Tex-Mex music of Chicanos from the border region between Mexico and Texas; and mariachi, a Mexican folk music that has become a popular entertainment genre (see chapter 7).
- Cajun music from the French-speaking people in southwestern Louisiana and zydeco music from the French-speaking black Americans in the same area (see chapter 7).
- Klezmer music from the Yiddish-speaking Jewish community (see chapter 8).

All this music has a significant following in the United States and has become, to varying degrees, an important part of American popular culture.

Reggae

It is impressive that music from small Caribbean nations like Cuba, Puerto Rico, the Dominican Republic, Trinidad, and Jamaica has had such a significant impact on the popular music of other countries worldwide, particularly through the genres of salsa, calypso, and reggae.

Reggae began in the urban slums of Jamaica in the mid-1950s with a Jamaican-style R&B known as *ska*. When musicians placed more emphasis on socioeconomic issues and to emerging Jamaican and African nationalism—and less emphasis on American trends—a more sophisticated Jamaican style known as *rocksteady* evolved. This led to an internationally popular music: reggae. Reggae had connections with Rastafarianism, black nationalism, and social reform and became part of the ideology of young people and the black power movement of the early 1970s.

Reggae was given a boost by at least three factors: (1) the popularity of a film, *The Harder They Come* (1968), starring Jimmy Cliff, (2) the development of the Jamaican recording industry and distribution networks, and (3) the rise to international prominence of Bob Marley, Jamaica's first reggae superstar. In addition to Marley, the most important artists of early reggae music included Jimmy Cliff, Bunny Wailer, and Peter Tosh.

In Jamaica, the disk jockey (DJ)—as opposed to live performances—was integral to reggae. DJs and reggae poets began chatting or reciting improvised lyrics over a backing track (recorded music without lyrics) or even chatting in interaction with a singer. This was one precursor of rap, and in the 1980s, the reggae audience merged with the audience for American hip-hop, causing a decline in the popularity of reggae music in Jamaica. However, urban American stores still stock large quantities of current reggae recordings.

Latino Music

Four popular styles in the United States that have roots in folk and traditional Latin-based or Hispanic music are salsa, bossa nova, Tex-Mex, and mariachi.

Listening Guide   No. 29

"Get Up, Stand Up"

CD1, Track 29, 3:26

Composer: Words by Peter Tosh, music by Bob Marley.

Performer: Peter Tosh.

Genre: Reggae.

Background: Reggae is a true fusion music—a blend of African, Cuban, Spanish, Jamaican, and American influences. Its focus is in the plight of the poor people, political activism, and the African heritage. Musically, it takes advantage of electronic instruments, including synthesizers.

Predecessors of reggae in Jamaica are found in Rastafarian philosophy and ska music. Current trends include top 40–type settings. Urban stores carry a great deal of reggae music.

The first superstars of reggae were Jimmy Cliff and Bob Marley and the Wailers. Later stars included Peter Tosh, who played with the Wailers; Ziggy Marley; Bunny Wailer; and Yellowman.

Goals

Recognize musical elements that contribute to the sound of reggae: melodic and harmonic characteristics.

Describe the rhythmic and metric organization.

Recognize the verse-chorus pattern in the musical organization.

Recognize the minor quality in the music.

Guide

Count the beat at a moderately fast tempo. The music is in verse-chorus form, each consisting of four 8-bar phrases. However, if you allow the lyrics to generate the rhythm, the music will still have a strong rhythmic impulse but a different feel. Because the words produce shifting accents, many downbeats are weak, and the meter becomes less precise.

0:00	Intro	Electric guitar; the guitar line descends to the minor tonic on the first count of the second phrase and again four bars later; this establishes the minor mode
0:15	Chorus	*Get up, stand up, stand up for your rights*
		Get up, stand up, don't give up the fight
		(both lines repeated)
0:42	Verse I	

—Continued

Listening Guide –Continued   No. 29

1:06		*So now we see the light*
		We gonna stand up for our rights
		(Phrase ends each verse.)
1:10	Chorus	
1:38	Verse 2	
2:05	Chorus	
2:33	Verse 3	
3:00	Chorus	Followed by fade

Reflections

Follow the vocal melodic line but also the bass and other accompaniment patterns. Describe how they interrelate.

Describe the degree of rhythmic vitality and how it was achieved.

How does the minor quality affect the style of the music? Does it enhance the meaning of the words?

Salsa—dance music in an Afro-Cuban style—has been popular since the 1970s. It is not a specific genre or form but rather a way of performing or arranging. Salsa was first created mainly by Cuban and Puerto Rican musicians in New York City. Then it was developed to a large extent by the commercial recording industry in New York, and now it is almost synonymous with Latin jazz. Salsa is to Latinos what soul is to African Americans.

For many Latinos, salsa is an expression of ethnicity and of links with their home-land. As with much American popular music, salsa lyrics are typically apolitical, with the notable exception of songs by Ruben Blades, who frequently sings about social ills, barrio life, American cultural dominance, and Latino solidarity.

The most popular salsa band leader was Tito Puente; the best-known salsa singer was Celia Cruz. Other well-known salsa artists include Willie Colon and Eddie Palmieri.

Bossa nova, a pop-jazz style derived from the Brazilian samba, was first brought to the United States in the late 1950s. It became internationally popular after the American jazz musicians Stan Getz and Charlie Byrd visited Brazil in the early 1960s, recorded bossa nova music by Antonio Carlos Jobim, João Gilberto, and Astrud Gilberto, and performed it on tour. Three early bossa nova hits were "The Girl from Ipanema," "Desafinado," and "Corcovado."

A popular Mexican-based dance music is the **Tex-Mex** (*tejano*) style of the border region between Mexico and Texas. This working-class music is an important symbol of ethnic identity for Texas Chicanos. It is commonly performed at their public dances. The traditional music is performed by a *conjunto*, a combo featuring button accordion and *bajo sexto*, a Mexican 12-string guitar. Modern groups usually add drums and sometimes alto sax. The dominant music is the *ranchera*, a modern country-and-western type of song; and the *corrido*, a more traditional story song or ballad. Typically, song texts are sentimental and superficial, not vehicles for social or political protest.

Tito Puente, a Latin-Jazz percussionist, was born in New York City of Puerto Rican heritage. In this 1992 photograph, Puente plays the timbales during a concert in New York City. His recordings of the mambo and the cha-cha earned him a wide recognition. In a long career, this popular band leader recorded over 100 albums and even was awarded a star on the Hollywood Walk of Fame.

A mariachi band is pictured performing in San Antonio, Texas.

Most of the Tex-Mex recordings come from local Chicano producers who are independent of the corporate giants of the recording industry. Important Tex-Mex artists include Lydia Mendoza, El Conjunto Bernal (Paulino Bernal), and Baldemar Huerta (Freddie Fender); three of the most popular recent artists are Flaco Jiménez (see Listening Guide 30), Little Joe Hernandez, and the Texas Tornados. Selena was a crossover artist, moving easily between border music and American pop.

Mariachi is originally a traditional Mexican folk music that in the twentieth century became an urban, entertainment music performed in restaurants and performance halls, at parades and folk festivals, and at weddings and parties in Mexico, the United States, and throughout the world.

The modern instrumentation typically includes violins; a folk harp; *vilhuelas, jarana,* or other small guitar; a *guitarrón* (bass guitar); and trumpets. Voices are sometimes used.

Listening Guide No. 30

"Ay Te Dejo en San Antonio" ("I'm Leaving You Here in San Antonio")

CD1, Track 30, 1:31

Performer: Flaco Jiménez, accordion; vocal duet with Toby Roirres. From the album *The Best of Flaco Jiménez* (1999).

Genre: Tex-Mex or *tejano.*

Context: A *conjunto* is a small performing group familiar to Chicanos of the American Southwest, particularly the working-class people who live along the Texas-Mexico border. *Conjunto* music is characterized by the sound of the *Norteño* accordion and the *bajo sexto,* a Mexican 12-string guitar.

The Texas Tornados playing Tex-Mex music at a winery in California in 1991. The performers in front are (left to right) Doug Sahm, *bajo sexto* (a Mexican 12-string guitar); Freddie Fender, electric guitar; and Flaco Jiménez, accordion.

Listening Guide –Continued   No. 30

"Ay Te Dejo en San Antonio" is a *ranchera* composed by Santiago Jiménez Sr. (Flaco Jiménez's father). It is also the title of the album that, in 1986, won a Grammy for Flaco Jiménez.

Flaco Jiménez is probably the most famous Tex-Mex musician. He was a member of the popular Texas Tornados and has recorded with, among others, the Rolling Stones, Dwight Yoakam, Ry Cooder, Doug Sahm, Linda Ronstadt, Emmylou Harris, and Los Lobos.

Goals

Recognize cadence patterns and the repetitive nature of this music.
Identify chord changes and the extremely simple harmonic progressions.
Describe the form.

Guide

This is a song about "cheating ways" and lost love. The first verse (translated from the Spanish) sets the tone:

I don't even want to kiss you or for you to kiss me,
or to look at you or even hear your voice,
because I found out that you have another lover,
and in Laredo you already had two others.

Count in a moderately fast two.

0:00	Instrumental
0:24	Verse 1
0:40	Chorus
0:50	Instrumental
1:14	Verse 2; (fade to 1:31)

Reflections

Describe the sound and style of the accordion in *conjunto* music.

Describe what makes this piece distinctive. Is it enjoyable to listen to? To dance to? Is this music important? Why or why not?

Listening Guide   No. 31

"Árboles de la Barranca" ("The Trees of the Ravine")

CD1, Track 31, 2:40

Performer: Nato Cano's Mariachi Los Camperos, from the album *¡Viva el Mariachi!* produced by the Smithsonian Institutions on its Folkways label (2002). It is a compilation of Los Camperos's recorded songs from the 1990s.

–Continued

Listening Guide –Continued   No. 31

Genre: A country song (*canción ranchera*) arranged for a mariachi.

Background: Cano was born in the state of Jalisco, Mexico. He began his mariachi career in Guadalajara, then settled for a long time in Los Angeles. The instrumentation for Los Camperos, in addition to the traditional mariachi instrumentation, includes a parody of a traditional Mexican brass band (*banda*). On this recording, the parody is created by the low-sounding brass instruments playing in unison.

Goals

Distinguish harp and guitar sounds and their respective musical functions.

Recognize the "brass band" sound and discuss its function. How is the sound produced?

Identify the meter—one beat or three beats to the bar. Is the meter consistent?

Identify what instruments are creating the sound of the brass band.

Guide

0:00	Intro	8 + 10	Harp, then trumpets
0:20	Verse	8 + 8 + 10	Vocal
0:50	Interlude	8 + 8	Harp with shouts, then trumpets
1:08	Verse	8 + 8 + 10	Vocal with "brass band," then vocal
1:38	Interlude	6 + 10	Harp with shouts, then trumpets
1:56	Verse	8 + 8 + 10	Vocal; second phrase only with brass band
2:25	Ending	6	Harp; ritard to cadence

Reflections

What aspects of this musical example surprise you?

In what ways does the brass band contribute to the musical style?

Does it detract?

What is the function of the brass band?

Would you enjoy a live performance of mariachi music? If so, would you enjoy it better in a concert hall, in a restaurant, or at a street festival?

Cajun and Zydeco Music

French refugees from Acadia (now Nova Scotia) settled in Louisiana in the second half of the eighteenth century. Since they were farmers and fishermen, they were not accepted in New Orleans by the upper-class French people already settled there. Eventually, they wound up in the swamp and bayou country of southwestern Louisiana.

The folk music of these white Cajuns consists of songs and **ballads** in French patois, or dialect. The fiddle, since the earliest days, has been the main instrument in Cajun dance music. Popular twentieth-century fiddlers were Dennis McGee, Dewey

Balfa, and Michael Doucet (the leader of Beausoleil, a well-known Cajun group). The accordion was added in the 1920s and is now an integral part of Cajun music. In the middle of the twentieth century, Cajun music became commercialized, and some of its earlier distinctiveness was lost as it took on more country or hillbilly characteristics. The steel guitar was even added to some Cajun bands.

In recent years, however, groups such as Beausoleil have helped bring back the spirit of traditional Cajun music. The sound and language are unique, and the music is lighthearted and zesty.

Black musicians also lived in Cajun country. Their music, for dancing with songs sung in French, was a Cajun style combined with the blues. This is **zydeco** music. The accordion has remained in the zydeco band, along with the electric guitar, electric bass, drums, occasional saxes, and the washboard—sometimes called the *rub board*. Important zydeco artists are Buckwheat Zydeco and, during their life, Rockin' Dopsie and Clifton Chenier. Chenier was considered the undisputed "king of zydeco." A number of these artists performed at folk and blues festivals across the United States.

Listening Guide   No. 32

"Tu Le Ton Son Ton" (excerpt)
CD2, Track 1, 2:10

Performer: Clifton Chenier, accordion, and his five-piece Red Hot Louisiana Band. From the album *60 Minutes with the King of Zydeco* (1986).
Genre: Zydeco.

Goals

Describe elements of contrast and repetition.
Identify chord patterns.
Identify the form.

Guide

12-bar phrases; moderately fast tempo.

0:00	Intro with three-beat pickup
0:03	Instrumental
0:22	Vocal
0:41	Vocal
0:58	Instrumental
1:17	Vocal
1:35	Instrumental
1:53	Vocal (fade)

Reflections

How is this commercial music? Folk music? Ethnic music?
What are the values in this music? Which ones can be shared across cultures?

Music of South America, Mexico, and the Caribbean

Traditional music of South America, Mexico, and the Caribbean was influenced by several factors:

- Indigenous folk culture.
- Popular and folk music styles derived mainly from Spanish and, in some cases, Portuguese and African practices.
- Instruments commonly used in popular and folk music.
- Christian churches and missionaries.
- Music schools and conservatories.
- European models of art music.
- Beginnings of nationalism in art music.

Indigenous Folk Culture

The folk and popular (**vernacular**) music of Latin America—Mexico and Central and South America—is derived mostly from the traditions of the **mestizo** people, natives of mixed Indian and Spanish ancestry. Mestizo music exists throughout most of Latin America. It is Latin America's main so-called indigenous music, the music of its natives since the Spanish conquest in the sixteenth century. This music was often derived from a combination of Spanish tunes and words with native dances. Other vernacular music is derived from people of African Hispanic heritage. The music of African derivation, based largely on dance, exists in the Caribbean islands, such as Cuba, Puerto Rico, Jamaica, and Trinidad, and in some parts of Latin America.

Several Latin American Indian groups, such as the Incas of Peru, had a high degree of social and political organization and apparently had strong musical traditions. However, very little pure Latin American Indian music exists today. Only a few indigenous groups remain relatively unaffected by European traditions.

The natives learned the songs of the Europeans, adapting these songs to their own ways of performing music. Natives also learned European ways of performing, adapting those practices to their own songs. Whatever the combination of influences, an original song or the source of a song often became obscure or unknown as subsequent versions became altered—a common circumstance in oral tradition folk music.

Musical Instruments

Native Latin Americans became proficient at making and playing musical instruments. The following instruments were widely used throughout the region:

- *Wind instruments* (**aerophones**): reed flutes, ocarinas, panpipes, *quenas* (vertical or end-blown flutes), and clay or conch-shell trumpets.
- *Percussion instruments* (**idiophones** and **membranophones**): rattles, rasps, claves, castanets, guiros, maracas, marimbas, xylophones, and drums of all sorts—includes bongos, conga drums, and steel drums.
- *String instruments* (**chordophones**): violins, *jaranas* (little guitars) and *guitarróns* (bass guitars), lutes, and harps.

Folk Songs and Dances

Much Latin American and Caribbean music is foot-tapping, finger-snapping music. It often has a strong rhythmic pulse and is frequently associated with dancing to

The group Tahuantin-suyo is an Andean folk ensemble. Notice the panpipes, a common wind instrument in Andean culture. In recent years, Andean musicians have performed in Peru and other parts of South America but also at folk festivals and fairs in the United States. In New York City, they have played at Carnegie Hall and Lincoln Center, as well as on Manhattan street corners and in subway stations.

such styles as the rumba and salsa (Cuba); samba, bossa nova, and lambada (Brazil); ska and reggae (Jamaica); cumbia (Colombia); calypso and soca (Trinidad); merengue (Dominican Republic); and huapango (Mexico). Although there are regional and stylistic variations, some generalizations can be made about Latin American folk and popular music:

- Harmonies are European in style, with prevalent tonic and dominant chords.
- Music is simple and repetitive, but differing, simple lines can be combined to create a more complex texture.
- **Chromaticism** is uncommon.
- The melodies encompass a limited range; a countermelody paralleling the melody at an interval of a third or a sixth is common.
- There is little or no improvisation or freedom of melodic and rhythmic interpretation in native Hispanic music, except salsa and Latin jazz. However, improvisation and freedom to add personal interpretation to a melody are common in Afro-Hispanic music.
- Phrases are often clear and regular.
- **Tonality,** for the most part, is major or minor—often both in the same song.
- Rhythm is usually regular, syncopated, and percussive, particularly in African-based music. The Latin sound is metric but sometimes ambiguous or obscure, at times generating more than one meter at the same time. Pulses or bars often have alternate divisions of twos and threes.

Many of the dances are instrumental folk songs (*sones*) written for popular ensembles, such as mariachi, *charanga*, and *conjunto*. Other songs (*canciones*) include narrative ballads or story songs, *rancheras* (cowboy or country songs), and lyrical love songs (*corridos*) and their religious counterparts (*alabados*). Call and response is common, as is the verse-refrain form. The verse (stanza) may be sung by a soloist and the refrain by more than one singer.

Listening Guide   No. 33

"Pajaro Campana" ("Bell Bird") (excerpt)
CD2, Track 2, 1:14

Performer: Sergio Cuevas of Paraguay, Indian harp.
Genre: Latin American folk music.

Goals

Identify the timbre of the harp and the plucked bass guitar. Describe differences among the several lines of music.

Describe the phrase structure. How clear are the cadences? What obscures and what strengthens them?

Describe the meter. How clear are the patterns of strong and weak beats? What obscures the clarity?

Guide

The music begins with the harp in free rhythm—isolated tones in descending melodic intervals, instruments being added, getting faster, and soon establishing a duple metric feeling (strong-weak/strong-weak). Counting from when the bass enters and the duple meter is established, the full texture continues for 14 bars with chords changing every other bar. After the 14 bars, the song begins and continues in a series of 8-bar phrases, each with the same chord structure.

0:00	Intro	Harp begins in free rhythm
0:19		Bass enters; duple meter established; fourteen 2-beat bars until song begins
0:29	Song	Bars 1 2 3 4 5 6 7 8
		Chords V – I – V – I – (fade)

Reflections

The bass often is playing a three-beat pattern against the duple meter (three against two), or is it a triple meter with the upper parts playing a two-beat pattern against the three-beat meter established by the bass? Or does the meter shift?

The ticklike sound occurs mostly on each beat.

Notice (1) much syncopation, mostly in the harp; (2) the extent to which the harp and bass lines are continually moving, even at the ends of phrases; and (3) the degree to which the chord patterns help establish the ends of phrases by returning to tonic chords on every seventh and eighth bar.

Religious Influences

From the early sixteenth century on, the musical life of the Latin American natives was dominated by the Roman Catholic Church. The missionaries taught them Gregorian chant and Renaissance polyphonic church music (see chapter 9). The Indians were ready and rapid learners and were adept at making and playing musical instruments. They participated in church activities and had a keen aptitude for imitating and assimilating European cultural traits.

The cathedral was the center of public life in the community. Natives were employed as church musicians but seldom for the more prestigious and better-paying positions of chapelmaster (choir director) or organist. Cathedral musicians, including native Indians and mestizos, became composers and performers of religious art music and of secular art concert music as well. They created songs of praise for religious fiestas and processions (in Latin and later in the vernacular) and, by the nineteenth century, musical plays, opera, chamber music, and salon music for piano.

Summary

World music, for many music educators and scholars, means music based on non–western European traditions and music from faraway, exotic places (chapter 8 presents world music from beyond the Americas, including the music of India, Japan, and southern Africa). But world music also exists close to home, within the United States and throughout the Western Hemisphere. Although it represents part of the heritage of our neighbors, we call it world music because it is unfamiliar to most Americans and because it is out of the mainstream of American music.

Native American music is based on compositional techniques, aesthetic values, and performance practices different from those of European-based music. Latin American classical music and popular music are based largely on European scales, tonalities, harmonic progressions, forms, and other aspects of the Western musical language. Some ethnic music in the United States is well known—for example, salsa and reggae. But some may be less known—for example, zydeco and Tex-Mex music. This chapter discusses some of the music and traditions of our neighbors to the south. Our jazz and popular music—for listening and for dancing—owe a great debt to the rhythms and the spirit of Caribbean and Latin American music.

8

Music Beyond the Americas

Chapter Outline

In This Chapter

How would you characterize music from the British Isles? From the Far East? From sub-Saharan Africa?

What are the differences between non-Western "classical" music and non-Western "popular" music?

What are the cultural and performance contexts in these regions?

What are the common instruments and instrumental ensembles in these regions?

Where are Western influences apparent? Not apparent?

To Americans, *world music* typically means styles centered in parts of the world other than western Europe and the Americas and to music derived from cultures and traditions other than our own. We sometimes refer to it as "non-Western" music (perhaps non-Western people refer to our music as "non-Eastern"). But if world music is indeed music of the whole world, then Western music, both classical and **vernacular,** is part of it.

However you define it, world music is not necessarily far away from us, for non-Western music and less familiar Western styles exist within the United States. In chapter 7, you saw that the music of Native Americans is indigenous to American culture yet is foreign to most of us. It is fair to say that we treat Native American music as world—or at least ethnic—music.

In this chapter, we consider music beyond the Americas, paying special attention to its impact on America's music. Like American society in general, American music is a product of a merging of cultures and musical styles from all parts of the globe. American music is a result of many cross-cultural influences, including these:

- The contributions of millions of immigrants from all parts of the globe.
- Expanding technology (sophisticated recording facilities exist in most parts of the world), worldwide distribution of recordings, and international concerts and tours by artists from many countries.
- The creative work of American composers, as well as jazz and rock musicians, who have studied the music of foreign cultures, often through books and recordings but increasingly through extended visits to other countries and studies with musicians from other world music cultures.

153

- The study of music from other cultures, which is increasingly accessible to U.S. students as growing numbers of colleges and universities offer world music experiences, both courses and performance opportunities (the instructors are often musicians and scholars native to the cultures that produced the music).

This chapter offers a brief sampling of the unique musics found in a variety of settings throughout the world, from large, metropolitan areas to small, isolated villages. You will learn about distinctive features that make this music sound different from "your own." If you are interested in the further study of world music, you might consider exploring these cultures in greater depth or studying the music of other cultures—perhaps Korea or Tibet, the countries of the South Pacific, the Caucasus region, or even the indigenous peoples of Alaska and Hawaii.

Goals for Listening

In addition to terms and concepts introduced previously, you will begin to recognize and explore additional instruments and instrumental combinations, modal sounds, octave skips, motives, melodic embellishments, tremolos, polyrhythms, layers of sound that sometimes seem unrelated, ostinato patterns, and call-and-response patterns. We also explore similarities and differences between music of various cultures and between non-Western and Western musical characteristics.

Music in India

India may seem a distant, exotic land, but Americans for years have imported Indian textiles, cloths, vases, tables, and lamps. Particularly since the 1960s, we have been influenced by India's religion and philosophy. We have learned about India's music from visits by Ravi Shankar and other accomplished artists and from the increasingly large numbers of Americans who have studied Indian music in India and returned to teach others.

India's music includes popular dance and film music, music for religion and rituals, and both classical and traditional music. Like most cultures, India has its work songs (songs that people sing while they work, to make hard work more tolerable), music for festive occasions, and songs for religious ceremonies and personal devotion. The folk, popular, and ceremonial repertoires are as varied as the peoples of India.

Classical Music

The music of India that westerners know best is **art music**—music that has been widely researched, recorded, and reported. Based on ancient traditions and associated with great artists, India's "classical" music was founded on a long-standing theoretical system and written about by Indian scholars for centuries.

The art music of India is highly developed, primarily improvisatory, and melodic. **Harmony** (chords and chord progressions) is not a valued part of the music. Simultaneous sounds result from the interaction of the melodic, plucked instruments and the sounds of other instruments or voices rather than from a conscious effort to use harmony as an end in itself.

Since the thirteenth century, the musical styles of India have been identified according to practices found in the north (Hindustani music) and in the south (Karnatic music). In examining these styles, we can identify differing musical characteristics and instrumental preferences, as well as many commonalities.

An aesthetic basis called **rasa** underlies all Indian art music. Rasa is not just the music but the power of the music to convey thoughts, feelings, moods, and images. Indians value the relationship of their music to nature, religious or philosophical beliefs, and time—the stages of life, the seasons of the year, the hours of the day.

In Hindustani classical music, the lead instrumentalist typically plays a sitar—a plucked stringed instrument. Added to the ensemble may be a sarod, also a plucked stringed instrument. The tabla player—a drummer—provides rhythm and energy. The **drone** is usually played on a stringed instrument called a tambura. The drone results from the constantly repeated, trancelike tones, played only on the open strings, that help to establish the main notes.

In Karnatic (south Indian) music, the lead may also be played on a plucked string instrument, perhaps the vina. The common Karnatic drum is the mridangam. Sometimes a second stringed instrument, perhaps a sarangi—a bowed instrument—serves in an accompanying role, and sometimes a solo singer adds a contrasting sound as well as text. Although there are distinct differences between Hindustani and Karnatic music, often these distinctions are blurred.

Precomposed songs are learned from memory. Although notated music exists, it is not valued or adhered to as in Western music. The music is organized by means of an established melodic pattern known as a **raga** and a rhythmic pattern known as a **tala.** The level of artistry is determined by the musician's ability to develop the melodic pattern, or raga, to its fullest extent and to explore all the rhythmic intricacies implied in the tala. A gifted student becomes a disciple of a guru (master teacher) and learns ragas and precomposed pieces through imitation and practice. The disciple must learn not only the broad repertoire of ragas and talas but also performance practices (such as **ornamentation**) and how to feel and think about the music.

The raga is the basic means by which the melodic aspects of a piece are determined. Western music is based on **scales** (a system of **pitch** organization), usually in a major or a minor key. A raga is a sequence of ascending and descending pitches similar to a scale, but it conveys much more than a scale. It can be thought of as a melodic shape rather than an abstract pitch structure. The raga can convey certain melodic patterns; pitch **registers** conceptualized as high, middle, or low; and ornamentations that make a particular raga immediately recognizable. It communicates to the performers and to the audience the mood and aesthetic character of the music.

The performer uses the pitches, sequence of pitches, melodic patterns, mood, symbol, and meaning of the raga to develop an extended improvisation. The best musicians are able to improvise raga performances based on an internalized set of rules that guide the choice of melodic figures, overall structure, and style. The improvised sections alternate with less freely improvised sections, which may be based on a precomposed melody or song.

The tala is the basic means of organizing the rhythm or durational aspects of Indian art music. It dictates to a performer the complete pattern or cycle of counts as well as the recurring subdivision within the cycle. For example, a tala may be 16 counts in length and have an internal subdivision of $4 + 4 + 4 + 4$, or it may have 14 counts with a subdivision of $5 + 2 + 3 + 4$. Two or more tala cycles may constitute a phrase. The drummer learns to improvise using a set of drum strokes and rhythmic patterns that subdivide the ongoing pulse of the tala. The drummer (or tabla player) learns to improvise sections that pull against the tala, creating tension, and then returns to patterns that correspond to the tala, releasing tension.

A raga performance can last 30 minutes or longer. It begins with the lead instrumentalist, the sitar player, performing a slow, rhythmically free, improvised statement of the raga in which the musician reveals its main characteristics. A second section provides increased and more repetitive rhythmic activity accompanied by the constant drone. A third section builds in speed and rhythmic intensity in anticipation of the next section. The final section firmly establishes the tala and is devoted to extended improvisation and interaction between the lead and the percussion and other accompanists. The structure of both the tala and the raga is applied in an increasingly fast, intricate, complex style. In raga performance, there is always a delicate balance between exciting virtuosic display and sensitive musicality.

Listening Guide   No. 34

"Bhimpalasi" (two excerpts)
CD2, Track 3, 3:40

Performers: Ravi Shankar, sitar; Chatur Lal, tabla; and N. C. Mullick, tambura.
Genre: Hindustani afternoon raga.
Context: The sitar is the lead instrument, the tabla is the percussion instrument, and the tambura is the drone instrument.

Goals

Recognize the timbre of the sitar and the tabla. Identify the drone sound.
Recognize when the music is in free rhythm and when it generates a sense of meter.

Guide

0:00	First excerpt: After a descending glissando, the sitar presents the raga in free rhythm, setting forth its pitches and its intended character; many slides, pitch-bending alterations, and ornaments enhance the melody; the drone continues throughout
0:52	The entrance of the tabla creates a distinct pulse and a more active rhythm
2:03	Second excerpt: The rhythm and the melodic improvisation become more complex

Reflections

Notice the improvisation and the melodic embellishments, such as glissandos and pitch bending.
Be aware of the sound of music based on a non-Western scale structure.

Popular Music

For many decades, listening to music from films and to music distributed in cassette form has been central to the popular music industry in India. The cassette was the primary medium for disseminating popular music, particularly to outlying, nonurban areas. Thus, India's music industry was known as the "cassette culture." India's more urban culture now includes much Western-style jazz and rock.

Films are produced annually by the hundreds, most of them in Mumbai. Much of their success depends on the male star, the director, and the music—each publicized widely. Plots are light and escapist. Almost all Indian films are musicals.

Instrumental music in these musicals may be produced by 100-piece orchestras or by small synthesizers, often combining Indian traditional music with Western styles. Most of the stars do not sing. "Playback" singers who record their music in advance of production perform the songs. Among the most famous playback artists is the legendary Lata Mangeshkar (still singing and recording as of this writing). The name of the film industry of India is Bollywood (bollywoodworld.com; bollywoodmusic.com).

Music in Japan

If you scanned the published list of musical events in modern Tokyo for almost any week of the year, you would find an abundance of concerts and club or restaurant performances appealing to a wide range of tastes—music by symphony orchestras and string quartets, jazz and rock groups, blues and bluegrass musicians, and even mariachi ensembles. The performers might be Americans or Europeans on tour, or they might be Japanese who grew up playing and listening to Western musical styles.

For more than 100 years, the Japanese school system, including university music schools and conservatories, has been teaching the music of Bach and Beethoven and Western **aesthetic** values, including the following:

- Thick **textures** as found in orchestras, bands, choirs, and **big band jazz.**
- Harmonies and chord progressions that give music **forward energy.**
- Major and minor tonalities with emphasis on the **tonic** and **dominant.**
- Dramatic changes within a composition: melodic contrasts and differing **timbres.**

Those Western values, however, are not easily applicable to traditional Japanese music, which is distinct in style and requires from westerners a different way of listening.

The Performance Context

In modern Japan, traditional Japanese music is performed in concert halls, theaters, and the courtyards and gardens of shrines and temples. When it is performed indoors, screens painted with images of nature—trees, flowers, ponds—create an illusion of natural settings. Japanese music is entwined with visual and dramatic effects. It is often part of theatrical productions that include dance, costumes, acting, colorful staging, poetry, and stylized movements. This is why Japanese music should be seen as well as heard. As in Western music, songs and instrumental pieces from theatrical productions find their way into concert halls for more people to enjoy. Thus, many visual and dramatic effects become part of concert performances.

Japan consists of many islands, a factor that has produced distinctive regional folk traditions and musical styles. Despite regional differences, however, Japanese folk music displays certain common practices and characteristics: a propensity for theatricals and festivals; visual effects such as elaborate costumes and grotesque masks; a high, tight-throated, nasal vocal quality; and a melodic style often accompanied by handclapping, drums, and flutes.

Musical Genres

The Japanese value small-group performances—all the parts heard separately (as in chamber music), rather than merged (as in orchestral music). A public performance usually involves from one to three musicians, except for the larger nagauta ensemble associated with Kabuki theater (see below). Traditional music is typically performed in traditional garb.

To appreciate traditional Japanese music, one listens for the skill and beauty with which a musician manipulates traditional materials rather than exploring new ideas. This contrasts markedly to the Western tendency toward experimentation and change rather than preservation of styles. The Japanese musician exercises restraint and control and strives to communicate the emotions of the subject rather than his or her own emotions. Musicians want to refine rather than to expand their limited tonal and instrumental resources. They choose to perfect a few meaningful musical ideas rather than to explore a wide range of sonic possibilities. They try to achieve the maximum effect from minimal resources.

Most Japanese music is learned by memory, from master teachers known as *sensai*. Notational systems exist but are sometimes quite vague and still need to be interpreted. The musical characteristics of traditional Japanese music include the following:

- Narrow range of dynamics.
- **Pentatonic scale,** commonly used with ornaments that provide minute deviations from the melody.
- Nonexistent or incidental harmony.
- Regular rhythm—not driving yet often quite free.
- Varied timbres, unblended but not striking; emphasis on delicate nuances.
- Melody and timbre as main values.
- Little or no improvisation.

Several important styles are representative of the Japanese musical tradition. Japan's first instrumental genre is the ancient court music known as **gagaku.** Music for theater is represented by the **Kabuki** tradition. We also discuss music for three Japanese instruments: the koto, shakuhachi, and shamisen.

Gagaku   The oldest documented orchestral music in the world, gagaku was performed at the Japanese imperial courts that flourished from the ninth through the eleventh centuries. It was a form of courtly entertainment that provided a total theatrical experience, including dance, masks, and visual effects.

Musically, gagaku was static, consisting of blocks of sound that had little forward movement. Its primary instruments were the hichiriki, a double-reed, oboelike instrument, and the sho, a mouth organ having 17 small pipes. Some gagaku music was purely instrumental; other types accompanied dancing. Gagaku music of both types is performed today.

Nagauta musicians perform on stage in a Japanese kabuki theater. The ensemble usually consists of perhaps a dozen musicians: a few drums, flutes, several shamisen players, and singers.

Kabuki   Kabuki theater grew out of the Noh tradition and also flourished outside the imperial household. Noh is a major form of classical Japanese music drama that has been performed since the fourteenth century. It still has wide appeal. Kabuki is melodrama that includes colorful dancing; an onstage music ensemble known as the **nagauta,** which provides the basic vocal and instrumental accompaniment; and narrative *gidayu* songs performed onstage with shamisen accompaniment. Kabuki theater also has an offstage music ensemble known as the *geza,* used for noise, sound effects, signals, and music not covered by the musicians onstage.

The nagauta has developed its own concert life independent of Kabuki theater. The orchestra usually consists of about a dozen musicians: three drums, a flute, several shamisen players, and singers. The nagauta emerged from combining the lyricism of shorter songs with the sustaining power of longer narrative music.

Koto, Shakuhachi, and Shamisen   The koto is a large, 13-stringed instrument. The Japanese learn to play the koto from venerable masters called *kengyo* ("maestro"). An accomplished koto player uses slides, scrapes, struck strings, and other techniques to produce ornaments and microtones typical of traditional Japanese music. The koto is the genteel instrument of Japan much as the parlor piano was the genteel instrument in nineteenth-century America. The presence of a koto in a Japanese home suggests good breeding and an artistic upbringing.

A shakuhachi is an end-blown flute whose ancestor is the bamboo flute of ancient Japan. It is common for ornaments and other deviations from a melody. This instrument is frequently used in combination with the koto. Flutelike instruments in general have universal appeal and are found in almost all cultures.

The shamisen is a three-stringed plucked instrument used by entertainers and amateurs. It is played as an accompanying instrument in much of the folk repertoire.

The koto, shamisen, and shakuhachi make up a common chamber music trio known as *sankyoku.* The musicians in this ensemble concentrate on the minute and delicate shadings and timbres that each of them can bring to the melodic line.

Japanese women in traditional dress play traditional Japanese instruments. Both are plucked stringed instruments: the koto, a "classical" instrument, is on the left, and the shamisen, a "folk" instrument, is on the right. The koto is a 13-stringed instrument, and the shamisen a 3-stringed instrument. The koto is used in Japanese traditional classical music, and the shamisen is used to accompany songs in Japanese puppet theater and also to accompany short, often evocative songs known as *kouta*, often sung by geisha.

Listening Guide   No. 35

"Kyo No Warabeuta"
CD2, Track 4, 4:29

Performers: Musicians of the Ikuta school of koto playing.
Musical instruments: Koto and shakuhachi.
Genre: Traditional Japanese music.

Goals

Compare and contrast the sound (timbre) of the koto with the sounds of familiar plucked instruments, such as the guitar.
Recognize the sounds and patterns of the koto in its various pitch ranges—that is, its various layers of sound.

Listening Guide –Continued

Describe the musical factors that delineate the sections of this music, such as changes of tempo, instrumentation, rhythms, and **motives.**

Recognize octave skips, tremolo (strumming), **tone bending, glissandos** (slides of pitch), and ritards.

Guide

The piece has many shifts of character and mood in several distinct sections. The music has a strong sense of pulse and meter at some times but not at others. Several melodic motives are recognizable, as are their subsequent modifications.

0:00	Koto—at a slow tempo
0:19	The shakuhachi enters with ascending four-note motive—with a pickup; ritard—at end
0:43	A three-note motive is soon repeated at a lower octave, at a still lower octave, and then with a tremolo played above the motive
1:09	A moderately fast section starts in a low register after a one-bar **vamp;** a ritard is followed by an *a tempo;* other motives are heard in high registers; and patterns are repeated in different octaves
2:16	A plucked tremolo begins the next section with sustained, lyrical melodies played on the shakuhachi at a moderately slow tempo; a single-line koto passage is heard in a low register
3:19	A koto passage begins the final section with high energy, a strong meter, and a faster tempo
3:42	The shakuhachi enters; soon the tempo slows and the piece comes to a quiet end

Reflections

What makes this music sound different from Western classical music?

Describe the relationships among melody, harmony, and rhythm. Which seem most important in this musical example?

Notice the stepwise motion in the melodies. How is this different from pitches connected by sliding motion (glissando)?

Music in Sub-Saharan Africa

This section focuses on the music of Africa south of the Sahara: the music of Nigeria and Ghana; of the Democratic Republic of the Congo; of Kenya, Uganda, and Tanzania; and of Zimbabwe, Namibia, and South Africa. The values and aesthetics of traditional cultures and the lifestyles of the people in this region are changing rapidly. The people are being torn between the pull of Western culture and the desire to preserve the uniqueness of their traditional cultures.

Listening Guide No. 36

A geisha playing her shamisen. A geisha is a woman trained in the traditional Japanese arts: dance, singing, etiquette, and playing a small folk instrument, usually the shamisen. Geishas serve as professional hostesses and entertainers at such events as parties and wedding receptions and in tea houses.

"Sado Okesa" (excerpt)
CD2, Track 5, 1:22

Performer: A geisha from Okayama City.
Genre: Traditional Japanese music.
Context: The geisha have popularized many Japanese folk songs.

Goals

Recognize the sound of a shamisen.
Describe the vocal quality.
Recognize ostinato.
Describe the metric feeling.

Guide

Count at a moderately slow pulse. The numbers represent the number of pulses to each pattern or phrase.

0:00	Intro	11 beats (6 + 5)
0:11	Vocal	16
		15
		8 + 11 + 4
		8 (fade)

Reflections

This love song has a lilting character and a regular rhythm. The vocal line, based on a gapped scale, is highly ornamented. The voice has a tight, nasal, stylized quality.

The accompaniment is played on the shamisen. Do you notice any similarities between the vocal quality and style and the sound of the shamisen?

As can be seen from the number of beats in a phrase or phrase group, there are no balanced phrases or regular patterns of contrast and repetition.

Notice the scale pattern, which features an interval wider than a whole step. The melody is based on a gapped scale.

Africa is a huge, complex continent in which over 200 different languages are spoken. Its musical diversity reflects the diversity of its people, as well as influences from other cultures. North Africa is a region of Mediterranean countries—Algeria, Morocco, Libya, Tunisia, and Egypt—whose cultures have been influenced largely by Islamic and Arabic traditions. The classical, popular, and folk music of North

Africa is derived primarily from Asian musical sounds and thus is distinct from the music of the rest of Africa.

We emphasize the music of Africa south of the Sahara—sub-Saharan Africa—because it has greatly affected American culture. Spirituals, blues, jazz, ragtime, and gospel all have roots in the music of southern Africa.

Music in Context

Typically, African music includes more than music. It may involve props, costumes, dancing, sculpture, crafts, and drama; all these elements increase opportunities for participation. Music is an outlet for social interaction and shared attitudes. It enhances social activities, is performed for amusement, or communicates important messages and feelings. Music may be a tribute to an individual, an offering to a deity, or a service to a potentate. It is created for specific purposes and is seldom performed out of context. For example, a religious song is performed only for a religious occasion; a work song is performed only in the context of the work; and dance music is performed only for dancing, not for listening.

Traditional music occupies a position of great importance in the cultures of sub-Saharan Africa and is an art in which nearly all Africans participate. African young people tend to reject traditional ways in favor of the Western influences found in urban environments, but their current music reveals considerable crossover among traditional African music, African popular music, and African American popular music.

Instruments

Africans use an enormous variety of musical instruments, the most common being percussion. Instrumental music is important, perhaps as important as vocal music. Common instruments include drums and rattles of all sizes and shapes, one-stringed bowed fiddles, musical bows, xylophones, mbiras, natural trumpets, and flutes. The mbira—also known as the kalimba, sansa, and thumb piano—has from 8 to 30 "keys" or metal reeds that are plucked by both thumbs. The length of each reed determines its pitch, and its resonator typically is a box with sound holes, although sometimes a gourd is attached.

Instruments are used to accompany singing, although some songs may be accompanied by rhythmic hand clapping. Instruments are used in ensembles, either drum ensembles or groups of instruments of different families. Performing groups may be spontaneous or organized, and they may be attached to occupational organizations, special households, or royal courts. They range in size from two or three musicians to large drum orchestras numbering in the hundreds; however, small groups are the most common. In some cases, drums have specific purposes and are not used for any other reason. Different drums may be associated with funerals, with gods, or with tribal chiefs.

The **idiophones**—instruments whose basic material of construction is the sound-producing agent—include rattles, metal or wooden bells and gongs, shells, log drums, clay pot drums, xylophones, and mbiras.

The sizes and shapes of **membranophones**—drums with heads of stretched skin—are innumerable. A drum may have a skin at both ends. If a drum is covered with skin only at one end, the other end may be open or closed. Drums may be played with sticks, hands, or a combination of the two. A common technique involves an intricate manipulation and alternation of fingers, thumb, and the heel of the hand in striking the drum head. Among the most important instruments in Africa are the master drums, which are used to lead ensembles and to signal important events.

The mbira is a common instrument in Africa, enjoyed by people of all ages. An mbira player plucks metal reeds with both thumbs (the instrument is also known as a thumb piano). The length of each reed (thin metal strips of varying lengths) determines its pitch. The reeds are attached to a resonator (a hollow box) to help amplify the sound and to make the quality of the sound more vibrant.

The **chordophones**—stringed instruments—include various forms of lutes, zithers, harps, and fiddles. Here, too, the shapes and sizes are innumerable. The number of strings and the tunings vary greatly from instrument to instrument. Most African stringed instruments are plucked rather than bowed, in accordance with the tendency toward strong rhythmic articulation.

The **aerophones**—wind instruments—include natural horns or trumpets that are made of wood, ivory, or animal horn, usually with no finger holes or valves. Also in this category are vertical and horizontal flutes and reed instruments.

Rhythm

Rhythm is the heart of African music; it is more integral than melody or harmony. Compared with African rhythmic textures, the most common Western rhythm seems simple and straightforward. In fact, rhythm in African music often sounds extremely complex to Western ears, as though a number of unrelated things are going on simultaneously.

Traditional African music is usually performed by drum ensembles, although solo singing is common and is often accompanied by drums or other folklike instruments. Singing tends to be earthy in quality, melodies have a limited range, and harmonic progressions are unimportant in traditional African music. However, melody and harmony have become important in the considerable quantity of African popular and folk styles influenced by contemporary Western music.

In 1959, this group of Nigerians played wooden, vertical flutes to accompany a dance festival.

The strong rhythmic articulation in African music is produced not only by drums and other percussion instruments but also by strings, winds, and voices. Very little African music is smooth or connected; in most music, individual tones are attacked strongly. Stringed instruments are plucked more often than bowed, and this technique contributes to the percussive quality of the music.

Listening Guide   No. 37

"Magonde" ("Song for the Chief")
CD2, Track 6, 1:37

Performer: Chabarwa Musunda Moyo Sinyoro of Rusapi, Zimbabwe.
Genre: Traditional mbira music from Zimbabwe.

–Continued

Listening Guide –Continued   No. 37

Context: "Magonde" is an old, traditional tune played on an mbira-type instrument known as *Njari dza MaNjanja.* It has 27 reeds and two manuals on a board with external resonators.

Goals

Describe the sound of the mbira.

Recognize ostinato patterns, syncopation, and multiple layers of sound.

Recognize the **vocables.**

Guide

0:00	An introduction of seven "chords"
0:04	A fast mbira ostinato pattern with a three-beat feeling that continues for nine "bars"
0:12	Mbira melody enters in a descending contour with the background patterns continuing; the melody is syncopated and has many rhythmic patterns that contrast with the accompaniment; both the melody and the accompaniment are played by one person on one mbira
0:27	Singer enters; his rhythms are in contrast to the mbira patterns; the mbira is played to some extent in dialogue with the singing

Reflections

Notice the interplay among the differing rhythms sounding at the same time, and notice the energy created by the syncopation. What Western instruments are most like the mbira?

Popular Music

As many sub-Saharan African societies became urbanized, Western music greatly influenced their popular cultures. The most important influences were American jazz, rock, and soul; African-Latin music from the Caribbean region, particularly calypso, reggae, and the rumba; and the Brazilian samba. Now, however, as African music itself is becoming more influential worldwide, African musicians are creating styles and songs that reflect both Western influences and their own national or regional traits and traditions.

The most popular styles are highlife, juju, and Afrobeat. Among the other significant styles are griot music, *mbaqanga, makossa,* and *mbube.* Important musical traditions and world-class artists have come from Nigeria, Ghana, Senegal, Cameroon,

Miriam Makeba, a popular singer from South Africa, gained an international reputation. She was recognized as a musician and a political activist who spoke out against apartheid. In 1966, she was awarded a Grammy for best folk recording of the year. In 1987, her popularity peaked when she appeared with Paul Simon on his Graceland Tour. Miriam Makeba contributed significantly to the introduction of African music to the West. She died in 2008.

Fela Kuti was an important Nigerian singer who used songs not only as entertainment but also as a means of political expression in the struggle for human rights. He was a composer and played saxophone and keyboards. His most popular musical styles were Nigerian highlife, Afro-soul, and most important, Afrobeat.

King Sunny Adé is another of the popular musicians from Nigeria. He is a singer, composer, and guitarist who is known as the "King of juju." Juju is perhaps the most popular and most durable Nigerian popular music genre. Adé first recorded in 1967 and achieved international stardom in the 1980s.

Listening Guide   No. 38

"Yo Lé Lé"
CD2, Track 7, 1:53

Performers: Youssou N'Dour and the Super Étoile: Youssou N'Dour, lead and background vocals; Mamadou (Jimi) Mbaye, lead guitar; Pape Oumar Ngom, rhythm guitar; Ousseynou Ndiaye, background vocals; Ibrahima Cissé, keyboards; Habib Faye, bass guitar and keyboards; Jean-Philippe Rykiel, keyboards; Fallilou (Gallas) Niang, drums; Assane Thiam, Senegalese talking drum; Babacar (Mbaye Dieye) Faye, percussion (sabar, djembe, and others) and background vocals; Thierno Koite, alto and soprano saxophones; and Issa Cissocko, tenor saxophone; plus additional horns.

Genre: Contemporary pop music from Senegal.

Context: Youssou N'Dour is from Senegal. He has gained wide exposure from his association with Peter Gabriel and his participation in the 1988 Human Rights Now World Tour with Gabriel, Sting, and Bruce Springsteen. The words to "Yo Lé Lé" are sung in English, Fulani, and Wolof. The phrase *Futa Toro* refers to a place in northern Senegal, the ancestral place of the Fulani people.

Goals

Identify elements of Western and African influences in this music.

Describe the relative importance in this music of melody, harmony, rhythm, and timbre.

Recognize ostinatos.

Youssou N'Dour and
the Super Étoile.

Listening Guide –Continued   No. 38

Describe elements of contrast and repetition.
Identify the form.

Guide

The song consists of a series of four melodic patterns that have other, mostly fragmented, lines superimposed, such as vocal, keyboards, trumpets, percussion, and other instruments.

0:00	Intro	"Futa Toro" chant—talking drums and vocal soon enter
0:53	Pattern 1	Vocal—"Yo Lé Lé"; repeated patterns
1:11	Pattern 2	Electric keyboards
1:21	Pattern 1	Main motive higher and slightly more melodic
1:31	Pattern 3	Trumpets; keyboards—fade

Reflections

Converting the pattern numbers to letter names, the patterns can be described as a b a c b c d c d (three separate "a b a" groups). Do the letter names add to or detract from your ability to perceive the form?
Could this be one long, free-form piece with constantly evolving patterns?
Describe your aesthetic reaction to this music.
What aspects of this music do you enjoy most? Least?
In what ways does this music have traditional indigenous elements?
Modern Western elements? Modern African elements?

Uganda, Zaire, and South Africa. These artists include Hugh Masekela, Miriam Makeba, Fela Kuti, Manu Dibango, Youssou N'Dour, King Sunny Adé, and Ladysmith Black Mambazo. Several of these artists have been successful in the United States. The career of Youssou N'Dour of Senegal received a big lift as a result of recordings produced by Mickey Hart, then drummer for the Grateful Dead. Hart had shown considerable interest in world music and global percussion.

Music in Eastern Europe

Over the centuries, the eastern European countries, through war and conquest and their struggles to be free, came under the influence of different nations and cultures. Their cultural roots include ancient Greece, Islamic nations, Asia, and western Europe. Their musical roots lie in the chants of the Greek Orthodox Church, the pentatonic modes of Mongolia, the complex rhythms and unique sounds of Arab and other Islamic music, and the musical language of western Europe. This cultural mix has resulted in a great diversity of styles; each country and sometimes each village has its own rich cultural heritage.

Traditional music from this region coexists with popular and sometimes classical music. In some cases, traditional music may have become less important or may no longer exist, for reasons such as the following:

- Urban influences and the shift to industrialization.
- Government control of traditional music in the most oppressive regimes.
- Changes in national and regional boundaries.
- Ethnic population shifts and changing loyalties.

Changes in boundaries and population shifts may have been brought about by civil wars and other political upheavals, as in the early 1990s in the Bosnian-Serb-Croatian regions of eastern Europe. If folk music grows out of the lives of the people, and if life is drastically and permanently disrupted, a new folk music, perhaps newly composed, may take its place.

Instrumental music is common, either as dance music or as an accompaniment to a song. The bagpipe, double recorder, and cimbalom (hammer dulcimer) have been common folk instruments. Modern, factory-made instruments include the button accordion, the fiddle, and several types of flutes.

Depending on the political climate, songs that reflect social and political conditions may have to fall in with state-approved ideology and goals—or go underground. Government-approved music may receive financial and other support (recordings, tours, international distribution), whereas sales of disapproved music may be taxed and will not receive such benefits. Governments tend to export the music they favor; thus the folk music available to Western audiences may not reflect the lives of the common people. Since the demise of oppressive communist governments in eastern Europe, however, authentic folk and traditional music has been recorded and is now more available to Western audiences.

Among the many "international" artists and groups from eastern Europe are Gheorghe Zamfir of Romania, panpipes performer; the Bulgarian Radio Women's Choir, with its distinctive musical pieces; Ivo Papasov, the Bulgarian jazz clarinetist, who, with his orchestra, performs Bulgarian folk dances, especially wedding music; and Márta Sebestyén, Hungary's leading folksinger, who is a popular *táncház* (dance house) artist. *Táncház*—the term originally meant a traditional village dancing place—is a movement that began in the 1970s in reaction to state-controlled "traditional" music. It was inspired by traditional songs and dances of the villages of Transylvania, a region of Romania with a large Hungarian population. Some *táncház* bands play Hungarian Gypsy music.

Listening Guide   No. 39

"Angelina"
CD 2, Track 08, 1:45

Performer: Koutev Bulgarian National Ensemble; Philip Koutev, director.

Genre: Bulgarian folk-concert music.

Background: Traditional Bulgarian music has a distinct sound that is rooted in Balkan folk traditions. These folk songs are frequently arranged for women's choirs and feature a very bright, open-throated sound. The most influential pioneer in Bulgarian women's chorus music is Philip Koutev.

Listening Guide –Continued   No. 39

The women in these choirs are skilled at combining the different timbres and techniques of their traditional folk songs with the complex structures and styles of Western classical composition. Thus, the ensemble is as much a classical choir as it is a folk ensemble.

Bulgarian music is often rhythmically varied, using common two-, three-, and four-beat meters and irregular meters of five or seven beats per bar. The sounds are derived from Western major and minor scales as well as chromatic and pentatonic scales. Further variety is achieved by using intervals known as microtones, sounds based on intervals of less than a half step that are not included in Western scales. These microtones give the music a "Middle Eastern" flavor.

Following the success of several different groups, including the Bulgarian National Folk Ensemble and the Magical Voices of Bulgaria, Bulgarian music has enjoyed a growing audience in Europe and the United States. The Koutev ensemble follows in this tradition.

Goals

Recognize the sound of non-Western scales in both the vocal and instrumental parts.
Describe the timbres of the voices and instruments.
Describe the relationship of the instrumental phrases to the vocal phrases.
Recognize the call and response between the soloist and the choir.

Guide

"Angelina" is arranged in paired phrases.

0:00	8-bar instrumental introduction, consists of two 4-bar phrases
0:12	Solo
0:18	Choral response
0:28	Instrumental
0:36	Solo
0:42	Choral response
0:51	Instrumental
0:59	Solo
1:06	Choral response
1:15	Instrumental
1:23	Solo
1:28	Choral response

Reflections

Describe the familiar and unfamiliar harmonies.
Does this music have a strong rhythmic impulse? Is it foot-tapping music?
Where would you place this music on a continuum ranging from easy listening to harsh sounding?
In what ways did you enjoy or not enjoy this listening example?

Indonesian Gamelan and Popular Music

Indonesia is made up of many islands in southeastern Asia, southwest of the Philippines and northwest of Australia. It includes hundreds of ethnic groups, and although Indonesian is the official language, Indonesians speak more than 200 separate languages. Java is the most populated island, with 100 million inhabitants in an area about the size of New York State. Its capitol is Jakarta, a city of 9 million.

Indonesia has many cultures of many different societal groups with shared language, traditions, and values. Thus, diversity is a prominent characteristic of Indonesia and of its music. This discussion of Indonesian music focuses on two genres: gamelan music and Indonesian pop.

A **gamelan** is a set of instruments—mostly gongs, drums, and metal mallet instruments (like a xylophone with metal bars). Wind and string instruments, singers, and dancers are sometimes added. The gongs may be forged bronze with elaborate carvings and decorations, or they may be homemade from whatever materials are available.

Gamelan orchestras provide music for recreation and entertainment. They may provide music for official ceremonies in palaces, music for dances or wedding receptions, or street music. Gamelans of all sizes (roughly from 4 to 30 musicians) play in a wide variety of settings in nearly every large city and village. Formal concerts for audiences are rare, however. Commonly, gamelan music is related to some form of poetry, drama, or dance.

The Balinese gamelans are the most highly developed and best known in the United States. This music is unlike any Western music. The instruments are different, as are the scales on which the music is based. Two scales, or tunings, are used:

Indonesian dancers perform gamelan music.

a five-tone scale and a seven-tone scale. Instruments are tuned to be out of tune—that is, out of tune to Western ears and not exactly compatible with the tunings of a piano. There is both traditional and newly composed gamelan music, but neither is performed publicly from notation.

It is not uncommon to hear gamelan music in the United States. Many gamelans have been organized at colleges and universities. Because this music is highly repetitive and can be played without formal training, gamelan music (of a sort) can occasionally be heard and performed in school classrooms by students using Orff or similar percussion instruments when gamelan instruments are not available.

Indonesian popular music is like popular music anywhere: diverse, commercial, hit oriented, star oriented, and distributed through the mass media, sometimes internationally. Most of it includes Western instruments, rhythms, and harmonies. Two of the most popular genres are *kroncong* and *dangdut*.

Kroncong, the old style, is enjoyed by the older generation and was popular in Indonesian films through most of the twentieth century. It was named for a ukulele-type instrument and became associated with patriotism and authentic Indonesian culture. *Kroncong* is a respectable, national popular music.

Dangdut, a popular style since the 1970s, is youth music, particularly appealing to Muslim lower- and lower-middle-class youth. It is music for dancing, films, religion (Islam), and sometimes protest (against social inequalities). It has been influenced by Indian rhythms (*dangdut* is the sound of the predominant rhythm, originally played on a tabla), by "authentic" Indonesian music (*kroncong*), and by Western pop and rock, using drum sets and electric guitars. Rhoma Irama, the first *dangdut* superstar, remains popular; his recordings and films have influenced Indonesian dress, behavior, and attitudes.

Listening Guide No. 40

Gendhing "Kodok Ngorek" (excerpt)
CD2, Track 9, 1:59

Performers: Music students from York University (UK) and members of the gamelan group led by Dr. Neil Sorrell, a leading authority on Javanese gamelan music.
Genre: Javanese Gamelan.
Context: Gamelan is associated with the traditional "classical" music of Indonesia, particularly the islands of Java and Bali. Its traditions date back many centuries. It has served many religious, political, and social functions. Gamelans perform for the royal courts, temples, shadow puppet theaters, concerts, and dances. Today, gamelan music is more widely performed in communities and, worldwide, through music departments of colleges and universities that maintain active gamelan ensembles.

Gamelan is ensemble music (from 3 or 4 musicians up to 15 or 20—or more). A gamelan orchestra consists primarily of a wide variety of percussion instruments and tuned gongs. The music is composed, but it is not notated in the Western sense. The pitches used do not match the major or minor scales of Western music. Dancing and singing are sometimes a part of gamelan music.

–Continued

Listening Guide *–Continued*   No. 40

Goals

Listen to the various layers of sound, each having equal importance to the other. Listen to the different percussion sounds, to the wide array of gong sounds, and to the unique vocal quality and performance style of the singer.

Guide

0:00	Percussion followed immediately by the entrance of the gongs— continues in a repeated, ostinato pattern
0:17	This same pattern continues with each note repeated, thus a greater sense of speed—tempo slows
0:52	Different gongs enter but more in the background
1:22	Voice enters in a sometimes quivering manner (fade)

Reflections

Gamelan music sounds so different to Western ears that it may sound other-worldly. Nevertheless, Western-influenced pop and rock music are flourishing in Java and in Bali, particularly in large metropolitan areas.

Could it be, as individual cultures become increasingly globalized, that gamelan music will become comfortable to our ears and a shared cultural experience? Will we soon be able to hear gamelan music on radio and television, at least on "educational" stations? Would you like this to happen?

Jewish Music

Jewish music reflects a multiplicity of traditions and shared cultural values: liturgical music, religious poems, secular songs, music from Islamic traditions, and new Jewish music from the modern state of Israel. To understand the distinct aspects of this music, we must consider the musical materials used, the background of composers, contexts in which the music was created and performed, and the text, language, and content of the songs.

Cultural Context

Prior to 1948, when the nation of Israel was created, the Jewish people were for many centuries spread throughout the world, without a homeland. Today, Jews live in more than a hundred countries, from the few who live in the Philippines to the millions who immigrated to the United States.

Wherever the Jews settled, they remained religiously separate, retaining their religious traditions and practices and holding on to many of the old styles and forms of Jewish religious music. At the same time, however, they absorbed much of the culture of their host countries. Consequently, modern Jewish music is a result of the Jews' commitment to adapt, to compromise, and to assimilate while retaining their ethnic values and traditions. This balance between ethnic preservation and acculturation has resulted in considerable cross-influence between Jewish traditions and other cultures.

It is impossible to imagine how different the music of the United States would be without the contributions of the Jewish people who came to America within the last hundred years. Irving Berlin, George Gershwin, Aaron Copland, and Leonard Bernstein are some of the twentieth-century Jewish American composers who contributed immeasurably to American music. Their music is "Jewish" because its composers were Jews, but it is also American. These composers captured the American spirit and helped shape what is considered characteristically American music.

Liturgical Music

The liturgical music emphasizes prayers and invocations and is transmitted by oral tradition. The music is typically **melismatic**—that is, several notes of the melody correspond to a single syllable of the text. The result of a melisma is a fast-moving melody and a slow-moving text. The songs are known as *cantillations* and are sung by a cantor. They may be sung unaccompanied or may be accompanied by an organ, an orchestra, or other instruments.

Klezmer Music

Klezmer music is primarily music of Yiddish-speaking Jewish immigrants in the United States. It is a popular American ethnic music, but it also is a long-standing part of the Jewish tradition.

A klezmer is a small band, or **combo,** put together to play popular music—from sad, reflective tunes to dance tunes. Klezmer bands are known to have wandered throughout eastern and central Europe as far back as the fifteenth century, playing Jewish tunes, Yiddish folk songs, and Gentile music for Jewish and Christian celebrations and other events.

The lifestyle of a traditional klezmer musician was insecure; he had no regular employment, no property, and no permanent place in society. His status was inferior, and he was not trained in music or music theory. Klezmer musicians are thought to have been highly creative and imaginative, with an excellent ear for music and a highly developed sense of rhythm. They absorbed and assimilated musical materials from their surroundings, becoming highly flexible entertainers.

Recent American klezmer bands include the Klezmorim, the Klezmatics, and the Klezmer Conservatory Band.

Listening Guide   No. 41

"Der Bosfer" ("The Bosphorous") (excerpt)
CD2, Track 10, 1:30

Composer: Kornienko Kornienko, a Ukrainian American musician.
Performer: Klezmer Conservatory Band, featuring Don Byron, clarinet. From the album *A Jumpin' Night in the Garden of Eden* (1988).
Genre: Klezmer.

–Continued

Listening Guide –Continued   No. 41

Goals

Listen for chord and key changes. Notice the lack of chord movement in the extended improvisation.
Identify the instruments and describe their roles.

Guide

0:00	a
0:14	b
0:20	a
0:28	c
0:41	b
0:48	Extended improvisation (fade)

Reflections

What mood is created in the extended improvisation?
How would you describe the mood or moods of this music?
Give reasons for your answer.

Celtic Music

It is easy to start with what Celtic music is not. It is not the music of the Celts, for the Celts as a people no longer exist. Beyond that, its defining characteristics are not so clear. The following descriptions come close:

- Celtic music encompasses the traditional music of Ireland, Scotland, Wales, Brittany (a northeast region of France), and a few other smaller regions of France and Spain whose people share a common bond with Celtic culture.
- Celtic music is now part of a multinational music industry; it is a "world music." It runs the gamut of styles from traditional or roots music to New Age.

Traditional music, as discussed in chapter 3, is the folk music of a people—music learned by memory and disseminated by oral tradition. It is music inherited from the past and is always changing according to the inclinations and creative instincts of the performers. It is not notation-based music. It is music whose origin is probably not known, but it is likely to have been in existence for generations, if not centuries, in one form or another.

Timothy D. Taylor, in his book *Global Pop: World Music; World Markets* (1997), traced the beginnings of modern Celtic music—or the success of Celtic music as an American popular music—to a Volkswagen commercial in 1993 that included background music by Clannad, a popular Irish band. The CD that included this music propelled Clannad to the top of the World Music charts, where the band remained for 55 weeks. Theirs was the best-selling world music album in 1993. Significantly, the sales of the Volkswagen Passat increased by 25 percent.

In 1995, the record label Narada introduced *Celtic Legacy: A Global Celtic Journey*. This recording made the charts and remained there for 52 weeks. It was one of *Billboard*'s top 10 Global Pop: World Music, World Markets music albums in 1995.

Having the word *Celtic* in the title of a CD became a craze. Thirteen such titles were on the charts in August 1996. Atlantic Records created a CD line called "Celtic Heartbeat," which included the music of Clannad. Ironically, the Irish did not, and do not, recognize "Celtic" as a category or genre.

Celtic music and traditional Irish music are overlapping but separate genres. Timothy Taylor describes Celtic music as media driven—a "virtual community." In contrast, Irish music is community based—the traditional or "roots" music of Ireland. In recent years, numerous traditional music festivals have been organized, particularly in France, Ireland, Scotland, England, and Wales.

If you buy "Celtic music," you may obtain traditional "roots" music that includes a harp, a bodhrán, and a singer, or you may get a traditional song surrounded by New Age sounds—in a setting wherein the traditional song has synthesized background accompaniment and a vocal quality that is no longer rough and rootsy. You also may hear traditional Irish music in pop or rock settings.

Artists desiring to maintain a rootsy character and not a multinational career strive for authenticity in village clubs and pubs and a local but knowledgeable constituency. Artists desiring international careers develop a style that has wide appeal and is grounded in effective management and marketing efforts.

Instruments

In traditional Celtic music, you hear everything from guitar to bouzouki, from bagpipes to uilleann pipes, and from fiddles to hurdy-gurdys. You may hear a Welsh harp or a Celtic harp. And you likely will hear a bodhrán, a violin (fiddle) or two, and a tin whistle or flute. Among the more common but perhaps less familiar instruments used in Celtic music are the bouzouki, a plucked string instrument of Greek origin, similar to a banjo; uilleann pipes, Irish bellows-blown bagpipes; and the bodhrán, a large Irish drum played with a small stick or the hand.

A traditional Celtic/Irish "band" is a small group of up to five or six musicians. They play songs ranging from love songs, to traditional Irish jigs and reels, to rock-oriented music.

Artists

In this section, we focus on four Celtic bands. Altan, Clannad, Solas, and the Chieftains are among the best, but many other Celtic bands are successful in their local communities, at regional festivals, and then on international tours.

Altan   Altan began in the early 1980s under the leadership of the Belfast flute player Frankie Kennedy and the singer and fiddler Mairead Ní Mhaonaigh. The duo soon added a bouzouki player, a flute player, and then a guitarist. This group shaped the current Altan sound. The band played clubs and festivals throughout Ireland and began its recording career in the mid-1980s, producing 18 CDs so far. In the early 1990s, Altan added an accordion player from Donegal—a center of traditional Irish music, particularly Donegal fiddlers. The group's award-winning CDs have been produced by Green Linnet, by Virgin Records, and most recently by Narada.

Clannad   Clannad, an Irish group, has created an interesting mix of concerts and recordings of traditional performances, including songs with lyrics in the members' native Gaelic language. Much of their output, however, is in English and incorporates elements of rock, jazz, and world music. Clannad is a family band from

The Chieftains perform Celtic music.

Gweedore, Donegal. The children—Maire, Pol, and Ciaran Brennan—began singing and playing instruments in their father's bar at an early age. Soon uncles Padraig and Noel Duggan joined, as did their sister Enya—who later went on to pursue her own very successful singing career.

During the 1980s, Clannad's success increased significantly through radio and recordings, concerts, and festivals. The group's songs ranked high on the charts. Arrangements featured more electronics. Bono, of U2, sang a duet with Maire ("In a Lifetime") on a track that charted in 1986 and in 1989. Four RCA albums followed, including a sound track to the animated film *Angel and the Soldier Boy.* The song "Theme from Harry's Game" was featured in the 1992 film *Patriot Games,* starring Harrison Ford. Other sound track work followed: *Last of the Mohicans* (1992) and *Message in a Bottle* (1999). Clannad won a Grammy in 1999 for the album *Landmarks.*

Solas   Solas, an acoustic quintet from the United States, performs traditional Irish music. Three of its members are from the United States, and the other two are New Yorkers born and raised in Ireland. Irish American Solas member Séamus Egan is a multi-instrumentalist (flute, tin whistle, low whistle, nylon-string guitar, four-string banjo, mandolin, bodhrán, and uilleann pipes). The other two Irish Americans are button accordion player John Williams and fiddler Winifred Horan. The two members from Ireland are vocalist Karen Casey and guitarist John Doyle.

Solas has produced eight CDs since 1996. The group's CDs—particularly their album *The Edge of Silence* (2002)—and live shows reveal the musicians' commitment not to limit themselves to a single genre but to expand the traditions they know so well. (See Listening Guides 42 and 43 beginning on the next page.)

The Chieftains   The Chieftains are the most famous and most durable (the oldest) of the internationally known Celtic/Irish bands. The group began in 1962 with Paddy Moloney, a uilleann piper from Dublin, who teamed with Martin Fay, fiddle and bones; Sean Potts, tin whistle; Michael Tubridy, flute and concertina; and David Fallon, bodhrán player, to record a one-time album for Claddagh Records under the name "The Chieftains." After a few personnel changes, the Chieftains played their first concert in the United States in 1972, returning with successful tours in 1973 and 1974. They added a harpist, Derek Bell, in 1973. In 1975, they decided to become a full-time professional group.

In the 1980s, the Chieftains toured the world, produced recordings, and added dancers (including Michael Flatley, in his pre-Riverdance days). They performed with dance troupes and symphony orchestras and on radio and television, and they even made a guest appearance on *Saturday Night Live*. Their first Grammy nomination came in 1987, and their first Grammy Award in 1989. They expanded into producing music for films, radio, and television.

In 1993, the Chieftains were one of the first groups to visit China; the visit was documented in the album and video *The Chieftains in China*. The group explored Galician music (from the predominant Celtic region in Spain) and its relationship to Irish traditional music. The 1990s brought many honors including Grammy nominations and six Grammy Awards between 1992 and 1999. In 1997, their CD *Santiago* won the Grammy for Best World Music album. The Chieftains frequently have collaborated with other artists—from Van Morrison and Bonnie Raitt to Diana Krall and Alison Krauss.

Since *The Chieftains 1* was released in 1965, the Chieftains have produced more than 30 recordings plus sound tracks and collections, in addition to concerts, tours, and film appearances. Theirs has been a truly remarkable career—and the Chieftains are not finished yet!

Listening Guide   No. 42

"Ailliú na Gamhna" (excerpt)
CD2, Track 11, 2:00

Performer: Solas: Karan Casey, vocals; John Doyle, guitars, mando-cello, vocals; Séamus Egan, flute, banjo, tin whistle, mandolin, bodhrán; Winifred Horan, fiddles; John Williams, button accordion, concertina.
Genre: Celtic.
Form: Verse-chorus.
Lyrics: Traditional; translated from the Gaelic by Oisin Ó Siochrú.

Goals

Notice the ornaments in the soloist's style. Only the words to verse 1 and the chorus in Gaelic and in English are printed.

0:00	Intro		
0:10	Verse 1		
	Is iníon d'aoire mé féinig gan amhras		*I'm a herdsman daughter, sure enough;*
	do bhíodh ina cónaí cois taobh na Laune,		*Who once lived down by the banks of the Leamhna,*

–Continued

Listening Guide –Continued   No. 42

| | Bhí bothán an bainne ag téamh agam | I had a cabin there, a window in the gable. |
| | 'sea ghlaofainn ar na gamhna. | While I heated the milk, I called in the calves. |

0:33   Chorus (*Curfá*)

Aililiú na gamhna, na gamhna bána,	Aliliú the calves, the pretty calves,
aililiú na gamhna, na gamhna b'iad a b'fhearr liom,	Aliliú the calves, I loved them the best,
aililiú na gamhna, na gamhna geala bána,	Aililiú the calves, the fine pretty calves,
na gamhna mainin shamhraidh ag damhsa ar na bánta.	Dancing in the meadow on a clear summer's morning.

0:55   Verse 2
1:18   Chorus
1:41   Instrumental interlude (fade)

Reflections

Is this style more closely related to American pop or to folk? Or is it unrelated to either?

Can you enjoy the music without translation? In other words, can you enjoy the music without understanding the meaning?

This performing group is based in the United States. Is Solas's music therefore American music?

Listening Guide   No. 43

"Tom Busby's" (excerpt)

CD2, Track 12, 1:18

Performer: Solas.

Genre: Irish jig.

Context: A fiddle is featured in a group of three songs: "Tom Busby's," "James O'Byrne's," and "The Four Posts of the Bed." An Irish jig is a dance in fast 6/8 time. The three jigs are performed without pause. Only the first jig is heard here.

Goals

Be aware of phrases and chord changes (as phrases change).

Be aware of the style of Irish fiddling in the context of playing a jig.

Listening Guide –Continued No. 43

Guide

Count in a fast two (two beats to the bar)—but with a feeling of high energy.

0:00	a	First two phrases—8 bars each
0:15	b	Next two phrases—8 bars each—pitched lower
0:26	a	Next two phrases—8 bars each—original pitch
0:39	b	Next two phrases—8 bars each—pitched lower—same pitch as second group
0:53	a	Next two phrases—8 bars each—original pitch
1:06	b	Next two phrases—8 bars each—pitched lower—same pitch as second group (excerpt fades)

Reflections

Is there an American dance that is the equivalent of or similar to the Irish jig?
Could the meter of this jig be analyzed differently? How?

Summary

Musical styles and musical languages differ from country to country, region to region, and culture to culture. Yet we find ourselves using the same descriptive language for all styles. For example, melody, harmony, rhythm, texture, and form are useful concepts in describing music of any and all cultures. Musical instruments used by many cultures may differ, but all are plucked, shaken, hit, blown, or bowed, giving us a common descriptive frame of reference.

The functions of music (why music exists in a culture), performance practices (setting, dress, degree of formality), and the relationship between performer and audience may differ among cultures. However, these issues are common to all cultures and provide a common vocabulary for studying world music.

Finally, all cultures value, use, create, perform, and listen to music in a variety of ways. By studying the music of other cultures, we become aware that music is important to people whose values regarding music and life may be quite different from our own. It can be a humbling but enriching experience to realize that Western music represents only a fraction of the world's musical styles and preferences.

PART four

*Listening to Western
Classical Music*

The classical music that is part of American culture has its roots in the history and traditions of western Europe. It developed through distinct yet overlapping historical periods. Each period brought changes in society and in common musical practice. These changes, both societal and musical, grew out of earlier developments such as the invention of printing from movable type, the invention of musical notation, the invention of new instruments, and the harnessing of electricity. Musical changes also resulted from shifting progressive and conservative attitudes on the part of composers, and from composers' desires to experiment.

Over time, musical aesthetics and styles evolved in historical periods during which creators of music emphasized personal feelings, imagery, and romantic notions about music. During other periods, composers took a more objective, intellectual approach, emphasizing form and structure, balance, and craftsmanship.

These contrasting changes resulted in specific periods in the development of Western music: Medieval (450–1450), Renaissance (1450–1600), Baroque (1600–1750), Classic (1750–1820), Romantic (1820–1900), and Modern (1900 to the present). These dates must be considered approximate, especially the beginning year of the Medieval period. All dates allow for the overlap of musical styles, composers, and influences.

Chapters 9 through 13 trace the development of Western classical music—that is, art music—from the beginning of the Christian era to the present. Chapter 13 focuses on twentieth-century European and American classical music. Information about significant women composers and their music is presented within the cultural context of the time that they flourished as composers.

Throughout modern history, women have been active as performers and composers, but, because of social customs based on gender distinctions, they often participated in music as amateurs rather than professionals. As performers, they were mainly singers or keyboardists.

The first well-known woman composer was Hildegard von Bingen (1098–1179), a nun and abbess in Germany. The first woman known to have published her own music and to have considered herself a professional composer was Maddalena Casulana (c. 1540–1590), in Italy. Francesca Caccini (1587–1645?) is believed to have been the highest-paid musician in the court of the Medici in Florence, Italy.

During the seventeenth and eighteenth centuries, women's roles in classical music expanded to include teaching and performing at court and in public concerts. The nineteenth and early twentieth centuries saw an even greater expansion of opportunities. Women composed music in every genre, including symphony and opera. They increasingly had their music published, though sometimes under a man's name. They performed throughout Europe; they studied in the newly established music conservatories and subsequently taught in these conservatories; and they became scholars of music and wrote about music.

When women were paid for their musical artistry and creativity, however, they were not compensated equally with men. They were denied many opportunities for performance, such as positions in symphony and opera orchestras. Perhaps most important, historians largely ignored their creative accomplishments.

Only in the past few decades has a vast quantity of research uncovered considerable information about the roles of women in Western classical music. Many of their works have been performed, published, and recorded. Improvements in the status of women in music, however, must be considered relative to previous conditions and opportunities. For example, many of these works have become known as a result of initiatives by women in establishing their own performing, recording, and publishing outlets.

We learn music and assess its quality as a result of considerable study and contemplation over time. Widespread availability with abundant opportunities to hear and study this music is necessary to the process.

Chapter Outline

In This Chapter

What are three significant aspects of the culture in the Medieval and Renaissance periods?

How would you describe the early notation of western European music?

How do monophonic and polyphonic music differ?

What were the important musical genres of the Medieval and Renaissance periods?

What was the role of the church in relation to music during these periods?

Who were the great composers of the Medieval and Renaissance periods?

Where were the centers of musical activity (cities or regions) during these periods?

To understand and discuss western European classical music, you can draw on your understanding of the terms and the musical concepts presented in previous chapters, but you will now have the opportunity to learn new terms and concepts, including notation, the Renaissance, Gregorian chant, polyphony, and the mass.

Prior to 1600, European culture was centered, for the most part, in the Roman Catholic Church, and this religious focus affected the era's music. Later, with the Protestant Reformation, came a movement from chants to singing hymns, which also profoundly affected the ways that people performed music.

Before the end of this period in the history of Western music, composers of music became well known in their own time, including composers such as Palestrina and Gabrieli, whose music remains widely performed today.

Goals for Listening

To help you begin exploring the sounds of Western classical music, chapter 9 includes three examples of chant, parts of a Roman Catholic Mass in Latin, an Anglican anthem in English, two secular choral pieces, and lute music. These examples will help you achieve several goals:

- Describe melodic shape (contour) and rhythm of chant.
- Understand the relationship of music and words.
- Recognize flexible pulse and rhythm.
- Describe phrase structure.
- Recognize and describe monophonic and polyphonic textures.
- Identify motive.
- Recognize imitation.
- Describe ornamentation.

In chapter 2, we used the word **texture** to describe the relative thinness or thickness of sound, and we explained that a few notes or lines of music at one time create thin texture and many notes or lines create a full, thick sound. There are three basic musical textures:

- *Monophonic.* Music consisting of a single, melodic line and no accompaniment or other horizontal or vertical sounds is described as a monophonic texture. **Chant** and other unaccompanied solo singing are examples of **monophony.**
- *Polyphonic.* Music consisting of two or more melodies sounding at the same time, having equal emphasis but not necessarily starting and stopping at the same time, is described as polyphonic. Any familiar song performed as a round, such as "Row, Row, Row Your Boat," is an example of **polyphony** or polyphonic music. The word **counterpoint** is commonly used to describe this compositional technique.
- *Homophonic.* Music consisting of one predominant melody (in the foreground) supported by a harmonic or chordal accompaniment (in the background) is described as homophonic. Almost all our popular music, folk music, and recent religious music are examples of **homophony.**

Combinations of textures are apparent in much music. Homophony may be present in polyphonic music, for example. The term we use to describe a specific work depends on which texture predominates.

The Beginnings of Western Music (until 1450)

Western European and American **art music**—classical music—and much of American **vernacular** music are part of a musical tradition that can be traced back to the theoretical writings and teachings of ancient Greek scholars. This period extends from the time of Pythagoras, about 500 B.C.E., to that of Ptolemy, around 200 C.E., and includes the teachings of Aristotle and Plato.

Western music was influenced by Greek music theory, not Greek practices—that is, by the doctrines and descriptions rather than the music itself. Greek scholars wrote about the nature of music, its place in the universe and in society, and its materials and principles of composition. They examined its effects on people and tried to define the relationships between music and mathematics, morality, poetry, education, and character or personality. The vocabulary the Greek writers used to discuss and describe music formed the beginnings of the musical vocabulary we use today. The history of Western practice, however, is traced not from the music of Greece but from music composed at the beginning of the Christian era.

Whereas the theory of Western music derives from the Greek philosophers, the religious ritual (liturgy) of the Roman Catholic Church and its music were borrowed and adapted from the Jewish synagogue services: the singing of hymns and Psalms, prayers, the position of the cantor (the chief solo singer), and **antiphonal** (responsorial) singing. As Christianity spread into Africa, parts of Asia, and Europe, its music absorbed elements from these diverse areas.

The first 1,400 years of Western music were dominated by the Roman Catholic Church. These centuries are typically divided into the Medieval period, or Middle Ages (up to the early fifteenth century), and the Renaissance (c. 1450–1600). Music in the Middle Ages was mainly vocal. Instrumental genres, including works for keyboard instruments, were not fully developed until around the sixteenth century.

The earliest historical information about secular music—that is, folk and entertainment music—dates from around the twelfth century. Secular music was not notated until the late Middle Ages. Because it was often related to dancing, it was more metric than sacred music and had a stronger rhythmic feeling. It also included instruments for accompanying songs and dances. Secular music was frequently performed in the context of other forms of entertainment, such as acting, storytelling, poetry, juggling, acrobatics, and dancing.

Secular music and drama were occasionally added to the church liturgy. By the thirteenth century, such insertions had developed into what are now known as liturgical dramas, and these eventually became entities in themselves that were performed outside the church. The two most common liturgical dramas, dating from the twelfth century (and available on modern recordings), are *The Play of Daniel* and *The Play of Herod*. These dramas used instruments such as flutes, trumpets, and percussion.

The liturgy of the early Western churches was varied, as local churches at first were relatively independent. The main musical style of religious music was **chant**, a type of song found in many cultures and traditions. Chants range from the intoning of a two-note melody to elaborate, **melismatic** melodies. In the Roman Catholic Church, chants were sung in Latin.

From the fifth to the seventh centuries, the church organized boy choirs, established schools for training boys and men as church musicians, and revised its liturgy and music. The most significant musical reform came during the papacy of Pope Gregory I at the end of the sixth century. Gregory established an order for the liturgy, assigning particular items to the various services throughout the church year. An outgrowth of this reform was the emergence of a uniform repertoire of chant for use by Roman Catholic churches in all countries. This repertoire became known as **Gregorian chant.**

Gregorian Chant

Gregorian chants are the earliest examples of Western classical music. These relatively short pieces were used in the liturgy of the Roman Catholic Church. At first, various regions developed their own distinct liturgies and repertoires. By the eighth century, however, regional variations had either disappeared or been absorbed into the single uniform practice established by the church leaders.

A chant was sung in Latin by a priest or a cantor, by the men and boys of the choir, or by the congregation. Originally, these monophonic chants were performed without instruments. By the thirteenth century, instrumental accompaniment was sometimes used. In recent years, much of the Catholic liturgy has been presented in the vernacular (the spoken language of the people), rather than in Latin, and set to music in accessible contemporary styles.

A chant (see Listening Guides 44, 45, and 46 in this chapter) is monophonic in texture, of relatively short duration, and sung in an unhurried manner. Its rhythm is fluid, reflecting the natural inflection of the mostly unmetered text. Its accents are compatible with the accents of the text—that is, there is no regular accent and no strong metric feeling. The earliest chants were not notated. Manuscripts containing notated chants date from the ninth century, and many were written down in beautiful calligraphy. The composers of Gregorian chants—mostly priests, monks, and nuns—are unidentified in these manuscripts.

The chant text can be given a **syllabic setting**, with one note to each syllable of text; a florid, melismatic setting, with several and sometimes many notes to a single syllable; or a combination of those two treatments. The shape of a chant melody is fairly flat, is mostly stepwise, and encompasses a small range. The illustration below shows a typically flat contour—a **conjunct** melody—and the relationship of notes to text. Notice both the melismatic and the more syllabic portions of the chant.

The scale patterns of Gregorian chants are derived from church **modes** (scales) that antedate the major-minor tonal system that we are familiar with. The church modes give the chants their oriental, mystical quality—a quality also found in much American traditional folk music and in recent jazz and popular music. The church modal system formed the basis of Western music for over a thousand years.

Chant was functional music. It was an aid to worship rather than music that people passively listened to. The several thousand chants make up a significant body of literature in Western music. Many have been used as bases for other types of musical compositions, such as the **polyphonic** settings of the Mass and sacred motets prevalent during the sixteenth century.

An excerpt of a chant is seen in Medieval notation (above), which can be compared with the same chant seen in modern, western European notation (below).

This fragment on the crucifixion of St. Andrew is a late-thirteenth- or early-fourteenth-century artwork created from tempera and gold leaf on vellum. The chant depicted in the work is from an antiphonary, which is a book of liturgical chants used by the choir and congregation in Catholic churches. The chants were usually antiphonal chants, or antiphons, sung by a single person (the cantor) and then repeated by the choir and the congregation.

Listening Guide

No. 44

Antiphon for Easter Sunday in Praise of Mary

CD2, Track 13, 0:51

Performer: Choir of the Vienna Hofburgkapelle.

Genre: Gregorian chant.

Context: Gregorian chants function as an integral part of the liturgy of the Roman Catholic Church. They are an aid to worship, with many having specific purposes in the ritual of the Mass. An antiphon is a commonly used liturgical chant sung as a refrain before, after, or sometimes between verses of a psalm or a canticle.

–Continued

Listening Guide –Continued   No. 44

Goals

Identify the musical characteristics of the chant, particularly its melodic shape, texture, and rhythm.

Recognize monophonic texture.

Recognize the relationship of music to words, noticing especially the phrasing and accents and whether the treatment of the words is melismatic or syllabic.

Guide

Latin text and English translation:

Regina caeli laetare, alleluia,	*Rejoice, Queen of the Heavens, alleluia,*
Quia quem meruisti portare, alleluia,	*Because He whom you were worthy of bearing, alleluia,*
Resurrexit, sicut dixit, alleluia.	*Has risen as He promised, alleluia.*
Ora pro nobis Deum, alleluia.	*Pray to God for us, alleluia.*

Reflections

Notice the flexible pulse. The music is nonmetric because it flows with the natural inflection of the text.

Although the chant is sung by a group of men rather than a soloist, the texture of this chant and the one in Listening Guide 46 is monophonic: A single melodic line exists by itself without accompaniment or supportive harmony.

Is this chant syllabic or melismatic? Why?

Listening Guide   No. 45

Kyrie eleison: "Magnae Deus potentiae"

CD2, Track 14, 1:45

Performer: Choralschola of the Niederaltaicher Scholaren; Konrad Ruhland, conductor.

Genre: Gregorian chant.

Goals

Identify the musical characteristics of the chant, particularly its melodic shape, texture, and rhythm.

Listening Guide –Continued　　No. 45

Recognize monophonic texture and then the two-part textures that start in unison, move away in parallel motion typically at intervals as wide as a fifth, then return to a unison ending.

Recognize the relationship of music to words, noticing especially the phrasing and accents and when the treatment of the words is melismatic or syllabic.

Notice the phrasing, which occasionally ends in the middle of a word, typically *eleison*.

Guide

Kyrie eleison.

Greek　　*Kyrie eleison. (Lord, have mercy upon us.)*
　　　　　Kyrie eleison.
　　　　　Christe eleison. (Christ have mercy upon us.)
　　　　　Kyrie eleison.

Reflections

Is this chant metric or nonmetric? Why?

Notice the frequency with which syllables of text are treated melismatically. Typically, how long are the melismas?

Maixant Ndeky, a Benedictine monk from Senegal, strums a *kora*. This traditional African instrument was made in the workshop of the Benedictine Monastery in Keur Moussa, Senegal. These Benedictine monks, however, typically sing their Gregorian chants accompanied by the sounds of a traditional African harp.

Notation

Notation—a system of visual symbols—was developed to reinforce the singer's memory of a chant melody learned from oral tradition. Notation was also developed to specify pitches so that chant melodies would be uniform throughout the far-flung Roman Catholic Church. See the illustration on page 188 for a comparison of medieval square notation with its counterpart in modern notation.

A system of notating music was also devised to convey several melodic lines of music for others to perform. This system specifies both pitch and rhythmic patterns in order to achieve accurate performances of increasingly complex music. Therefore, singers were taught to read this notation.

Notation was a great aid in the teaching of polyphonic music. By the thirteenth century, music in three parts had become common, and the person who created a piece of music (the composer) was no longer always anonymous but began to be acknowledged in the notated manuscripts. An important region for the development of notation was northern France. The first known composers of notated polyphony were Léonin and Perotin.

Polyphonic Music

The ninth through the thirteenth centuries saw fundamental changes in Western music. Composition was becoming structured, adhering to certain principles and techniques. Chant was not only an entity in itself but was becoming the basis of other compositions. By the eleventh century, musicians had added a second melodic line to a chant, creating vertical sounds—**harmony**—and polyphonic texture. The melodies moved with the same rhythm or, more commonly, had contrasting rhythms and a contrasting sense of movement (one melody moving faster than the other). Polyphony became a common technique.

The various melodic lines of Renaissance polyphonic music (see the next section) were considered equal in importance. In this music (unlike music consisting of a melody with accompaniment), no line was dominant. Each line was a singable melody, rhythmically independent from the other lines. In the illustration on page 193, notice that each voice enters separately in a rising contour and that the words *absalon fili mi* are not sung at the same time. It was common for composers to write in **imitative counterpoint**—that is, each voice entered separately but imitated the voice that had started the previous phrase. This technique was usually worked out so that each voice would begin with the same melodic and rhythmic pattern, perhaps on a different pitch, and then soon deviate from the pattern. Because the melodic lines were moving independently, the strong beats fell at different times. The music was metered, but the rhythmic independence among the lines minimized the metric feeling, The result was a gentle, flowing rhythm. The polyphony shown in this illustration is imitative. Notice the identical contour of each entrance of *absalon fili mi*.

Polyphony may give unity to a piece but also may make it sound more complex and challenging than a homophonic song with a single-line melody supported by an accompaniment. The multiple independent lines and overlapping imitative parts also tend to obscure the text, a problem particularly disadvantageous to the liturgy. Renaissance choral polyphony may be challenging, but those who know the music consider it beautiful and noble and rank it among the most inspired choral music in Western literature.

By the end of the sixteenth century, composers of both sacred and secular choral music were paying more attention to vertical sounds—to harmonies or chords. In fact, much choral music, especially secular music, placed sufficient emphasis on its

This excerpt is from a motet composed by Josquin des Prez (c. 1440–1521); it represents the notation of imitative, polyphonic choral music. Each line enters independently, one after the other, and each has the same melodic shape with the same text but starting at different times.

harmonic aspects to be considered homophonic rather than polyphonic. This is in contrast to thirteenth- or fourteenth-century works, which had independent lines and in which vertical sonorities were quite incidental and of little concern.

The Renaissance (1450–1600)

The Renaissance in Europe saw a magnificent flourishing of knowledge and productivity in the arts and letters. This was the age of Michelangelo and Leonardo da Vinci, Raphael and El Greco, Luther, Shakespeare, and many other great artists and writers. The Renaissance was also the golden age of polyphonic choral music created by the first significant group of great composers, a group that included Josquin des Prez, Giovanni Pierluigi da Palestrina, and Giovanni Gabrieli.

The Renaissance was a period of humanism, optimism, and reform. Artists and scholars expanded their interests into secular society, and patronage of the arts began to shift from the church to the courts. Developments that were important in shaping Western culture occurred during the Renaissance. The use of gunpowder and the

The Cathedral of Notre Dame in Paris dates back to the twelfth century. During this time, composers in and around Paris were creating polyphonic, liturgical music, a practice which led to the more sophisticated development of the sacred choral polyphonic repertoire of the fifteenth and sixteenth centuries.

compass changed the course of history. Printing techniques invented by Gutenberg in the fifteenth century soon led to the dissemination of printed music and books about music.

Choral and Vocal Music

Choral music is music in which more than one singer sings each part—for example, a choir of sopranos, altos, tenors, and basses (SATB). *Vocal music* usually means either a solo piece for one singer with or without accompaniment or an ensemble work in which there is one singer to each part. Three choral genres that became established by the end of the Renaissance were the mass, the motet, and the madrigal.

Mass   The part of Catholic liturgy that has produced the most important sacred music is the **Mass,** particularly music for the Ordinary of the High Mass.

In a Low Mass, the priest intones or recites the prayers, and the congregation remains silent. In contrast, in a High Mass, the liturgy is recited and sung by a choir either in Gregorian chant or in a combination of chant and polyphonic choral settings. A High Mass consists of the Proper, the parts of the Mass that vary according to the season of the church year or the particular event being commemorated, and the Ordinary, the parts that do not vary.

The Ordinary is often sung by a choir. Its five sections are the *Kyrie, Gloria, Credo, Sanctus* and *Benedictus,* and *Agnus Dei.* Polyphonic settings of these sections constitute much of the great choral literature in Western music, some of it (such as J. S. Bach's Mass in B Minor) intended not for liturgical use but for concert performance. This music has been sung in churches and concert halls by Catholic, Protestant, and secular choirs—sometimes with the Latin text preserved, sometimes in translations into the vernacular.

Polyphonic settings of the Mass have been composed consistently since the late Middle Ages. The first important polyphonic setting was the *Messe de Nostre Dame*, composed in the mid-fourteenth century by a Frenchman, Guillaume de Machaut (c. 1300–1377). The significance of this work was its **unity**. Previously, there had been little concern for the relationships among style, mode, or thematic idea from one section of the Ordinary to another. Machaut, however, regarded his mass as a single composition.

Two other important composers of masses are Josquin des Prez and Giovanni Pierluigi da Palestrina. Josquin (c. 1450–1521), a Franco-Belgian, worked many years in Italy. His best-known mass is *Missa L'homme armé*. The most influential work of the Italian composer Palestrina (c. 1525–1594) is the *Missa Papae Marcelli*. Josquin and Palestrina rank among the greatest of the early composers. Polyphonic settings of the Mass were most prevalent through the sixteenth century, particularly in Italy.

Listening Guide   No. 46

"Benedicta es"
CD2, Track 15, 2:11

Performer: The Tallis Scholars; Peter Phillips, director.
Genre: Chant.
Context: This chant is not a part of the Gregorian repertoire and is not a specific part of the Catholic liturgy. It is known as a sequence—an addition to the liturgy. However, it has all the musical characteristics of chant described in this chapter.

Goals

Recognize monophonic texture, a flexible rhythm with no sense of meter, and an essentially stepwise melodic contour with a very small range.

Describe the syllabic setting evident in this example.

Recognize aurally the phrase structure indicated in the figure on page 196 and described below in the "Guide."

Guide

The six verses are in pairs. The music changes in every other verse, so the form can be described as a a b b c c; an *Amen* concludes the chant. Much unity results from the fact that only the first phrase of each verse changes; subsequent lines are the same as those in the first verse. The first four verses each have three lines of text; the fifth and sixth verses each have four lines. The figure depicts the melodic contour and phrase relationships.

–Continued

Listening Guide –Continued   No. 46

Benedictus es, caelorum Regina,   a

et mundi totius Domina,   b

et aegris medicina.   c

Tu praeclara maris stella vocaris,   a

quae solem justitiae paris,   b

a quo illuminaris.   c

Te Deus Pater, ut Dei Mater   d

fieres, et ipse frater   b

cujus eras filia.   c

Sanctificavit, Sanctam servavit,   d

et mittens sic salutavit: b

Ave plena gratia.   c

Per illud Ave prolatum   e

et tuum responsum gratum   e

est ex te Verbum incarnatum,   b

quo salvantur omnia.   c

Nunc Mater exora Natum   e

ut nostrum tollat reatum,   e

et regnum det nobis paratum   b

in caelesti gloria.   c

Amen.   A—men

Listening Guide –Continued   No. 46

Reflections

What is a syllabic setting? A melismatic setting? Describe the setting of this chant.

Notice the slurs in the first phrase, the only place in the chant where more than one note of music equals one syllable of text, other than in the *Amen.*

Does this music convey feeling, mood, and emotion?

Notice the duration of pitches. Notes are equal in length with the exception of a longer note at the end of each phrase.

Listening Guide   No. 47

"Gloria," from Missa Benedicta es

CD2, Track 16, 3:37

Composer: Giovanni Pierluigi da Palestrina (c. 1525–1594).

Performer: The Tallis Scholars; Peter Phillips, director.

Genre: Renaissance Mass.

Context: This polyphonic setting of the second part of the Ordinary of the Mass is based on the chant "Benedictus es" (see Listening Guide 46).

Goals

Follow the respective voice parts—soprano, alto, and bass—and the cantus firmus, or fixed melody.

Recognize polyphonic texture and points of imitation.

Describe the vocal-choral quality, with particular regard to the use of vibrato.

Guide

The music begins with the chant "Gloria in excelsis Deo." The polyphonic setting can be counted in a slow two or a moderately fast four.

	Part 1		
0:00	Chant	"Gloria in excelsis Deo"
0:08	Bar 1	First theme begins in the alto: "Et in terra pax . . ."
0:21	Bar 7	Points of imitation among tenors and basses
	Bar 11	Now six-part polyphonic texture

–Continued

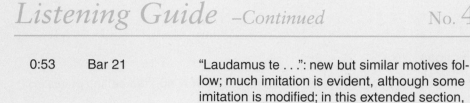

0:53	Bar 21	"Laudamus te . . .": new but similar motives follow; much imitation is evident, although some imitation is modified; in this extended section, polyphonic interplay, mostly in six-part texture, continues until the final cadence
Part 2		
2:47	A brief excerpt	"Qui tollis peccata mundi miserere nobis" is included to illustrate the remarkable contrast with part 1 in both style and mood

Reflections

Imitation of a motive might be modified through small changes in pitch or rhythm, but the basic idea of the motive is evident. A goal is to recognize points of imitation—that is, points where imitated motives or melodies begin.

Notice that this piece combines restrained dignity with a highly expressive, uplifting quality. It exhibits cerebral polyphonic control yet a tender, human spirituality. To what extent can these moods be conveyed despite a polyphonic texture in which the words, for the most part, cannot be understood? In what ways can music communicate without text?

Describe the vocal quality and how it contributes to the spiritual mood. How do you respond to this music?

Motet   A **motet** is a sacred polyphonic composition, usually sung in Latin without accompaniment (a cappella). It is a choral genre intended to be sung by choirs of trained singers, rather than by congregations. During the Renaissance, a motet usually had from four to six independent melodies, in contrast to the more common three-part texture of thirteenth-century motets.

The thirteenth-century polyphonic motets were composed anonymously in France and England, frequently in three voices with a different text in each voice—either in Latin or in the vernacular. One voice, usually the tenor, was based wholly or partly on a chant. It was slow, whereas the other composed melodies were more rhythmically active. The chant that was used as the basis for polyphonic composition—in either a motet or a section of a mass—was known as the **cantus firmus,** or fixed melody. Because the cantus firmus had no liturgical function, it was frequently sung in the vernacular or played on an instrument.

The popularity of the motet spread throughout western Europe. The cantus firmus continued to be borrowed not only from the chant repertoire but also from popular songs of the day. Composers freely borrowed melodies, texts, or fragments of either from existing sources. Motets usually were not intended to be sung as part

This is the basilica of St. Mark in Venice, Italy. Giovanni Gabrieli
(c. 1525–1594), organist and choir director at St. Mark's and also
a noted composer, was influenced by the architecture of St. Mark's.
He was able to place two or more choirs and an instrumental group,
usually brass instruments, to create polychoral music (multiple choirs
of voices). Choirs often sang antiphonally—singing in alternation or
one in response to the other.

of the liturgy but became a common repertoire for trained choirs in church services
and concert settings. They are still performed in those settings today.

Renaissance choral music culminated in the great **polychoral motets**—motets for
multiple choirs—of Giovanni Gabrieli. Although polychoral music was established
before Gabrieli, he was able to exploit it most effectively in his work for St. Mark's
Cathedral in Venice. St. Mark's was built in such a way that Gabrieli, who was the
choirmaster and a noted composer, could have two or more independent choirs
placed to allow music to be sung antiphonally—that is, with two or more choirs
singing in alternation or one in response to the other. St. Mark's had two great
organs, and Gabrieli was interested in writing sacred choral music that included not
only the organ but a variety of wind and string instruments; thus, he composed motets and other choral pieces for several choirs with numerous independent melodic
lines. These works also featured **homorhythmic** sections in which the text was sung
by all voices at once, making the words more understandable.

Gabrieli's use of instrumentalists performing lines that were independent of
the voices and his use of multiple choirs contrasting with each other and with the

instruments became basic principles of the Baroque style that emerged at the turn of the seventeenth century (see chapter 10). Gabrieli's music and the natural acoustics of St. Mark's must have provided a thrilling and exalting musical experience.

Madrigal   The Renaissance madrigal (see Listening Guide 48) typically is in four or five parts with one singer to a part; thus, it is considered vocal chamber music. A **madrigal** is a secular composition, reflecting the growing independence of the arts from the church. In the vernacular, the poetic text is about love, a pastoral theme, or some other secular topic. The music, usually more metrical and lively than a motet, combines elements of ancient modal scales with the harmonies of modern major tonalities and combines polyphonic and homophonic textures.

Madrigals, which flourished in Italy and England, were sung at court festivities, social gatherings, and meetings of learned societies. Because the madrigal did not have to adhere to the strictures of the church, composers were more free to experiment with bold harmony, pictorial and expressive writing, or even contrasting a solo part with a harmonic bass line or with a chordal background (a technique that would become more common in Baroque music).

Listening Guide   No. 48

"Now Is the Month of Maying"

CD2, Track 17, 2:03

Composer: Thomas Morley (1558–1603).
Performer: John Rutter and the Cambridge Singers, from the album *Olde English Madrigals and Folk Songs at Ely Cathedral* (1984).
Genre: Renaissance madrigal.
Context: Morley was an English composer known primarily for madrigals. He wrote the first music instruction book in the English language.

Goals

Be aware of the shifting of polyphonic and homophonic textures.
Identify the metric organization.
Recognize the equal emphasis given to each vocal part (SATB).
Recognize imitation and modified imitation.

Guide

"Now Is the Month of Maying" is a madrigal for four voices. Although the voices move polyphonically, even imitatively, they come together more frequently in

Listening Guide –Continued   No. 48

homophonic texture than they typically would in the sacred polyphonic music of the same period. The text follows; notice in each verse that each pair of lines is repeated.

Now is the month of maying,
When merry lads are playing. Fa la, etc.
Each with his bonnie lass
Upon the greeny grass. Fa la, etc.

The Spring, clad all in gladness,
Doth laugh at Winter's sadness. Fa la, etc.
And to the bagpipes sound
The nymphs tread out their ground. Fa la, etc.

Fie then why sit we musing,
Youth's sweet delight refusing? Fa la, etc.
Say dainty nymphs and speak,
Shall we play barley break? Fa la, etc.

Reflections

Differentiate between texture in which several melodic lines are equal in emphasis (polyphony) and a single, dominant line that is supported by a secondary chordal texture or accompaniment (homophony).

Compare the mood and style (musical characteristics) of this piece with the mood and style of the piece by Palestrina (Listening Guide 47). In particular, describe the degree of rhythmic vitality and the dominance of one texture over another.

What makes music sound sacred? What makes it sound secular?

Listening Guide   No. 49

"Il est bel et bon" ("My husband's fine and good")

CD2, Track 18, 0:55

Composer: Pierre Passereau (flourished 1509–1547), composed in 1534.
Performer: The Scholars of London.
Genre: French chanson.
Context: Passereau composed mainly French chansons. A chanson is vocal chamber music with a secular text. The melodies for many chansons, including this one, were taken from currently popular tunes.

–Continued

Listening Guide –Continued   No. 49

Goals

Be aware of the shifting of polyphonic and homophonic textures.
Identify the metric organization.
Recognize the equal emphasis given to each vocal part (SATB).
Recognize imitation and modified imitation.

Guide

The piece is lively, and it is sung a cappella. Count in a moderately fast two.
The texture is polyphonic throughout.

0:00	*Il est bel et bon, commère, mon mari.*	*He is a good fellow, gossip, my husband.*
	Il était deux femmes toutes d'un pays,	*There were two women of the same neighborhood,*
	Disans l'une a l'autre: avez bon mari?	*Saying to one another: have you a kind husband?*
0:19	*Il ne me courouce, ne me bat aussi:*	*He does not annoy me, neither does he beat me;*
	Il fait le ménange, il donne aux poulailles	*He does the housework, he feeds the hens*
	Et je prene mes plaisirs.	*And I take my pleasures.*
0:32	*Commère, c'est pour rire*	*Gossip, it is funny*
	Quand les pouilles crient:	*When the hens cluck:*
	Petite coquette, qu'est-ce ci?	*Little coquette, what is this?*
0:45	(Repeat of first verse)	

Reflections

Differentiate between texture in which several melodic lines are equal in emphasis (polyphony) and a single, dominant line that is supported by a secondary chordal texture or accompaniment (homophony).

Compare the mood and style (musical characteristics) of these pieces with the mood and style of the piece by Palestrina (Listening Guide 47). In particular, describe the degree of rhythmic vitality and the dominance of one texture over another.

What makes music sound sacred? What makes it sound secular?

Instrumental Music

Instrumental music—music for drums and other percussion instruments, lyres, and various kinds of flutes—must have existed before recorded history. By the twelfth century, it had an important part in many liturgical dramas. The development of offset printing facilitated the spread of secular, instrumental music. During the Middle Ages and Renaissance, instrumental music typically was more metric, livelier, and less polyphonic than sacred liturgical music, and it was probably created not for its own sake but for its important role in accompanying singing and dancing.

The harp, lyre, psaltery, and viele were instruments in common use in the Middle Ages. The viele, a bowed instrument, was a forerunner of the viol, itself a forerunner of the violin. Instruments common in the Renaissance were recorders, viols, shawms, krummhorns, cornetts, and lutes. The most common keyboard instruments were the harpsichord and the clavichord. The organ as we know it today became popular during the sixteenth century.

For the most part, Renaissance instrumental music modeled itself after the vocal style, and it was common to have an instrument either double or substitute for a vocal part. Music was sometimes written for a **consort** of similar instruments, such as soprano, alto, tenor, and bass recorders or a group of viols of various ranges.

By the sixteenth century, instrumental music had developed to the point that composers wrote pieces specifically for instruments, and the first instrumental genres evolved: the ricercar and the canzona. Although the stylistic distinction between these genres is blurred, the ricercar was generally written for keyboards or for an instrumental ensemble and was modeled after the polyphonic motet; the less sober canzona was similar to the madrigal or to the French chanson. It usually was entertaining, fast moving, metric, and contrapuntal in a light and easy manner.

The Reformation

In 1517, Martin Luther set in motion events that led to the splitting of the Christian church into two major divisions: Catholic and Protestant. The Protestant Reformation and the Catholic Counter-Reformation had a dramatic impact on the history of music. In the Calvinist version of Protestantism, congregations sang texts in the vernacular, rather than in Latin—particularly Psalms that adhered rigidly to the Bible. The texts were rhymed, metrical translations of Psalm texts that were published in **psalters** (see chapter 4). Among the best-known and most widely used psalters were the *French Psalter* (1562), the *Scottish Psalter* (1564), and the *Ainsworth Psalter* (1612). Editions of these books became important sources of hymn singing in American churches, beginning with the *Ainsworth Psalter*, which the Pilgrims brought to New England in 1620.

In 1534, the Church of England separated from the Roman Catholic Church, paving the way for even more church music to be sung in the vernacular. The anthem, sung in English, became the Anglican counterpart of the Latin motet.

Of course, the Roman Catholic Church countered with its own reforms (the Counter-Reformation). Palestrina's music is considered especially important because it established a model for making liturgical music more worshipful and dignified and easier to understand.

Featured Composers

One of the earliest known composers is Hildegard of Bingen (1098–1179), a nun, abbess, mystic, poet, writer on medical and scientific matters, and composer of

77 religious songs, numerous chants, and a lengthy music drama. Although she lived in Germany at a time when women were forbidden to teach or hold authority over men, many of her song texts were focused on women, inspiring them to exercise power in a material world.

By the end of the Renaissance, numerous composers, some well known and widely performed today, were successful and influential in the development of Western classical music. Three of the greatest are discussed on pages 206–208. Others include Orlando di Lasso, Thomas Tallis, Tómas Luis de Victoria, Thomas Morley, and John Dowland.

Listening Guide No. 50

A close-up photo of a lute, a widely used instrument in the late Renaissance. Many variations and uses of the lute exist, particularly as a folk instrument in many nations and cultures. Such instruments may look like a lute, play like a lute, and sound like a lute but will have a different name. The unknown lutenist pictured above is not the performer of "The Frog Galliard" described in this guide.

"The Frog Galliard"

CD2, Track 19, 2:02

Composer: John Dowland (1563–1626).

Performer: Jakob Lindberg, lutenist. Recorded in 1995.

Genre: Song for solo lute.

Context: John Dowland was an English composer who wrote almost 90 lute songs and many other pieces that include the lute. This galliard is derived from Dowland's song "Now, O Now I Needs Must Part." A galliard is a lively dance in triple meter.

Jakob Lindberg was born in Sweden, developed his first serious interest in music from the Beatles (according to Lindberg's own liner notes accompanying this recording), and studied lute at the Royal Academy of Music in London.

Goals

Identify (1) the original theme, (2) phrases in which this theme is repeated, (3) the several contrasting phrases, and (4) the phrases having an antecedent-consequent relationship.

Follow the bass line, and determine how consistent it is from phrase to phrase.

Describe the relationship of melodic contour to phrase structure.

Listening Guide –Continued   No. 50

Describe techniques of ornamentation evident in this music.
Describe the aesthetic mood of this music.

Guide

Triple meter at a moderate tempo. Essentially **diatonic.** Eight phrases of eight bars each, grouped in four phrase groups.

0:00	Phrases 1–2	Antecedent phrase; a descending motive with a melodic line rising in pitch then returning down to the cadence; open cadence at the end of the first phrase; the consequent phrase similar to the first but ends on a closed cadence
0:30	Phrases 3–4	Antecedent-consequent pattern; a variation of the previous material
0:59	Phrase 5	In a new key; a new melodic motive with the same style and texture
1:15	Phrase 6	Almost an exact repeat of the first two phrases
1:30	Phrases 7–8	Seventh phrase derived from the fifth phrase; ritard and descending line to final cadence

Reflections

Compare these plucked sounds with those of modern and more familiar-sounding instruments, such as the guitar or banjo.

Discuss the technique of variation in music.

Which parts of this music would be considered relatively simple and which parts relatively complex?

Listening Guide   No. 51

"If Ye Love Me"
CD2, Track 20, 1:58

Composer: Thomas Tallis (c. 1510–1586) for the Anglican liturgy.
Performer: The Tallis Scholars; Peter Phillips, director.
Genre: Anglican anthem.
Context: Anglican music is a product of the Reformation.

–Continued

Listening Guide –Continued   No. 51

Goals

Describe the vocal quality and interaction of voices (vocal textures).

Recognize shifting textures (homophony, polyphony).

Recognize clear cadences using common chord progressions (not common in Tallis's time).

Guide

A cappella. Pure, unadorned vocal quality. Flowing, gentle quality. A mix of homophonic and polyphonic textures.

If ye love me, keep my commandments,	Homophonic setting; chordal
And I will pray the Father,	Polyphonic setting; points of imitation; no clear V–I cadence
And He shall give you another comforter,	Polyphonic setting; points of imitation; a clear V–I cadence
That He may abide with you forever,	Polyphonic setting; points of imitation; open cadence on V
E'en the spirit of truth.	Polyphonic setting; points of imitation; closed cadence (V–I); last two phrases repeated; open and closed cadences; ritard at the end

Reflections

What is the primary function of this music? In what other ways can it appropriately be used?

Describe your aesthetic reactions to this music and the reasons for those reactions.

Is Renaissance choral music best sung in Latin?

Josquin des Prez   Josquin (c. 1440–1521) was born in the border region between France and what is now Belgium. He became a successful court musician and composer, particularly in Italy. Much of his music was published in printed collections; it includes 18 masses, 100 motets, and 70 secular songs with French texts (chansons).

Because the mass offered few opportunities for experimentation, Josquin used the motet to create his most innovative and influential works. In his motets, he was able to use a variety of texts and to develop a new compositional style with flowing melodies, rich harmonies, and less restricted rhythms. Through this music, he was able to convey a humanistic attitude—an attitude of the Renaissance—that provided a wide range of expression.

Josquin's genius lay in his ability to combine the intricacies of polyphonic composition with emotional expression. In so doing, he was able to transcend the limits of the musical language of his time. He was one of the great composers of the Renaissance.

Giovanni Pierluigi da Palestrina Palestrina (c. 1525–1594) was born near Rome, where he spent his entire professional life as a choirmaster and composer. He spent his last 24 years at St. Peter's Cathedral. His music is primarily sacred and includes 102 masses, 450 motets and other liturgical compositions, and 56 spiritual madrigals with Italian texts.

Palestrina's music is characterized by its purity (detached from secular influences) and its appropriateness to the formal ritual of the Roman Catholic liturgy. It serves as the model of the best in sixteenth-century imitative counterpoint, capturing the essence of the conservative elements of the Counter-Reformation. Palestrina set out to show through his music that polyphony is not necessarily incompatible with a reverent spirit or an understanding of the text.

Palestrina's contrapuntal texture is not overly elaborate; his melodies are diatonic, mostly stepwise, and easily singable. A large number of his sacred polyphonic pieces are for four voices, each given equal importance. **Cadences** (ends of phrases)

This portrait shows Giovanni Pierluigi da Palestrina, sixteenth-century Italian composer

overlap because of the polyphonic textures. Palestrina incorporates much chordal, homorhythmic writing with clearly perceivable chord progressions. These sections end with strong, full cadences that generate tonic-dominant relationships and clear tonal centers. His compositions signal a shift away from modal writing and foreshadow the emerging major-minor tonal system that would become fully established in the seventeenth century.

Giovanni Gabrieli   Gabrieli (c. 1557–1612) was the organist and choirmaster at St. Mark's Cathedral in Venice from 1585 until his death. He was also an exemplary composer of sacred works for multiple choirs and for combinations of voices and wind and string instruments.

Performances by multiple choirs positioned in different areas of a church did not originate with Gabrieli and did not begin in Venice, but they flourished in Venice because of the design of St. Mark's and the receptiveness of the people to the grandiose music of multiple choirs with contrasting instrumental sonorities. In his music for multiple choirs, Gabrieli used the antiphonal dialogue technique (echo) and chordal homorhythmic writing contrasted with rich contrapuntal textures. His music places him at the border between two historical eras. Like Josquin, he was a master of the older polyphonic Renaissance style whose use of contrasting sonorities foreshadowed essential qualities of the Baroque era to follow.

Listening Guide   No. 52

"Jubilate Deo"

CD2, Track 21, 3:35

Composer: Giovanni Gabrieli (c. 1557–1612).

Performer: The Canadian Brass and the Berlin Philharmonic Brass.

Genre: Motet.

Context: This motet, originally composed for eight voices, was published in 1613 in Venice. It is not a polychoral motet (a piece for two or more separate choirs—see page 199), but a piece for eight separate parts. Listeners, however, will perceive the effect of polychoral writing in the contrasting sounds of instruments, such as trumpets and horns and upper and lower brass instruments.

This is a transcription. It is common to transcribe pieces so that they can be performed in a medium (such as brass instruments here) different from the original (voices). The notes are identical to the original, so only the timbre and the spirit have changed. The brass quality and the spirited performance change the mood from the typically more somber, slower sacred motet to the almost dancelike character of this instrumental version.

Listening Guide –Continued   No. 52

Goals

Recognize motives and points of imitation.
Describe the varying textures.
Describe the rhythmic characteristics and metric organization.
Recognize the syncopated motives.
Identify the sounds of the trumpets, horns, trombones, and tubas.
Recognize the sectional organization of this motet.

Guide

Count in duple meter, two beats to the bar, at a moderate tempo.

Part 1
0:00	Bar 1	First motive stated by the trumpet; immediately imitated by the second trumpet; ascending scale; descending leap
	Bar 3	Descending, stepwise motive in a quick dotted rhythm
	Bar 5	Fast ascending motive; tuba enters
0:11	Bar 9	Quiet second theme with a syncopated motive begins in the horns; it ends with a series of loud separated chords preparing the return of another quiet, syncopated motive in the horns; the last passage of this part begins with a three-note motive featuring a descending skip followed by very clipped dotted notes; a strong cadence ends the first part

Part 2
1:07   Soft, four-note, stepwise motive, beginning with a pickup, appears in quick repetitions; followed by a soft syncopated passage, repeated at a higher pitch level; this is extended in full texture without syncopation to a cadence

Part 3
1:45   This part starts with the melody in the horns, in a thin texture; it continues with material derived from previous motives; this extended passage concludes on a strong cadence, followed immediately by a soft passage with slower rhythmic movement

–Continued

Listening Guide –Continued   No. 52

Part 4

2:43   The first of two alternating passages enters with a loud descending pattern: five bars in a fast triple meter, counted in one, with no cadence; this is answered by a four-beat passage at a slightly faster pulse, highlighted by repetitions of a descending, two-note motive, ending on a strong cadence; after two alternations of these passages, the motet ends on a strong IV–I cadence

Reflections

In what ways is this piece polyphonic, homophonic, or both?

Compare and contrast this motet with the previous polyphonic pieces.

Typically, motets are sacred polyphonic choral compositions. Describe your reaction to this instrumental version.

Summary

Although the beginning of Western music can be traced to ancient civilizations, our examination of Western music starts with the beginning of Christianity and the liturgy of the Roman Catholic Church. Gregorian chant, in common use in the church since about 500 C.E., represents the first body of music literature in Western civilization.

The addition of a second line and then a third or more lines to Gregorian chant created polyphonic texture. By the sixteenth century, the texture had stabilized at four or five parts, and most polyphonic compositions were created independently of a chant. The development of notation facilitated this kind of composition. Notation allowed composers to communicate more complex music so that others could perform it. By 1600, advances in printing had greatly facilitated the dissemination and preservation of music. Printing also greatly expanded the communication of information and ideas about music.

The Renaissance saw the first professional composers and performers of classical music—that is, people who created and made music for their livelihood. The initial employers were the churches; later, the aristocracy became important employers of musicians. Creators of music became known for their talent and their contributions. The most outstanding of them are among the best-known composers today.

The main genres after Gregorian chant were choral settings of the Mass, the Renaissance motet, and Italian and English madrigals. Instrumental music was used mainly to accompany dancing and folk and popular songs. When instrumental music did exist as a separate entity, it was patterned after choral music. No distinct instrumental genres had yet emerged.

This early period of Western music, dominated by the influence of the Roman Catholic Church, culminated in the golden age of choral music—the music of Josquin, Palestrina, and Gabrieli.

The Protestant Reformation opened new directions in sacred music: Music in Protestant churches was sung in the vernacular in hymn style by the congregation rather than chanted in Latin by the priest or sung by the choir as in the Roman Catholic Church. The Reformation also began the rich tradition of Protestant polyphonic choral music, much of it based on hymn or chorale melodies, in much the same way that earlier polyphonic music was based on Gregorian chants.

10 *Music of the Baroque Period (1600–1750)*

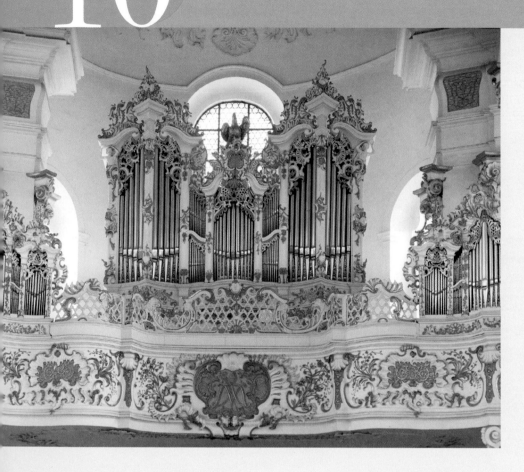

In This Chapter

What are the most prominent genres of the Baroque period?

What are the most prominent compositional techniques?

Who are the best-known composers of the Baroque era?

What are the components of Baroque opera?

Where can you hear Baroque music today?

During the Baroque period, music flourished in the regions that are now Italy, France, Germany, and England. The era was marked by pomp and splendor, a dynamic and dramatic spirit, and artistic expressions full of color and movement. It was romantic and grandioso, an age of innovation and adventure. This era saw major contributions in science, philosophy, and the arts from individuals such as Galileo, Newton, Descartes, Spinoza, Milton, Rubens, and Rembrandt.

Not only the churches but also the aristocratic courts were major patrons of the arts during this time. The rulers of the royal courts were wealthy monarchs who built magnificent palaces and maintained court composers and musicians for orchestras, chapel choirs, and opera companies. Although folk music, entertainment music, and music for churches remained popular, secular classical music abounded, performed mostly for the courts and the upper class.

In addition, some city governments joined the churches and courts as centers of music and culture and as employers of musicians. Musicians were needed to meet the demand for church music, entertainment at the courts, and festivals, ceremonies, and other public occasions in the cities. Audiences were interested in and enthusiastic about the music of local contemporary composers.

During this era, Protestant churches became firmly established and added significantly to the repertoire of Western music. Protestant music involved a significant shift away from Renaissance polyphonic pieces that were sung in Latin and based on Gregorian chants or other known melodies. They shifted to various compositional forms based on the Lutheran chorale. Among these forms were the following:

- Lutheran **chorale** melodies sung by a congregation in unison and in the vernacular. These were analogous to modern hymn tunes.

- Polyphonic settings of chorale melodies performed by a choir, with the text in the vernacular.
- Chorale harmonizations in a simple, chordal, homophonic, **strophic,** hymnlike style for congregational singing. (These existed by the end of the seventeenth century.)

The Baroque period gave us the beginnings of opera, which incorporated the aria and recitative to help carry the dramatic action forward. This period brought a proliferation of keyboard works for harpsichord and organ, the fugue as the primary polyphonic compositional technique, the oratorio and cantata as important choral genres, and the concerto as an important instrumental genre.

Goals for Listening

In this chapter, you will continue to develop your understanding of polyphonic and homophonic textures, melismatic and syllabic settings of text, and melodic embellishment and **ornamentation.**

Musical Characteristics

New techniques of composition, new musical forms, the development of opera and the orchestra, and the establishment of the major-minor tonal system are hallmarks of the Baroque period. It now was common for composers to write music with specific tone colors and instruments in mind. Judging from the music composed during the late Baroque period (the first half of the eighteenth century), we can see that instrumentalists became more proficient than ever before, placing greater emphasis on technical skill and virtuosity. Organists and other keyboard performers added to the notated music by improvising harmonies or embellishing a melodic line according to certain prescribed practices.

During the Baroque period, many genres and forms emerged, particularly for keyboards and other instruments that remain in use today. Many of the instruments and musical sounds that we know and feel comfortable with came into common use during this period.

Texture

A significant development in the Baroque period was the emphasis on harmonic or chordal writing (*homophonic* texture), with one predominant melody and subordinate lines or an accompaniment (harmonic background). This was a change from the older style of composition that emphasized the combination of two or more equal melodic lines (*polyphonic* texture). Composers still wrote polyphonic music, but many now created music with homophonic texture, an essential ingredient in the development of opera. By the late Baroque, polyphonic textures were common in instrumental and keyboard music, as well as in sacred choral works.

Major-Minor Tonal System

Another important development was the major-minor tonal system. The basis of composition shifted from the system of church **modes** to the major-minor tonal system (**tonality**)—the system of scales and keys that produces the sounds with which

Americans are most familiar. This is the system of the **tonic,** or chord of rest, and the **dominant,** or chord of movement.

We can hear the tonic, the stable home tone or tonal center of a key; and we can hear **modulation,** a change of tonality from a key of stability (the tonic) to a key of contrast or instability (frequently, but not always, the dominant). The tonal system allows for diatonic writing (notes in the key) and additional color and modulation through chromatic or altered tones (notes outside the key). Much Baroque music is diatonic.

Continuo

The **continuo** had a significant role in Baroque performance practice. It typically involved two instruments: a keyboard (organ or harpsichord) and a bass instrument (a cello or similar instrument). The keyboard player filled in or improvised harmonies based on chord symbols and a bass line. The player of the bass line (usually a cellist) played a simple, continuous, notated bass line that emphasized the principal notes of the harmonies or chords (a concept similar to the **walking bass** in jazz).

The keyboard improvisation is sometimes known as "realizing" harmonies (bringing them into reality, as a jazz pianist or guitarist does). By harmonically supporting one or more instrumental or vocal melodic lines, the continuo provided a harmonic basis for the new homophonic tonal (rather than modal) music.

A form of musical shorthand (chord symbols) was devised to assist the keyboard player. The notes of the chords were not written out; rather, numbers were placed below the notes of the bass line, identifying the chord tones so that the keyboardist could realize the harmonies. The shorthand was called **figured bass.** The bass line itself was known as **basso continuo.** Such improvisation expanded in scope, becoming a high art and a coveted skill among keyboard performers in the late Baroque period. See page 216 for an example of a continuo with figured bass.

Word Painting

Word painting began during the Renaissance as composers realized that music could convey the moods and meanings of a text, expressing a wide range of ideas and feelings. Triumph or resurrection, for example, might be described musically in a very different manner from death or crucifixion. During the Baroque period, the interest in word painting became more pronounced, and the technique became more sophisticated. Composers went to great lengths to depict not only specific images but also the emotions of a text, to mirror the text in the music as literally as possible.

Other Musical Characteristics

Baroque music is music of contrasts: of voices and instruments, of loudness and softness, of changes of key (modulations), of section A and section B as in a **da capo aria,** and of a small group of instruments and a large group within the same piece. Rhythm is regular, metric, and often energetic. A steady pulse is often maintained in the bass. Baroque pieces were sometimes derived from popular and court dances, and this practice increased the tendency toward a dynamic rhythm. Yet the strong metric feeling is in contrast to the free rhythm of the recitative and the free rhythm common in improvised passages, especially in keyboard works.

Figured bass—a musical shorthand—is the name given to the numbers below the bass line, as shown above. These numbers identify the chords and the chord tones that the keyboardist should play.

Melody is often perceived as a continuous expansion of an idea, without short, regular phrases. Dynamics (levels of loudness) are contrasting and abrupt, achieved by adding or taking away instruments or voices rather than by gradually changing the loudness of the music. This technique is known as *terraced dynamics*.

Instruments

During the Baroque period, for the first time in Western music, instruments became equal in importance to the voice, for both composers and listeners. Orchestras were made up of instruments similar to those of today, but there existed no standard set of instruments or instrumentation. The Baroque orchestra was not as large or as varied as the modern symphony orchestra, and the instruments generally were smaller and quieter than their modern counterparts. The primary instruments were of the violin family plus trumpets, oboes, and flutes.

The lute was a popular plucked instrument, and the primary keyboard instruments were the harpsichord and organ. The fortepiano, forerunner of the modern piano, had been invented but was not well enough developed to be widely used during the Baroque period.

Musical Forms and Genres

New musical forms or genres that developed in the Baroque period ranged from keyboard works and **chamber music** to multimovement orchestral pieces, large choral works, and operas. Older forms, of course, continued. Renaissance polyphony and imitative counterpoint were adapted to Baroque instrumental music.

This ornate, French harpsichord, built in 1681, is on display in the Victoria and Albert Museum in London.

Opera

The development of **opera,** around 1600, resulted from several factors:

- Renewed interest among scholars in the classical Greek tragedies and a desire among a small group of scholars in Italy to set dramatic works to music with costumes and staging.
- Heightened interest generally in drama and theatrical elements in music.
- The tendency in the early Baroque period for composers to use music to depict the meanings of words and the emotions of the text.
- A shift from polyphonic to homophonic texture (an accompanied melody) that presented words in an understandable manner (an expressive solo singing style).
- Creation of the aria and recitative, which carried the dramatic action forward and developed the plot. Arias also provided a way to display vocal virtuosity.

The first operas were produced around 1600 in Italy. The most important and durable early operas were *Orfeo* by the Italian composer Claudio Monteverdi, produced in 1608, and *Dido and Aeneas* by the English composer Henry Purcell, produced in 1689. In the late Baroque, the great German composer George Frideric Handel wrote operas in the Italian style that were produced in England. Also, England saw the beginnings of ballad opera, the genre that satirized Italian opera. Ballad operas included popular tunes or ballads and enjoyed tremendous popularity both in Europe and, later, in the Americas.

Orchestral Works

The two orchestral forms that reached their peak in the late Baroque period were the **concerto** and the concerto grosso. The concerto featured one solo instrument playing

Angus Wood (Aeneas) and Deborah Humble (Dido) were photographed during a dress rehearsal of Purcell's *Dido and Aeneas*. This production took place in 2004 in Sydney, Australia.

with orchestra; the concerto grosso featured a small group of soloists, usually two or three. The element of contrast between the soloist or soloists and the orchestra was germane to these as well as other Baroque forms. Both concerto forms were in three movements—fast-slow-fast—with the slow movement in a contrasting key.

Listening Guide   No. 53

"When I Am Laid in Earth"
(Dido's Lament from *Dido and Aeneas*)
CD2, Track 22, 3:41

Composer: Henry Purcell (1659–1695).

Librettist: Nahum Tate.

Performer: Gillian Fisher, soprano, and The King's Consort (two violins, viola, cello, double bass, and chamber organ), directed by Robert King.

Genre: Opera aria.

Context: From *Dido and Aeneas,* the most famous seventeenth-century English opera, comes the era's most famous **aria.** Based on Virgil's *Aeneid,* the opera centers on two people who fall deeply in love. Aeneas is called away on "government business," and Dido cannot cope. This aria is her lament, after which she dies. The opera's premiere took place at a girls' school outside London in 1689.

Goals

Follow the text of this solemn, mournful aria from Purcell's only full opera.

Recognize the structural principle tying this piece together: a **ground bass** (sometimes called merely a *ground*)—here, 11 repetitions of a four-bar pattern in the bass line. Notice that the vocal phrases do not always coincide with the ground patterns. Sometimes the vocal line begins at the end of the ground. Each ground pattern leads to a strong V–I cadence.

Guide

The introduction to the aria is an instrumental statement of the ground. The first part of the pattern descends chromatically (in half steps).

The text follows:

When I am laid in earth, may my wrongs create
No trouble in Thy breast;
Remember me, but ah! Forget my fate.

Reflections

Describe how the ground pattern and the vocal line (including the text) each contribute to the mood of the aria–the lament.

Another widely used genre was the French **overture.** Originally intended to create a festive atmosphere as an opening to an opera, it later became an independent instrumental genre. The French overture was in two parts: the first in a slow, majestic, homophonic style and the second in a faster yet serious polyphonic style. The second part often ended with a reference to at least the rhythm of the opening section.

The **dance suite** was sometimes written for orchestra, sometimes for keyboards. It is a set of contrasting dances combined to form a single multimovement work. The main dances are the allemande, courante, sarabande, and gigue, but most dance suites have a flexible format that can accommodate other dances and perhaps movements other than dance forms.

Listening Guide   No. 54

Concerto Grosso, op. 6, no. 8
(*Christmas* Concerto) (IV, V, VI) (excerpt)
CD2, Tracks 23, 24, 25 (Part IV, 0:59; Part V, 1:31; Part VI, 1:23)

Composer: Arcangelo Corelli (1653–1713).
Performer: Kammerorchester Carl Philipp Emanuel Bach;
Hartmut Haenchen, conductor.
Genre: Concerto grosso.

Goals

Describe a Baroque instrumental style.

Identify the various meters, phrase structures, textures, and points of contrast and repetition.

Identify diatonic melody and harmony in each movement.

Compare the styles of the three movements.

Guide

Track 23

Movement IV:		Triple meter in a fast three or a moderately slow one; dancelike; crisp, rhythmic drive; diatonic in a major key; small string orchestra
0:00	Phrase group 1	8 bars; open cadence
		8 bars; open cadence
0:16	Phrase group 2	8 bars; open cadence
		12 bars with four-bar extension; closed cadence
0:37	Phrase group 3	Repeat of second phrase group

Track 24

Movement V:		Duple meter in a moderately fast two; starts with a pickup on the second beat; an aggressive, stylized dance

Listening Guide –*Continued*   No. 54

0:00	a	24 bars
	a	4 bars
	a	4 bars
	b	16 bars: ascending then descending motives with the last four bars repeated
0:23	a	24 bars: first section repeated with ornamentation
0:47	b	22 bars (11 + 11): contrasting style; ascending sequence in the second half
1:09	a	21 bars: first section repeated but modified after the first statement; ends with cadence on bar 20 followed by a one-bar extension and a ritard; moves directly to the sixth movement

Track 25

Movement VI "Pastorale" (excerpt):	In a slow two, with each beat subdivided in three (a 6/8 meter); the mood is quiet and pleasant
0:00	10 bars (5 + 5): second half; same mood but a different pitch area (around the dominant)
0:22	13 bars (5 + 8): first half of the melody in lower strings in the tonic key; second half of the melody in high strings with a descending sequence in two-bar patterns; ends in the key of the dominant
0:51	8 bars (2 + 2 + 4): two bars on the dominant; two bars on the tonic; four bars, descending contour to the key of the dominant
1:08	Quiet and sustained; fades in bar 5

Reflections

Notice the sudden changes in dynamics and thus the absence of gradual crescendos and decrescendos.

To what extent is this music homophonic? Polyphonic?

Chamber Music

The typical forms for a small number of instruments are the church **sonata** and the chamber sonata, both written for various combinations of instruments. Such sonatas typically included either one solo instrument with continuo (solo sonata, three performers) or two solo instruments with continuo (**trio sonata,** four performers).

These compositions usually had contrasting sections or movements, frequently in dance forms. The church sonata is usually a four-movement work in a slow-fast-slow-fast pattern. The chamber sonata is the ensemble form of the dance suite, although composers frequently incorporated additional dances or movements other than dances, such as a prelude or an aria.

This photograph shows an interior view of the Wieskirche (Wies Church) in Wies, Germany. The emphasis on ornate construction and decoration was common in the Baroque era.

Keyboard Works

Important single-movement keyboard compositions of the Baroque were toccatas, preludes, fantasias, and fugues; they were written for the harpsichord or clavichord (forerunners of the piano) or for the organ. The toccata and prelude were improvisatory in character, sometimes having a contrapuntal middle section and sometimes paired with a fugal composition in a performance. The fantasia was a larger, more complex work that might present a series of contrapuntal variations on a single theme.

Fugue is a compositional technique that may be used within any composition but often describes the structure of an entire piece (see Listening Guide 55). A fugue is an imitative contrapuntal form built on one or two themes. The theme is stated alone and then restated, usually in two or three other voices accompanied by intricate contrapuntal lines in voices that previously had stated the theme. This material continues in contrapuntal interplay, including restatements of the original theme, material based on motives of the original theme, and new but closely related themes. The fugue represents the highest form of Baroque polyphonic music.

Other keyboard works include the chorale prelude, an organ work based on a chorale tune that serves as a theme for a set of variations; the passacaglia and chaconne, both of which use a repeated bass line (ground bass) as the basis of the composition; and the dance suite, discussed previously as an orchestral genre.

Listening Guide   No. 55

Fugue in C Minor, no. 2, from *The Well-Tempered Clavier*, Book 1
CD2, Track 26, 1:36

Composer: Johann Sebastian Bach (1685–1750).
Performer: Davitt Moroney, harpsichord.
Genre: Fugue.

Goals

Recognize the five-note motive, polyphonic texture, and entering voices.
Recognize contrasting patterns and motives.

Guide

Count in a slow four. The subject (theme) is based on a five-note motive that opens the fugue. The music starts with a two-note pickup on the second half of the first beat; thus, the first beat of music falls just after the downbeat (the motive begins: "and a two").

The letters A, B, and C (below) identify the approximate initial entrances of each voice. The first statement of the subject (A) is in the middle voice (compared with the pitch areas to follow), the second entrance (B) is in the high voice, and the third entrance (C) is in the low voice.

```
(1) – 2 – 3 – 4 – 5 – 6 – 7 – 8 –
     A     B          C
```

After the entrances are made, the subject is developed in a variety of ways, including varying the subsequent entrances of the motive and making the setting more chromatic and unstable. Ritards lead to the final cadence.

Reflections

Listen for the five-note motive throughout the piece as Bach has developed the fugue. Follow the "voices" even when you are listening to instrumental music.

Be aware of the sound of the minor tonality and the shift of the last chord from the expected minor sound to major, offering a surprise chord quality in the context of the previous minor tonality.

This fugue features complex, contrapuntal interplay according to principles common to many fugues from the Baroque era.

What are the emotional and intellectual qualities of a fugue?

Choral Music

The two major choral forms of the Baroque period were the **cantata** and the **oratorio**. Both were dramatic forms, but the oratorio was of much larger proportions and usually was longer and more complex. The oratorio was intended for concert performance, the cantata for a worship service. Both usually were sacred works, and the cantata became an integral part of the German Lutheran service. Secular oratorios and cantatas did exist, however. One of the best-known secular cantatas is J. S. Bach's "Coffee" Cantata.

Cantatas and oratorios consisted of vocal solos (arias and recitatives), solo ensembles, choruses, and instrumental accompaniment. The **aria** typically was more songlike, melodic, and metric than the recitative. The **recitative** had a more important part in oratorios than in cantatas. As in opera, it was an important technique describing the action in a way that all listeners could understand. It was sung in free rhythm, declaiming words in a natural inflection with a minimal accompaniment of simple chords. Soloists often introduced their arias by means of the recitative. A narrator as a dramatic character was sometimes included, particularly in the oratorio. The solo ensemble was a small group of solo voices.

The choruses (sung by a choir) were often contrapuntal, even fugal. The accompaniment for the cantata was frequently an organ, occasionally with a small group of other instruments. An organ or an orchestra accompanied the oratorio.

Listening Guide   No. 56

Le Sommeil d'Ulisse (excerpt)

CD2, Track 27, 2:53

Composer: Elisabeth-Claude Jacquet de la Guerre (c. 1666–1729).
Performer: John Ostendorf, baritone, and the Bronx Chamber Ensemble, conducted by Johannes Somary.
Genre: French cantata.
Context: These miniature movements represent many compositional practices of the Baroque era.

Goals

Compare and contrast recitatives and arias.
Recognize homophonic texture and contrasting textures (full orchestra or small ensemble).
Describe the basso continuo.
Recognize dotted rhythms.

Guide

Three parts of a French cantata for voice, strings, and continuo:

Listening Guide –Continued   No. 56

0:00   1. Prelude (instrumental)
            In a moderately fast four; after a strong descending opening
            motive, a second passage starting in the third bar has a stepwise
            ascending contour, then descends; the full orchestra contrasts
            with the sound of a few instruments; the melody is supported
            harmonically by the bassoon and the harpsichord

0:23   The contrasting lighter section features dotted rhythms and
            short, echolike question-answer fragments; a ritard leads to the
            final cadence

1:07   2. Recitatif (vocal, with continuo)
            A flexible pulse accommodates the rhythm of the text; very
            thin-textured accompaniment

1:43   3. "Air de Mer" ("Song of the Sea") (vocal, with continuo)
            In a strong triple meter; crisp, dotted rhythms prevail in the basso
            continuo; a ritard leads to the final cadence

Reflections

Listen for diatonic, **conjunct** melodies; series of chord progressions; and broken
chords in the harpsichord accompaniment during the recitative.

The French cantata was lively, dramatic chamber entertainment. Its plots, often
mythological, were usually sketchy, but its music was elegant, compact, and
refined.

Featured Composers

The most famous Baroque composers, Bach and Handel, rank among the greatest
creators of Western classical music.

Johann Sebastian Bach

A member of an illustrious German musical family, Bach (1685–1750) lived and
worked in Germany. The first part of his professional career was mainly in Weimar,
where he was court organist and chamber musician to the duke of Weimar and
composed his most significant organ music. Bach then went to Cöthen, where
he was chapelmaster and director of chamber music for the prince of Anhalt; at
Cöthen he composed important chamber and orchestral music. He ended his career
in Leipzig, where he was cantor of St. Thomas's Church and School and composed
his monumental choral works.

Bach was a master of Baroque forms and genres, and in his work these forms realized their fullest potential. The organ music he composed remains among the best

This monument to Johann Sebastian Bach is located outside the Thomaskirche in Leipzig, Germany. For much of Bach's life, he taught, composed music, played organ, and directed church choirs in Leipzig.

of organ literature. His tonal counterpoint in choral music, chord progressions in chorale harmonizations, and fugues for keyboard instruments continue to be studied, perhaps more than those of any other composer. Among Bach's most impressive gifts was his phenomenal grasp of the technique of composition, particularly his mastery of the grand art of polyphony and the newer art of tonal harmony.

Bach's most important and enduring works include Mass in B Minor, *St. Matthew Passion,* and church cantatas, of which he composed more than 300; numerous chorale preludes, toccatas, fugues, and other works for organ or harpsichord; *The Art of Fugue, Goldberg Variations,* and *The Well-Tempered Clavier* for keyboard instruments; six suites for unaccompanied cello; and six *Brandenburg* Concertos for various soloists and orchestra. Bach's music was not performed much in the years immediately after he died, but it was rediscovered in the early nineteenth century. Today, his music is played in churches and concert halls throughout the world.

Listening Guide

No. 57

Cantata no. 140, *Wachet auf* (*Sleepers, Awake!*) (VII, I)

CD2, Tracks 28, 29 (Part VII, 1:24; Part I, 2:18)

Composer: Johann Sebastian Bach (1685–1750).

Performer: American Bach Soloists.

Genre: Church cantata.

Context: Bach composed this cantata in 1731. "Wachet auf," the chorale tune, was composed by Philipp Nicolai (1556–1608). This cantata has seven parts:

  I. Instrumental introduction and polyphonic setting of the chorale tune

  II. Recitative—tenor

 III. Duet—soprano and baritone

 IV. Chorus—based on the chorale tune

  V. Recitative—baritone

 VI. Duet—soprano and baritone

VII. Final chorus—stately chorale setting (see pages 228–229)

The cantata was written for four-part choir: soprano, alto, tenor, and bass. The instrumentation specified was horn, two oboes, taille (alto oboe), violino piccolo (small violin), two violins, viola, and continuo (cello, bassoon, and organ).

    In this Listening Guide, part I of the cantata, a polyphonic setting of the chorale tune, and part VII, the chorale, are presented in reverse order so that the chorale setting may be heard first.

Goals

Recognize the hymnlike setting of a Lutheran chorale.

Recognize a homophonic piece based on a chorale tune. Be able to identify the chorale melody and to describe its relationship to the other voices.

Recognize a polyphonic chorus based on a chorale tune. Be able to identify the chorale melody and to describe its relationship to the other voices.

Guide

Track 28

Part VII:	The final chorus of the cantata—a chorale setting written in a hymnlike style with all voice parts moving in nearly the same rhythm; most of the parts that do move against the primary rhythm are in the bass voice; the form is a a b; count in a moderately slow four (a slash denotes a break in the forward energy, either a pause within the phrase or a phrase ending)

–Continued

Listening Guide –Continued   No. 57

Homophonic setting of the chorale melody "Wachet auf," from part VII of Cantata no. 140 by J. S. Bach.

Listening Guide –Continued　　　No. 57

–Continued

Listening Guide –Continued   No. 57

Section A	1–2–3–/–4–5–6–/–7–8–/	(three phrases)
Section A	1–2–3–/–4–5–6–/–7–8–/	(three phrases)
Section B	–1–2–/–3–4–/–5–/–6–7–8–9–/	(four partial phrases)

Track 29

Part I:		The instrumental introduction to the cantata and a poly-phonic setting of the first two sections of the chorale tune; in triple meter, counted in a moderate three
0:00		The instrumental introduction begins with repeated dotted rhythms in an alternating, question-answer dialogue in the upper strings and oboes, followed by ascending scalar melodic patterns in the oboe and violin; the continuo provides the harmonic basis and rhythmic impulse
0:28	Phrase 1	The voices begin on the final cadence of the intro-duction; the chorale tune is heard in the soprano voice and horn in a simple, slow rhythm; phrases are separated by instrumental material, and each phrase is always surrounded by faster-moving, intricate, in-dependent lines with much imitation, usually in short, melodic fragments
0:50	Phrase 2	
1:14	Phrase 3	
2:00	Phrase 4—fade	

Reflections

Be aware of outer voices (sopranos and basses) and inner voices (altos and tenors). Notice the moving parts in which other voices move for a beat or two in faster rhythm over the notes of the soprano melody.

Identify recurring motives, imitation, and contrasting sounds. Be aware of the various layers of sounds—that is, the various lines, whether vocal or instrumental.

The polyphonic chorus is based on the chorale tune. It is the most elaborate and complex of all the movements of this cantata. Notice that the tune is in a slower rhythm than the other parts, and its phrases are separated.

George Frideric Handel

A native of Germany, Handel (1685–1759) mastered the Italian musical style, particularly in opera, and achieved his most notable successes during the nearly 50 years he spent in England. Unlike Bach, Handel was internationally famous during his lifetime. Initially, he was known as a composer and producer of Italian operas in England, but his most lasting fame was as a composer of oratorios. His best-known work is *Messiah*.

George Frideric Handel was a German composer who spent
most of his life in England and composed Italian opera.

Handel is also well known for his instrumental music in almost all the usual
Baroque forms—notably, concerto grossos, harpsichord suites, organ concertos, and
two orchestral pieces (now widely recorded): *Water Music* and *Music for the Royal
Fireworks*. Handel composed for a wide audience and became a master in the grand
style of the late Baroque.

Listening Guide   No. 58

Music for the Royal Fireworks (II, IV)
CD2, Tracks 30, 31 (Movement II, 2:00; Movement IV, 2:43)

Composer: George Frideric Handel (1685–1759).
Performer: Tafelmusik Baroque Orchestra.
Genre: Ceremonial music.
Context: Handel composed this work in 1749 to accompany a fireworks display
celebrating the end of the War of the Austrian Succession (1740–1748). It was
scored for large numbers of brass, wind, and percussion instruments, but not
many strings. The original ensemble may have been more like a band than an
orchestra. This piece has five movements:

  I. Ouverture
 II. Bourrée

–Continued

Listening Guide –Continued   No. 58

III. La Paix
IV. La Réjouissance
 V. Menuet I and II

Goals

Describe the mood of "Bourrée," and explain what evokes this mood.
Describe the mood of "La Réjouissance," and explain what evokes this mood.
Describe the instrumentation. How does it change throughout each movement?

Guide

Track 30

Movement II, "Bourrée": Duple meter at a moderate tempo; stately

0:00	a	winds only
0:12	a	section repeated
0:23	b	winds only
0:42	b	section repeated
1:00	a	strings
1:11	a	section repeated
1:22	b	strings
1:40	b	section repeated

Track 31

Movement IV, "La Réjouissance": Duple meter at a moderate tempo; brass, winds, and percussion dominate the sound

0:00	a	strings, brass, and percussion
0:18	a	section repeated—woodwinds and horns
0:35	b	strings, brass, and percussion
0:58	b	woodwinds and horns
1:20	a	all instruments
1:38	a	section repeated
1:55	b	all instruments
2:16	b	section repeated

Reflections

Imagine the performance **venue** for this music. Concert hall? Church? Arena? Salon?
Is this piece a work of art (art music)? Why or why not?
Compare this music with the other examples in this chapter. Which pieces did you like, and why?

Other Notable Composers

The most important composer of the early Baroque era was Claudio Monteverdi (1567–1643), known originally for his madrigals in Renaissance polyphonic style and later for more innovative madrigals. He was also known for operas composed in the new Baroque style. In addition to *Orfeo*, he wrote *The Return of Ulysses* and *The Coronation of Poppea*. All three are still performed today by university and professional opera companies for stage productions and recordings.

Any list of notable Baroque composers must also include the following individuals:

- Arcangelo Corelli (1653–1713) was a violin virtuoso known for his development of modern violin techniques, his trio sonatas, and his contribution to the concerto grosso form (see Listening Guide 54).
- François Couperin (1668–1733) was an important French composer of harpsichord music and chamber music and the author of an authoritative method book on playing the harpsichord.
- Elisabeth-Claude Jacquet de la Guerre (c. 1666–1729) was an immensely successful French composer and harpsichordist whose work is popular today, particularly her harpsichord works and cantatas (see Listening Guide 56).
- Henry Purcell (1659–1695) was England's foremost native composer of the seventeenth century. His success rested on numerous anthems and other religious works, trio sonatas, and his opera *Dido and Aeneas* (see Listening Guide 53).
- Antonio Vivaldi (1678–1741) was probably the most celebrated of all Italian composers. He wrote operas, oratorios, and church music, but his fame rests on his concerto grossos and solo concertos, of which he composed more than 400.
- Georg Philipp Telemann (1681–1767) was a prolific German composer of church music (masses, motets, oratorios, and more than a thousand cantatas), operas, keyboard pieces, and instrumental music (concertos, sonatas, overtures, and chamber music).

Summary

Sacred polyphonic choral music dominated Western music through the late Middle Ages and the Renaissance. The emphasis in the Baroque period was divided fairly equally between choral and instrumental music and between sacred and secular music.

The use of the major-minor tonal system, homophonic texture, and orchestral writing became standard practice during the Baroque period. Instruments as we know them today became common, laying the foundation for the symphony orchestra and chamber ensembles, such as the string quartet that became standard during the Classic period (see chapter 11).

The Baroque period also gave us the beginnings of opera, incorporating the aria and the recitative with their ability to carry the dramatic action forward. This period introduced a proliferation of keyboard works for harpsichord and organ, the fugue as the primary polyphonic compositional technique, the oratorio and cantata as important choral genres, and the concerto as an important instrumental genre.

Many Baroque-era composers are well known today: Corelli, Couperin, Lully, Monteverdi, Purcell, Telemann, and Vivaldi. But the giants were Johann Sebastian Bach and George Frideric Handel.

11 Music of the Classic Period (1750–1820)

Chapter Outline

The sounds of the **art music** created in the late eighteenth and early nineteenth centuries—in the Classic period—are familiar to Americans who listen to "classical" music (broadly defined) or have been exposed to it as part of their formal education. Many of the pieces and composers of this period are household words. This music is widely performed by school, community, and professional musical organizations; it is heard on so-called classical music radio stations; and American consumers frequently purchase such recordings. Even those who know very little about art music usually know something about Mozart, Haydn, and Beethoven, particularly through their works, such as Beethoven's Fifth Symphony and his *Moonlight* Sonata, Haydn's *Surprise* Symphony, and Mozart's *The Magic Flute* or *The Marriage of Figaro*.

The Classic period (1750–1820) is the beginning of the modern era. Developments during this time laid the groundwork for the musical practices of the next 150–200 years. Among these developments are the sonata, symphony, and string quartet; the instrumentation of the modern symphony orchestra; and public concerts available to everyone. The arts during the Classic period were centered in the royal courts and urban communities of Austria and Germany. This was a sophisticated, aristocratic society. The courts valued artistic and social status and demanded the best in entertainment. But this period also saw an increase in community concert halls and opera houses as music became more available to common people through public performances. Although Catholic and Protestant church music continued to be created, the church's influence on the direction of Western music declined. Instead, the Classic period saw a rise in instrumental music.

235

Goals for Listening

As you learn to identify and recognize by ear the themes, modulations, and repetitions that are typical of Classic-period music, you will find the following terms helpful:

- Dynamics: In music, **dynamics** refers to the loudness level: *forte* (loud), *piano* (soft), *mezzo piano* (medium soft), *crescendo* (gradually get louder), and *decrescendo* (gradually get softer).
- Form: The **form** is the shape or structure of a piece of music. Forms that are generic—that is, common in many musical styles—include the two-part or **binary** (a b) form and the three-part or **ternary** (a b a) form. An a a b a form is ternary because of its return to the theme. Among the more complex forms found in western European classical music are the sonata form, the minuet and trio, the rondo, and the theme and variations.
- Scales: A **scale** is an ascending or descending series of tones organized according to a specific pattern of **intervals**. In Western music, a piece is said to be **diatonic** if most of the tones of the piece are derived from a single scale. Frequently, notes that are not part of a standard scale are added to create interest and color. The addition of many nonscale tones may obscure the tonality of a piece and create a tonally unstable feeling; such music is said to be **chromatic**.
- Tempo: The **tempo** is the speed at which music is performed. To describe tempos or changes of tempo, musicians use terms such as *allegro* (fast), *andante* (moderate tempo), *largo* (slow), *accelerando* (get faster), *ritardando* or *ritard* (get slower), and *rubato* (interpret the music in a highly expressive manner).

Musical Characteristics

The Baroque period was a time of opulence, splendor, ornamentation, decoration, and emotional expression. In contrast, the Classic period reflected the emotional restraint, balance, clarity, symmetry, clear and precise formal structure, and simplicity of the Age of Reason.

In classical music, melody predominates and all other factors are subordinate to it. Thus, to the composer of the Classic era, homophonic texture was much more important than contrapuntal or polyphonic writing. Melodies were typically lyrical, with smooth, stepwise contours; phrases ended with obvious tonic-dominant cadences; and diatonic melodies prevailed and, to a large extent, reflected the underlying harmonies. Rhythm was for the most part uncomplicated and predictable.

Music was tonal, in a major or minor key, for harmonic practices were a logical extension and refinement of the tonal system established during the Baroque period. Tonality was clear. Chord progressions used the most common, most basic harmonies, which to a large extent are easily recognizable. The chords revolved around what had come to be common practice in the use of the primary tonic, **subdominant**, and dominant chords, with the continued use of dissonances, such as the dominant seventh chord, that demanded resolution.

Modulations to new keys were common, and key relationships—from one phrase group to the next, from one section to the next, and even from one movement of an extended work to the next—took on new significance. New keys introduced instability that was resolved only when the tonal center returned to the original tonic. This interest resulted in a strong preference for the a b a structure, with section a in the tonic key, section b in a contrasting key, and then a return to the tonic key. The concepts of **unity** and **variety,** of contrast and return, were valued and applied most commonly in the forms developed during the Classic period.

Instruments

The Classic period was an age of instrumental music. The families of instruments in modern orchestras and bands became standard: strings, woodwinds, brass, and percussion. The Baroque continuo and figured bass were no longer needed, for all parts were now written out. The pianoforte (a forerunner of the piano) displaced the harpsichord in popularity and was used as a solo instrument or as an equal member in chamber ensembles.

The instrumentation of the modern orchestra and of the string quartet and other chamber ensembles became standard during this period. The orchestra included a string section (consisting of first and second violins, violas, cellos, and double basses), winds in pairs (flutes, clarinets, oboes, bassoons, trumpets, horns, and sometimes trombones), and timpani, the only widely used percussion instrument. Chamber ensembles consisted of a wide variety of string, wind, and piano combinations, usually ranging from three to eight musicians (trios to octets). Typical ensembles included the string quartet (two violins, one viola, one cello), piano trio (violin, cello, and piano), and piano quintet (string quartet plus piano).

Genres

The genres of the Classic period emerged from Baroque-period genres, then stabilized sufficiently in terminology and concept to become models of formal structure on which much music would be based for the next 150 years. The descriptions given in this chapter apply to common practice; there are, however, many exceptions to each generalization.

The Emerson Quartet is seen performing in New York City in 2004. Members of the group are Eugene Drucker, violin; Lawrence Dutton, viola; David Finckel, cello; and Philip Setzer, violin.

Instrumental

The primary instrumental genres of the Classic period are multimovement works, usually with three or four movements: the **sonata** for one or two instruments, the **symphony** and **concerto** for orchestra, and **chamber music** (for a string quartet or other small chamber music group). In chamber music, each part is played on only one instrument. In orchestral music, more than one instrument may play each part—for example, 6 double basses might play the bass part, or 12 violins might play the violin part.

Typical multimovement works have the following arrangement and structure:

Movement I	Fast: sonata form.
Movement II	Slow: A broad a b a form is common; sometimes a theme-and-variations form.
Movement III	Dance: usually a minuet and trio or, later, a scherzo and trio; this movement was typically omitted in most three-movement sonatas and in concertos.
Movement IV	Fast: usually a rondo; sometimes sonata form.

The sonata is a work for one or two instruments. Solo piano sonatas are the most common. Sonatas for two instruments are usually written for an orchestral instrument and piano; of these, violin sonatas are the most common. It is not accurate to describe sonatas as works for solo instrument with piano accompaniment because the piano is usually as important as the other instrument.

The concerto features a solo instrument playing with a full symphony orchestra. It is usually in three movements. A dance movement is not included, for the texture of solo with orchestra does not lend itself to the spirit of dance. A Classic-period concerto often features a **cadenza:** The orchestra stops, and the soloist engages in an extended virtuoso passage highlighting his or her technical abilities. The cadenza has an improvisatory character and may include long passages in free rhythm.

The symphony is a work for full symphony orchestra, usually in four movements and featuring the varied tone colors of all the orchestral instruments.

The most common chamber music ensemble of the Classic period is the string quartet (two violins, viola, and cello). As mentioned previously, chamber music as a genre encompasses works for a variety of small ensembles, from trios to octets, including some that combine strings and piano and some that involve wind instruments.

Vocal, Choral, and Opera

The primary vocal, choral, and dramatic genre of the Classic period was opera. Composers continued to write oratorios, masses, and other sacred choral works, but by the late eighteenth and nineteenth centuries, these genres no longer reigned supreme as they had in the time of Bach and Handel.

The opera of the Classic period strengthened the relationship between music and drama and between singers and orchestra. Instead of the Baroque opera's recitatives, arias, and choruses, which interrupted the natural flow of the dramatic action, Classic opera presented ongoing music and continuous drama arranged in scenes. The recitative and aria were still used (see Listening Guide 59), but their accompaniment was more complex; it was intended to enhance the atmosphere of the text rather than be totally subservient to the singer. The recitative provided narrative, and the aria provided commentary on the plot. Solo ensembles and choruses, along with staging, costumes, and orchestral accompaniment, enhanced the plot and added musical and dramatic interest. In the Classic period more than in the Baroque, the opera orchestra was used to create a mood that would support the drama. The orchestra was given lyrical melodies rather than mere accompaniment patterns, and it became a more integral part of the drama.

The most famous operas of the Classic period are those by Mozart, including *The Marriage of Figaro*, *The Magic Flute*, and *Don Giovanni*. Classical choral works include Haydn's oratorio *The Creation*, Mozart's *Requiem*, and Beethoven's *Missa Solemnis*.

Listening Guide   No. 59

"E Susanna non vien! . . . Dove sono," from *The Marriage of Figaro*, Act III

CD2, Track 32, 6:41

Composer: Wolfgang Amadeus Mozart (1756–1791).

Performer: Karita Mattila, soprano, and the Maggio Musicale Fiorentino Orchestra; Zubin Mehta, conductor

Genre: Opera; recitative and aria.

Context: This is Italian *opera buffa,* a type of comic opera. The libretto, by Lorenzo da Ponte, the imperial court poet in Vienna, was based on Beaumarchais's play *Le Mariage de Figaro.* The story involves love and conflict between the aristocracy and lower classes. The complex plot is laid out in act 1 and developed and resolved in subsequent acts. This is an opera with a unified story about human beings whose feelings and behavior are delineated and developed and whose major problems are resolved in the end. The substance, subtleties, and nuances of Mozart's music support the character development and give the story a timeless quality.

Figaro and Susanna, who plan to be married, are personal servants to the count and countess Almaviva. The count pursues Susanna. Figaro finds out and plots against the count. The countess, though not comfortable with subterfuge—wishing only that her love for the count were enough to keep him fulfilled—conspires against the count. Susanna, though promising to comply with the count's wishes, joins the countess in conspiring against him. In this recitative and aria, the countess is onstage alone; she contemplates this turn of events while waiting to hear from Susanna.

Goals

Describe the vocal style of a great opera singer; compare it with the style of a great folk, jazz, or pop singer.

Describe the range of expression in this aria.

Describe vocal techniques that exemplify the text and those that have little to do with the text.

—Continued

Listening Guide –*Continued*   No. 59

Guide

0:00	Recitative	Free rhythm, dictated by the words and their meanings; dramatic and declamatory yet with a wide range of expression; thin texture in the orchestral accompaniment
1:54	Aria	Duple meter in a very slow two, perhaps better felt in four; some changes of tempo; wide range of expression but essentially lyrical and melodic
	a	Two phrases (8 + 10); phrase 2 modified; an open-closed cadential pattern

Reflections

Discuss a variety of ways music is used in drama and drama in music.

Think about the various roles of individuals who make opera, such as the composer, librettist, producer, costumer, designer, conductor, orchestral musician, stage director, and vocal coach.

Forms

The formal structures discussed in this section—all used in instrumental music—were common in classical music but were seldom strictly adhered to. They became flexible models and the basis of much nineteenth- and twentieth-century music. The challenge for listeners is to recognize the factors that create form, such as contrast and repetition and changes in mood, tonality, or instrumentation.

Sonata Form

During the Classic period, the **sonata form** was commonly used in the first movement of sonatas, symphonies, concertos, and string quartets. A typical first movement in sonata form includes an exposition, development, and a recapitulation and sometimes an introduction and coda.

The *exposition* presented the primary theme in the tonic key, followed by a secondary theme in a contrasting key, sometimes in a contrasting mood. Sometimes a short transition section moved the music from one key to the next. The second section could end in the new key—that is, it did not return to the tonic key but ended with a feeling of expectancy. The exposition was sometimes repeated.

In the *development* section, the composer's imagination could flourish. This music was based on prior material, such as a melodic fragment of the first theme or perhaps the second theme or even both themes. The fragments became the basis of experimentation, in which the composer used an idea and let it grow. Tonal centers might be obscure or might change frequently. The pitch contour of melodic fragments might be altered. Dynamics, rhythms, harmonies, and tempos might be modified, or a fragment might be passed from instrument to instrument, from a high- to a low-pitch area, from the brass to the woodwinds. Contrapuntal imitation might be inserted in an essentially homophonic texture, or the density (thickness) of the texture might be varied by increasing or decreasing the number of instruments playing at any time. Any or all of these devices created unstable, restless music—a dramatic sense of conflict and tension that at some point demanded a return to stability.

The *recapitulation* provided the return to stability: a return to the tonic key, the primary theme of the exposition. Sometimes it was a literal repetition of the exposition, except that the second theme area usually was kept in the tonic key rather than modulated to a new key as in the exposition. At other times, the recapitulation was modified in a variety of ways, particularly at the point of bringing the movement to a close.

A *coda* was the concluding section, in effect serving as an extension of the tonic ending but building up to and creating anticipation of the final cadence.

The formal structure of the sonata form can be outlined as follows:

Introduction.

Exposition: often repeated.
  A. Home key—stability.
  B. Contrasting key—instability and expectancy relative to section A.

Development: an expansion of the exposition; music derived from previous material—instability and expectancy.

Recapitulation: return to the tonic key—stability.
  A. Home key—stability.
  B. Home key—stability.

Coda.

Listening Guide   No. 60

Symphony no. 39 in E-flat Major (IV) (excerpt)
CD3, Track 1, 4:15

Composer: Wolfgang Amadeus Mozart (1756–1791).

Performer: Bavarian Radio Symphony; Rafael Kubelik, conductor.

Genre: Symphony in sonata form.

Context: Mozart composed Symphony no. 39 in 1788. The fourth movement is in sonata form and includes an exposition (two thematic areas), development, and a recapitulation. It clearly exemplifies the most important principles of sonata form: (1) contrast and repetition and (2) development.

Goals

Understand the basic characteristics of sonata form.

Be aware of the principles of stability and instability, tension and release, and contrast and repetition.

–Continued

Listening Guide –Continued   No. 60

Recognize the strong, identifiable, nine-note motive at the beginning, and be aware of the development of that motive.

Be aware of modulation (change of key) and return to the home key (tonic).

Guide

Count in a moderately fast two. The movement starts with the opening theme. Refer to the score on page 243.

0:00		Exposition	
	a	8 bars	Main theme area; diatonic melody; soft; strings; open cadence
		7 bars	Loud; full orchestra; closed cadence on the first bar of the next section
		26 bars	Starts simultaneously with the end of the previous phrase; first eight bars repeated, then extends to a cadence; the following material serves as a bridge to the second theme
0:37	b	6 bars	Second theme area is in a new key; soft; motive adapted from the first theme; thin texture; violins answered by woodwinds
		20 bars	Modified theme leads into a dialogue between flute and bassoon ending with a strong cadence in the key of the dominant (B-flat major)

1:02	Concluding section—37 bars	
	First segment (11 bars)	Loud; thick texture (full orchestra)
	Second segment (20 bars)	Thin texture; dialogue between oboe and bassoon
	Third segment (6 bars)	Full texture to a final cadence of exposition

1:36	Exposition repeated
3:12	Development—motivic development; the main motive passed around from instrument to instrument, altered in many ways; modulating; unstable; varying textures
3:58	Recapitulation—return to the material, style, and form of the exposition (fade)

Reflections

Recognize changes, contrasts, and returns, particularly the return to the stable, tonic key after the unstable development section. Equate instability with tension and stability with release of tension.

Identify and remember the initial motive in order to recognize it in its many manifestations as the piece unfolds.

Listening Guide –Continued   No. 60

Part of a full score (the complete instrumentation), which the conductor of a symphony orchestra uses when conducting an orchestra. The top lines are woodwinds (flute, clarinet, and bassoon), the middle lines are brass (horns and trombones and timpani), and the bottom lines are strings (1st violin, 2nd violin, viola, cello, and double bass). This work is the beginning of the first movement of Symphony no. 39 by Mozart.

Theme and Variations

The form of any large instrumental work or movement that is built on the statement of a theme followed by a series of variations on that theme is known as **theme and variations.** Variations are achieved by changes in tempo, dynamics, articulation (separated or connected notes, known as staccato or legato), tonality, mode (a shift from major to minor), instrumentation, and texture. The variations might be continuous, without clear stops, or sectional, with clear breaks between variations.

Minuet and Trio

The **minuet and trio** is a stately dance movement in triple meter. It is usually the third movement of a symphony or string quartet. A carryover from the stylized dance forms popular during the Baroque period, the minuet was the only dance form that remained popular during the Classic period. In the nineteenth century, the minuet and trio was often replaced by a scherzo and trio, also in triple meter but played at a fast tempo with great rhythmic drive.

The minuet is in two parts with repeats; the trio is in a contrasting mood, also in two parts with each part repeated. The minuet returns but is traditionally played without repeats. Contrasting key relationships and returns to the tonic are important in this form. A common minuet and trio form can be depicted as follows:

Minuet (part I)	A	a	Repeated
		b a	Repeated
Trio (part II)	B	c	Repeated
		d c	Repeated
Minuet (part I repeated)	A	a b a	

A boy and girl are shown dancing the minuet, a stately dance in three-quarter time (or in triple meter). The dance and the dress suggest an aristocratic setting of the eighteenth century. In this picture, a flutist provides the music for the dance.

Listening Guide

**String Quartet in C Major, op. 76, no. 3
(*Emperor* Quartet) (II) (excerpt)**

CD3, Track 2, 2:47

Composer: Franz Joseph Haydn (1732–1809).

Performer: Tátrai Quartet.

Genre: Chamber music in theme and variations form.

Context: One of the last of Haydn's 82 string quartets, the *Emperor* Quartet was composed in 1797, when Haydn was 65. The second of the four movements includes a hymn that Haydn was asked to write for the birthday of Emperor Francis II. It became the Austrian national anthem.

Goals

Describe theme and variations form.

Recognize the sounds and musical lines of each instrument.

In each variation, recognize and describe how Haydn changes the setting of the theme.

Distinguish between staccato and legato styles, and between simple and elaborate melodies.

Identify uses of tension and release.

Guide

Second movement—theme and variations (comments are provided for the theme and the first four of seven variations); a hymnlike melody; in a moderately slow four, starting with a two-beat pickup on the third beat.

	Main theme		
0:00	a	4 bars	Primary phrase
0:15	a	4 bars	Repeat
0:30	b	4 bars	Contrasting phrase
0:47	c	4 bars	New melodic motive starts on a high note, then descends to V–I cadence
1:03	c	4 bars	Repeat
1:19	Variation 1		For two violins; melody in the second violin; fast moving; florid first violin part; shifting staccato and legato passages
2:28	Variation 2		Melody in cello; legato harmonization in the second violin; harmonic "fill" in the viola; more elaborate, syncopated countermelody in the high first violin part (fade)

–Continued

Listening Guide –Continued　　　　　No. 61

Reflections

Be aware of the varying roles or styles given to the instruments, considering such issues as foreground and background roles, simple and elaborate lines, and melody and countermelody.
Recognize polyphonic and homophonic textures.
Discuss the values of the theme and variations form.

Rondo

The principle of contrast and return is integral to the **rondo.** It is based on three or more contrasting theme areas, in which changes are made in melody, mood, and tonality. Each change is followed by a return to the original section. The concluding movement of a sonata, symphony, or string quartet is frequently in rondo form, which might be depicted structurally as follows:

a b a c a   or   a b a c a b a   or   a b a c a d a

Featured Composers

The most significant composers of the Classic period were Franz Joseph Haydn, Wolfgang Amadeus Mozart, and Ludwig van Beethoven. Haydn and Mozart were Austrians. Beethoven was born in Germany but spent much of his life in Austria. The music of all three continues to be performed today, after 200 years, by amateur and professional symphony orchestras, chamber groups, choral organizations, and opera companies throughout the world. Their music is also available on audio recordings numbering in the thousands. More than 2,000 compact discs or sets featuring the works of Haydn, Mozart, and Beethoven are available. Almost 1,000 of these recordings are by Mozart alone.

Franz Joseph Haydn

Haydn (1732–1809) is the best example of a composer who worked successfully within the aristocratic patronage system. For 30 years, he was court composer to the prince of Esterhazy in Austria. He wrote music for every occasion the court demanded and had a court orchestra and opera company at his disposal—an ideal situation for a composer.

Though not a revolutionary, Haydn devised many new ways of putting music together—much to the delight of those who bought his compositions and attended his concerts. His works were known throughout the German-speaking world and in France, Spain, Italy, and especially England, where he achieved his greatest fame and fortune. His imagination, inventiveness, craftsmanship, and productivity are most evident in his sonatas, symphonies, and string quartets.

Franz Joseph Haydn.

Haydn's music built on the past but incorporated emerging romantic impulses and brought the Classic style of the late eighteenth century to the pinnacle of sophistication and perfection. Haydn was an innovative champion of new forms, yet his music was logical and coherent. He drew on the folk songs of his native Austria and on the dance music of the Baroque era. He also drew on the dramatic power of modulation and changes of tonality, taking to new heights the concept of thematic development and motives as building blocks of composition.

Haydn enriched the literature of Western art music. His compositions include 104 symphonies, approximately 35 concertos for various solo instruments, 82 string quartets, and 60 sonatas for solo piano. His most famous symphonies are no. 94, the *Surprise;* no. 100, the *Military;* no. 101, the *Clock;* no. 103, the *Drum Roll;* and no. 104, the *London.* Of his string quartets, perhaps op. 76, no. 3, the *Emperor,* is his most famous. Best known among his many concertos are those for cello, harpsichord, organ, trumpet, and violin. He also composed several widely performed masses and two oratorios, the most famous being *The Creation.*

Wolfgang Amadeus Mozart

Mozart (1756–1791), a product of the Austrian aristocratic system, was a prodigiously gifted child. He received a superior education from his father, Leopold, a court musician, and also from his extensive travels in Italy, France, England, and Germany and stays at the Austrian imperial court in Vienna. Although his childhood involved considerable travel with his father, it was at times serene. His adult life was more tumultuous. Sacrificing the security of the patronage system for personal freedom and the risks of earning a living from commissions, concerts, and the sale of his published music, he often had to struggle for recognition and income.

Wolfgang Amadeus Mozart.

Mozart was a genius with few peers in Western music. He was prolific and inventive, composing in almost every popular form of the day. He brought to his music unmatched lyricism and profound expressiveness. Devoted listeners can gain deeper insights into his music from repeated hearings. His works convey the elegance of court music at its best. They are sophisticated and urbane, reflecting the cosmopolitan culture of Salzburg and Vienna.

Mozart died when he was 35, yet he created more than 600 compositions in his lifetime. The final six symphonies are especially noteworthy. The last three—no. 39, no. 40, and no. 41 (the great *Jupiter* Symphony)—were not commissioned, nor were they performed in his lifetime, yet they now rank among the most substantial of his instrumental works.

Mozart wrote 25 piano concertos, seven violin concertos, and concertos for bassoon, clarinet, horn, flute, flute and harp, and oboe. His "entertainment" music—the divertimentos and serenades—continues to be popular, especially the Serenade in G, commonly known as *Eine kleine Nachtmusik*. His most unusual works may well be those written for the glass harmonica, an instrument invented by Benjamin Franklin; the sound was similar to that created by musical glasses.

Mozart's chamber music continues to be widely performed; it includes 23 string quartets, a quintet for clarinet and strings, a quintet for piano and winds, and piano quartets and quintets (piano with strings). Professional solo pianists are likely to have at least one of his 17 piano sonatas in their repertoire. His *Requiem* stands out among his many excellent choral works.

The Magic Flute, The Marriage of Figaro, and *Don Giovanni* are Mozart's most famous operas. He had an affinity for opera and was able to combine the best of the Italian and Germanic traits that dominated opera styles of his era. His gift for creating beautiful, lyrical melodies was combined with a strong sense of drama. With his collaborators, he infused opera with a sense of humanity, deep feeling, and character development. Real, recognizable human beings rather than stereotypical caricatures were central to Mozart's operas. More than lively tunes with light accompaniment, his music provided emotional and dramatic support for the characters and the plot.

Ludwig van Beethoven

Beethoven's earliest music is in the Classic style, but his later works—and, according to many scholars, his superior works—have many characteristics associated with the Romantic period that followed. For this reason, Beethoven is frequently considered both a Classic and a Romantic composer or, perhaps more accurately, a composer who exemplifies a transition from the Classic to the Romantic style.

Beethoven (1770–1827) began his career in the employment of the court at Bonn in his native Germany. At the age of 22, he moved to Vienna, where he would spend the rest of his life. Beethoven earned a comfortable living from the sale of his compositions; thus, he was independent of the exclusive patronage of the aristocracy.

The creative lives of many great composers can be divided into discrete periods. In Beethoven's case, scholars identify three periods: (1) During his first 32 years—his education and formative years—he became established as a great composer. (2) In his middle period (1802–1824), he produced many of his most famous works. (3) In his final years (1824–1827), when he became totally deaf, he produced fewer but intensely serious and personal works.

Beethoven freed music from the restraints of classicism by creating works that are models of subjective feeling and personal expression. His works influenced not only his contemporaries but also composers of later generations. He made significant contributions to nearly every musical form and every medium of musical expression, from the solo sonata, to the symphony, to grand opera.

Ludwig van Beethoven.

Beethoven's music can be beautiful and tender, but much of it is heroic, tempestuous, and powerful. It can be energetic, unpredictable, and highly emotional. His techniques for creating his powerful, personal statements include fragmentation of themes, harmonic clashes, and sustained tension. His later works, compared with those of Mozart and Haydn and his own earlier works, can be lengthy. In fact, the first movement of his Ninth Symphony lasts longer than his entire First Symphony. Beethoven was an innovator in many ways. His outstanding innovations include his use of the human voice in a traditionally instrumental work, as in his Ninth Symphony, and his dramatic, coloristic use of the piano, as in his *Appassionata* Sonata.

Beethoven's numerous famous works include nine symphonies, of which nos. 3, 5, and 9 are considered monuments of symphonic literature; five piano concertos, of which no. 5, the *Emperor* Concerto, is best known; a widely performed and recorded violin concerto; 32 piano sonatas, of which the *Pathétique* (see Listening Guide 62), the *Appassionata,* and the *Moonlight* are best known; chamber music, including 16 string quartets, 9 piano trios, and a quintet for piano and winds; numerous concert overtures, including *Egmont* and *Prometheus;* an opera, *Fidelio;* and a great choral masterpiece, *Missa Solemnis.*

Listening Guide   No. 62

Piano Sonata no. 8 in C Minor, op. 13 (*Pathétique* Sonata) (III)
CD3, Track 3, 2:33

Composer: Ludwig van Beethoven (1770–1827).

Performer: Vladimir Horowitz, piano.

Genre: Sonata in rondo form.

Context: The *Pathétique* Sonata (1799) is one of Beethoven's most respected and best-known works. It maintains many of the traditional Classic-period ideals of clarity and balance. However, with its dramatic contrasts, its powerful chords, and its range of emotions, this sonata foreshadowed the nineteenth-century romantic spirit. It also foreshadowed the intensely personal expression of Beethoven's own later, more mature works. The *Pathétique* has three movements:

  I. Grave; Allegro di molto e con brio
  II. Adagio cantabile
  III. Rondo: Allegro

Goals

Recognize the contrasting moods in the third movement of this sonata.
Discuss the musical characteristics that affect these changes.
Recognize shifts in major and minor tonalities.
Describe melodic contour as a means of identifying motives and themes.

Listening Guide –*Continued*   No. 62

Guide

Third movement: rondo form (abacaba); lively, dancelike; in the tonic key of C minor.

0:00	a	The opening statement (theme) in the key of C minor—extended phrase
0:21	b	Contrasting material in a major key; a strong chord is followed by an ascending then descending motive, then aggressive triplet patterns, then simple, quiet, blocked chords; the aggressive triplet patterns return and conclude with a climb to a high note over a dominant chord and a scale descending to this unstable chord that is resolved with the return of the opening statement—a pattern that is to recur several times
1:16	a	In the tonic minor key
1:35	c	Second contrasting section; in a major key; legato motive with wide skips and mild syncopation; staccato scales; arpeggio patterns that build in energy and intensity; an ending similar to the end of the second theme, with a long high note and descending scale to a sustained, unstable chord
2:30	a	In the tonic minor (fade)

Reflections

Why do classical pieces tend to be long and popular pieces short? Discuss exceptions.

Referring to characteristics of Beethoven's music discussed on pages 249–250, in what ways can the music in this excerpt be considered "beautiful and tender" or "tempestuous and powerful"? How would you describe this music?

Summary

The Classic period was an outgrowth of the aristocratic life of Austria, but it also saw the decline of the aristocracy throughout Europe, the rise of the middle class, the beginnings of the Industrial Revolution, and the urbanization of Western societies.

Musically, Bach and Handel exemplified the culmination of all that went before; their deaths marked the end of an era. With the music of many Germans, Austrians, and Italians, but particularly the music of Mozart, Haydn, and Beethoven, a new style emerged, resulting in a tremendous wealth of literature: symphonies, concertos, and string quartets; piano sonatas; operas and oratorios; and the standardization of the sonata, rondo, and other forms. The instrumentation of the symphony orchestra became standard, as it remains today.

In many respects, the mid- to late-eighteenth century—the Classic period—signals the beginning of the modern age in music.

12 Music of the Romantic Period (Nineteenth Century)

Chapter Outline

The composer Ludwig von Beethoven was an individualist, often defying the preferences of his artistic patrons and rejecting the rigidity of Classic-period musical forms. Caught up in the spirit of the French Revolution and the rise of the capitalistic middle class, he sought through his music to express his own convictions with emotion and imagination. Beethoven wanted his music to be different.

These attributes of Beethoven mirror the attributes of the Romantic period as a whole; it was a time when artistic expression became highly individual and personal, and also highly emotional. One composer's beliefs and practices often contrasted markedly with those of another composer. Consequently, the Romantic period was not characterized by uniform musical expression.

The business aspect of music became an important factor in the Romantic period as the aristocratic **patronage** system fell into decline. Instead of being employed by the royal courts, composers and performers had to find their own audiences and publishers. They had to sell their music to the public, literally and figuratively. This change created new jobs in the music profession for concert managers (or impresarios, as they were then known), music publishers, and music critics.

For an artist, a dynamic and colorful personality and dazzling displays of technical skill were significant assets in interesting the public and selling one's work. The greatest virtuosos—whether performers, conductors, or composers—became celebrities of their time.

Much of the music of the nineteenth century was so technically demanding that it could not be performed by amateurs. The demand for professional musicians created a demand for teachers; thus, the teaching of music became an established profession.

The nineteenth century was also a time of musical polarities, featuring works of tradition and of experimentation, classical forms and new forms, music for huge orchestras and intimate pieces for a solo instrument or voice, music expressing nationalism and internationalism, and absolute music and program music. A composer might work at one of these extremes or at any point between extremes.

Feelings of nationalism emerged in the late nineteenth century largely as a reaction against the dominance of German romanticism throughout Europe. These feelings reflected a desire for national, regional, or ethnic identity and were expressed through music in a style that became known as nationalistic music. Romantic composers who wrote lasting nationalistic music were mostly from Russia and eastern Europe; they included Rimsky-Korsakov, Dvořák, and Smetana.

Nationalistic music has definable national or regional characteristics. It is concert art music in which composers incorporate elements that reflect any of the following:

- Cultural characteristics of a national group rather than of humankind in general.
- Folk and popular music and traditions.
- History, tales, and legends of a nation.
- Patriotism and the glories and triumphs of a nation and its people.

Goals for Listening

Continue to develop your listening skills by recognizing the following musical characteristics:

- Familiar-sounding melodies and chords: Recognize diatonic and consonant melody and harmony.
- Complex-sounding melodies and chords: Recognize dissonance, chromatic tension and resolution, and chromaticism.
- Expressive qualities: Identify a ritard or an accelerando, and a crescendo or a decrescendo. Identify rubato.
- Structure: Recognize thematic contrasts and repetitions as a means of identifying form, and recognize changes in tonality, modality (major or minor), tempo changes, changes of mood, a strophic setting of a text, and other characteristics that composers use to organize music.
- Identify compositional devices: arpeggios, tremolos, and sequences.
- Compare a Romantic style of music, such as can be recognized in any of the musical examples in this chapter, with a Classic style, such as can be recognized in the music of Mozart or Haydn.

The Listening Guides in chapter 12 include a lied (art song), a solo piano piece, choral music, symphonic music, a concerto, chamber music, and program music.

Musical Characteristics

Music created for its own sake, without any extramusical connotations, is known as **absolute music.** Genres such as the sonata, symphony, and concerto provide examples. In the nineteenth century, however, **program music**—music created to depict moods, images, and characters and to tell stories—became a prevailing interest. Program music reflects composers' and the audiences' interest in poetry, the unity of music and words, and the use of music to create imagery suggested by a text. Romantic composers went to greater lengths than their predecessors to create music without text that could stimulate subjective feelings, moods, and images of places or things, and to associate specific musical ideas with characters in a story.

Music in the nineteenth century was primarily **homophonic,** with a predominance of singable, lyrical, "romantic" melodies. Folk melodies or melodies in a folk style also became common as composers sought not only new modes of expression but also ways to reach wider audiences. Melodies were usually related to underlying harmonies and harmonic progressions, particularly in the first half of the century. The second half of the century saw an increase in **chromaticism** and **dissonance** in an attempt to create musical **tension** and to intensify emotion. Much music was highly emotional, with strong contrasts, unexpected chords, and long buildups to exciting climaxes. The increase in chromaticism and dissonance brought with it a decrease in tonal clarity—a weaker sense of tonal center. By the beginning of the twentieth century, **tonality** in much music was obscure or nonexistent.

Rhythm in nineteenth-century music, compared with that from the previous century, was frequently less regular and more complex. This was increasingly so in the second half of the century. Composers avoided the regular stress on each downbeat and used more polyrhythms, more syncopation, and more changes in tempo. Changes in tempo included accelerandos (getting faster), ritardandos (getting slower), and rubato (a slight speeding up and slowing down that creates a flexible pulse and a highly expressive manner). The increase in complex rhythm brought with it a decrease in the sense of meter.

The nineteenth-century orchestra was bigger, more lush, and thicker in texture than the Classic-period orchestra. The use of instrumental tone color became an art in itself—the art of orchestration. Composers used individual instruments and combinations of instruments not only to play melodies and harmonies but also to create special, unique sonorities. As the Industrial Revolution dawned in the early nineteenth century, manufacturers sought ways to enhance the resonance and range of all orchestral instruments. New instruments were added to accommodate the need for new expression and new tone colors.

Forms and Genres

The multimovement sonata, whether a solo piece, symphony, concerto, or chamber work, continued to be a basic structure in the Romantic period, as were the sonata form and other Classic forms discussed in chapter 11. These, however, were flexible models that few composers held to rigidly. Forms were not as precise or clear and not as symmetrical or balanced as in the music of Classic-period composers. Phrases tended to be longer and less regular than in Classic music. Internal **cadences** were frequently less clear, suggesting ongoing movement or momentum rather than an obvious ending to a phrase or a section.

Instrumental Forms and Genres

Although many composers excelled in writing symphonies, concertos, and chamber works, other forms and genres emerged during the Romantic period: the symphonic poem, forms derived from stage productions (the overture, prelude, suite, and incidental music), and instrumental chamber groups other than string quartets and piano trios—specifically, string sextets and woodwind quintets (flute, oboe, clarinet, horn, and bassoon).

The **symphonic poem,** a one-movement work with contrasting moods, is derived from music that describes something (program music)—in contrast to symphonies and concertos, which usually do not have any nonmusical associations (absolute music).

The overture or prelude begins an opera or a ballet (see the next section). The suite is an orchestral arrangement of songs or dances from an opera or a ballet. Incidental music was performed between acts of a production. These instrumental works were often performed as symphonic concert pieces, sometimes becoming better known than the original stage productions.

Opera and Ballet

Opera, which combined music, poetry, drama, and visual effects, had a tremendous impact in the nineteenth century and became an important medium of Romantic expression. The great nineteenth-century composers of opera were Verdi, Wagner, Rossini, Puccini, and Richard Strauss. Opera flourished during the eighteenth and nineteenth centuries in France, Germany, and Italy. Today, it continues to appeal to a public that enjoys music with action, plots, and spectacle—attributes not typical of symphonic or chamber music. Operas still include arias, recitatives, solo ensembles, choruses, and orchestral accompaniment. The orchestra plays the overture, preludes to acts, any incidental music, and the accompaniments of singers and dancers.

Grand operas, with their large number of singers, elaborate scenery and effects, and serious, complex plots, often included visual diversion such as pageantry and ballet. Comic operas and operettas, in contrast to grand operas, generally were lighter in mood, less complex, and often satirical, and they frequently included spoken dialogue.

The **libretto** is the text of an opera—the lyrics, the poetry. It is created to allow the plot to be interrupted, perhaps enhanced, by the various songs, choral numbers, and dances. Whereas singers in choruses are identified as sopranos, altos, tenors, and basses, solo singers in operas are known as coloratura, lyric, or dramatic sopranos; mezzo-sopranos; contraltos; lyric or dramatic tenors; baritones; and basses (also basso profundo, or deep bass).

Opera is very popular in the United States, with professional opera companies in nearly every metropolitan area. In addition, there are performances by many regional semiprofessional or amateur companies and by departments or schools of music in colleges and universities.

Another form of stage production that became popular in the nineteenth century was the **ballet,** which at first was part of opera and then became an independent genre. It featured both solo and ensemble dancing and represented the highest form of the art of dance. Tchaikovsky composed the most memorable music for ballet in the nineteenth century, including *Sleeping Beauty, Swan Lake,* and *The Nutcracker.*

Keyboard Forms and Genres

Along with the large orchestras and orchestral forms and the elaborate stage productions, there emerged new small-scale compositions known as **miniatures:** (1) short **character pieces** for solo piano and (2) the solo song with piano accompaniment.

One-movement miniatures, exemplified by the solo piano works of Chopin, are expressive, at times lyrical and dramatic, and often technically demanding. These impromptus, nocturnes, mazurkas, polonaises, preludes, waltzes, and études have their own distinctive mood and character. They rank among the best solo piano literature from the nineteenth century. Today, they remain in the repertoire of concert pianists and are studied by the vast majority of advanced piano students.

Songs

The songs, known as art songs or **lieder** (singular **lied**), are best exemplified in the works of Schubert, who wrote over 600 of them. Most are short and are set to the works of German poets, notably Johann Wolfgang Goethe. The German poets' interest in creating lyric poetry stimulated composers' interest in creating art songs. The emergence of the piano in the nineteenth century as the primary keyboard instrument in concert halls and homes also contributed to the development of the art song. The piano's expressive power was well suited to enhancing the varying moods and images of the art song.

German lieder are known for their beautiful, expressive melodies. Many are **strophic** (that is, the music is the same for each verse of the poetry), but in some songs, the music changes to reflect changes of character or mood. Today, art songs from the nineteenth century are presented regularly in recitals by both professional and amateur singers.

Featured Composers

The music of at least 20 nineteenth-century composers is performed regularly in concerts and on stage in the United States each year. Almost all are men. It is unfortunate but not surprising that the two most prominent women artists and composers of the nineteenth century are usually presented in history books not as musicians in their own right but in relation to the male composers who were important in their lives. These women were the concert pianist and composer Clara Schumann, who was married to Robert Schumann, and the composer and pianist Fanny Hensel, the sister of Felix Mendelssohn.

Clara Wieck Schumann (1819–1896) was born into a musical family, received the best musical education, and married the composer Robert Schumann, who encouraged her pursuits as a concert pianist, composer, and teacher. Clara Schumann wrote mainly songs, choral works, chamber works, and piano pieces, many of them intended to show off her dazzling skill as a pianist. She also wrote a piano concerto. Through her long career as a teacher and performer, she influenced future generations of pianists.

Fanny Mendelssohn Hensel (1805–1847), a prolific composer and a skilled pianist, was encouraged to develop her talent but not to become a professional musician or to have her compositions published. Most of her works were songs and piano pieces, although she did write a few choral, orchestral, and chamber works (see Listening Guide 63).

Even those who claim to have but a minimal knowledge of western European classical music have some acquaintance with the most prominent Romantic composers. Seven of these composers are discussed below; these discussions are followed by a brief listing of other important composers of the period.

Listening Guide   No. 63

A portrait of Fanny Hensel, who was Felix Mendelssohn's sister, painted in 1829 by Fanny's husband, Wilhelm Hensel. It is located in the Staatliche Museum in Berlin, Germany.

Trio for Piano, Violin, and Cello in D Minor, op. 11 (I) (excerpt)
CD3, Track 4, 5:28

Composer: Fanny Mendelssohn Hensel (1805–1847).
Performer: Macalester Trio.
Genre: Chamber music.
Context: Fanny was the older sister of Felix Mendelssohn. They were devoted to each other and respected each other's music. Fanny was a gifted pianist as well as a composer. Fanny's father, Abraham, encouraged Felix to become a professional while advising Fanny that music, for her, "will always remain an ornament [and should not] become the foundation of your existence and daily life." She married a Prussian painter, Wilhelm Hensel, and became a housewife. Nevertheless, she composed more than 400 works, some of which were published under Felix's name.

Fanny Hensel composed oratorios, cantatas, other choral works, songs, vocal and instrumental chamber music, piano pieces, and orchestral music. This trio, opus 11, was published in 1850. The piano part is extremely virtuosic; the violin and cello parts are more lyrical.

Goals

Differentiate the sounds of the violin and cello.
Recognize arpeggio and tremolo passages, and differentiate them from the more scalar (stepwise) passages.
Identify themes, dotted rhythms, sequences, chromaticism, and modulations.
Differentiate the harmonically stable from the less stable sections.

Guide

Sonata form.

0:00	First theme: The motive of this quiet theme, stated first by the violin and cello in octaves, is characterized by a dotted rhythm with a wide, ascending skip, answered by an equally wide descending skip; the motive occurs over ascending and descending arpeggios, then fast shimmering scale passages on the piano

Listening Guide –Continued   No. 63

0:52	The lengthy transition to the second theme begins with a brilliant descending scale passage on the piano, followed by a descending sequence and a harmonically unstable section settling quietly in F major
1:35	Second theme: In F major; this lyrical melody, stated first in the cello, then the piano and violin, is related to the first theme in its wide chromatic skips; the accompaniment, however, rather than the fast arpeggios and scales heard previously, is an extended tremolo
2:34	Descending piano arpeggios, answered by a simple ascending scale motive in the violin, signal the second half of this theme, which is heard in F minor in a descending stepwise pattern; this idea soon becomes fragmented and unstable
3:46	Development: Ascending piano arpeggios signal the beginning of the development section as fragments of the first theme are soon heard
5:14	After the second theme is heard, the excerpt fades

Reflections

What special skills, if any, are required to listen to chamber music?

In what ways is this music Classic? In what ways is it Romantic?

This music has not been performed very often. Why? Does it deserve more hearings?

Johannes Brahms

Brahms (1833–1897) was born in Germany but moved to Vienna at the age of 30 and lived there for the rest of his life. He worked mostly as a freelance composer and pianist. He became world famous and was part of a midcentury controversy between the traditionalists, of whom he was the acknowledged master, and the musical revolutionaries, led by Richard Wagner. Such controversies were fed by the propensity of composers like Schumann and Wagner to function also as music critics and essayists.

While touring, Brahms met and became friends with Robert and Clara Schumann—a friendship that shaped the course of his artistic and personal life. He fell in love with Clara and was torn between his love for her and his loyalty to Robert. Evidently, he was also torn between love and freedom, for even after Robert died, Brahms never married Clara (or anyone else). Still, his friendship with Clara continued until her death in 1896.

Brahms's music is passionate. It is often introspective, mellow, and full of rich, dark sonorities. His melodies are lyrical, even when they have complex rhythms or

Johannes Brahms plays piano in his study. Brahms' work was influenced by the techno-logical development of the piano, which attained its modern form during his lifetime. Sometimes referred to as the most Classic of all the Romantic composers, Brahms' work was heavily influenced by the works of Beethoven, as well as the earlier Classic composers Mozart and Haydn. Brahms decided to give up on composing at age 57 but was unable to hold to his decision; before his death seven years later, he produced several masterpieces including two clarinet sonatas and the Four Serious Songs.

intricate polyphonic textures. His phrases can be irregular, at times conflicting with the prevailing meter. Devoted to the principles of the sonata form, Brahms was a Romantic in his emotional expressiveness but a Classicist in his formal organization. His orchestral music was full and massive. He was interested in absolute music, writing little program music except for his songs and choral works.

Brahms is best known for his four symphonies; a violin concerto; two piano concertos; Hungarian Dances; the *Liebeslieder* waltzes; important trios, quartets, quintets, and sextets; two serenades; the *German Requiem;* sonatas for piano, cello, violin, and clarinet; and numerous short piano pieces, songs, and choral works.

Listening Guide   No. 64

"How Lovely Is Thy Dwelling Place," from *German Requiem*
CD3, Track 5, 5:39

Composer: Johannes Brahms (1833–1897).
Performer: Atlanta Symphony Orchestra and Chorus; Robert Shaw, conductor.
Genre: Chorus from a requiem.
Context: The word *requiem* traditionally refers to the Roman Catholic Mass for the Dead. Brahms, however, created his own text, selecting Bible passages not used in the traditional funeral liturgy. He called his work "A German Requiem"; it is an extended work for soloists, chorus, and orchestra. "How Lovely Is Thy Dwelling Place," the best-known chorus from this work, is often sung as a choir anthem in church services.

Goals

Listen not only for the melody but for the interplay of all the parts.
Identify **word painting:** *lieblich* (lovely); *freuen sich in dem* (crieth out); *die loben dich immerdar* (praise Thy name).
Recognize and distinguish between homophonic passages and polyphonic passages.

Guide

German text and English translation (Psalm 84:1, 2, 4):

Wie lieblich sind deine Wohnungen, Herr Zebaoth!	*How lovely is Thy dwelling place O Lord of Hosts!*
Meine Seele verlanget und sehnet sich nach den Verh fen des Herrn;	*My soul, it longeth, yea fainteth For the courts of the Lord.*
mein Leib und Seele freuen sich in dem lebendigen Gott.	*My soul and body crieth out, Yea, for the living God.*
Wohl denen, die in deimem Hause wohnen;	*O blest are they that dwell within Thy house;*
die loben dich immerdar.	*They praise Thy name evermore.*

Reflections

In what ways does the music reflect or reinforce the text?
How does this piece reflect the Romantic spirit? Does it in any way reflect the Classic spirit?
Would this piece be effective if you substituted a secular text? For example, could it be made into a love song? Why or why not?

"Young Girls at the Piano" was painted in 1892 by Auguste Renoir. It is located in the Musee d'Orsay in Paris, France.

Frédéric Chopin

Chopin (1810–1849) was born and educated in Poland but spent his entire professional life in Paris. He was a virtuoso pianist but did not seek to develop an extensive concert career. He preferred private performances in the aristocratic salons and intimate gatherings of wealthy Parisians. In Paris, Chopin was profoundly influenced by his lover, George Sand (her pen name). She was a feminist with whom he lived for nine years. Many of his greatest and best-known works were created during this period.

Chopin is known almost exclusively for his études, preludes, waltzes, scherzos, polonaises, and nocturnes—short, one-movement piano compositions known as miniatures. His miniatures, many of which are virtuoso pieces, included stylized dances (not intended for dancing) and pieces that reflected the spirit of the Polish people. He also composed extended works, such as three solo piano sonatas and two piano concertos.

Chopin formed his unique compositional style by creating the following:

- Elaborate, decorative melodies.
- Bold, colorful harmonies with daring dissonances, unresolved tension, and unusual modulations.
- A rhythm not restricted by a regular pulse (a strict beat) but characterized by increased application of **rubato** (a flexible pulse).

Listening Guide   No. 65

Prelude, op. 28, no. 6 in B Minor

CD3, Track 6, 1:52

Composer: Frédéric Chopin (1810–1849).

Performer: Murray Perahia, piano.

Genre: Piano miniature.

Context: Chopin's 24 preludes, each in a different major or minor key, have no structural or stylistic similarity, whereas his other sets of pieces, such as his polonaises, nocturnes, and ballades, have common musical characteristics.

   The preludes are varied in style and mood. They may be short, miniature pieces or extended works having contrasting moods, and they may range in emotion from quiet serenity to chromatic restlessness. They are examples of absolute rather than program music.

Goals

Differentiate between absolute and program music. Compare this prelude with Schubert's lieder (see Listening Guide 66 in this chapter).

Listen for the phrase structure and points of repetition, contrast, and return.

Recognize rubato, arpeggios, inner and outer voices on the piano, and left-hand and right-hand pitch areas on the piano.

Guide

0:00	A	The right hand plays a repeating note over a cello-like melody played by the left hand.
0:32	A'	The opening idea repeats but then leads into an extended episode based on a melodic fragment from the opening sections. The opening idea reappears at the close.

Reflections

The nineteenth-century conductor and pianist Hans von Bülow called this prelude "Tolling Bells" because of the repeated notes prominent throughout. Do you think this is program music? Why or why not?

What musical characteristics in this piece allow us to classify it as Romantic?

In what ways is Prelude no. 6 different from Beethoven's Piano Sonata no. 8 (see Listening Guide 62, page 250).

Discuss the relationship between right-hand and left-hand functions in this prelude.

Felix Mendelssohn

Mendelssohn (1809–1847) came from a wealthy, educated German family of high social and cultural status. His home was a gathering place for musicians and intellectuals. He was surrounded by the finest opportunities for an aspiring musician, including the resources of a private orchestra. He was widely traveled and became famous throughout Europe and England.

Mendelssohn's music had wide appeal. It was traditional and closely aligned to Classic ideals of form and structure. His Classic spirit was reflected in his orderly, elegant, graceful expression; his Romantic spirit showed through primarily in the emotional expressiveness and sentimentality of his melodies. Mendelssohn is best known for his *Scotch* and *Italian* symphonies, the oratorio *Elijah*, the Violin Concerto in E Minor, the *Hebrides* Overture, and incidental music to *Midsummer Night's Dream*.

Franz Schubert

Schubert (1797–1828) was endowed with a prodigious natural gift for music. He composed 143 songs before he turned 19 and 179 more works the following year, including major choral and symphonic pieces. His entire adult life, however, was a struggle against illness and poverty. Without position or patronage, he led a precarious existence, depending on the generosity of friends, a few commissions, the sale of a few pieces to publishers, and some private teaching.

Schubert is best known for his more than 600 lieder. These art songs embody a wide range of feelings, from elegant simplicity to bold, dramatic expression, and from simple, folklike songs to elaborate ballads of great musical sophistication. The outstanding qualities of his compositions are lyrical melodies, colorful harmonies, and sensitivity to the poetic expression of the texts. "The Erlking," "Who Is Sylvia?" (in the next Listening Guide), and "Serenade" are among his best-known solo songs. Some of his most important songs are found in his two song cycles (sets of songs with a common unifying factor), *Die schöne Müllerin* and *Winterreise*.

Schubert's nine symphonies reflect Classic ideals of form and structure yet are infused with the songlike qualities of Viennese romanticism. Of these works, no. 8, the *Unfinished* Symphony (a symphony in two movements), and no. 9, *The Great*, are the most important. His short piano pieces, including the impromptus, the 22 solo piano sonatas, and *Moments Musicaux*, are widely performed today. His best chamber works include the string quartet *Death and the Maiden*, the *Trout* piano quintet, the Quintet in C for strings, and two piano trios. Among his well-known choral works is Mass in G.

Listening Guide   No. 66

"An Silvia" ("Who Is Sylvia?")

CD3, Track 7, 3:00

Composer: Franz Schubert (1797–1828).

Performer: Matthias Goerne, tenor; Alexander Schmalcz, piano.

Genre: Lied (art song).

Context: Schubert had a remarkable gift for creating melodies that were expressive, emotional, dramatic, sad, or mysterious. Such melodies epitomize the essence of romanticism. His songs for solo voice and piano accompaniment ranged from short, simple pieces to extended, more dramatic, emotionally complex works.

Listening Guide –Continued   No. 66

The text to "An Sylvia" was taken from Shakespeare's *Two Gentlemen of Verona*. The music is elegant and simple.

Goals

Recognize diatonic melody.

Recognize diatonic, consonant harmony.

Be aware of expressive qualities in music.

Use the terms *lied* and *lieder* correctly.

Guide

A simple accompaniment combining a bass ostinato in the left hand and repeated chords in the right hand supports one of Schubert's most beloved songs. It is strophic (the same music is used for each verse of poetry). Three musical phrases make up each stanza. Solo piano introduces and concludes the song and separates each stanza.

The text is from Shakespeare and was translated into German by one of Schubert's friends. It honors Sylvia, extolling her beauty, her grace, and her kindness, but it does not tell us who Sylvia is. The text follows:

Was ist Silvia, saget an,	*Who is Sylvia? What is she*
Daß sie die weite Flur preist?	*That all our swains commend her?*
Schön und zart seh ich sie nahn,	*Holy, fair, and wise is she,*
Auf Himmelsgunst und Spur weist,	*The heaven such grace did lend her*
Daß ihr alles untertan.	*That she might admired be.*
Ist sie schön und gut dazu?	*Is she kind as she is fair?*
Reiz labt wie milde Kindheit;	*For beauty lives with kindness:*
Ihrem Aug' eilt Amor zu,	*Love doth to her eyes repair*
Dort heilt er seine Blindheit	*To help him of his blindness:*
Und verweilt in süßer Ruh.	*And, being help'd, inhabits there.*
Darum Silvia, tön, o Sang,	*Then to Sylvia, let us sing,*
Der holden Silvia Ehren;	*That Sylvia is excelling;*
Jeden Reiz besiegt sie lang,	*She excels each mortal thing*
Den Erde kann gewähren:	*Upon the dull earth dwelling;*
Kränze ihr und Saitenklang!	*To her let us garlands bring.*

Reflections

Why are such simple pieces called art songs rather than folk songs?

Describe the accompaniment.

Differentiate between a song that is strophic and one that is not. Discuss the advantages and disadvantages of each.

Adriana Suarez, as the Snow Queen, and Paul Thrussell, as the Snow King, dance in a pas de deux in a dress rehearsal of Boston Ballet's *The Nutcracker*.

Pyotr I'yich Tchaikovsky

The most famous Russian composer, Tchaikovsky (1840–1893) was appointed a professor of composition at the Moscow Conservatory at age 25. He had a wealthy patron, Mme. Von Meck, whose support enabled him to leave his teaching position and devote his life to composition.

Tchaikovsky's music is both nationalistic and international, capturing the spirit of Russian folk song but also influenced by Italian opera, French ballet, and German symphonies and songs. His music is tuneful, accessible, sometimes exciting, and sometimes sentimental, and it remains tremendously popular. It has an appealing directness and a wide range of emotional expression. This is music full of beautiful melodies, striking contrasts, powerful climaxes, and passionate emotions.

Tchaikovsky's best-known works include his violin and piano concertos; his symphonies, particularly nos. 4, 5, and 6 (the *Pathétique*); the *1812 Overture;* and *Romeo and Juliet,* a symphonic overture-fantasia (see Listening Guide 67). His ballets—*Swan Lake, Sleeping Beauty,* and *The Nutcracker*—and orchestral excerpts taken from these ballets are also very well known.

Listening Guide   No. 67

Romeo and Juliet (excerpt)

CD3, Track 8, 9:12

Composer: Pyotr I'yich Tchaikovsky.

Performer: New York Philharmonic; Leonard Bernstein, conductor.

Genre: Symphonic poem.

Context: The concert overture was a favorite musical genre of many nineteenth-century composers. It is a one-movement concert piece not associated with a stage production but based on a nonmusical idea such as a literary work. In this sense, it is considered program music. Listeners can appreciate *Romeo and Juliet* on its own merits, however, whether or not they know its relationship to Shakespeare's play.

Goals

Describe the style and character of the two primary themes.

Recognize the thick, lush texture of the Romantic-period orchestra.

Describe musical climaxes and how they are achieved.

Guide

Composed for large symphony orchestra; in sonata form.

Introduction

0:00	a	Opens with a slow, somber melody in chordal texture played on the clarinets and bassoons; features an ascending stepwise motive in a simple, direct rhythm
0:34		Mysterious, dramatic passage begins in the low strings; rises to thick texture with full orchestra; ends with a series of sustained high pitches in the woodwinds over ascending harp arpeggios
2:00	a	Descending pizzicato strings introduce a restatement of the opening theme in a new guise; theme is stated in the woodwinds to the accompaniment of pizzicato, running notes in the strings
2:49	b	Mysterious second theme suddenly reappears in the lower strings; moves to higher strings
4:07		Transition: Introduction is extended to its greatest point of intensity; loud chords derived from the opening theme; suddenly quiet; intense, repeated chords lead to the exposition

–Continued

Listening Guide —Continued   No. 67

Exposition

5:25	a	Conflict theme: sharp, crisp, syncopated motive; loud, fast; full orchestra; extends with full orchestra, then drops out suddenly at transition to the second theme; features an ascending three-note motive in thin texture; restless harmonies; resolution repeatedly delayed and finally resolved at the beginning of the love theme
7:43	b	Love theme: first part; lyrical, romantic—one of the best-known melodies in classical music; opens with English horn and viola; light texture, small orchestra; simple chordal accompaniment in horns
8:05		Love theme: second part; provides a gentle, rocking motion; violins; straight rhythm in groups of four beats, but each group starts on the fourth beat of each bar
8:57		Love theme—first part (fade)

Reflections

Discuss in what ways this is program music and in what ways it is absolute music.

How is this music—the rhythm, phrasing, cadences, textures, and so on—different from that of Mozart or Haydn? What makes this music Romantic in character?

Listen to the work in its entirety to appreciate the range of Tchaikovsky's musical expression, such as the ways he develops and extends the themes and builds musical climaxes and massive sonorities.

Giuseppe Verdi

Verdi (1813–1901) was the greatest figure of Italian opera, a national hero. He had a wealthy patron and a secure job, and he became world renowned. He was famous in America and was invited to help open Carnegie Hall in 1891.

Verdi composed for a population whose main source of musical enjoyment was opera. He maintained the traditions of the aria and recitative and included choruses and ensembles as in earlier operas. Conventional harmonies and predictable rhythms and meters characterize most of his music, but he enriched his operas with superb melodies and a strong theatrical sense.

Verdi's early operas have little continuity of dramatic action and, in some cases, are nationalistic and political. His next operas—*Rigoletto, La Traviata,* and *Il Trovatore*—are among his best-known and most durable works. They are in the repertoire of almost every opera company today. His later operas, including *Aïda,* provide more drama and spectacle, richer harmonies, and a more important orchestra than do his earlier operas. In these works, he lessened the differences between the aria and the recitative. The librettos are invariably unhappy, with tragic endings. Real-life passions and emotions are conveyed through both heroes and villains. The dramatic action is typically swift moving, energetic, and full of conflict and tension. His operas still have these characteristics.

Among Verdi's few nondramatic works are two large, successful choral compositions: the *Te Deum* and the *Requiem.*

Richard Wagner

Wagner (1813–1883) was a German composer of opera who was caught up in the revolutionary movements of his time. He was raised in a theatrical family but was practically self-taught as a musician and composer. He studied the scores of previous masters, notably Beethoven. Active in the revolution of 1848, he was forced to flee his country and took up exile in Switzerland. While there, he set forth his theories about art, describing an ideal art form in which music, drama, poetry, and stagecraft would all have equal emphasis. He called this form *music drama* rather than *opera.* In the German town of Bayreuth, a theater designed by Wagner was built to produce his operas, and to this day, it serves as a center for lovers of Wagnerian opera. As a composer and author, Wagner expressed an artistic philosophy that influenced both contemporary and future musicians, as well as other artists and writers.

Wagner's music dramas were symphonic in nature, with strong emphasis on orchestral color—notably, the powerful brass instruments. The music was continuous, and the dramatic flow was not interrupted by arias, recitatives, and ensembles in the traditional sense. Wagner used chromaticism, dissonance, vague cadences, and unresolved tension. Much of his music had nearly no sense of tonality and no sense of symmetry or balanced phrase structure. He made extensive use of the leitmotiv, a recurring musical motive associated with a character or a mood. It contributed unity to his music in the absence of more traditional forms and structures.

Wagner's theories are exemplified in his cycle of four operas known as *The Ring of the Nibelung,* which took 20 years to complete, and in *Tristan and Isolde,* a work of great beauty, sustained tension, and dramatic expression. Wagner was his own librettist, demonstrating his ideas about the unity of the arts. He was aided greatly by a wealthy patron, King Ludwig II of Bavaria, who helped him complete *The Ring* and create a lavish production of the cycle in Munich in 1876.

Other Notable Composers

Among other important composers of the Romantic period are Hector Berlioz, Antonín Dvořák, Edvard Grieg, Franz Liszt, Gustav Mahler, Giacomo Puccini, Sergei Rachmaninoff, Nicolay Rimsky-Korsakov, Gioacchino Rossini, Robert Schumann, Bedřich Smetana, and Richard Strauss.

Listening Guide
No. 68

Piano Concerto no. 2 in C Minor (I) (excerpt)
CD3, Track 9, 4:33

Composer: Sergei Rachmaninoff (1873–1943).

Performer: London Philharmonia Orchestra: Esa-Pekka Salonen, conductor; Yefim Bronfman, piano.

Genre: Piano concerto.

Context: This excerpt from one of the most popular concertos of the Romantic period provides an example of the virtuosity of many nineteenth-century solo performers, particularly pianists. This example represents only a part of the first movement of this concerto, which has two other movements. (The total time of the first movement is approximately 10 minutes; the entire concerto lasts approximately 33 minutes.)

Traditionally, the orchestra begins a concerto—in effect, introducing the pianist. This concerto begins with the piano.

Goals

Define *virtuosity,* and recognize it in the music.

Notice the interaction between the piano and the orchestra—when the soloist is predominant and when the orchestra is predominant.

Notice when the pianist is playing in a virtuosic manner. Describe the style when it is not virtuosic.

Guide

0:00	Introduction—piano only—slow; brooding yet gentle—strength increases
0:22	Piano increases the speed of the notes, then orchestra enters; piano in the background
1:45	Piano in the foreground—lyrical melody
2:00	Contrasting section in virtuosic style—piano flourishes—pounding
2:26	Lyrical melody enters—expressive, much **rubato** (flexible rhythm)
3:58	Oboe lead, then piano (fade)

Reflections

Discuss what it means to be a virtuoso.

How does this example reflect virtuosic performance? Are there parts of this example that do not reflect virtuosity?

Summary

The nineteenth century produced an amazing number of great composers and great works that are known, loved, and listened to by people worldwide. The purpose of this chapter is to draw attention to the characteristics of nineteenth-century romanticism and to the composers and their compositions that best exemplify these characteristics.

Nineteenth-century music is many people's introduction to the world of Western classical music. It is this music, along with the music of Mozart and Haydn in the Classic period, that we usually are exposed to first. These sounds are familiar, and the music is to a great extent accessible at first hearing. Also, these works wear well. They can unfold subtleties and reveal new insights on repeated hearings, and their ability to communicate feelings and to evoke responses among large numbers of people has spanned generations, even centuries. These are the attributes that characterize a great work of art in any medium or style.

13 Music of the Twentieth Century

Music, like the other arts, reflects the society in which it was created. Thus, music in the twentieth century was characterized by complexity, experimentation, a multiplicity of styles and directions, new forms, new symbols for expressing musical language (new notational systems), and multicultural influences. Which styles, forms, musical language, and composers will withstand the test of time and survive to influence twenty-first-century composers, performers, and listeners remains to be seen.

Chapter 13 introduces several trends important in the twentieth century and the composers associated with these trends. Many contemporary composers cannot easily be classified. In their search for originality, they at times have experimented and discovered new possibilities but at other times have returned to practices of the past. When a composer returned to an old style, the music usually combined elements of the old with new musical languages of the day. Still other **avant-garde** composers branched out in new directions, perhaps minimizing influences from the past, and have developed new musical languages, compositional techniques, and aesthetic ideas.

As radical and extreme as much contemporary music may seem, it does not represent any greater leap from the past than some of Monteverdi's music relative to Palestrina's, Beethoven's music relative to Haydn's, or Wagner's music relative to Brahms's. Stravinsky's ballet music of 1910–1913 was considered radical and barbaric at the time but now is ranked among the classics of the twentieth century (see Listening Guide 70, page 281).

Classical music from all historical periods is readily available on broadcasts, in recordings, at concerts, and over the Internet. Through recordings, scores, books, and musicological research, present-day audiences for classical music know the music of the past, and for the first time in history, many listeners prefer the music of the past to the music of contemporary, living composers. In fact, many twentieth-century composers created music not for the general public but for highly trained professional musicians, scholars, and other composers. This has been an ironic aspect of contemporary Western classical music: It speaks in a contemporary language to a public that prefers the eighteenth- and nineteenth-century musical language.

We can only speculate what the musical environment of the twenty-first century will be like and how audiences will respond to the new music of this new century.

Goals for Listening

In this chapter, you will notice several trends:

- More emphasis on texture and timbre than on melody and harmony—and on new instruments and new uses of old instruments.
- Asymmetrical rhythm and phrasing—and less emphasis on regular rhythm and balanced phrases.
- More than one key sounding simultaneously (polytonality), obscure tonality, or no sense of tonal center.
- Melodies that are often jagged, with wide skips (angular).
- **Tone clusters:** three or more adjacent tones sounding simultaneously.

Listening experiences in this chapter include impressionistic program music by Claude Debussy (page 277), experimental music (at the time it was written) by the Russian-French-American composer Igor Stravinsky (page 281), and a traditional-sounding orchestral piece with jazz elements by the French composer Darius Milhaud (page 298).

General Characteristics

About the only generalization one can make about modern classical music is that it is diverse and often complex. Contemporary composers have written for every conceivable medium from a single solo instrument to a huge symphony orchestra. They have written for conventional orchestra instruments and for unconventional instruments, adding them to the orchestra or creating new ensembles. A number of composers even expected performers to play conventional instruments in unconventional ways.

By the end of the Romantic period, the typical symphony orchestra had grown to more than twice the size of the orchestra of Mozart's time. Romantic composers wrote for larger numbers of string instruments and also added more brass, woodwind, and percussion instruments. Instrumental compositions had become much longer and more involved, but new short forms for both piano and voice had emerged as well.

Chromaticism had increased, and harmony had become complex, at times blurring tonality to the extent that there was no tonal center. Melodies were longer, phrases were less clear, and form was more difficult to discern.

To a great extent, twentieth-century composers emphasized timbre and rhythm rather than melody and harmony, creating a need for a different way of listening to music. Silence became a conscious compositional device in modern music, and not simply a time for a performer to rest. Silences frequently have a powerful aesthetic impact because of their length and their place in the music.

The organization and form of modern classical music are also diverse and often complex. The music ranges from totally controlled to free and improvisatory. In controlled music, the composer gives detailed instructions about how the music should be played. In music that is freer, performers sometimes are instructed to improvise passages—though usually within certain guidelines and restrictions. Much of this music is organized in time segments and is measured in seconds rather than by bars and phrases.

The horizontal pitch organization is typically angular and **disjunct,** moving in wide intervals or skips rather than in the smooth, **conjunct** manner of traditional-sounding melodies with a stepwise contour. Melodic lines span wide, even extreme, ranges. Frequently, these melodies cannot be described as singable. In modern music, it is less common than in earlier music to find balanced phrases, symmetrical patterns, forward energy culminating in clear cadences, and regular meter. Traditional tonic-dominant chord progressions are rare. Dissonance is the rule, and unresolved dissonances and sustained tension are common.

Modern art music may be tonal, but typically the sense of a major or minor key is obscure. Some music lacks any sense of key; some may be in two or more keys at the same time. Frequently, pitches are based on scales other than major or minor. They may incorporate scales found in other cultures or scales invented by the composer. The five-tone pentatonic scale and a whole-tone scale that excludes half steps are common in some modern pieces. Many modern composers, however, are experimenting with a return to tonality.

Essentially, the musical language of today is extremely different from the language common in the nineteenth century. For much contemporary music, new notations had to be devised to accommodate new sounds and new concepts. It is a language with which many people feel uncomfortable, perhaps because it is a language they haven't completely come to understand.

Stylistic Developments and Featured Composers

Most developments in the history of Western art music have come logically from past practices, as composers sought to create new, inventive music while building on existing forms. The continuum ranged from conservative composers such as Mendelssohn and Brahms to innovators such as Berlioz and Wagner.

New developments occurred because composers reacted against what they considered the excesses of the past or a particular style then popular. New developments also occurred because of external circumstances: economic factors, shifts in patronage, or political upheavals.

As we look back on the twentieth century from our vantage point in the early twenty-first, we can identify important composers and see a number of influential styles and techniques that rightfully are considered major new developments in the history of Western music. All the composers discussed here have created works that fall outside the category under which they are presented, but all are well known for their music and their influence in that particular category. Note, too, that there are numerous twentieth-century composers of significance; those presented here represent a sample rather than an inclusive list.

Impressionism: Claude Debussy

Impressionism is an artistic style derived from the philosophy and practice of a group of French painters, notably Monet and Renoir, toward the end of the nineteenth century. Impressionism in music was a reaction against the intellectual Germanic music of Brahms, Wagner, and Mahler. This new impressionistic music is best typified in the works of Claude Debussy and is marked by the delicate sonorities of flute, harp, and strings rather than massive sounds of brass and by subtle shadings rather than dramatic contrasts of tone color. And although you will hear exceptions to any generalization, impressionistic music is generally sensuous and beautiful and seldom harsh.

Debussy (1862–1918) was an adventurous French composer who rejected many of the established musical styles, forms, and techniques. He sought to evoke moods and to convey impressions of images and feelings rather than to produce literal descriptions. Although he is considered an impressionist, he did not set out to compose impressionistic music; others gave his music that label.

Perhaps more than any other composer, Debussy personifies the transition from nineteenth-century romanticism to the diverse and more complex practices of the twentieth century. He wrote in nearly every medium, but his piano and orchestral music stands out. Among his best-known works are *Prelude to the Afternoon of a Faun* (1892–1894) for orchestra; *Nocturnes* (1893–1899), a set of three descriptive pieces for orchestra; *La Mer* (1903–1905), a large programmatic three-movement orchestral work (see Listening Guide 69); *Syrinx* (1912) for unaccompanied flute; *Images for Piano*, books 1 and 2 (1905, 1907); and *Preludes for Piano*, books 1 and 2 (1910–1913). He also composed one string quartet, one opera, and "Clair de Lune," his most popular piece.

Claude Debussy.

Listening Guide   No. 69

"Jeux de vagues," from *La Mer*
CD3, Track 10, 7:17

Composer: Claude Debussy (1862–1918).

Performer: New Philharmonia Orchestra; Pierre Boulez, conductor.

Genre: Multimovement orchestral work.

Context: This impressionistic work for symphony orchestra has three movements:

I. De l'aube a midi sur la mer (From Dawn to Noon at Sea).

II. Jeux de vagues (Play of the Waves).

III. Dialogue du vent et de la mer (Dialogue between the Wind and the Sea).

The orchestra, in addition to the normal string section and winds in pairs, includes piccolo, English horn, a third bassoon and contrabassoon, two additional horns, a third trombone, and a tuba. The percussion section includes three timbales, gong, cymbals, triangle, two harps, and a glockenspiel.

This "symphony" paints a tonal landscape, evoking Debussy's impression of the wind and sea. The music conveys the surges and swells of the waves, with moods ranging from serene when the sea is calm to furious during the storms.

This musical example is the second movement, "Play of the Waves"; it is light and playful. Listen to musical details as specified in the Guide but also to the overall sounds, letting the "soundscape" create images in your mind.

Goals

Be aware of texture, timbre, and mood more than clearly stated melody and harmony.

Recognize chromatic and dissonant harmony.

Recognize asymmetrical meter and phrasing.

Describe impressionism.

Recognize music whose tonality is obscure and whose sounds are derived from scales other than major or minor.

Guide

Downbeats are often obscure, resulting at times in ambiguous meter.

0:00	Introduction	Quiet; sustained winds and harp arpeggios followed by a descending flute; repeated staccato notes in the trumpets that signal the start of the first theme
0:16	Theme A	Stated in English horn (motive is an ascending, four-note, whole-tone scale, which is then repeated and extended); answered by an oboe in high range, with an ascending harp arpeggio; music builds in intensity then recedes, descending to low trills in the cellos, signaling the beginning of the second theme

–Continued

Listening Guide –Continued   No. 69

0:53	Theme B	Stated in upper strings (shimmering, flat contour); followed by harp arpeggios and horns in dialogue; repeated staccato notes in high woodwinds signal the start of the third theme
1:34	Theme C	Long, legato theme stated in English horn; joined soon by solo horn; short, loud brass figures accompanied by a flurry of descending, ostinato figures passed between high woodwinds and high strings; solo clarinet, then solo violin, then solo horn followed by an increasingly animated passage; suddenly quiet as the oboe line is accompanied by a countermelody in flute and horn; legato strings and horns with flute arpeggios; staccato horns and trumpets signal the return of the theme; theme C restated in cellos; staccato figures continue; music builds and subsides
3:26	Theme A	Stated in oboe and clarinet; builds to a peak—solo trumpet—then subsides; dialogue in the upper woodwinds, beginning with oboes and English horn, then clarinet and flute; descending string scales answered by ascending scales in the woodwinds with a horn melody; occasional brief trumpet solos; builds to a climax; subsides to quiet, sustained trills in upper strings
4:44	Theme B	Stated in flute then oboe; legato passage in violas and cellos; horns and clarinets soon added; theme restated in oboes and bassoons; many lush ascending and descending passages in strings over ascending pizzicato scales in cellos, contrasting with fragments in upper woodwinds, horns, and trumpet solos; builds to a huge climax; sound subsides and texture thins
6:02	Coda	Ascending and descending harp arpeggios; answered by sustained horns with fragments of the first theme; ends with slow harp figures and one final statement of theme A in oboe; short, ascending lines by the harp, then flute in the low range, a glockenspiel arpeggio, and finally a single tone on the harp

Reflections

The music is chromatic, with little sense of tonality or traditional chord progression. Melodies seem to emerge and recede, flowing in and out of the sound fabric, ranging from a light, airy texture to the sonority of the full orchestra.

Experimental Music: Igor Stravinsky

In every generation, a small group of composers tries new styles, techniques, forms, timbres, or concepts in order to develop a new approach to composition, new aesthetic notions, or a new language for expressing music. These composers are said to be in the **avant-garde.** Their pieces, being experimental, have varying impacts. For some experimentalists, the musical outcome of an experiment is far less significant than the process of the experiment itself. In other words, such compositions are considered more important as musical ideas than as music.

The work of experimentalists ensures that music continually evolves. Usually, the pieces considered most representative of a specific musical style are not the initial experimental pieces but those that follow. These later pieces show the influence of the experimentalists but also likely blend new concepts with tried and acceptable practices. It is not unusual for pieces by an experimentalist to gain wide acceptance as these concepts and techniques are refined in his or her own subsequent compositions.

The term *creative process* suggests a certain amount of experimentation, but some composers create in bold, innovative ways while others create in a language that is known and proven acceptable. Typically, composers settle into one end or the other of this continuum, depending on where they feel most comfortable and have the best prospects for success.

Igor Stravinsky (1882–1971) was a Russian composer who lived and worked in Russia, Switzerland, France, and, for the last 32 years of his life, the United States. He became an American citizen in 1945. A legendary figure, he is regarded as one of the great composers of the twentieth century.

Stravinsky's fame began around 1910 in Paris, where he composed three large-scale ballets for Diaghilev and the Ballets Russes (Russian Ballet): *The Firebird, Petrushka,* and *The Rite of Spring.* The collaboration produced revolutionary ballet and ballet music. As frequently happens, however, his ballet music has been kept

The "Rite of Spring" is performed on stage in London.

alive mainly through orchestral versions of these three major works. Each became a classic of the twentieth-century symphonic repertoire.

Because the global economy was adversely affected by World War I, Stravinsky for a time created smaller works, such as *The Soldier's Tale* (1918), a theater piece with an "orchestra" of seven solo instruments that incorporated elements of jazz, ragtime, marches, a waltz, a tango, and a fiddling dance. Then, in the early 1920s, he began composing **neoclassical** music, such as *Symphonies of Wind Instruments* (1920) and *Concerto for Piano and Wind Orchestra* (1924). Other neoclassical works include the opera-oratorio *Oedipus Rex* (1927); *Symphony of Psalms* (1930), a three-movement sacred work for chorus and orchestra that omits violins, violas, and clarinets; and *Symphony in Three Movements* (1945), one of Stravinsky's most original works. An opera, *The Rake's Progress* (1951), written when he was nearly 70, was the culmination of Stravinsky's neoclassical period.

Stravinsky then embarked on what we now refer to as his modern period—a time during which he produced experimental works. He continued his compositional activity into the 1960s, but most critics agree that his greatest and most memorable works came from his earlier ballets and his neoclassical period (the first quarter of the twentieth century).

Stravinsky's contributions lie in several areas:

- His rhythmic imagination and complexity. He explored irregular meters and shifting accents to create imbalance, minimizing the effect of the pulse and regular metric feeling.

This pen and ink sketch of Stravinsky was drawn by Jean Cocteau; he titled it "Le Sacre du Printemps" ("The Rite of Spring"). Cocteau was a French artist who collaborated with Stravinsky in designing and producing several theatrical works.

- His innovative approach to orchestration. He used extreme ranges and unusual combinations of instruments.
- His ability to produce tonal music in new ways.
- His success in creating new music from old material, particularly Baroque and Classic forms and techniques, and from other existing styles, such as jazz and ragtime rhythms and Russian folk melodies.

Listening Guide   No. 70

Le Sacre du Printemps (The Rite of Spring) (opening scene)
CD3, Track 11, 8:21

Composer: Igor Stravinsky (1882–1971).

Performer: Cleveland Orchestra; Pierre Boulez, conductor. Recorded in 1991.

Genre: Concert piece from a ballet.

Context: The music for the ballet was composed between 1911 and 1913 and first performed by Ballets Russes in Paris in 1913. *Le Sacre du Printemps* is Stravinsky's third ballet. Although its first performance met with a riotous response, the work became a classic of twentieth-century music. The harsh dissonance, sharp rhythms, irregular meters, and unusual use of conventional instruments in this ballet and in Stravinsky's other early works influenced countless composers throughout the twentieth century.

Igor Stravinsky.

    Le Sacre du Printemps is in two parts. This example includes the beginning of part 1 (the entire concert version lasts more than 33 minutes).

Goals

Recognize dissonant harmonies, unusual melodies, and asymmetrical rhythm and phrasing.

Recognize ostinato patterns.

Be aware of varying degrees of tension and how they were achieved.

Describe various timbres and instruments.

–Continued

Listening Guide –Continued   No. 70

Guide

0:00	Introduction	Thin texture; quiet; woodwinds: high bassoon solo
0:45		English horn solo
1:14		Clarinet solo; then oboe solo; then English horn solo with bass clarinets; sound diminishes
1:55		Motives passed from instrument to instrument
2:25		Oboe, then joined by clarinet and English horn; trumpet enters; texture thickens and energy builds; ends suddenly
3:03		Solo bassoon returns
3:36	Omens of Spring: Dances of the Youths and Maidens	Harsh dissonant chords with off-beat accents sound in the strings followed by an English horn ostinato; more dissonant chords; descending trumpet line; texture thins but energy intensifies; off-beat dissonant chords return with a different accompanying motive, primarily in trombones and bassoons
4:55		Patterns move from instrument to instrument creating a fragmented texture; previous motives are heard, especially the English horn ostinato; a lyrical melody is heard in the horn—then, after descending trumpet lines, on the flute; texture thickens; loudness increases, then softens and builds again gradually to its greatest intensity
6:56	Ritual of Abduction	Begins with strings—answered by low thuds in timpani and bass drum; followed immediately by fast notes on solo trumpet; frenetic energy—motives passed around quickly from instrument to instrument; many punctuated chords, percussion thuds; ends with a loud string tremolo and a quiet flute tremolo

Reflections

Notice the lack of dominant-tonic chord progressions. Functional harmony was not a large part of twentieth-century musical language. This is unconventional tonal music, and any sense of key center is achieved by ways other than through traditional chord movement and cadences.

To a large extent, *Le Sacre* avoids regular pulse and metric feeling. At times, you may have a sense of suspension in time—of a lack of forward energy. At other times, the music moves forward, building to powerful climaxes.

This music deviates from the common practices of the eighteenth and nineteenth centuries and helped pave the way for a twentieth-century, if not a twenty-first-century, western European language for classical music.

Atonal Music and Serialism: Arnold Schoenberg

In traditional tonal music, compositions are usually organized around patterns of whole steps and half steps that establish key centers: the major or minor scales. **Atonality** results when establishment of a tonal center is deliberately avoided. It provides an alternative approach to the major-minor tonal system.

Serialism, known as **serial composition** or **12-tone technique**, evolved as a systematic means of organizing atonal music. It emerged in the 1920s and revolutionized music.

The essence of serialism is a set of pitches typically consisting of the 12 tones of the chromatic scale—that is, each half step within the octave. This set of pitches, a tone row, is the basis of the composition; by its nature, it avoids key centers. The tone row is subsequently used in various forms in its entirety; a tone is not repeated until the entire row is completed. In addition to its original order of pitches, the row may be used backwards, upside down, or upside down and backwards. The art is in the imaginative manipulation of the row: rhythmically, melodically, harmonically, in varying textures and timbres, and in contrasting dynamics.

The first and most important composer associated with serialism was Arnold Schoenberg, although few composers, including Schoenberg, adhered to it strictly— and only then in a few pieces.

Schoenberg (1874–1951), an Austrian, became a leader of contemporary musical thought in the 1920s. He assumed an important post as professor of composition in Berlin in 1925. After the rise of Hitler, he moved to the United States and became an American citizen in 1940. His longest post was as professor of composition at the University of California at Los Angeles, where he remained until his retirement at age 70.

Schoenberg's first compositions were in a highly chromatic but tonal post-Romantic style reminiscent of Brahms, Mahler, and especially Wagner. His most important early work is *Verklärte Nacht* (1899). In his next stage as a composer, Schoenberg rejected the major-minor tonal system entirely and created atonal pieces. Schoenberg's outstanding pieces from this period are *Five Pieces for Orchestra*, op. 16 (1909), and—perhaps his most popular work—*Pierrot Lunaire* (1912), for female reciter and an ensemble of five players playing eight different instruments. The reciter "sings" in an unusual style that combines speech and singing. From 1914 to 1920, Schoenberg produced few works. Instead, he contemplated ways of organizing the 12 tones of the chromatic scale in some cohesive system, which ultimately resulted in serialism.

Schoenberg's most famous serial compositions date from the late 1920s. His first composition based solely on a single row is *Suite*, op. 25, for piano. *Variations for Orchestra* (1928) is considered one of his best serial compositions. An entire opera, *Moses and Aaron* (1930–1932), is based on a single tone row. He continued to write serial music throughout his career, at times experimenting with combinations of tone row technique and tonality in the same piece.

In Schoenberg's atonal and serial music, the melodies tend to be predominantly disjunct rather than stepwise; the texture is sometimes polyphonic. Rather than the huge resources of post-Romantic music, Schoenberg preferred small orchestras and chamber ensembles of both standard and unconventional instrumental combinations. His phrases are of irregular length, and he deliberately avoided melodic repetition and chord progressions. The music sounds complex and fragmentary. Unity is achieved in different ways in different pieces, often through some transformation of short motives.

In Vienna, Schoenberg gathered students around him, the most talented being Anton Webern and Alban Berg, both of whom became noteworthy composers. In fact, composers since Schoenberg have experimented and produced important compositions in which other musical factors were serialized, basing their compositions not only on tone rows but on specific sequences (rows) of nonrepeated, contrasting dynamic levels, note values, or timbres. When several factors are serialized, the music is said to be **totally controlled music.** Little creativity is left to the composer once the serial decisions are made; the growth of the composition is determined in great detail by the previous decisions establishing the various rows.

Atonality and serialism are controversial. Some people think that this music is too cerebral, too complex, and emotionless. Others feel that serial composition is the logical path on which to base future musical developments. However, few composers in the late twentieth century based entire compositions on a single row of 12 tones; instead, most worked more flexibly as they applied the principles of cohesive organization suggested by Schoenberg's revolutionary system.

Electronic Music: Edgard Varèse

Although primitive electronic instruments existed in the first half of the twentieth century, electronic music as a medium did not exist until the 1950s. The impetus came from the development of magnetic tape recording. Technicians in Paris experimented with **musique concrète,** a name given to the technique of manipulating tape-recorded sounds from existing natural sources. Recorded sounds generated from musical instruments or voices could be altered by changing the speed of the tape, playing it backward, and cutting and splicing it. The altered sounds, perhaps combined with natural sounds, could then serve as sources for a composition.

The next development in electronic music was sound-generating equipment and synthesizers in which the electronic sound generation was combined with sound modification. Composers could now control every detail: rhythm, dynamics, pitch organization, timbre, reverberation (echo), and even the way a tone was begun and released (attack and decay). What the composer created was immediately on tape, ready for any listener; no performer was necessary. Synthesizers are common today. They are greatly reduced in size and operational complexity and are used in the performance of classical, jazz, rock, and commercial music.

Most electronic music today is created for live performance. The performance may include one or more standard instruments with prerecorded tape or a standard instrument using tape for sound modification, such as digital tape delay. Early experiments involved not only live performers with electronically generated sounds but also real or modified tape-recorded sounds from nature, such as the sound of fire, water, birds, or whales.

Computer-generated music and computer-assisted music are no longer innovative, except as new developments and improvements occur. Through **MIDI (Musical Instrument Digital Interface)** technology, software programs now make both computer-generated music and computer-assisted music easy for professionals and amateurs. In addition, sophisticated software programs make the preparation of music scores relatively easy.

Edgard Varèse (1883–1965) was one of the prominent early composers of electronic music. Born and educated in Paris, in 1915 he came to the United States, where he spent his entire career. Like Henry Cowell, Aaron Copland, and others, Varèse actively promoted new music, helping to make it more accessible and well known, and thus building an audience for it. Varèse and others used a variety of means to promote this new, perhaps experimental, music: They conducted new works, wrote articles and books, and participated in classes and seminars. By doing so, they helped people understand and appreciate the new music.

Varèse accepted any sound—whether perceived as pitches or noise—as potential material for musical composition. In the 1920s, he used a wide variety of percussion instruments and even sirens. In the 1950s, he incorporated electronically taped sound sources. His music is frequently described as static sound masses or as collages of sound having little to do with chord progressions or melodic movement.

His most influential music was composed in the 1920s and 1950s. The earlier music, reflecting his lifelong interest in science and technology, included *Hyperprism, Octandre, Intégrales, Arcana, Ionization, Density 21.5,* and *Ecuatorial.* His later music, incorporating manipulated taped sounds, is best represented by *Déserts* and *Poème électronique. Ecuatorial* is a unique piece composed in 1934 that uses primitive electronic instruments: originally a theremin and, in a later version, an ondes Martenot.

Other successful and influential composers of electronic music include Milton Babbitt, Mario Davidovsky, Otto Luening, and Morton Subotnik.

Chance Music: John Cage

Chance music, sometimes called *indeterminate music,* represents a compositional style at the opposite end of the spectrum from totally controlled serial music. The composer does not control all the details of a composition. Chance music allows the performer to participate in the creative process.

This process can include the random selection of sounds, selection by chance, or improvised passages within the structure of a composition. However, it is not uncontrolled music. Although details are left to the performer, the overall structure is indicated in a score. A work in which techniques of chance are applied is never performed the same way twice.

The influence of John Cage (1912–1992) is felt not only through his music but also, and perhaps more, through his writings. Like his predecessors, Cage explored new sounds and new ways of organizing sound. He is best known for influence in areas that fall under the category of the following broad terms: prepared piano, chance music, and silence.

Whereas some composers have extended concepts of serialism to gain total control of every nuance of sound, Cage reduced control, allowing the outcome of a performance to be unpredictable. Rather than put things together, Cage was willing to let things happen. He is well known for a piece whose "instrumentation" was no more than multiple radios set at different places on the dial, including static. He accepted the sounds, whatever they were, as the piece of music.

Cage's early work emphasized percussive sounds, including the piano. His best-known technique was to alter the sound of the piano by placing screws and other items inside, touching the strings in ways that affected the sound. His most famous work in this technique is *Concerto for Prepared Piano and Chamber Orchestra* (1951).

Cage became aware that there is no such thing as silence because we always hear some sounds—the sound of our own bodies; air circulating; people moving, breathing, or coughing. These sounds become sources of sound for music. Today, more than at any time in music history, silence has become a conscious part of composition. Cage has helped us understand it better.

Nationalism: Béla Bartók

Nationalism, introduced in chapter 12 (see page 254), became a major theme for a number of late-nineteenth-century composers, particularly from Russia and eastern Europe. Many twentieth-century European composers incorporated nationalism in their music. Among the most noted of these was Béla Bartók.

Bartók (1881–1945), one of the greatest Hungarian composers, taught piano at the Budapest Academy of Music for 27 years (1907–1934) and gave recitals throughout Europe. An intense anti-Nazi, he felt compelled to leave Hungary and in 1940 immigrated to the United States. He settled in New York City, where he died in 1945.

Early in his career, Bartók became interested in the nationalist movement that had spread throughout Europe. He sought to preserve the folk music of Hungary and to let the world know that Hungary possessed a traditional folk repertoire that included more than Gypsy music. He traveled to small villages and rural communities during the first decades of the twentieth century and recorded the people's songs on cylinder machines. Bartók succeeded because he lived with the peasants for a time and gained their confidence and trust. As a result, he was able to develop a treasury of folk songs numbering in the thousands, including songs collected and recorded as he moved into other parts of eastern Europe and northern Africa. This folk music was to have a profound effect on Bartók's compositional style.

Béla Bartók.

Bartók's highly individual style combines the spirit of eastern European folk music, Classic-era forms, and the musical language of contemporary Europe—a language he expanded in exciting and innovative ways. His music transcends many styles, techniques, and systems. It is tonal, often modal, and sometimes polytonal. It frequently slides into highly chromatic atonality because Bartók did not adhere rigidly to the major-minor tonal system. His harmony is dissonant and often harsh, and his rhythms are vital and often pounding, nonsymmetrical, and syncopated. He sometimes treats the piano as a percussion instrument, using pounding chords and **tone clusters** as elements of rhythm. His scoring for instruments brings imaginative tone colors, particularly from the many percussion instruments that he frequently uses.

Among Bartók's greatest compositions are works for piano and for orchestra. *Mikrokosmos* (1926–1937) is a set of 153 piano pieces in six books at varying levels of difficulty. They not only have pedagogical value but summarize his compositional styles and the styles of European composition flourishing at the time. His *Music for Strings, Percussion, and Celesta* (1936) is another of his greatest works. His six string quartets (1908–1939) rank among the finest works in the chamber music repertoire.

Bartók's best-known compositions are from the years he spent in the United States, although they were not happy years. He was poor, felt isolated and unaccepted, and could not get his music performed. He received few commissions and eventually developed leukemia. While he was hospitalized, he received the commission that led to *Concerto for Orchestra* (1943), his most popular work. His last completed work was his Third Piano Concerto (1945). Ironically, after Bartók's death, his music became popular in the United States, and he became famous.

Other composers of note who wrote nationalistic music include Ralph Vaughan Williams (England), Zoltán Kodály (Hungary), Heitor Villa-Lobos (Brazil), and the two American composers discussed in the following section.

Nationalism: Charles Ives and Aaron Copland

Nationalism in music emerged in the late nineteenth century among a group of composers from eastern Europe and Russia—Rimsky-Korsakov, Mussorgsky, and Dvořák, among many others. Charles Ives was one of the most prominent of American nationalistic composers; another was Aaron Copland.

Composers of **nationalistic music** at times quote directly from the folk repertoire or compose in a manner that reflects folk rhythms or the moods of this music. To create American nationalistic music, a composer might use, for example, Native American melodies and rhythms. To create an orchestral piece based on Cuban dances, one might incorporate native Cuban dance rhythms and instruments, such as claves, guiro, or bongos.

Before the 1920s, American composers sometimes quoted folk tunes, spirituals, and other vernacular music, but European-style music dominated. After the 1920s, certain composers, notably Aaron Copland, sought a style that would be immediately recognizable as American. **Americanist music** would become a matter of national pride and would also reach a broad audience. The composer begins with the premise that certain events, places, or characteristics—musical or other—are important and known to a large segment of Americans and are suggestive of America. These are things that do not apply to other nations or regions; they are national rather than universal.

Americanist music might convey a sense of the wide open spaces; it might reflect vernacular elements, such as the syncopated rhythms of jazz and popular music; or it might connote religious, folk, or patriotic themes. Perhaps the ideal of a distinctively American musical style was derived from the notion that America was a "melting pot" in which various cultures blended into one "American" society. However, even at the time this nationalistic music was being composed, America already was too diverse for such a blending. Although many immigrants—individuals and groups— were thoroughly assimilated into mainstream society, others retained distinctive characteristics such as their taste in food, their songs and dances, their dialect, and their values.

The music of mainstream America and of its ethnic groups was a mosaic of styles—diverse and enriching. The mosaic also included the many American composers who developed their own style without a consciously American flavor. These composers focused more on abstract, experimental music—perhaps electronic and, more recently, computer music. Others focused on atonality and serialism, and still others on earlier styles and structures—neoclassical or neoromantic. Many of these composers produced works with more than one focus. Yet all this was American music, created in America by Americans. Diversity is the core of the American musical language.

To a large extent, we must listen to much twentieth-century music, such as the music of Charles Ives, differently from the way we listen to the music that preceded it. The emphasis is more on texture, color, and rhythm than on melody, harmony, or thematic development. By definition, when music considered experimental is new, it is not in the mainstream repertoire—that is, it is not known and appreciated by the general public—although some of it gradually becomes part of the mainstream.

Charles Ives (1874–1954) was perhaps the first great innovator in twentieth-century American classical music. He was followed by Edgard Varèse and Henry Cowell, composers who also helped shape the mid-twentieth-century avant-garde movement, particularly in America. In the 1950s, the music and writings of Cowell's student John Cage and Varèse's work in the newly developing electronic medium gave impetus to experimentation.

Charles Ives.

Ives was well educated in music, with a degree from Yale. Working in Connecticut and New York, far from the major European music centers, he developed a style that was outside the generally accepted European tradition. One of America's rugged individualists, Ives felt that he could be freer and more independent as a composer if he did not have to depend on music for his livelihood, so he worked in his family's insurance business. His music represents nearly every major compositional innovation in the twentieth century, but Ives "discovered" the new techniques decades ahead of everyone else.

Ives experimented musically but was guided by larger issues. To him, music was more than sounds. It was the spirit that emanated from its creator, a musical manifestation of life itself. Ives's music was infused with quotations of melodies or fragments of melodies from familiar American vernacular music, mostly hymns, patriotic songs, and marches—re-creating sounds from life. He did not think of this use of quotations as producing nationalistic music; rather, he was using available materials to create something larger. He recognized that all of life is vital and substantial and that art and life do not need to be separate. In this way, his music synthesized American classical and vernacular traditions.

Ives stopped composing in 1921, and he has been well known only since the 1940s. Full recognition of his work came even later, after his death in 1954.

Although much of Ives's music is extremely complex, and some of it hard to perform and listen to, his works now are widely recorded and performed, particularly some choral pieces and songs from the nearly 200 that he wrote. His instrumental music is widely recognized. Particularly noteworthy are his four symphonies, the third of which was awarded the Pulitzer Prize in 1947; *Three Places in New England,* a set of tone poems; and *The Unanswered Question,* for trumpet, four flutes, and an offstage string orchestra. Of his two piano sonatas, Sonata no. 2 (*Concord*) is best known.

Aaron Copland (1900–1990), without a doubt, is the best-known and most successful American composer of classical music. His nationalistic music has been especially successful in contributing to the development and vitality of American music. He was the first of the idealistic Americans in Paris in the 1920s who wanted to elevate American music and help shape the American musical personality.

Aaron Copland.

Copland was interested in merging elements of classical and vernacular music. He wanted to do more than quote hymns, spirituals, or American Indian chants, as others before him had done. His genius was in using vernacular, often regional, elements to formulate more universal thoughts that could represent the whole country.

Copland was interested in innovation, but not at the expense of the past. He felt that although music had to move ahead, it should be built on past practices. He was influenced, as were other Americans in Paris in the 1920s, by Stravinsky, whose first musical achievements had taken place in Paris 15 years earlier. Stravinsky's influence was neoclassicism—he combined a new musical language with old forms, structures, and values.

In the 1920s and 1930s, along with Henry Cowell, Roger Sessions, Edgard Varèse and others, Copland organized concerts that featured new, often experimental, works by American and sometimes contemporary European composers. Copland also wrote about this music to help people understand it. There was an audience for these concerts for a while, but in the mid-1930s, the audiences began to dwindle. The gap between composer and listener began to widen as composers became ultra-modern, abstract, and separated from the tastes of the public. As audiences for the new music declined, Copland became concerned about composing in a vacuum. In the late 1930s, he began to explore ways of reaching a wider public, of composing with artistic integrity but in a more accessible language.

From this approach came Copland's tone poems, ballet music, music for films and radio, and patriotic works reflecting the American spirit and drawing on vernacular forms. This music includes cowboy songs, popular Mexican songs, church music, jazz, and blues. It was the music of rural America with urban rhythms and harmonies. It allowed Copland to develop a distinct and enduring style.

Copland's best-known ballets are *Billy the Kid* (see Listening Guide 71), *Rodeo*, and *Appalachian Spring*. His patriotic music includes *Fanfare for the Common Man* and *Lincoln Portrait*. His best-known movie music was for *The Red Pony* and *Our Town*. Copland also experimented with serial composition, particularly in the 1950s, and his piano music ranks among the best abstract modern works.

Listening Guide   No. 71

Billy the Kid (excerpt)
CD3, Track 12, 3:58

Composer: Aaron Copland (1900–1990).

Performer: New York Philharmonic; Leonard Bernstein, conductor.

Genre: Ballet, orchestral version.

Context: The music for Copland's ballet *Billy the Kid* derives from the western European concert music tradition. It is American music in one sense because the composer is American. It is American in another sense because the story and many of the tunes Copland uses in this ballet are derived from the songs and traditions of the American people and from American folk traditions.

Listening Guide –Continued No. 71

Goals

Recognize and describe texture, timbre, and dynamics.

Describe various layers of sound, such as bass lines, inner voices, and other supportive lines.

Recognize patterns in the music as it develops, particularly patterns in the treatments of meter, repeated musical ideas, and contrast.

Be aware of rhythmic vitality, and identify ways in which it is achieved.

Distinguish between the sound of a solo instrument and the sound of a group of instruments.

Guide

0:00	First theme, a four-note motive, sounds soon in the solo horn, then the flute; oboe answers
0:21	As this section begins to extend and expand, building on the original motive, the quiet mood is accompanied by a two-note descending interval featuring off-beat thumps in the timpani and other low instruments
0:59	Section increases in intensity and loudness, culminating in cymbal crashes, timpani, and brass instruments
1:14	Energy suddenly diminishes, builds again in a similar manner with the two-note motive appearing melodically in higher-range instruments, and then ends abruptly as the next section begins
2:04	Contrasting section features a folklike melody introduced by the piccolo; wind instruments then enter a dialogue with the brasses, passing parts of the melody back and forth; pungent dissonances add interest and excitement
2:56	Section extends in a more regular, dancelike style, followed by irregular rhythms and much syncopation
3:07	Strings present the melody; trombones answer; strings play it again but this time are followed by the trumpets; soon only fragments of the melody are heard in various instruments; section subsides to a quiet ending

Reflections

Be aware of the density of instrumentation. Describe the sound—a few instruments produce thin texture while many instruments usually produce a full, thick texture.

Listen for contrasting sections and changes of tempo (speed), range (high or low pitch areas), and musical thoughts (phrases).

–Continued

Listening Guide –Continued   No. 71

The folklike melodies, usually presented only in fragments, are often passed from instrument to instrument. Identify the instruments from their sounds.

Describe the meter and rhythm. Can you tap your foot to the music? Is there a regular beat? Is it danceable music, or does much of it have only the "feel" of music to be danced to?

Discuss the texture of a string quartet (see Listening Guide 3, page 36, and Listening Guide 61, page 245), and compare it with the texture of the symphony orchestra heard in this example. Is one texture always thin and the other always full?

Additional American Composers

This section discusses a variety of diverse and successful American composers: two mid-twentieth-century women (Amy Beach and Ruth Crawford), two mid-twentieth-century African Americans (William Grant Still and Ulysses Kay), a composer of experimental music who was considerably ahead of his time (Henry Cowell), a very well known composer of Tin Pan Alley songs and very popular opera and other classical music (George Gershwin), and a Pulitzer Prize–winning female composer (Ellen Taaffe Zwilich).

Amy Cheney Beach   Beach (1867–1944) had a successful career as a performer and composer, a significant accomplishment in her time. Her *Gaelic* Symphony was the first symphony by an American woman. She was also the first woman to have her music premiered by the Handel and Haydn Society of Boston and the New York Philharmonic Orchestra. Much of her music is recorded and available.

Beach's compositions for solo piano, in particular, may sound conservative to our contemporary ears. Works such as "By the Still Waters" and "From Grandmother's Garden" incorporate impressionistic sounds and are programmatic. Her instrumental music, including a piano concerto, a string quartet, and a piano quintet, is more innovative and complex.

Ruth Crawford   Crawford (1901–1953) was an active and important composer when, in the early 1930s, she married Charles Seeger, a distinguished **ethnomusicologist** and collector of folk songs. She stopped composing because of family responsibilities and chose to concentrate, along with her husband, on American folk music.

In the 1920s, Crawford was in the vanguard of musical developments such as the serialization of elements other than pitch. In 1930, she was the first woman to be awarded a Guggenheim Fellowship, which enabled her to study in Berlin and Paris. She composed songs, suites for various instruments, the nine Preludes for Piano, a well-known string quartet, and a woodwind quintet.

Listening Guide   No. 72

Symphony no. 1 (III)

CD3, Track 13, 4:00

Composer: Ellen Taaffe Zwilich (b. 1939).
Performer: Indianapolis Symphony; John Nelson, conductor.
Genre: Symphony for orchestra.
Context: Zwilich won the Pulitzer Prize for Music in 1983 for this work; she was the first woman to win this coveted prize.

Goals

Recognize the main motives and elements of contrast and repetition.
Identify entrances of main theme areas.
Be aware of the sounds of modern, tonal music.

Guide

0:00	First theme area	Fast, vibrant, forceful; begins with timpani, followed by the main ascending motive and by many staccato repeated-note patterns as well as wide-ranging passages; ends with a bell
1:14	Contrast	Slow and quiet; descending, stepwise pattern
1:38	Return	Timpani, then the original ascending motive
1:52	Second contrast	Begins with a bell; legato, soft, and slow
2:34	Return	Fast and sprightly, making use of the earlier repeated-tone patterns; intensity builds; range of the violins is at times extreme; ends conventionally, providing a clear sense of tonic

Reflections

This movement has characteristics of a rondo (a b a c a), but without traditional sounds or formal clarity.
Compare the musical characteristics of this piece, particularly the orchestral sonorities, with those of Stravinsky, Brahms, and Bach.

Ellen Taaffe Zwilich   Zwilich (b. 1939) has composed solo works, chamber music for various ensembles (her String Quartet of 1974 received much acclaim), and music for orchestra. Her style combines modern musical language with links to the past. She likes to develop large-scale works based on a germinal idea, and she values the richness and variety of modern orchestras.

Ulysses Kay   An African American composer, Kay (1917–1995) was one of the most honored of all American composers. He received a Fulbright Scholarship, a Guggenheim Fellowship, and the Prix de Rome. He had a successful career as a moderately conservative tonal composer. Much of his music is in small forms, but he also composed operas and music for television and films. Much of his work could be considered neoclassical because of its form and orchestral balance.

Henry Cowell   Cowell (1897–1965) was influential as a composer, a teacher, an author, and a promoter of new music. Some of his values and practices, which he developed in the 1920s, became commonplace by the 1950s.

Cowell was committed to exploring ways of merging Western music with the folk and traditional music of other cultures. He searched for new sources of sound and new ways of organizing sound, and he created new notation to communicate his new techniques.

One of his most famous compositional devices, dating from as early as 1912, is the tone cluster—several adjacent pitches played simultaneously. On the piano, a cluster is often achieved by depressing the keys with the fist or the entire forearm. Cowell found new sources of sound in numerous percussion instruments and in using the piano as a percussion instrument—by means of tone clusters and also by plucking, strumming, scraping, and hitting the strings inside the piano.

Among the best known of Cowell's more than 5,000 compositions are a number of symphonies, a series of pieces titled *Hymn and Fuguing Tunes*, and music for solo piano.

George Gershwin   A Tin Pan Alley composer of songs, musicals, and film music, Gershwin (1898–1937) was also a composer of jazz-oriented classical music. Indeed, he was one of the most popular and most effective of all American composers. His classical music is widely known, universally loved, and extensively performed. It includes *Rhapsody in Blue* for piano and orchestra (1924), Concerto in F for piano and orchestra (1925), *An American in Paris* for orchestra (1928), three Preludes for Piano (1926), and *Porgy and Bess*, a folk opera (1935) (see "Summertime," from *Porgy and Bess*, Listening Guide 18, page 93).

George Gershwin.

Symphony conductor JoAnn Falletta is currently the conductor of the Buffalo Philharmonic Orchestra. She has served as guest conductor of symphony orchestras throughout the world, including the Philadelphia Orchestra, the National Symphony in Washington, D.C., the San Francisco Symphony, the Saint Paul Chamber Orchestra, and orchestras at Tanglewood, the Hollywood Bowl, Wolf Trap, and Interlochen.

Listening Guide   No. 73

Preludes for Piano, no. 1
CD3, Track 14, 1:26

Composer: George Gershwin (1896–1937).
Performer: Michael Tilson-Thomas, piano.
Genre: Piano miniature.
Context: In 1926, Gershwin composed his Preludes for Piano to play at his own recital at the Hotel Roosevelt in New York City. The three pieces are usually performed as one three-movement composition in a fast-slow-fast order. They are in contrasting keys.

Goals

Recognize jazz and Latin elements in a classical context.
Recognize the vamp.

Guide

This prelude opens with a blue note motive. The left-hand vamp precedes the entrance of the opening theme, and the accompaniment takes on a distinctively Latin flavor.

Reflections

The prelude is in a classical form and context but incorporates the syncopated, bluesy sounds of the popular music and jazz of the 1920s.
Compare this piece with the prelude by Chopin (see Listening Guide 65, page 263).

William Grant Still, a prominent and award-winning African American composer. He was the first African American to compose a major symphonic work and have it performed by a major American orchestra.

William Grant Still   One of the best-known African American composers, Still (1895–1978) had a career that took him from his home state of Mississippi to New York City and Boston. He worked or studied with W. C. Handy in Memphis, Eubie Blake and Noble Sissle on Broadway, George Chadwick at the New England Conservatory, and Edgard Varèse in New York. While Still was a staff arranger and composer for radio stations in New York City, he came into contact with such famous entertainers as Artie Shaw, Sophie Tucker, and Paul Whiteman.

A Guggenheim Fellowship, awarded in 1934, enabled Still to devote more of his time to classical composition. Settling in Los Angeles, he pursued an active career in composition. He produced operas, many orchestral works, and vocal, keyboard, and chamber pieces. His style, conservative and consonant, combined elements of French impressionism and Afro-American music. His most representative and perhaps best-known work is the *Afro-American Symphony*, composed in 1930.

Neoclassical Music

Many twentieth-century composers valued form and structure; in some cases, they returned to the common practices and aesthetic values of the past. These composers are known as neoclassicists. Other composers, though not primarily neoclassicists, often created one or more pieces in a neoclassical style.

Neoclassical music may be derived from past practices, but its language is not. A neoclassical piece by Stravinsky, perhaps the best-known neoclassical composer, does not sound like Mozart, but it may reflect classical ideals of control, order, emotional restraint, adherence to formal structure, minimal instrumentation, and transparent texture.

Minimalism

Minimalism is a style of composition that seeks the greatest effect from the least amount of material. It emerged in the late 1960s with the music of composers Philip Glass and Terry Riley, in part as a reaction against the complexities of serialism and other twentieth-century styles that lacked melodic shape, tonal clarity, and perhaps audience appeal.

The technique of minimalism is to take a musical pattern or idea and repeat it incessantly, creating slow, subtle changes in rhythm, chord movement, or other musical elements. The rhythmic activity may be fast, but the rate of change in the activity is slow. The technique represents a way of controlling music other than through serialization, and it also represents a return to tonal music in that the repetition generates clear centers of tonal feeling.

Minimalist music allows the listener to concentrate on few details, thus enhancing perception. Its adherents have a kinship with jazz, rock, and the music and ideas of India and Africa. Time will tell if minimalism has a significant impact on the long-term development of Western classical music.

Traditional Sounds

Not all twentieth-century music is abstract, complex, or challenging to listen to. In the early part of the century, composers such as Stravinsky returned to practices of the past, yet they created their music using a context and a fresh musical language that made it sound as though it belonged in the twentieth century. Other composers preferred a return to nineteenth-century Romantic aesthetics, forms, and techniques. They wrote program music, symphonies, or concertos, and they created personalized, expressive music with singable melodies. Their music is tonal with relatively simple rhythms, conventional playing or singing ranges, and traditional instrumental combinations. Their harmonies are colorful—even bold—but generally within the accepted structure of the major-minor tonal system.

Composers may have adopted a traditional style because of their own comfort with accepted practices or perhaps from a desire to counter the complexities of other modern music by simplifying musical language. Some were also motivated by a desire not to alienate audiences but rather to provide music that listeners would find accessible and enjoyable—and, of course, would pay to hear in concerts or on recordings.

Folk songs and regional ethnic music have inspired many composers. As mentioned previously, Bartók became intimately involved in folk music. Whereas some composers incorporated the spirit of folk music rather than specific songs, others used specific folk material—melodies, rhythms, and dances—as the basis of a composition. In these cases, because of the literal reference to folk material, such music frequently was tuneful, rhythmically comfortable or even exciting, and created in a traditional rather than an experimental context.

Many of the great composers found a balance between innovation and a style that would find wide acceptance. Interestingly, such acceptance sometimes came decades later, even after the composer's death. However, composers whose music is never forward-looking seldom contribute much to the development of music. It was the great innovators like Monteverdi, Beethoven, Wagner, and Stravinsky who gave vitality to music.

Listening Guide   No. 74

La Création du Monde, op. 81 (excerpt)

CD3, Track 15, 5:03

Composer: Darius Milhaud (1892–1974).

Performer: Branford Marsalis, alto saxophone, and the Orpheus Chamber Orchestra—from the album *Creation* (2001).

Genre: Classical orchestral piece.

Context: This was the first piece of classical music to incorporate jazz elements—in the early 1920s.

Branford Marsalis is a jazz musician, having performed with great jazz artists during the 1980s, such as Art Blakey, Clark Terry, his brother Wynton Marsalis, and Herbie Hancock. In 1985, he joined Sting's pop/rock group; by 1986, he was heading his own quartet; in 1992, he became musical director of Jay Leno's *Tonight Show.* As of this writing, his versatility is demonstrated on five classical CDs, including *Creation.*

Milhaud's *La Création du Monde* (*The Creation of the World*) was premiered in 1923, before the jazz-influenced pieces of George Gershwin: *Rhapsody in Blue* (1924) and *Porgy and Bess* (1935). *La Création* was originally a ballet but is now more frequently heard as a concert piece. This is an excerpt; the total work lasts over 17 minutes.

Goals

Listen carefully to parts other than the solo instrument, and describe how they support the melody.

Describe Marsalis's playing style.

Discuss the effect of the last chord of the excerpt in relation to the preceding material.

Guide

0:00	Part 1	Alto sax solo; gentle rocking pattern supports the melody; soft syncopated pattern in the trumpets provides contrast; notice strong percussion beats
0:50		Similar to above—repetition of style and mood
1:36		Long, ascending scale increasing in loudness followed by descending scale in different style, decreasing in loudness and speed
2:14		Slow—quiet mood—moving parts supporting the melody; ends with an ascending scale pattern in upper strings
2:39		Suddenly loud—change of mood, part of it like a fanfare; brass, percussion
2:54		Quiet mood—descending, tempo slows

3:14		Extended quiet section—sax solo—rocking accompaniment; double bass countermelody; descending scales; tempo slows to full cadence
4:21	Part 2	More jazzy style: increased energy; percussion; double bass solo; syncopated polyphonic texture, solo entrances: trombone, alto sax, trumpet; fade

Reflections

In what ways is this piece classical, and in what ways is it jazz? Or is it both? Neither? Would you answer differently if considering only part 1 or only part 2?

To the extent that you feel *La Création* is effective as a jazz-influenced piece, would it have been equally as effective if the primary solo material had been written for an instrument other than alto saxophone, such as violin, clarinet, or trombone? What other instruments would have worked as well as the alto sax?

Summary

In the twentieth century, for the first time in the history of music, the public was more interested in dead composers than in those still living and writing music. One major reason for this preference is clear: The century saw advances in scholarly research on music from previous eras and in the availability of all kinds of music (both published and recorded). Consequently, the public had more access to music from the past than ever before. In addition, though, the twentieth century was an age of experimentation in which composers felt free to do their own thing—express what they felt, try new techniques, and create new notations. They valued artistic integrity above the need to appeal to the masses or sell more music. This priority led to the creation of some music that, while innovative and artistic, was not appealing to the general public. For the most part, the audience was less important to the twentieth-century composer than it was to composers in previous eras. Likewise, the modern composer's music is less important to the contemporary audience.

It is also important to keep in mind that the twentieth century was the era of two world wars and the beginning of the nuclear era, which holds the continual threat of more devastation. The century generated a rapidly advancing technology that affected every facet of people's lives and a communications industry that brought daily information about tragedy and turmoil from around the world. In music as well as the other arts, the creation of artistic works reflected this unsettled world.

APPENDIX A

A List of Recommended DVDs and Videos
Supporting the Philosophy of The World of Music

Alison Krauss and Union Station—"Live"

DVD. Rounder, 2003. Two discs. Contemporary bluegrass—chapter 6.

This performance was filmed in HD at the Louisville Palace in Louisville, Kentucky.

Andreas Vollenweider—"The Magical Journeys"

DVD. A PBS program, 2006. Two discs. World music—chapter 8.

The Zurich Chamber Orchestra is conducted by André Bellmont. Other musicians include Abdullah Ibrahim, piano; Xiaojing Wang, Chinese erhu; Carly Simon, vocals; Djivan Gasparyan, duduk; David Lindley, lap and steel guitars; and Andi Pupato, percussion. Vollenweider plays piano, gu-cheng, Chinese flute, kora, ocarina, and other instruments; he also was the primary composer and arranger. (No music on this video was composed by Bach, Beethoven, or Brahms!)

J. S. Bach—Organ Concert in St. Thomas Church (Leipzig, Germany)

DVD. Ullrich Böhme, organist. Baroque music—chapter 10.

The St. Thomas Church and the organ are important pieces of European culture both musically and historically.

Beethoven—Symphony no. 9

VHS. Image Entertainment, 2001. Music of the classic period—chapter 11.

This is a live recording of Beethoven's Symphony no. 9 in D Minor (the Choral Symphony), from the Gewandhaus concert halt in Leipzig, Germany. It features Kurt Masur conducting the Gewandhaus Orchestra and Chorus, with soloists Venceslava Hruba-Freiberger (soprano), Doris Soffel (mezzo), James Wagner (tenor), and Gwynne Howell (bass).

Blues Masters—"The Essential History of the Blues"

VHS. Rhino Home Video, 2002. Traditional blues—chapter 3; jazz—chapter 5; popular music—chapter 6.

Artists include Son House, Leadbelly, Bessie Smith, Ethel Waters, Billie Holiday, Muddy Waters, and B. B. King. Songs include "Levee Camp Blues," "St. Louis Blues," "Pick a Bale o' Cotton," "Hoochle Coochle Man," and "Shake, Rattle and Roll."

Chick Corea—"Piano Legends"

VHS. VAI Jazz Video Collection, 2001. Jazz—chapter 5.

Jazz pianist Chick Corea traces the history of jazz piano from its early ragtime beginnings through the swing and bebop eras to modern times. Artists include Earl Hines, Fats Waller, Art Tatum, Oscar Peterson, Marian McPartland, Thelonious Monk, and Chick Corea.

Dave Brubeck—"Rediscovering Dave Brubeck"

DVD. Image Entertainment. Hedrick Smith Productions, 2001. Jazz—chapter 5.

"Down from the Mountain"

DVD. Artisan Entertainment, 2002. 98 minutes. Bluegrass music—chapter 6.

Artists include T-Bone Burnett, composer of "O Brother, Where Art Thou?" Musicians include Emmylou Harris and Alison Krauss and Union Station.

This documentary centers on a bluegrass concert in Nashville, Tennessee, given by the bands that contributed to the *O Brother, Where Art Thou?* movie sound track. It provides a brief history of folk and bluegrass music.

Ella and Basie '79—"The Perfect Match"—Norman Granz's Jazz in Montreux

DVD. Laser Swing Productions. Red Distribution, 2004. Jazz—chapter 5.

This features a live performance by vocalist Ella Fitzgerald and big band leader Count Basie at the prestigious Montreux Jazz Festival in 1979.

Eric Clapton—"Crossroads Guitar Festival"

DVD. Reprise Records, 2004. 210 minutes. Two discs. Popular music—chapter 6.

Numerous guitar legends gathered in June 2004 at the Cotton Bowl in Dallas, Texas, to play a benefit for Eric Clapton's Crossroads Center. Artists include John Mayer, B. B. King, Robert Cray, Carlos Santana, and James Taylor.

"Gael Force" (Celtic music)

DVD. Image Entertainment. 100 minutes. World music—chapter 8.

Artists include the Chieftains, Sinead O'Connor, Clannad, Afro Celt Sound System, Christy Moore, Sharon Shannon, Allan, and Mary Black. Recorded at Dublin's Point Theatre.

Handel's *Messiah*—250th Anniversary Performance

VHS. Universal Music & Video, 2003. Baroque music—chapter 10.

This performance was recorded in 1992 at the Point Theatre in Dublin, Ireland, the city where *Messiah* was originally performed in 1742.

Hildegard von Bingen, "In Portrait"

DVD. Opus Arte, 2003 (www.opusarte.com). *Ordo virtutum* (*The Ritual of the Virtues*), an opera ("A Renaissance Woman in a Renaissance Time"). Two discs. Music to 1600—chapter 9.

"The Ladies Sing the Blues"

VHS. V.I.E.W. Video, 2004. Jazz—chapter 5; popular music—chapter 6.

Artists include Bessie Smith, Billie Holiday, Sarah Vaughan, Ethel Waters, and Dinah Washington. Songs include "St. Louis Blues," "Darkies Never Dream," "When You Lose Your Money Blues," "Lean Baby," and "You're Mine You."

Leonard Bernstein Conducts *West Side Story* (1985)

DVD. Universal Music & VI, 2002. Music of the twentieth century—chapter 13.

This documentary follows Leonard Bernstein as he records the first-ever complete recording of his musical theater masterpiece. Virtually the entire recording takes place in a New York recording studio with a pickup orchestra, session singers, and headliners Kiri Te Kanawa (Maria) and José Carreras (Tony).

"Live at the Montreal Jazz Festival"

DVD. Universal Video, 2004. Jazz—chapter 5.

This concert features Diana Krall and includes songs such as "The Girl in the Other Room," "East of the Sun," "Devil May Care," and "Love Me Like a Man."

"Live in Rome"—The Tallis Scholars, Peter Phillips, Conductor

DVD. Harmonia Mundi, 2004. Renaissance music—chapter 9.

This live concert took place in the Roman Basilica, the surroundings perfectly suiting the works performed. The program is complemented by artworks that hang in the Basilica.

Metropolitan Opera Centennial Gala

DVD. Geneon Entertainment, 1999. Western classical music—chapters 9–13.

In celebration of the one-hundredth anniversary of the Metropolitan Opera, almost one hundred of the world's leading singers, seven conductors, and the Met Orchestra, Chorus, and Ballet perform in two separate programs. Artists include José Carreras, Placido Domingo, Luciano Pavarotti, Leonard Bernstein, and Kathleen Battle.

Norah Jones, Jazz Piano, and the Handsome Band—"Live in 2004"

DVD. Bluenote Records, 2004. Jazz and popular music—chapters 5 and 6.
Special guests include Dolly Parton and Gillian Welch, among others.

Paratore—*Twentieth-Century Music for Two Pianos*

DVD. Geneon Entertainment, 2000. Twentieth-century American classical music—chapter 13.

A live concert featuring piano versions by duo-pianists Anthony and Joseph Paratore of four groundbreaking works by twentieth-century composers: Stravinsky's revolutionary piece *The Rite of Spring*, Gershwin's *Rhapsody in Blue* and his *Concerto in F,* Ives's rarely performed work "Three Quarter-Tone Pieces," included as a tribute to Ives and his musical vision.

Paul Simon—"Graceland: The African Concert"

DVD. WEA, 1999. American popular music—chapter 6; world music—chapter 8.

This video of Paul Simon's Graceland Tour features music from South Africa as well as nine songs from Simon's Grammy-winning *Graceland* album. Taped in Harare, Africa, songs include "Township Jive," "Gumboots," Soweto Blues," "Homeless," "Graceland," "You Can Call Me Al," and "Diamonds on the Soles of Her Shoes."

Piano Extravaganza

DVD. BMG, 2004.

Organized to help commemorate the tenth season of the Verbier Festival and Academy in Switzerland, the event featured the "Birthday Festival Orchestra," with eight world-class pianists playing arrangements of existing piano literature. Arrangements of this literature were for varying numbers but none for eight pianos. The Grand Finale was an impressive arrangement of "Happy Birthday, Verbier Festival and Academy."

The pianists included Emmanuel Ax, Claude Frank, Lang Lang, and James Levine, as well as Leif Ove Andsnes, Nicholas Angelich, Martha Argerich, Evgeny Kissin, Mikhail Pletnev, and Steffan Scheja.

The Three Pickers

DVD. Rounder Records, 2003. 85 minutes; color; surround sound. Popular music (bluegrass)—chapter 6.

Artists include Earl Scruggs, Doc Watson, and Ricky Skaggs with Alison Krauss. Songs include "Soldier's Joy," "What Is a Home Without Love?" "Down in the Valley to Pray," and "Foggy Mountain Top."

The "Up in Smoke" Tour

DVD. Eagle Vision, 2001. Popular music (rap/hip-hop)—chapter 6.

This DVD features live performances from the 2000 "Up in Smoke" Tour, starring Ice Cube, Eminem, Dr. Dre, and Snoop Dogg.

A Vision Shared—A Tribute to Woody Guthrie and Leadbelly

DVD. Sony Music Distribution, 2000. American traditional music—chapter 3; American popular music—chapter 6.

Artists include John Mellencamp, Sweet Honey in the Rock, Pete Seeger, Arlo Guthrie, Taj Mahal, Little Richard, Emmylou Harris, Bruce Springsteen, U2, Willie Nelson, and Bob Dylan. Songs include "Do Re Mi," "Sylvie," "Alabama Bound," "Vigilante Man," "Bourgeois Blues," "Rock Island Line," "Hobo's Lullaby," and "This Land Is Your Land."

The measure of the impact on American music and culture of Woody Guthrie and Leadbelly can be gauged by their friends who, through interviews and performances, paid tribute by means of this historic recording.

APPENDIX B

Classification of Instruments according to Methods of Tone Production

Different cultures produce not only different musical styles but different instruments. Using a common "world music" method of classification, this appendix describes musical instruments from throughout the world. This classification is helpful because language based on western European culture—such as *brass, woodwinds, strings,* and *percussion*—does not always suffice in describing or even including many instruments.

Acoustics, the science of sound, can be applied to the construction of all sorts of performance halls, studios, and audio equipment. Acoustical principles can apply also to the construction of musical instruments, and it is on this basis that instruments worldwide are classified here.

The basic sound-producing mechanism of an instrument is the vibration of the material of which it is made. Vibrations are set in motion by energy exerted by a performer through an elastic medium. This process of generating musical sound may include a bow or finger that starts a string in motion (violin or guitar), lips that vibrate ("buzz") into a cupped mouthpiece (trumpet) or cause a wooden reed to vibrate (clarinet), or sticks that are hit on a stretched skin (snare drum) or a wooden or metal bar (marimba or xylophone). The resulting sound-producing vibrations cause the material that the instrument is made of to vibrate sympathetically (at the same speed), such as a box (violin or drum) or a tube (flute or trumpet). This sets air into motion inside and outside the instrument that, if received by an aural system (the outer and inner ear), can be perceived as sound.

Chordophones (Stringed Instruments)

The basic sound-producing mechanism of string instruments is the vibration of the string by plucking or bowing. The vibrations are transmitted by a bridge to the belly and back of the instrument, causing the wood to oscillate sympathetically with frequencies present in the vibrating string.

The strands of the bow are usually hairs from the tail of a horse that grip the string during bow strokes. Sound is produced when the bow grabs or a finger pulls (plucks) a string. The string, when it reaches its maximum point of elasticity, moves in the opposite direction as far as it can, then returns as far as it can, thus setting up vibrations that continue only if given additional stimulus from bowing or plucking.

The piano consists of individually tuned strings encased in a wooden body. The keyboard has 88 keys, 36 black and 52 white, which when depressed cause hammers to strike the strings. The upper notes of the keyboard consist of three strings per hammer, while the lower ones have one or two strings. When pressed, the left pedal (soft pedal) moves the entire keyboard slightly to the side so a hammer that would normally strike three strings hits only two. The middle pedal (sustain pedal) on many grand pianos (absent from most uprights and from some grand pianos) sustains only the keys that are being held at the time the pedal is pushed. It simply acts as a damper pedal for the notes in the low range.

A.   Violin family
    1. Violin (fiddle)
    2. Viola
    3. Violoncello (cello)
    4. Double bass (string bass, bass fiddle)
B.   Viols
C.   Sarangi
D.   Harps
E.   Zithers
    1. Dulcimer (plucked, hammered)
    2. Autoharp
    3. Koto
    4. Cimbalom
F.   Lutes
    1. Sitar
    2. Shamisen
    3. Mandolin
    4. Biwa
G.   Guitars
    1. Banjo
    2. Guitarrón
    3. Charango
    4. Tambura
    5. Ukelele
    6. Dobro
H.   Keyboards
    1. Piano
    2. Harpsichord

Aerophones (Wind Instruments)

The trumpet and trombone of the brass family use basically cylindrical tubes. As in the woodwinds, conical tubes are also used in brasses, although the acoustical difference between conical and cylindrical tubes is not as dramatic for brass instruments as for reed instruments. Three primary elements determine the characteristic tone quality of woodwind instruments:

1. The source of the sound—for example, the vibration of the reed in clarinets and saxophones.
2. The size and shape of the bore (wood or metal tube—the body of the instrument).
3. The size and position of finger holes or keys.

A. Flutes
 1. Piccolo
 2. Flute (alto flute)
 3. Panpipes
 4. Shakuhachi
 5. Recorder (soprano, alto, tenor, bass)
B. Reeds
 1. Single reed
   a. Clarinet (soprano, alto bass)
   b. Saxophone (soprano, alto, tenor, baritone)
 2. Double reed
   a. Oboe
   b. English horn
   c. Bassoon
 3. Free reed
   a. Harmonica (mouth or folk harp)
   b. Accordion
C. Pipe organs
D. Brass
 1. Trumpet
   a. Cornet
   b. Flugelhorn
 2. Horn (or French horn)
 3. Trombone (bass trombone)
 4. Euphonium (baritone horn)
 5. Tuba (sousaphone)

Idiophones and Membranophones (Percussion)

Of all the instrument families, the percussion family has the greatest variety of sound, in both dynamics and sound quality. Basic to percussion is sound that is produced by striking the instrument, whether it is a marimba, timpani, a cymbal, or a drum. Important in considering percussion instruments are the unique timbres of the many instruments and the unique attack and decay of the sound.

Idiophones

A. Clappers
 1. Claves
 2. Castanets
 3. Cymbals (also a hitter)
B. Shakers
 1. Maracas
 2. Rattles
C. Hitters
 1. Xylophone
 2. Marimba
 3. Vibraphone (vibes)
 4. Steel drums
D. Pluckers
 1. Mbira (sansa, kalimba)

Membranophones

A. Double head
   1. Snare drum
B. Single head
   1. Bongos
   2. Timpani (kettledrums)
   3. Tabla

Electrophones (Electronic Instruments)

With the technological explosion beginning in the 1950s came the development of many new instruments and ways to make music. In the 1950s, the tape recorder became influential in the creation of classical music. Electronic music originally resulted from the taping of sounds from nature and from the environment and the taping of sounds of both traditional and nontraditional musical instruments. Music was created by manipulating these taped sounds (for example, by changing the direction and speed of the tape and by tape splicing), selecting the new sounds, and organizing them into a piece of music recorded on another tape.

Subsequently, electronically generated sounds (by means of a synthesizer) became common, first in classical music, then in rock music and jazz. Now, synthesizer keyboards, as well as guitar and drum synthesizers, are purchased as traditional instruments.

Electronic technology includes computer applications, MIDI technology, and sampling. MIDI (Musical Instrument Digital Interface) is the technology that allows an electronic musical instrument to "speak" to a computer, and vice versa. The sampling feature can be found on many small, inexpensive electronic keyboards, as well as on highly sophisticated, expensive models. A musician can digitally record and store in memory one or more sounds, and these "samples" can be retrieved as a sound source for later playback on a synthesizer or some other electronic instrument. The quantity of sound samples is limited only by the capacity of the computer memory.

Much electronic music today, whether in live or in recorded performance, combines electronically produced sounds with sounds from traditional instruments. One example pertains to existing and new pipe organs that now can have electronic enhancements, including MIDI and hundreds of sampled sounds of additional organ pipes of various pitches and timbres. The ultimate benefits include a vastly increased variety of sounds that can be stored and changed electronically, thus instantly.

A. Keyboards
   1. Synthesizer
   2. Electronic organ
   3. Pipe organs with electronic enhancements
B. Guitars
C. Drum machines (drum synthesizers)

Descriptions of Representative Instruments

Accordion: A portable, free-reed aerophone with keyboard for melody and buttons for chords. Its wind is supplied by bellows worked by the player's arm; the bellows compress and expand the air supplied to the reeds.

Autoharp: A zither that has a series of chord bars that lie across all the strings. Grooves in the bars are placed to allow strings that produce pitches in the chosen chords to vibrate while other strings of nonchord tones are damped to prevent vibration. The autoharp is commonly used in elementary school music programs and in the performance of folk music of the southern mountains.

Banjo: A plucked chordophone of African origin, with a long, guitarlike neck and a circular, tightly stretched parchment of skin or plastic against which the bridge is pressed by the strings.

Baritone: *See* euphonium.

Bass fiddle: *See* double bass.

Bassoon: A double reed tenor or bass instrument made of a wooden tube doubled back on itself. It dates from the seventeenth century. The contrabassoon plays one octave lower than the bassoon.

Bongos: An Afro-Cuban, single-head membranophone usually played in pairs. The two are of the same height but of different diameters and are joined. Bongos are often played in jazz and rock groups featuring Latin American rhythms.

Cello: *See* violoncello.

Charango: A small guitar from South America. Made of dried armadillo shell or carved wood, is used mainly by the Indians and mestizos in the Andean mountains. Most models have 10 strings tuned in pairs.

Clarinet: A single-reed woodwind instrument dating from the late seventeenth century. The clarinet family consists of the soprano in E-flat, soprano in B-flat and A, alto in E-flat, bass in B-flat, and contrabass in B-flat. The soprano B-flat clarinet is common in many parts of the world and is an important melody instrument in western European and American bands, symphony orchestras, chamber music ensembles, and jazz groups.

Claves: Idiophones consisting of two cylindrical hardwood sticks that are clapped together. They are usually used in the performance of various Latin rhythms.

Cornet: A trumpetlike instrument that has a bore and bell slightly different from the common trumpet's and achieves a more mellow tone. In early decades of the twentieth century, it was the main melodic high brass instrument in European and American concert bands and American Dixieland groups.

Cymbal: An idiophone of indefinite pitch. It is a round metal plate that can vary in size and is hit with a stick or played in pairs (clapped together: crash cymbals). The high hat and ride cymbals are common in jazz.

Double bass: The bass instrument of the violin family. It is the standard bass instrument of the symphony orchestra (the bass section). At least one is found in many symphonic bands, and it is standard in any traditional jazz combo or big band. In modern jazz and rock, it has largely been replaced by the electric bass or bass guitar. The double bass is often known as the bass, bowed bass, stand-up bass, acoustical bass, bass fiddle, or string bass.

Drum machine: A drum synthesizer used in modern jazz and rock groups. Some groups carry the traditional drum set and the drum "synth."

Dulcimer: A name applied to certain zither-type instruments. Certain dulcimers are plucked with the fingers. Others are hammered (strings are struck with curved mallets).

Electronic organ: *See* organ.

English horn: An alto oboe that looks similar to an oboe but is larger and has a bulb-shaped bell. It has a slightly more mellow sound than the oboe.

Euphonium (baritone horn): A valved brass instrument that has the same playing range as the trombone.

Fiddle: A generic name for a bowed instrument having a neck. It is the common name for the violin, particularly when used to play folk or country music.

Flugelhorn: Similar to the trumpet but with a bore and bell that give it a more mellow, sweeter tone. It is a favorite melody instrument among some jazz artists.

Flute: A woodwind instrument generally made of either wood or metal. There are two types of flutes: vertical flute (recorder, panpipes) and transverse flute (the flute in general use today in American bands and orchestras).

Gong: An idiophone in the form of a circular, shallow, metal plate that can vary in size and is hit usually with a soft-headed beater. It is hung vertically, and its tone characteristically swells after the gong is struck.

Guitar: A flat-backed, plucked chordophone of Spanish descent. It is traced from the thirteenth century and is now used worldwide in folk, jazz, popular, and classical styles of music.

Guitarrón: A bass guitar used in Spain and throughout Mexico and Latin America. It is common in modern mariachi groups.

Harmonica: A free-reed aerophone. The reeds are placed in a small, rectangular box. Grooves lead from the reeds to openings on one of the long sides of the box into which the player exhales or inhales air. The player changes pitches by moving his or her mouth back and forth along the side of the box.

Harp: A chordophone with ancient heritage. Its strings are placed perpendicular to the soundboard (sound resonator). Generally, harps are triangular in shape and are placed on the floor and played vertically. Concert harps have pedals to play chromatically altered tones and all the major and minor keys. Folk harps typically are smaller and do not have these pedals and the tonal flexibility.

Harpsichord: A keyboard instrument characterized by a mechanism whereby the strings are plucked rather than struck as with the piano. It has one or two manuals and less capacity than the piano for expressive contrasts. It dates to the Renaissance and was a popular Baroque keyboard instrument.

Horn: A generic name for a variety of lip-vibrated wind instruments of the trumpet family with or without valves. It is also a name for a specific brass instrument whose bore spirals and culminates in a large, flaring bell. This instrument is sometimes known as the French horn.

Kalimba: *See* mbira.

Kettledrums: *See* timpani.

Koto: A long zither with 13 strings, each with a movable bridge, traditionally placed horizontally on the floor. It is sometimes considered the national instrument of Japan.

Lute: An ancient plucked or bowed chordophone with a round back and a neck (instruments in the guitar family have flat backs). The tuning pegs in many versions were placed perpendicular to the neck. The lute family includes the Arabic ud, the Japanese shamisen, the mandolin, and instruments of the viol and violin families.

Mandolin: A plucked chordophone of the lute family. It dates from the early eighteenth century and is in common use today, mainly in Italy and in the United

States. Although it is chiefly used in folk and country music, it occasionally is used in classical compositions.

Maracas: A pair of gourd rattles, most commonly oval gourds usually containing dried seeds or beads. They are originally of South American Indian cultures but are now commonly used in playing Latin American dance rhythms.

Marimba: An idiophone (xylophone) consisting of tone bars under which are gourd or tubular resonators. The bars are hit with sticks (mallets). Its antecedents are instruments from sub-Saharan Africa.

Mbira (thumb piano, kalimba, sansa): An African, plucked idiophone consisting of tuned metal tongues (as are common in music boxes) and sometimes gourd resonator boxes. The ends of the tongues are free to vibrate as they are depressed and released (plucked) by the thumbs of the performer.

Oboe: A double-reed, woodwind instrument whose tone can be described as nasal and piercing. The oboe is often used as a solo instrument in the classical symphony orchestra, modern symphonic bands, and woodwind chamber ensembles.

Organ (pipe organ, electronic organ): The pipe organ is a wind instrument consisting of one or more ranks (sets of pipes) of individual wooden or metal pipes. Each pipe produces a specific tone color at a specific pitch. Each rank consists of a set of pipes for each tone quality. An organ usually has from two to four manuals (keyboards). The largest organs have thousands of separate pipes. The tones are generated from air supplied by a blower supported by action that is dictated by the organist at the keyboard and that directs the air to the appropriate pipes. The various tone colors of the electronic organ are generated by electrical circuitry rather than air pressure. These sounds are similar to those of the pipe organ. In fact, some electronic organs, by means of computer technology, now nearly duplicate pipe organ sounds.

Panpipes: Sets of end-blown flutes of different pitches combined into one instrument. There are no finger holes; the player changes pitches by blowing air across the end-holes of the different pipes. Panpipes are used in all regions of the world. They often are associated with the Inca civilization of the Andes Mountains in Peru and Bolivia.

Piano: A keyboard instrument whose strings are struck by rebounding hammers. Its origin dates back to the early eighteenth century. In the second half of the eighteenth century, the piano replaced the harpsichord as the popular keyboard instrument in Western classical music.

Piccolo: A small, transverse flute. It sounds an octave higher than written and often doubles the flute part an octave higher.

Pipe organ: *See* organ.

Rattles: Any shaken idiophone.

Recorder: An end-blown, vertical flute used from the Middle Ages until the eighteenth century that has seen a resurgence in popularity in modern times. Often, recorders come in sets that consist of descant (soprano), treble (alto), tenor, and bass recorder.

Sansa: *See* mbira.

Saxophone: A single-reed, woodwind instrument made of metal. The family of saxophones includes the soprano in B-flat, alto in E-flat, tenor in B-flat, baritone in E-flat, and the less common bass in B-flat. The alto and tenor saxophones are the most common and are integral to band instrumentation and to jazz ensembles. They are occasionally used in symphony orchestras.

Shakuhachi: An end-blown Japanese flute usually made of bamboo with five finger holes. With roots in China dating back to the tenth century, it is used today as a solo instrument and as part of various instrumental ensembles, sometimes with koto and shamisen.

Shamisen: A three-stringed, long-necked Japanese lute. It is used as part of ensembles, sometimes with koto and perhaps the shakuhachi, and is used also to accompany traditional Japanese songs.

Sitar: A large, fretted, long-necked lute. It has from four to seven metal strings, movable frets, and several drone strings. The sitar is the main melody instrument in music of northern India.

Snare drum: A side drum with a set of snares (wires) stretched across the lower head. The tension of these wires can be adjusted to change the quality of sound.

Sousaphone: A type of tuba used in marching bands. It is distinguished by its shape that wraps around the body for ease in carrying and its overhead, widely flaring bell.

Steel drum: A tuned idiophone usually made from an oil drum. Steel drum bands were first popular in the Caribbean, particularly Trinidad, and are now popular in the United States.

String bass: *See* double bass.

Synthesizer: An electronic instrument capable of generating and processing a wide variety of sounds (drums, keyboard, and guitar).

Tabla: A pair of small, tuned, hand-played drums of north and central India, Pakistan, and Bangladesh. They are used to accompany both vocal and instrumental art, popular, and folk music. They are particularly well known in music of northern India as a frequently intricate accompaniment in raga performances.

Tambura: A long-neck, plucked lute of India. It has four wire strings used only for drone accompaniments in both classical and folk styles.

Timpani (kettledrums): A single-headed drum consisting of a large, bowl-shaped, resonating chamber or shell (usually of copper). The large head can be tightened or loosened to produce different pitches. It is struck with a pair of mallets. A band or orchestra usually uses a pair of timpani of different sizes. Some music calls for four timpani, with the additional ones extending the pitch range higher and lower.

Trombone: A brass aerophone characterized by a telescopic slide with which the player varies the length of the tube, thereby manipulating the pitch. It is a common harmony and melody instrument in the tenor range used in bands, orchestras, brass chamber music, and jazz ensembles of all kinds.

Trumpet: A treble brass instrument played with a cup-shaped mouthpiece. Its brilliant tone makes it an ideal melody instrument in bands, orchestras, chamber music ensembles, and jazz groups. It is found frequently in Mexican and Latin American popular music groups. Various versions of the trumpet, many made from animals' horns, date from ancient times and are found in many cultures. The invention of the valves in 1813 as a means of changing pitch made it the versatile and popular instrument it is today.

Tuba: The bass instrument of the brass family.

Ukulele: A small guitar originally from Portugal but popularized in America through Hawaiian music.

Vibraphone (vibraharp or "vibes"): A xylophone with metal bars and metal resonator tubes suspended below each bar that help to sustain the tones. An electric motor drives propellers affixed at the top of each resonator tube that produces its characteristic pulsating pitches (vibrato).

Viol: A bowed string instrument with frets usually played vertically on the lap or between the legs. The viol was built in three sizes: treble, tenor, and bass (viol da gamba). It flourished in Europe in the sixteenth and seventeenth centuries and subsequently became one of most popular Renaissance and Baroque instruments. By the middle of the eighteenth century, it had been replaced by the more resonant violin family of instruments.

Viola: The alto or tenor member of the violin family. The viola is slightly larger than the violin and creates a slightly more mellow sound.

Violin: The soprano and most prominent member of the violin family. Its versatile, expressive quality is unequaled. The history of the violin dates to the early seventeenth century in Cremona, Italy. It was here that the first great violin makers worked: Niccolò Amati, Antonio Stradivari, and Giuseppe Guarneri. The violin is the main melody instrument of the Western symphony orchestra and of chamber music ensembles such as the string quartet. The violin is also used in folk music (fiddle), in jazz (both acoustic and electric versions), and in music of many other cultures.

Violoncello (cello): The tenor or bass instrument of the violin family. Its beautiful, lyrical quality makes it ideally suited to play melody as well as harmonic and bass lines.

Xylophone: A percussion instrument consisting of two or more wooden tone bars of varying lengths to produce varying pitches. The bars are struck with knobbed sticks. Modern versions have the bars laid out similarly to a piano keyboard with each bar having a metal resonator suspended below it. With roots in Asia, the xylophone was introduced in the Americas by Africans.

Zither: A folk instrument, but also a class of chordophones whose strings are stretched between two ends of a flat body, such as a board or a stick. The hammered dulcimer, piano, and harpsichord are board zithers.

GLOSSARY

A

Absolute music Music created for its own sake without extramusical connotation. Examples include such genres as the sonata, symphony, concerto, and string quartet, as well as preludes, fugues, études, and other works whose titles point to only form or function. *Also see* program music.

Accent A stress or emphasis on a particular tone.

Acculturation The blending of cultures. The process by which one culture assimilates or adapts to the characteristics and practices of another.

Acoustics The science of sounds and the physical basis of music.

Aerophone A wind instrument. The sound-producing agent is air set in vibration either within the body of the instrument or outside the instrument. (*See* the appendix, p. 306.)

Aesthetics The study of the emotional and expressive aspects of music.

Airplay The number of times a popular song is broadcast on radio. Airplay can generate record sales and can contribute to making a song a hit.

Americanist music Concert art music written in a style immediately recognizable as American. Ives, Copland, and other American nationalistic composers frequently incorporated familiar patriotic, folk, and religious tunes, as well as elements of jazz and popular music, into their classical compositions. *Also see* nationalistic music.

Aria A lyrical song found in operas, cantatas, and oratorios. It may comment on the text presented in a recitative that precedes it. *Also see* recitative.

Arrangement A setting (rescoring) of a piece of music for a genre or an ensemble for which it was not originally intended, such as a pop song arranged for big band or an orchestral piece arranged for wind ensemble.

Art music Music that is formal, sophisticated, urban, and appreciated by an educated elite. It is music derived from a cultivated tradition based largely on notated music. A certain amount of musical training is needed in order to create and perform art music.

Art song *See* miniature.

Assimilation The process whereby immigrant groups gradually adopt the characteristics of the host society. Also the process by which a primitive culture is modified by contact with an advanced culture.

Atonality The avoidance of tonal centers and tonal relationships in music. It results in highly chromatic, dissonant music without traditional, functional chord progressions, modulations, and tuneful melodies. Dissonances stand alone and are not resolved to consonances as in traditional music.

Avant-garde composers Experimental composers who are in the forefront of musical developments and are leaders in the development of new and unconventional musical styles. They experiment with untried techniques, forms, timbres, and concepts in devising new approaches to composition, new aesthetic notions, or a new language for expressing music.

B

Ballads Songs with a story having a beginning, middle, and end. The music is strophic and may have many stanzas. A ballad singer is a storyteller.

Ballet Stage production featuring formal, stylized dance performances with a story or a unified theme. It has, at times, been part of opera but also developed popularity as an independent genre in the nineteenth century.

Bar   *See* meter.

Basso continuo   *See* continuo.

Bebop   A combo jazz style that emerged in the 1940s. It is characterized by high energy, virtuoso solo improvisation, complex rhythmic patterns, and more novel and chromatic harmonies than were used in previous styles. *Also see* combo.

Big band jazz   Music for a large jazz ensemble, usually 12–20 musicians. It is notated music that may be original compositions but more frequently is arrangements of preexisting songs. Arrangements are scored for the brass section (trumpets and trombones), the sax section, and the rhythm section. *Also see* chart (sense 2).

Binary   *See* form.

Black gospel   *See* gospel music.

Bluegrass   A style of country music that combines a return to the rural, folk traditions of hillbilly music and the urban, commercial music that is part of our national popular culture. Typical bluegrass instrumentation includes the acoustic guitar, fiddle, mandolin, bass fiddle, and banjo—no electric instruments.

Blues   A style of music that has exerted considerable influence on jazz, rhythm and blues, soul, rock, and other forms of recent American popular music. The word *blues* can refer to a three-line poetic stanza, a 12-bar musical structure with a specific chord progression, a scale having the flatted blues notes, or a melancholy, soulful feeling.

Boogie woogie   A piano jazz style popular in the late 1920s and 1930s. It is characterized by a left-hand ostinato figure underlying a rhythmically free and highly syncopated right-hand melodic texture. Most boogie woogie pieces are based on the standard 12-bar blues chord progression.

Bossa nova   A popular music of Brazilian origin that is rhythmically related to samba but with complex harmonies and improvised, jazzlike passages.

Break   A stop of the music in a jazz piece during which a soloist improvises, usually for two bars. A break occurs at the end of a phrase, providing transition to the next phrase.

Bridge   The "b" phrase of an a a b a form—that is, the contrasting phrase in a song form or in the chorus of a verse-chorus form. Used primarily in traditional popular songs and jazz—the standards.

Broadside   A song written on one large piece of paper with or without music notation. These songs, which flourished during the eighteenth and nineteenth centuries, described current events and functioned somewhat like newpapers in communities and regions. Originally written down, many broadsides were eventually passed on by word of mouth, thus becoming part of the oral tradition.

C

Cadence   A point of repose at the ending of a musical phrase.

Cadenza   An unaccompanied passage in free rhythm in which the soloist displays his or her virtuosity. *Also see* concerto.

Cantata   An extended solo or choral work that flourished during the Baroque era. It was intended for the German Lutheran worship service, although some cantatas have secular texts. Choral cantatas, particularly those by J. S. Bach, include harmonized chorales, polyphonic choruses, arias, recitatives, solo ensembles, and instrumental accompaniment.

Cantus firmus   A term meaning "fixed melody" that denotes a preexisting melody, often a Gregorian chant, which a composer from the Renaissance used as the basis of a polyphonic composition.

Chamber music   Works for solo instruments performing together in small ensembles, such as a string quartet, a woodwind quintet, or a piano trio. Each part is played on one instrument (no doubling). In the Classic era, the string quartet (first and second violins, viola, and cello) became the standard chamber music genre. The quartet typically was a four-movement work with a fast-slow-dance-fast pattern, although many exceptions to this pattern exist.

Chance music   A compositional technique whereby a composer does not control all the details of a composition, allowing the performer to make creative choices through improvisation or other means of selecting sounds within the structure of the composition. John Cage was a major influence in developing chance music.

Chant   A simple song found in many cultures and traditions. It is a monophonic song without accompaniment, of relatively short duration, of limited melodic range, and with a fluid pulse reflecting the rhythm of the text. Gregorian chants, sung in Latin, are used in the liturgy of the Roman Catholic Church. They date from the end of the sixth century C.E., when Pope Gregory I is believed to have ordered the collection and classification of chants to be used throughout the far-flung church.

Character piece   *See* miniature.

Chart   (1) A weekly record of sales of songs in a variety of categories, such as rock, jazz, rhythm and blues, and country. A chart is used to measure a song's popularity. The most widely used charts are produced by *Billboard*. (2) The written or printed arrangement of a popular song or a jazz tune for an ensemble, such as a rock group, studio orchestra, or a jazz band.

Chorale   Originally a hymn tune of the German Lutheran Church sung by the congregation in unison and in German (rather than Latin). It was an outgrowth of the Reformation and the rise of Protestantism. Chorale tunes, especially during the Baroque era, were used as the basis for other compositions: They were harmonized in four-part settings for singing by choirs and congregations; they were used as the basis of sacred polyphonic compositions for trained choirs; and they formed the basis of organ pieces known as chorale preludes.

Chord   A meaningful (as opposed to random) combination of three or more tones. The primary chords in western European harmonic practice are the tonic (I chord), the subdominant (IV chord), and the dominant (V chord).

Chordophone   A stringed instrument. The sound-producing agent is a stretched string that is plucked or bowed. (*See* the appendix, p. 305.)

Chromatic   Proceeding by half steps, using sharps or flats. Notes outside a standard major or minor scale. A melody is chromatic if many of its pitches are not derived from the standard major or minor scale.

Church modes   Scales consisting of seven tones with a variety of patterns other than major and minor scales. They were commonly used in medieval and Renaissance church music. *Also see* scale.

Combo   A small jazz group, usually from three to six musicians.

Comping   The syncopated chords and melodic figures played by a jazz pianist while accompanying a solo improvisation, adding rhythmic punctuation and vitality.

Concerto   A three-movement work for solo instrument and orchestra that emerged during the Baroque period and has been a common instrumental genre ever since. The concerto grosso was an important genre of this period that featured a small group of soloists with orchestra. The arrangement of the movements is fast-slow-fast. Many concertos since the Baroque era include a cadenza. *Also see* cadenza.

Conjunct   *See* melody.

Consonance   A relatively stable, comfortable sound that seems to be at rest in contrast with a dissonant, restless sound. *Also see* dissonance.

Consort   A group of similar instruments—such as soprano, alto, tenor, and bass recorders—that provide a homogeneous sound.

Context   Social, economic, and political circumstances prevalent in a society that may influence the nature of a creative work.

Continuo   A technique for providing a harmonic basis in the new homophonic music of the Baroque period. It was a style of accompaniment for a singer or one or two solo instruments. The basso continuo, or bass line, provided the underlying structure for the harmonies, and it usually was played on a cello. The chords were not completely notated and were improvised on a keyboard instrument, usually a harpsichord. The performer determined what chords to play from the bass line and the figured bass. The figures were numbers written below certain notes of the bass line as a musical shorthand to indicate the harmonies.

Contour   The shape of a melody, whether smooth (made up primarily of small intervals) or jagged (characterized by wide skips).

Contrast   A departure from that which has been presented. A phrase or section that is different from what preceded it. To achieve contrast, the music has different tonality, rhythm, melody, tempo, dynamic level, articulation, or mood.

Cool jazz   An outgrowth of and reaction to bebop. Cool jazz arrangers and performers strived to maintain the musical qualities of bebop while making their music more accessible to their audience. They adopted many elements from classical music, including the use of orchestral instruments not commonly used in jazz, such as the flute, oboe, and French horn. *Also see* bebop.

Counterpoint   The compositional technique of creating polyphonic texture. The word is frequently used as a synonym for *polyphony*. *Imitative* counterpoint is the creation of two or more independent melodic lines, with each entrance beginning with the same melodic shape at the same or a different pitch level.

Culture   A group of people, a society, characterized by the totality of its arts, beliefs, customs, institutions, and all other products of work and thought.

D

Dance suite   A multimovement work for keyboard or orchestra. It includes contrasting, stylized dances popular in the Baroque period. The principal dances are the allemande, courante, sarabande, and gigue.

Diatonic   In Western music, the eight tones of a standard major or minor scale. A melody is diatonic if most of its pitches are derived from these eight tones.

Disjunct   *See* melody.

Dissonance   An active, unstable sound. *Also see* consonance.

Dixieland   The first popular jazz style. It was characterized by group improvisation (clarinet, trumpet, and trombone) supported by a steady ragtime rhythm.

Dominant   A chord built on the fifth degree of the major or minor scale.

Downbeats   The first beat of each measure in Western notated music.

Drone   An instrument whose primary purpose is to play a low sustained pitch, perhaps a constantly repeated pitch that produces a trancelike quality. In Hindustani music of India, the pitch is achieved by playing the open strings of the tambura, helping to establish the main notes of a raga.

Duple meter   A rhythmic pattern in which alternate beats are stressed (strong-weak-strong-weak). *Also see* meter.

Duration   The length of time a pitch sounds. *Also see* rhythm.

Dynamics   The level of loudness. *Also see* loudness.

E

Electrophone   An electronic instrument. The tone is produced, modified, or amplified by electronic circuits. (*See* the appendix, p. 308.)

Embellishment   *See* ornamentation.

Ethnic   Pertaining to people who are not part of a mainstream population but are recognized as a group on the basis of certain distinctive characteristics, such as religion, language, ancestry, culture, or national origin.

Ethnomusicologist   A scholar of music in culture—of world music; one who studies ethnomusicology; one who researches the music of a culture, writes about it, and teaches others about it.

Ethnomusicology   A study of music in culture, considering the context of music in a society, music as it relates to human behavior, and the general attitudes of a people about their music.

F

Fasola system   A system in which the initial letters of four syllables—*fa, sol, la,* and *mi*—are placed on the staff, each representing a different pitch. The fasola system was used in nineteenth-century America to aid in the immediate recognition of scale degrees and to help people read musical notation. *Also see* notation.

Fermata   To hold a tone or chord longer than is indicated by its note value.

Fiddle tune   A song from oral tradition used to accompany country dances. The song has a shape and character more appropriate for playing on the fiddle than for singing. Fiddle tunes are frequently played by string bands, bluegrass groups, or solo fiddlers.

Field recording   A scholarly or professional recording of folk or traditional music made in the environment where the performers typically make music, rather than in a professional recording studio.

Figured bass   *See* continuo.

Fill   Melodic movement and embellishment in jazz while the main melody sustains a tone, such as at the end of a pattern or a phrase.

Folk music   Usually of unknown origin and enjoyed by the general population, informal, aesthetically and musically unsophisticated music that communicates directly and obviously to large groups within a culture or a subculture, such as a nation or an ethnic minority. It is usually preserved and transmitted by memory (oral tradition). Also known as *traditional music.*

Follies   *See* vaudeville.

Form   The shape or structure of a piece of music. Form is determined primarily by patterns of contrast and repetition. A two-part form is *binary* (a b)—no repetition. A three-part form is *ternary* (a b a)—the first theme is followed by a contrasting section, after which the first phrase or section is repeated. A 32-bar song form is a a b a—four phrases with the third phrase in contrast to the first two, after which the first phrase is again repeated. *Also see* minuet and trio; rondo; sonata form; theme and variations; 12-bar blues; verse-chorus.

Forward energy   The tendency in some music to have momentum—that is, to move from one point to the next, such as from the beginning of a phrase to its conclusion.

Free jazz   A style that is almost pure improvisation without adherence to predetermined chord structures, meter, or melodic motives. Musicians interact musically with each other, build on what others in the group are doing, and are free to create according to their musical instincts.

Frequency   The rate of speed of sound waves.

Fuging tune   A four-part hymn with a short middle fugal section in which each voice enters at a different time, one after the other. *Also see* fugue.

Fugue   An imitative polyphonic composition that originated as a keyboard genre during the Baroque period. It is, however, a compositional technique used during and since the Baroque in both choral and instrumental music. A fugue is built on a single theme whose entrances appear imitatively in several voices (melodic lines at different pitch levels), usually three or four, and then are developed in intricate contrapuntal interplay. *Also see* counterpoint.

Funk   A distinctive style using polyrhythms, syncopated bass lines, and short vocal phrases.

Fusion   A synthesis of elements of jazz and rock; style of modern jazz.

G

Gagaku   An instrumental music genre of the imperial courts of ancient Japan. It is the oldest documented orchestral music in the world.

Gamelan   An Indonesian orchestra, particularly from the islands of Bali and Java, composed of various-sized drums, metal xylophones, and gongs. Gamelan music has a long history and has influenced composers of Western classical music, as well as jazz and rock performers.

Genre   A category of music, such as symphony, hymn, ballad, mass, march, and opera.

Glissando   Producing a sliding contour on an instrument or voice.

Global perspective   A worldwide point of view, including awareness of and respect for the lifestyles, traditions, values, and arts of other nations and cultures.

Gospel music   Protestant religious music usually associated more with rural, folk roots than with urban, European traditions. American gospel music has evolved in such a way that distinct stylistic differences exist between the gospel music of white and black Americans. We now distinguish between *black gospel* and *white gospel* styles. White gospel includes camp meeting songs, hymns and songs for revival services, and music from the pentecostal tradition.

Gregorian chant   *See* chant.

H

Hard bop   The bebop style of the 1950s and 1960s. Hard bop retained the intensity, complexity, harmonic imagination, and speed of the bebop of Charlie Parker and Dizzy Gillespie. Counted among this second generation of bebop musicians are John Coltrane, Sonny Rollins, Clifford Brown, Ornette Coleman, and Cannonball Adderly. Some musicians and scholars use the word *hard bop* to describe any of the jazz styles that followed bebop, including the funky, gospel jazz of Horace Silver, Art Blakey, and Herbie Hancock, and the cool jazz of Miles Davis, Gerry Mulligan, and the Modern Jazz Quartet. None of these musicians, however, played in only one style.

Harmony   Pitches heard simultaneously in ways that produce chords and chord progressions.

Head arrangements   Arrangements that are not notated but are worked out in rehearsal and, eventually, played by memory in traditional jazz style.

Hillbilly   A style of popular song derived from the rural, southern folk tradition and from sentimental songs of the late nineteenth century. It represents a merging of rural and urban influences and a regional, ethnic music made popular nationally and successful commercially.

Homophony   *See* texture.

Homorhythmic   Multiple horizontal lines moving with the same rhythm in all parts.

Hymnody   A body or a collection of hymns of a time, place, or church.

I

Idiophone   A percussion instrument that is struck, shaken, plucked, or rubbed. (*See* the appendix, p. 307.)

Imitative counterpoint   *See* counterpoint.

Immigrant   A citizen of a foreign nation who emigrates to another nation and establishes residence, finds employment, becomes part of the culture of that economy, and brings to the host nation part of his or her past culture, whether cuisine, music, dance, language, or religion. The United States is, to a large extent, a nation of immigrants or the descendants of immigrants.

Impressionism   A style of music, exemplified in the works of Debussy, that avoids explicit statement and literal description but instead emphasizes suggestion and atmosphere, evokes moods, and conveys impressions of images and feelings.

Improvisation The process of simultaneously composing, performing, and listening to music.

Indigenous Native to a culture; the original people in a region.

Instability *See* tension.

Intensity The energy that generates the amplitude or height of sound waves.

Interval The difference in pitch between two musical tones. *Also see* pitch.

J

Jam session An informal, usually "after hours" gathering in which jazz musicans come together to improvise and enjoy themselves making music. Because the jamming musicians are not obligated to an employer or to a paying audience, they have the freedom to explore and share their musical ideas.

K

Kabuki A Japanese theater style with music that is considered a genre of traditional Japanese music. Important components of Kabuki music are the narrative *gidayu* songs with shamisen accompaniment and the nagauta ensemble of drums, a flute, several shamisens, and singers. The nagauta became an important concert genre, independent of Kabuki theater.

Key *See* tonality.

L

Lead The soloist in a jazz arrangement or performance.

Lead sheet A notated melody with chord symbols, usually of a popular song or jazz tune, on which a musical performance is based. A means of structuring a performance in lieu of notating all parts for the entire piece.

Libretto The words to an opera or other musical stage production. The person who writes the story is the librettist.

Lied (plural: **lieder**) *See* miniature.

Lining out A call-and-response style of hymn singing whereby a minister or song leader sings one line at a time and the congregation sings it back, usually adding embellishments and often at a much slower tempo. Lining out is derived from rural, folk traditions and was brought to the United States from the British Isles.

Loudness The degree of intensity or energy producing a sound. The loudness or softness of a tone.

Lyrics The words to a popular song. The person who writes the lyrics is a lyricist.

M

Madrigal A Renaissance secular contrapuntal work for several voices that originated in Italy and later flourished in England.

Mainstream Having the prevailing characteristics of a society.

Mariachi A popular Mexican folk music ensemble that includes a harp, violins, various sizes of guitars, and sometimes trumpets.

Mass (1) The Roman Catholic worship service. A High Mass is composed of the Proper and the Ordinary. The Proper varies from Sunday to Sunday throughout the church year. The Ordinary remains the same and consists of the *Kyrie, Gloria, Credo, Sanctus* and *Benedictus,* and *Agnus Dei.* Much of the great choral literature in Western music is polyphonic settings of various sections of the Ordinary. (2) A musical setting for the Ordinary.

Measure *See* meter.

Melisma A setting of a text to music in which one syllable of text is given a series of musical notes. *Also see* syllabic setting.

Melody A succession of musical tones, usually of varying pitch and rhythm, that has identifiable shape and meaning. A melody may be characterized by its smooth, *conjunct* shape that moves mostly stepwise or by its *disjunct,* angular shape resulting from frequent use of wide intervals (skips). It may comprise a wide or a narrow range of pitches.

Membranophone A percussion instrument whose sound is produced by the vibration of a stretched membrane, either skin or plastic. (*See* the appendix, p. 307.)

Mestizo Natives of Mexico and South America having mixed Indian and Spanish blood.

Meter The organization of rhythm into a pattern of strong and weak beats. Each pattern constitutes a *bar* (a *measure* in notated music). Each strong beat is the downbeat of a bar. Groups of patterns can compose a phrase (such as an eight-bar phrase). Music is *nonmetric* if no rhythmic pattern can be perceived. *Also see* duple meter; mixed meter; triple meter.

MIDI (Musical Instrument Digital Interface) A means for providing electronic communication between synthesizers and computers or other synthesizers. It enables sounds to be stored in memory until needed.

Miniature   A small-scale composition, such as the art song and character piece, that became popular in the Romantic era, perhaps as an alternative to the massive size and sounds of the symphony orchestra. The *art song* is a solo song with piano accompaniment. Commonly known by the German word *lied* (plural, *lieder*), it is exemplified by the songs of Schubert that he set to German poetry. The *character piece* is a one-movement work for solo piano. It is exemplified by the works of Chopin, such as his impromptus, nocturnes, mazurkas, études, polonaises, and preludes.

Minimalism   A style of composition whose creator attempts to achieve the greatest effect from the least amount of material. It is typically based on many repetitions of simple patterns, creating slow, subtle changes in rhythm, chord movement, or other musical elements. Phillip Glass, a contemporary American composer, has been considered the leading exponent of minimalist music.

Minstrel show   A variety show, popular in the nineteenth century, that included songs, dances, and comical skits. Lively, syncopated minstrel songs formed the nucleus of the minstrel show. A product of the merging of rural American folk traditions with urban, composed music, the minstrel song can be considered the first distinctively American musical genre. *Also see* vaudeville.

Minuet and trio   A stately dance movement in triple meter in a b a form. It is often the third movement of a symphony or string quartet. A scherzo and trio form is similar but has a faster tempo and increased rhythmic energy; its function is the same as that of the minuet and trio.

Mixed meter   Combinations of duple and triple meter (shifting strong beats). *Also see* duple meter; triple meter.

Mode   A scale, key, or tonality.

Modulation   To change from one key to another, frequently by harmonic progression. *Also see* tonality.

Monophony   *See* texture.

Motet   A sacred, polyphonic composition with a non-liturgical text. It flourished during the Renaissance and was sung without accompaniment (a cappella) in Latin by trained choirs, typically in four or five parts. Polychoral motets were written for multiple choirs or choirs divided into two or three distinct groups performing singly (in alternation) and jointly in the full ensemble.

Motive   A short melodic pattern or phrase that is used for further development and sometimes as the basis of a section of music or a complete composition.

Motown sound   A style of black popular music derived more from black gospel than from blues or jazz traditions. It featured a studio-controlled sound (Motown Records) designed to make black music widely popular and profitable.

Musique concrète   The compositional technique of manipulating tape-recorded sounds of existing natural resources. The sounds of recorded instruments, voices, or other sound sources are altered by changing tape speed or direction and by cutting and splicing the tape. These altered sounds, perhaps combined with original sounds, serve as the sound source for an electronic music composition. Edgard Varèse pioneered musique concrète, which predated electronically generated or synthesized sounds.

Mute   A device placed on an instrument to alter its tone, usually to soften it; most common in instruments of the violin family (placed on the bridge) and in trumpets (inserted in the bell).

N

Nagauta   An ensemble that provides the basic accompaniment on stage in Kabuki theater, a highly stylized Japanese form of music drama. The ensemble has perhaps a dozen musicians, including three drums, a flute, several shamisen players, and singers.

Nashville sound   The sound of hillbilly music produced by sophisticated recording techniques and arrangements controlled by the recording studios to ensure the popularity and commercial success of their songs. It minimizes the country twang of the singers, reduces the emphasis on fiddle and steel guitar, and includes background singers.

Nationalistic music   Concert art music that reflects national or regional rather than universal characteristics. The music may describe something derived from the folk or popular traditions of a nation; its history, tales, or legends; its cultural characteristics; or a place that is important to the nation or region. *Also see* Americanist music.

Neoclassicism   A style of modern composition that is based on established forms and structures of the past and particularly on the aesthetics and musical values of the Classic era.

Nonmetric   *See* meter.

Notation   The use of written or printed symbols to represent musical sounds. Notation makes possible the preservation and dissemination of music by means of writing.

Note bending   *See* tone bending.

O

Octave   The musical interval, spanning eight different pitches, between the first and last tones of a diatonic scale.

Opera   A dramatic stage production that involves soloists who sing arias and recitatives, solo ensembles, choruses, dancing, dramatic action, costumes, staging, and orchestral accompaniment. It began at the beginning of the Baroque era and evolved into a genre that continues in popularity throughout the Western world, particularly in Italy.

Oral tradition   The passing down of music by word of mouth from one generation to the next.

Oratorio   An extended, sacred choral work intended for concert performance. It emerged during the Baroque era and has been a common genre since. It is of large proportions, lengthy (many lasting up to three hours), and dramatic in nature, sometimes including the character of a narrator as a soloist. Polyphonic choruses, arias, recitatives, solo ensembles, and orchestral accompaniment are common components of oratorios.

Ornamentation   An *embellishment* of a melody; adding notes for decoration according to established and commonly accepted performance practices; found in western European classical music, music of many nations and cultures, and all forms of popular music and jazz.

Ostinato   A rhythmic or melodic pattern repeated many times.

Overture   A festive opening to an opera or other musical stage production. It sets the tone, sometimes identifies principal themes and characters, and prepares an audience for the opening scene. Overtures have become popular concert pieces, sometimes achieving popularity and subsequent performances where the stage production did not. Because of this popularity, many composers have written overtures as independent concert pieces. In the Baroque era, the French overture was a popular instrumental genre, and in the Romantic period, the concert overture assumed even greater popularity.

P

Patronage   A common source of income for composers. In the sixteenth to eighteenth centuries, the church or the courts provided employment; in the nineteenth century, often a wealthy patron provided employment; and in the twentieth century, the university provided employment for many composers.

Patterns   Groupings of notes having an identifiable character that, when used repeatedly, help to give form and style to a musical work.

Pentatonic scale   A five-tone scale that serves as the basis of much music throughout the world.

Perceptive listening   Listening to music attentively in an attempt to understand the musical processes and structure that give the music its characteristic qualities.

Phrase   A section of music with a recognizable beginning and ending; a complete musical thought.

Piracy   Copying music illegally, whether using cassettes, CDs, DVDs, or downloads.

Pitch   The highness or lowness of a tone produced by a single frequency. A melody consists of sounds perceived as *registers*: high, middle, or low—or soprano, alto, tenor, or bass. A melody has a range of pitches: the lowest pitch to the highest. *Also see* melody.

Polychoral motets   *See* motet.

Polyphony   *See* texture.

Program music   Music that depicts images, moods, stories, characters, and other nonmusical associations. It includes all music with text and many instrumental forms common during the Romantic period, including the symphonic poem and some symphonies that were created with programmatic associations. *Also see* absolute music.

Psalm singing   Congregational singing of rhymed, metrical versions of the Psalms set to hymn tunes. Psalm singing was prevalent in early America. The hymnbooks in which the settings were published, with words only or with hymn tunes, were called *psalters*. The singing of fuging tunes was a type of Psalm singing popular throughout the eighteenth century. *Also see* fuging tune.

Psalter   *See* Psalm singing.

Pulse   The recurring beat of the music.

R

Raga   The basic means by which the melodic or pitch aspects of the classical music of India are determined. Ragas convey not only melodic shape but mood and aesthetic character, and they provide the basis for extended improvisations. The moods they represent usually are related to temporal elements, such as seasons of the year or times of day (morning or evening ragas).

Ragtime   A style of music first popular in the first two decades of the twentieth century. It is characterized by a strongly pulsated, nonsyncopated bass line that supports a highly syncopated right-hand melody. Ragtime remains popular today.

Range   *See* pitch.

Rap   A style of black popular music that, in the 1980s, emerged from the inner city to become mainstream—an ethnic style becoming nationally popular. The rhythm is highly repetitive; the poetry is recited in a highly rhythmic manner. Electronic keyboards, sampled sounds and rhythms, drum machines, and prerecorded tracks are common in rap music.

Rasa   An aesthetic basis that underlies much of the art music of India.

Recitative   A vocal solo in opera, cantatas, and oratorios that declaims the text in a sung-speech manner, in free rhythm with minimal accompaniment, so that all listeners can understand the words. It frequently introduces an aria. *Also see* aria.

Reggae   A synthesis of rock, rhythm and blues, and Latin American and African rhythms. Reggae originated in the poor sections of Jamaican cities and has become an internationally popular music genre. Many of the songs reflect black nationalism and social reform and are rooted in Rastafarianism and its spiritual leader, Haile Selassie, late emperor of Ethiopia. The original superstar of reggae is Bob Marley.

Register   *See* pitch.

Repetition   A return to previously stated material. A pattern, phrase, or section that is presented again either exactly or modified but retaining basic characteristics.

Resolution   *See* tension.

Revues   *See* vaudeville.

Rhythm   The organization of time in music, creating patterns of long and short durations of pitches to achieve desired degrees of rhythmic energy—the rhythmic impulse.

Rhythm and blues (R&B)   A style of black popular music that originally featured a boogie woogie–style piano accompaniment in blues form, a blues singer, and electric guitar. Later, the term *R&B* referred to any blues-based black popular music. Today, urban R&B is not necessarily blues based.

Riff   Short, syncopated patterns usually written for specific groups of instruments in a big band jazz arrangement. Riffs provide punctuated background material while another section or soloist is playing the melody or improvising. Occasionally, an entire chorus consists of riffs without a recognizable melody.

Rock and roll   An underground, antiestablishment, and protest music that emerged in the 1950s and evolved into a phenomenally successful commercial product. It was derived primarily from a merging of black and white traditions (rhythm and blues and hillbilly) and appealed mostly to teenagers for both listening and dancing. Influenced by the Beatles, Who, Rolling Stones, Pink Floyd, and other British groups, rock and roll (now known as rock) assumed a new character that featured advanced electronic technology, sophisticated arrangements, and extreme visual impact and onstage behavior. Rock transformed American popular music and gave rise to the formed study of popular culture.

Rockabilly   The form of popular music in the 1950s that resulted from the influence of hillbilly singers on the new rock and roll music.

Rondo   A musical form consisting of two or more contrasting theme areas, each followed by a return to the opening theme. No common rondo structure may be depicted as a b a c a and a b a c a b a. The rondo is commonly used as the spirited final movement of Classic-era sonatas, symphonies, and string quartets.

Rubato   A flexible pulse—not restricted by a steady beat. Contributes to a highly expressive style.

S

Salon music   A type of piano music popular throughout the Western Hemisphere during the nineteenth century. Reflecting European practices, salon music was short, simple pieces published as sheet music. Often it was created in the style of marches or dances, such as the tango, habanera, conga, polka, bolero, or waltz.

Salsa   A popular music of Latin American origin that has absorbed characteristics of rhythm and blues, jazz, and rock.

Sampler   Method by which, by means of MIDI technology, samples of sounds can be recorded and stored in memory to be recalled and performed. The sampled sound is expanded for performance to include the entire range of the keyboard.

Scale   An ascending or descending series of tones organized according to a specified pattern of intervals.

Scat singing   Improvised jazz singing using a variety of vocal sounds rather than lyrics. Its purpose is to improvise a vocal solo line in the manner of a lead instrumentalist.

Score   A printed version of a piece of music. Often refers to the version used by a conductor that depicts the music to be played by all performers—the full score.

Sections   *See* big band jazz.

Sequence   A melodic pattern repeated several times either a step lower or a step higher than the preceding statement.

Serial composition (12-tone technique)   A set of nonrepeated pitches—a tone row—used as the basis for organizing the vertical and horizontal arrangement of pitches throughout a composition. A system created and refined by Schoenberg, rows originally consisted of all 12 tones of the chromatic scale. Serialism was created as an alternative to the major-minor tonal system, and it was a means for organizing the chaotic chromaticism prevalent in late-nineteenth-century German Romantic music and early-twentieth-century atonal music. An extension of the 12-tone technique includes the serialization of note values, timbres, or dynamics. Music in which all these aspects are serialized, including pitch, is known as *totally controlled music*.

Shape-note system   An aid in learning to read music popular in nineteenth-century America. Each pitch of a hymn tune was represented on the staff by a note whose head had a distinctive shape. Each shape represented a specific pitch of the scale.

Sidemen   A jazz combo typically put together by the leader. The hired musicians were known as sidemen.

Singing schools   Schools established to introduce and teach singing from musical notation. Their primary purpose was to improve the state of hymn singing in America—that is, to elevate the rural, folk-based hymn derived from oral tradition to the urban, European, notation-based hymn sung in a refined style.

Sonata   In the Baroque period, a multimovement work written for a solo instrument and continuo; also the trio sonata written for two solo instruments and continuo; since the Classic era, a multimovement work for piano or for a solo instrument with piano. The typical order of movements is fast-slow-dance-fast.

Sonata form   A structure that composers in the Classic era and since have commonly used for the first movement of a sonata, symphony, concerto, or string quartet (or other similar chamber music work). It includes three main sections—the exposition, development, and recapitulation—and often begins with an introduction and ends with a coda. The exposition has two theme areas in contrasting keys. The development is based on material from the exposition. The recapitulation is a return to previous material stated in the exposition.

Song form   A 32-bar a a b a chorus (verse). *Also see* form.

Soul   Any popular music performed by blacks for black audiences. Soul combines elements of R&B, jazz, and black gospel.

Sound source   Any elastic substance capable of generating sound waves that can be perceived as music, such as any conventional band or orchestral instrument, any instrument identified in the appendix, or any material in the environment used to generate sounds to be incorporated in a piece of music. This material may include pots and pans; taped sounds of water, fire, birds, or whales; or things that people become aware of in a classroom that can be used in an original piece of music.

Spiritual   A religious song usually of a deeply emotional character that was developed especially among African Americans in the southern United States.

Stability   *See* tension.

Standard   A song that has sustained popularity through decades and generations, transcending changing styles and tastes.

Stop-time   A jazz technique in which the rhythm section stops playing for one or more beats each measure while a soloist continues to play.

Stride   Originally a solo piano style growing out of ragtime. Its predominant characteristic is the strongly pulsated "boom-chick," a left-hand rhythmic and harmonic foundation over which, in the right hand, is usually a highly syncopated dazzling display of improvisation with fast runs and arpeggios. Fats Waller is well known for his stride style. Later pianists such as Art Tatum were rooted in the stride style but incorporated a more advanced harmonic vocabulary and, with both hands, covered the entire range of the piano with their dazzling displays.

Strophic   A musical structure in which the same music is used for each stanza of a ballad, song, or hymn.

Structure   The way in which parts are arranged to form a whole; the form of a piece of music.

Style   External characteristics of music developed through the creative process that distinguish one piece from another, characteristics that are determined by the composer's use of musical elements, formal design, and emotional expression.

Subdominant   A chord built on the fourth degree of a major or minor scale.

Swing   A manner of performance that, in part, separates jazz from other styles of music. It is a manner that generates heightened energy and rhythmic vitality.

Syllabic setting   A setting of a text to music in which one syllable of text is given one note of music. *Also see* melisma.

Symphonic poem   A programmatic, one-movement work for symphony orchestra with contrasting moods. It became popular during the Romantic period.

Symphony   A multimovement work for symphony orchestra. The typical order of movements is fast-slow-dance-fast. This pattern was standard in the Classic period but less adhered to in the Romantic and Modern eras.

Syncopation   The occurrence of accents in unexpected places, usually on weak beats or on weak parts of beats.

T

Tala   The basic means for organizing the durational aspects—the rhythm and meter—of the classical music of India. They involve cycles of counts with regular or irregular subdivisions. For example, a 16-count cycle may be subdivided 4 1 4 1 4 1 4, or a 14-count cycle may be subdivided 5 1 2 1 3 1 4.

Tempo   The rate of speed at which music is performed.

Tension   A perception of instability in traditional Western music that suggests the need for release of tension or resolution. It is often marked by increased harmonic or rhythmic complexity, dissonance, modulation away from the tonic, or a rise in pitch or dynamic level. A lessening of complexity or loudness, a lowering of pitch, a decrease in complexity, and a return to consonance or tonic can create stability, resolution, or release of tension.

Ternary   *See* form.

Tex-Mex   A style of music originating in southern Texas.

Texture   (1) The density of sound; the number of simultaneously sounding lines. Music can have a full, thick texture or a thin, transparent texture. (2) The manner in which the horizontal pitch sequences are organized. A single-line melody with no accompaniment or other horizontal or vertical sounds has a monophonic texture. Two or more independent, simultaneously sounding melodies having equal emphasis have a polyphonic texture. A melody that is dominant with other lines supporting the main melody has a homophonic texture.

Theme   A short melody or phrase that has a sense of completeness—a complete musical thought; a theme usually ends with a cadence. A theme often is the unifying musical idea of a piece or section of a piece.

Theme and variations   An instrumental form in which a stated theme is followed by a series of variations on that theme.

Timbre   The characteristic quality of the sound of a voice or instrument.

Tin Pan Alley   A period of popular songwriting that began the 1890s and whose most productive years were the 1920s and 1930s. Many of America's most beloved songs—the standards—are part of the Tin Pan Alley tradition. The phrase *Tin Pan Alley* also referred to the part of the music industry devoted to the sale of popular songs. The name comes from the nickname given to the street in New York City where nearly every publisher of popular music was located in the early twentieth century.

Tonality   The gravitational pull of music toward a tonal center; the key of the music—for example, C major or C minor.

Tone bending   Altering a pitch slightly according to established performance practice, such as in pop or jazz music.

Tone clusters   Three or more adjacent tones sounding simultaneously.

Tone quality   *See* timbre.

Tonic   The first and most important note of the major or minor scale; the tonal center of a piece of music; a chord built on the first note of a scale.

Totally controlled music   *See* serial composition (12-tone technique).

Traditional music   *See* folk music.

Tremolo   Rapid repetition of a tone, often produced in string instruments by quick up-and-down strokes of the bow. In Listening Guide 35, p. 160, the tremolo is achieved on the koto by plucking the strings.

Trio sonata   *See* sonata.

Triple meter   A rhythmic pattern in which the first of every three beats is stressed (strong-weak-weak-strong-weak-weak). *Also see* meter.

12-bar blues   A musical phrase of 12 bars, usually divided into three 4-bar segments using a specific set of chord progressions. Some blues melodies have 8 or 16 bars. *Also see* meter.

12-tone technique   *See* serial composition.

U

Unity   Music that does not ramble and is cohesive, with an exact or a modified repetition of themes and patterns.

V

Vamp   A short, repeated pattern used as an introduction to a song or as a transition between verses or phrases—often a pattern of repeating one or two chords.

Variety   Music that departs from previously stated themes and creates points of contrast.

Vaudeville   A variety show consisting of unrelated acts by singers, dancers, comedians, jugglers, child performers, trained animals, and actors. It replaced the minstrel show as America's most popular stage show. New York City was the center of vaudeville; the most sophisticated shows were produced on Broadway. These shows were variously known as revues, vanities, scandals, and follies, of which the most famous were the Ziegfeld Follies, produced from 1907 through 1932. *Also see* minstrel shows.

Venue   A place to perform, such as an auditorium, nightclub, bandstand, arena, or church.

Vernacular   The most familiar and most used language of the people of a nation, region, or a cultural group. Vernacular music is the common musical language of a people.

Verse-chorus   A form in which there are different texts to each verse and a return to the chorus after each verse.

Vibrato   An oscillating variation of pitch that enhances a tone, providing richness and warmth particularly to sustained pitches or to a slow, lyrical melody.

Vocables   Words in Native American songs having no meaning and intended only as vocal sounds.

W

Walking bass   A jazz bass line played on each beat, frequently with some embellishment and emphasizing the main tones of the underlying chord structure.

Western swing   A style of country music that became popular as the popularity of hillbilly music moved westward. It features a larger instrumental ensemble that includes saxes, brass, and a standard jazz rhythm section.

White gospel   *See* gospel music.

Word painting   A technique common in the Baroque period of conveying in the music the moods, emotions, images, and meanings suggested by a text.

Z

Zydeco   The popular dance and entertainment music of the black Americans living in southwestern Louisiana. Their songs, often sung in a French dialect, combine Cajun music and the blues. Common instruments include the button accordion and rub board (washboard), in addition to electric guitar, electric bass, and drums. Zydeco has become nationally popular from appearances in the 1970s and 1980s by zydeco artists at folk and blues festivals nationally. The original superstar of zydeco was Clifton Chenier.

BIBLIOGRAPHY

American Music—General

Cox, Christoph, and Daniel Warner (eds.). *Audio Culture: Readings in Modern Music*. New York: Continuum, 2004.

Crawford, Richard. *America's Musical Life: A History*. New York: Norton, 2001.

Ferris, Jean. *America's Musical Landscape*. New York: McGraw-Hill, 2002.

Heintze, James R. (ed.). *Perspectives on American Music since 1950*. New York: Garland, 1999.

Hitchcock, H. Wiley. *Music in the United States: A Historical Introduction*. Upper Saddle River, NJ: Prentice-Hall, 2000.

Kingman, Daniel. *American Music: A Panorama*. New York: Schirmer Books, 2003.

American Vernacular Music (Chapters 3–6)

Boyer, Horace Clarence. *How Sweet the Sound: The Golden Age of Gospel*. Washington, DC: Elliott and Clark, 2000.

Brackett, David. *The Pop, Rock, and Soul Reader: Histories and Debates*, 2nd ed. New York: Oxford University Press, 2009.

Cantwell, Robert. *Bluegrass Breakdown: The Making of the Old Southern Sound*. Urbana: University of Illinois Press, 2003.

Filene, Benjamin. *Romancing the Folk: Public Memory and American Roots Music*. Chapel Hill: University of North Carolina Press, 2000.

Garofalo, Reebee. *Rockin' Out: Popular Music in the USA*. Upper Saddle River, NJ: Prentice-Hall, 2002.

Gioia, Ted. *Delta Blues: The Life and Times of the Mississippi Masters Who Revolutionized American Music*. New York: Norton, 2008.

Lornell, Kip. *Introducing American Folk Music*. New York: McGraw-Hill, 2002.

Neal, Mark Anthony. *What the Music Said: Black Popular Music and Black Popular Culture*. New York: Routledge, 1999.

Peretti, Burton W. *Jazz in American Culture*. Chicago: Ivan R. Dee, 1997.

Roberts, John Storm. *Latin Jazz: The First of the Fusion, 1880s to Today*. New York: Schirmer Books, 1999.

Starr, Larry, and Christopher Waterman. *American Popular Music, from Minstrelsy to MP3*. New York: Oxford University Press, 2007.

World Music (Chapters 7–8)

Broughton, Simon, Mark Ellingham, and Richard Trillo (eds.), with Orla Duane and Vanessa Dowell. *World Music: The Rough Guide*. Vol. 1, *Africa, Europe and the Middle East*. Vol. 2, *Latin and North America, Caribbean, India, Asia, and Pacific*. London: Rough Guides, 1999.

Fairchild, Charles. *Pop Idols and Pirates: Mechanisms of Consumption and the Global Circulation of Popular Music*. Burlington, VT: Ashgate, 2008.

Fletcher, Peter. *World Musics in Context: A Comprehensive Survey of the World's Major Musical Cultures*. New York: Oxford University Press, 2004.

Garland Encyclopedia of World Music (9 vols.). New York: Garland, 1998.

Miller, Terry E., and Andrew Shahriari. *World Music: A Global Journey.* New York: Routledge, 2006.

Nettl, Bruno, et al. *Excursions in World Music.* Upper Saddle River, NJ: Prentice-Hall, 2001.

Peretti, Burton W. *Lift Every Voice: The History of African Music.* Lanham, MD: Rowman and Littlefield, 2009.

Roberts, John Storm. *Black Music of Two Worlds: African, Caribbean, Latin, and African-American Traditions.* New York: Schirmer Books, 1998.

Roberts, John Storm. *The Latin Tinge: The Impact of Latin American Music on the United States.* New York: Oxford University Press, 1999.

Sawyers, June Skinner. *Celtic Music: A Complete Guide.* New York: Da Capo Press, 2001.

Schechter, John M. (ed.). *Music in Latin American Culture: Regional Traditions.* New York: Schirmer Books, 1999.

Stokes, Martin, and Philip Bohlman (eds.). *Celtic Modern: Music at the Global Fringe.* Lanham, MD: Scarecrow Press, 2003.

Stoltzoff, Norman C. *Wake the Town and Tell the People: Dancehall Culture in Jamaica.* Durham, NC: Duke University Press, 2000.

Taylor, Timothy D. *Beyond Exoticism: Western and the World.* Durham: Duke University Press, 2007.

Tenzer, Michael, with foreword by Steve Reich. *Gamelan Gong Kebyar: The Art of Twentieth-Century Balinese Music.* Chicago: University of Chicago Press, 2000.

Titon, Jeff Todd (ed.). *Worlds of Music: An Introduction to the Music of the World's Peoples.* Belmont, CA: Schirmer/Thomson Learning, 2006.

Western European and American Classical Music (Chapters 9–13)

Kuhn, Laura Diane. *Music since 1900.* New York: Schirmer Reference/Gale Group, 2001.

McCutchan, Ann. *The Muse That Sings: Composers Speak about the Creative Process.* New York: Oxford University Press, 1999.

Salzman, Eric. *Twentieth-Century Music: An Introduction.* Upper Saddle River, NJ: Prentice-Hall, 2002.

Schwartz, Elliott, and Barney Childs (eds.), with Jim Fox. *Contemporary Composers on Contemporary Music.* New York: Da Capo Press, 1998.

Steinberg, Michael. *Choral Masterworks: A Listener's Guide.* New York: Oxford University Press, 2005.

Whittall, Arnold. *Exploring Twentieth-Century Music: Tradition and Innovation.* New York: Cambridge University Press, 2003.

Music Technology

Alexander, Alison. *Taking Sides: Clashing Views in Mass Media and Society.* Boston: McGraw-Hill Higher Education, 2009.

Cann, Simon. *Rocking Your Music Business: Run Your Music Business at Home and on the Road.* Boston: Course Technology Cengage Learning, 2009.

Fries, Bruce, and Marty Fries. *Digital Audio Essentials.* Sebastopol, CA: O'Reilly, 2005.

Knopper, Steve. *Appetite for Self-Destruction: The Spectacular Crash of the Record Industry in the Digital Age.* New York: Free Press, 2009.

Van Buskirk, Eliot. *Burning Down the House: Ripping, Recording, Remixing, and More.* New York: McGraw-Hill/Osbourne, 2003.

CREDITS

Photo Credits

Chapter 1

p. 4, © Craig Aurness/Corbis; p. 6L, © Aris Messinis/AFP/Getty Images; p. 6R, © Kelly-Mooney Photography/Corbis; pp. 7, 8, © AP/Wide World Photos; p. 10, © Jack Vartoogian/FrontRowPhotos; p. 12, © AP/Wide World Photos; p. 13, © Corbis; p. 14, © Dat's Jazz

Chapter 2

p. 18, © Tibor Bognár/Corbis; p. 23, © Peter Turnley/Corbis; p. 24, © Ellen Senisi/The Image Works; p. 25, © Jack Vartoogian/FrontRowPhotos; p. 34, © Stephan Boitano/Getty Images; p. 36, © Bettmann/Corbis

Chapter 3

p. 42, © Neal Preston/Corbis; p. 45, Photograph of Ann Warner recording Frank Profitt courtesy of the Frank and Ann Warner Collection. Rare Book, Manuscript & Special Collections Library, Duke University; p. 51, © Hulton Archive/Getty Images; p. 52, © Neal Preston/Corbis; p. 53, © AP/Wide World Photos

Chapter 4

p. 56, © Frank Mullen/Getty Images; p. 60, White Spirituals in the Southern Uplandism by George Jackson Pullen; p. 61, From Music Division, Library of Congress, Washington, DC. Reprinted by permission; p. 63T, Photo by Joel Richardson/© 1980 The Washington Post. Reprinted with permission; p. 63B, © Underwood & Underwood/Corbis; p. 64, © Jack Vartoogian/FrontRowPhotos; p. 69, © Frank Micelotta/Getty Images

Chapter 5

p. 72, © Thierry Orban/Corbis Sygma; p. 74, © Hulton-Deutsch Collection/Corbis; pp. 75, 79, © Bettmann/Corbis; p. 80, © Ray Avery; pp. 82, 84, 85, © Bettmann/Corbis; p. 88, © Jack Vartoogian/FrontRowPhotos; p. 90, © Dennis Stock/Magnum Photos; p. 91, © AFP/Getty Images; p. 93, © Derick A. Thomas/Dat's Jazz/Corbis; p. 96T, © Tad Hershorn/Hulton Archive/Getty Images; p. 96L, © James L. Lance/Corbis; p. 96R, © Neal Preston/Corbis

Chapter 6

p. 100, © AP/Wide World Photos; pp. 104, 107, © The Granger Collection, New York; p. 108, © Bettmann/Corbis; p. 114, © The Hampton University Museum, Hampton, Virginia; p. 115, © AP/Wide World Photos; p. 116, © Rick Diamond/WireImage/Getty Images; p. 118L, © AP/Wide World Photos; p. 118R, © Neal Preston/Corbis; p. 119, © Stephen Lovekin/Getty Images; p. 120, © Michael Ochs Archive/Getty Images; pp. 121, 122L, 122TR, © AP/Wide World Photos; p. 122BR, © Neal Preston/Corbis; p. 125, © AP/Wide World Photos; p. 127, © Mitchell Gerber/Corbis; p. 128, © AP/Wide World Photos

Chapter 7

p. 132, © Danny Lehman/Corbis; p. 135, © Joseph Sohm/The Image Works; p. 143T, © AP/Wide World Photos; p. 143B, © Joseph Sohm/ChromoSohm, Inc./Corbis; p. 144, © Tim Mosenfelder/Getty Images; p. 149, © Jack Vartoogian/FrontRowPhotos

Chapter 8

p. 152, © John Reader/TimeLife Pictures/Getty Images; p. 159, © Jack Vartoogian/FrontRowPhotos;

p. 160, © Underwood & Underwood/Corbis; p. 162, © Michael Masian Historic Photographs/Corbis; p. 164, © Elsa Peterson/Stock Boston; p. 165, © Keystone Features/Getty Images; p. 167T, © ArenaPal/Topham/ The Image Works; p. 167BL, © Bernard Bisson/Corbis Sygma; p. 167BR, © Lynn Goldsmith/Corbis; pp. 168, 172, © Jack Vartoogian/FrontRowPhotos; p. 178, © AP/Wide World Photos

Chapter 9

p. 184, © Joel Gordon; p. 189, Courtesy St. Louis Art Museum, Museum Purchase; p. 191, © AP/Wide World Photos; p. 194, © Scala/Art Resource, NY; p. 199, © Erich Lessing/Art Resource, NY; p. 204, © Nik Wheeler/Corbis; p. 207, © Scala/Art Resource, NY

Chapter 10

p. 212, © Erich Lessing/Art Resource, NY; p. 217, © Victoria & Albert Museum, London/Art Resource, NY; p. 218, © Patrick Riviere/Getty Images; pp. 222, 226, © Vanni/Art Resource, NY; p. 231, © Scala/Art Resource, NY

Chapter 11

pp. 234, 237, © AP/Wide World Photos; p. 244, © Bettmann/Corbis; p. 247, © The Art Archive/Corbis; p. 248, © Bettmann/Corbis; p. 249, © Caesco Pictures

Chapter 12

p. 252, © AP/Wide World Photos; p. 258, © Bildarchiv Preussischer Kulturbesitz/Art Resource, NY; p. 260, © Bettmann/Corbis; p. 262, © Erich Lessing/Art Resource, NY; p. 266, © AP/Wide World Photos

Chapter 13

p. 272, © Robbie Jack/Corbis; p. 276, © Bettmann/ Corbis; p. 279, © Robbie Jack/Corbis; p. 280, © Bettmann/Corbis; p. 281, © Marvin Koner/Corbis; p. 286, © Keystone/Hulton Archive/Getty Images; p. 288, © Bettmann/Corbis; p. 289, © AP/Wide World Photos; p. 294, © Renato Toppo/Corbis; p. 295, Courtesy Genevieve Spielberg Inc.; p. 296, © AP/Wide World Photos

INDEX